Trading Communities in the Roman World

Columbia Studies in the Classical Tradition

VOLUME 37

The titles published in this series are listed at brill.com/csct

Trading Communities in the Roman World

A Micro-Economic and Institutional Perspective

By

Taco T. Terpstra

BRILL

LEIDEN • BOSTON
2013

Cover Illustration: Marble plaque dedicated by Iulius Aurelius Heliodorus to the Palmyrene gods Malachbel and Aglibol. Capitoline Museums, Rome (author's photograph).

Library of Congress Cataloging-in-Publication Data

Terpstra, Taco T.
Trading communities in the Roman world : a micro-economic and institutional perspective / by Taco T. Terpstra.
pages cm. — (Columbia studies in the classical tradition, ISSN 0166-1302 ; 37)
Includes bibliographical references and index.
ISBN 978-90-04-23860-2 (hbk. : alk. paper) — ISBN 978-90-04-24513-6 (e-book) 1. Rome—Commerce—History. 2. Microeconomics. 3. Social archaeology—Rome. 4. Rome (Italy)—History—To 476. I. Title.

HF377.T47 2013
381.0937—dc23

2012044489

This publication has been typeset in the multilingual "Brill" typeface. With over 5,100 characters covering Latin, IPA, Greek, and Cyrillic, this typeface is especially suitable for use in the humanities. For more information, please see www.brill.com/brill-typeface.

ISSN 0166-1302
ISBN 978-90-04-23860-2 (hardback)
ISBN 978-90-04-24513-6 (e-book)

Koninklijke Brill NV incorporates the imprints Brill, Global Oriental, Hotei Publishing, IDC Publishers and Martinus Nijhoff Publishers.

This book is printed on acid-free paper.

Printed by Printforce, the Netherlands

CONTENTS

PREFACE

This book is the reworked version of my doctoral thesis, written at Columbia University between 2006 and 2011. However, the seed for this book was sown when I studied the Sulpicii archive during my MA in Classics at Groningen University. The Sulpicii archive is the only ancient source I actually recall reading for the first time. My mentor at Groningen, Willem Jongman, introduced me to this material in a peculiar setting, which I still remember vividly. Visiting friends in Cambridge and on my way to a May Ball at one of the colleges, I went to see Wim, who was spending a semester at the University. He had just checked out Camodeca's edition of the Sulpicii archive from the library—a recent publication at the time—and showed it to me, sitting in his garden. In the chilly spring dusk, seated on a plastic lawn chair, uncomfortably dressed in white tie, I leafed through the pages. Even reading the Sulpicii documents only cursorily that first time, I was fascinated with them: their content provides the kind of direct evidence for business in the Roman world that is exceedingly rare. I decided then and there I wanted to study the archive.

Working in Pompeian archaeology for many years, and becoming familiar with the general area where the tablets were found, made the archive even more evocative to me. I have often stood under Pompeii's Porta Stabia, gazing at the road leading into Pompeii, wondering if the people I knew from the archive ever walked that street. I like to think that they did, although as the archaeological section of the Chapter 1 makes clear, chances are this is just my fantasy.

The topic for this book grew out of a number of practical questions I developed reading the Sulpicii documents, and out of simple curiosity: how did Roman merchants, not just the merchants in the archive but in the Roman world in general, manage to trade around the Mediterranean Basin and beyond, while information and goods traveled only slowly? Why did they use Roman law and Roman courts if there was no state mandate to that effect and the state did not enforce the courts' verdicts? I did not find satisfactory answers to those questions in the literature, so I decided to devise them myself. Because of the scarcity of data on the Roman economy, I needed a general framework to slot the limited ancient sources into. During my doctorate I was able both to develop the theoretical framework I needed—an exercise that allowed me to engage with economic theory, a subject since long of interest to me—and expand on the evidentiary data pool for my model.

A note on the system of references to secondary literature used in this book: for authors cited with surname, year, and page numbers, e.g. Camodeca (1994) 104–109, the full reference can be found in the bibliography. Works not separately listed there, such as the entries in Eva Steinby's *Lexicon Topographicum Urbis Romae*, are cited with initial, surname, year, and page numbers, e.g. E. Papi ([in: Steinby V] 1999) 10–12. If the pages referred to are in a journal, the author's initial and surname along with the abbreviated journal title are given, e.g. R. Lanciani, *N.d.sc.* (1881) 114. A full list of journal abbreviations used in this book is given below. A full list of abbreviations of the epigraphic corpora is also included.

I could not have written this book alone, and in the course of writing it have incurred many debts of gratitude. First and foremost I am deeply indebted to William Harris and Roger Bagnall who, during my years at Columbia, have provided me with essential guidance, feedback, and criticism. Their professional mentorship has been a constant reminder to me of just how lucky and privileged I was, working with scholars of their stature.

A number of people have contributed to this work with enthusiastic and critical comments. I would like to thank in particular: Justin Dombrowski, Emily Holt, Willem Jongman, Marco Maiuro, David Ratzan, Peter Temin, and Arjan Zuiderhoek. All of them have read parts or all of the manuscript, and have provided me with valuable feedback. My deep gratitude also goes to Ronald Findlay and Adam Kosto. I am very thankful to both for lending me their expertise and for giving me advice; this book is much the better for it. I would also like to thank Jessica Goldberg for allowing me access to her (at the time) unpublished *Past & Present* article, and for providing me with helpful reading suggestions. The usual disclaimer applies of course: any remaining flaws and mistakes in the argument or in the handling of sources are wholly mine.

I would further like to express my gratitude to Columbia University for providing me with a W. Stuart Thompson Memorial Fellowship for research at the American Academy in Rome during the academic year 2008/2009. I would not have been able to write the third and fourth chapters of this book as they now stand without this generous support. I would also like to thank Columbia's Center for the Ancient Mediterranean for providing me with the opportunity to visit Turkey's west coast during the Center's field-trip in June 2008. The knowledge acquired on that trip has been of great help to me in writing Chapter 5. My gratitude also goes to the Stanwood Cockey Lodge Foundation, which financed the imaging work in this book.

Finally I would like to thank my parents who, throughout my long journey from MA student to Ph.D. candidate at Columbia, have been an invaluable source of inspiration and support to me. Their encouragement has been crucial; their sense of pride has been heartwarming. This book is dedicated to them.

ABBREVIATIONS

AdI = *Annali dell'Istituto di corrispondenza archeologica*
AE = *L'Année épigraphique*
AION = *Annali dell'Istituto universitario orientale di Napoli*
AJA = *American Journal of Archaeology*
AM = *Mitteilungen des deutschen archäologischen Instituts, athenische Abteilung*
ANRW = *Aufstieg und Niedergang der römischen Welt*
BCH = *Bulletin de correspondance hellénique*
BÉFAR = *Bibliothèque des écoles françaises d'Athènes et de Rome*
Bull.Com. = *Bullettino della commissione archeologica comunale di Roma*
Cah.Glotz = *Cahiers du centre Gustave-Glotz*
CB = William M. Ramsay, *Cities and Bishoprics of Phrygia* volume I, part 2 *West and West-Central Phrygia* (Oxford, 1895)
CIG = *Corpus Inscriptionum Graecarum*
CIL = *Corpus Inscriptionum Latinarum*
CIS = *Corpus Inscriptionum Semiticarum*
CJB = *Collection du Centre Jean Bérard*
CRAI = *Comptes-rendus des séances de l'Académie des inscriptions et belles-lettres*
Eph.Ep. = *Ephemeris Epigraphica: Corporis Inscriptionum Latinarum Supplementum*
Epigraph. = *Epigraphica: Rivista italiana di epigrafia*
FIRA = Salvatore Riccobono, Giovanni Baviera, Contardo Ferrini, Giuseppe Furlani, and Vincenzo Arangio-Ruiz, *Fontes Iuris Romani Antejustiniani*, 3 vols. (Florence, 1940–1943)
I.Anaz. = Mustafa H. Sayar, *Die Inschriften von Anazarbos und Umgebung* (= *Inschriften griechischer Städte aus Kleinasien*, vol. 56) (Bonn, 2000)
I.Cos = Mario Segre, *Iscrizioni di Cos* (= *Monografie della scuola archeologica di Atene e delle missioni italiane in Oriente*, vol. 6) (Rome, 1993)
I.Did = Albert Rehm, *Didyma II: Die Inschriften* (Berlin, 1958)
I.Délos = André Plassart, Jacques Coupry, Félix Dürrbach, Pierre Roussel, and Marcel Launey, *Inscriptions de Délos*, 7 vols. (Paris, 1926–1972)

IG	= *Inscriptiones Graecae*
IGRR	= René Cagnat, Jules Toutain, Pierre Jouguet, and Georges Lafaye, *Inscriptiones Graecae ad Res Romanas Pertinentes*, 3 vols. (Paris, 1911–1927)
IGUR	= Luigi Moretti, *Inscriptiones Graecae Urbis Romae*, 4 vols. (Rome, 1968–1990)
I.Eph.	= Hermann Wankel and Reinhold Merkelbach, *Die Inschriften von Ephesos* (= *Inschriften griechischer Städte aus Kleinasien*, vols. 11–17) (Bonn, 1979–1981)
I.Knidos	= Wolfgang Blümel, *Die Inschriften von Knidos* (= *Inschriften griechischer Städte aus Kleinasien*, vol. 41) (Bonn, 1992)
ILS	= Hermann Dessau, *Inscriptiones Latinae Selectae*, 3 vols. (Berlin, 1892–1916)
I.Magn.	= Otto Kern, *Die Inschriften von Magnesia am Maeander* (Berlin, 1900)
Inv.	= Jean Cantineau, Jean Starcky, and Michel Gawlikowski, *Inventaire des inscriptions de Palmyre* (Beirut, 1930–)
I.Porto	= Giulia Sacco, *Iscrizioni greche d'Italia: Porto* (Rome, 1984)
IRT	= Joyce M. Reynolds and John B. Ward-Perkins, *The Inscriptions of Roman Tripolitania* (Rome, 1952)
I.Strat.	= Mehmet Çetin Şahin, *Die Inschriften von Stratonikeia* (= *Inschriften griechischer Städte aus Kleinasien*, vols. 21/22) (Bonn, 1981–1990)
I.Trall.	= Fjodor B. Poljakov, *Die Inschriften von Tralleis und Nysa* (= *Inschriften griechischer Städte aus Kleinasien*, vol. 36,1) (Bonn, 1989)
JöaI	= *Jahreshefte des österreichischen archäologischen Instituts in Wien*
JRA	= *Journal of Roman Archaeology*
JRS	= *Journal of Roman Studies*
MAAR	= *Memoirs of the American Academy in Rome*
MAMA	= William M. Calder, Josef Keil, William H. Buckler, *Monumenta Asiae Minoris Antiqua* (London, 1928–)
MEFRA	= *Mélanges de l'école française de Rome: Antiquité*
MemLinc	= *Memorie. Atti della accademia nazionale dei Lincei, classe di scienze morali, storiche e filologiche*
MGR	= *Miscellanea greca e romana: Studi pubblicati dall'Istituto italiano per la storia antica*
N.d.sc.	= *Notizie degli scavi di antichità*

OGIS	=	Wilhelm Dittenberger, *Orientis Graeci Inscriptiones Selectae: Supplementum Sylloges Inscriptionum Graecarum*, 2 vols. (Leipzig, 1903–1905)
OLD	=	Peter G.W. Glare (ed.), *The Oxford Latin Dictionary* (Oxford, 1996)
PAAR	=	*Papers and Monographs of the American Academy in Rome*
PAPS	=	*Proceedings of the American Philological Association*
PCPS	=	*Proceedings of the Cambridge Philological Society*
PASA	=	*Papers of the American School of Classical Studies at Athens*
P.Mich.	=	*Michigan Papyri*
P.Oxy.	=	*The Oxyrhynchus Papyri*
Puteoli	=	*Puteoli, studi di storia antica*
RDGE	=	Robert T. Sherk, *Roman Documents from the Greek East*: Senatus Consulta *and* Epistulae *to the Age of Augustus* (Baltimore, 1969)
REL	=	*Revue des études latines*
RendNap	=	*Rendiconti dell'Accademia di archeologia, lettere e belle arti di Napoli*
SEG	=	*Supplementum Epigraphicum Graecum*
TPSulp.	=	*Tabulae Pompeianae Sulpiciorum* (= Camodeca [1999])
ZPE	=	*Zeitschrift für Papyrologie und Epigraphik*

INTRODUCTION

This book investigates Roman trade. More specifically, it investigates the trading communities that facilitated Roman trade, taking a micro-economic and institutional approach to the subject. Abstract though this approach may seem, the problems addressed are concrete and down-to-earth. The leading question behind the work as a whole can be summed up in a single sentence: how did trade operate in the Roman Empire under conditions of imperfect government enforcement and imperfect information? In the course of this book I will elaborate further on this question, but let me briefly explain what I mean here.

The Roman state commanded awe-inspiring powers of physical violence and did not shy away from using them. However, unlike modern states it did not employ the powers at its disposal to enforce private contracts drawn up by ordinary individuals. The Roman legal system, in that sense, can be said to have been 'imperfect'. A party to a contract confronted with a default could not call upon the help of the Roman authorities to make a contractual partner honor his obligations. Of course, he could take a defaulter to court, but even with a favorable verdict in hand the vindicated litigant was still pretty much on his own. Ordinarily, no police or military unit would have been available to back him up in putting the court's ruling into effect.[1] This is not to say that such help will never have been granted. There will doubtless have been instances where the Roman administration—whether central or provincial—for whatever reason thought it expedient to lend some muscle to an individual litigant. But the point here is that any such help would have been random and arbitrary; it could not be relied upon. Government enforcement simply did not form part of the Roman legal institution in the way it forms part of the legal institution of, for instance, the United States.

Since the lightning-fast means of communication we take for granted were unavailable to the Romans, information could only move as fast as sails and legs would allow. The slowness with which information traveled formed a serious constraint on overseas business, a constraint felt increasingly with growing distance. For anyone intending to enter into a transaction with someone in a far-away place it was difficult to assess risk;

[1] See in general, Nippel (1995).

the data were few, and evaluating their accuracy was a slow and challenging task. How, then, was Empire-wide trade conducted if merchants could not count on third-party enforcement of their contracts, and could not easily gather information on trading conditions in overseas locales? This book offers a model of how such trade operated. In the briefest of terms, the argument put forward is that information circulated within small but far-reaching groups defined by their members' shared geographical origin; the loss of a member's reputation or trading position within the group formed the instrument of contract enforcement.

In broad outline, the discussion moves geographically outward from the imperial center, consisting of three main parts. The first looks at trade at an *intra*-community level in a city at the very heart of the Empire: Puteoli (Chapter 1). Within a relatively small community, information will have been readily available, although government enforcement was still lacking. I argue that in the Puteolan community, Roman law was the default mode for economic interaction and conflict resolution, a situation that was the result of a 'path-dependent' process; the rules of the Roman imperial legal system had become deeply embedded as a social convention, creating further behavior that conformed to that particular convention. The 'embeddedness' of the rules ensured that they would be followed continuously, in effect ensuring enforcement of private contracts.

The second part brings the wider world outside Italy into the discussion, focusing on long-distance *inter*-community trade. The goal of this second part is to study how traders from the provinces managed to do business in Italian cities. Chapter 2 builds on the findings from the first chapter, analyzing how merchants from other communities managed to trade in Puteoli. It argues that exchange was conducted through local 'colonies' of immigrant merchants domiciled permanently in the city. Chapter 3 then addresses the question of how long-distance trade networks operated internally, and how behavior was regulated within them. The chapter takes Ostia as an example, considering most of all the evidence from the so-called 'piazzale delle corporazioni'. Both chapters employ micro-economic theory as a framework, and both draw on comparisons with other historical situations. Chapter 4 then tests the model proposed for inter-community exchange in Puteoli and Ostia on the largest data-set available, that from the city of Rome.

Finally, the last part (Chapter 5) moves out from Italy, studying the mirrored situation from Chapters 2–4, namely Roman merchants doing business overseas. It takes the Roman province of Asia as a case-study, arguing that Roman traders settled there in order to facilitate exchange, just as provincial traders did in Italy. However, the chapter also investigates the most conspicuous difference between provincials coming to Italy and Romans moving to the provinces, namely the role of the Roman state. Provincials coming to live in Italian cities would not see magistrates from their native region or local government there. In the provinces, on the other hand, a Roman governor and his staff were present to administer legal affairs. The fact that Roman resident traders would encounter Rome's imperial officials in their new environment seems to have put them in a more favorable position than their provincial counterparts migrating to Italy. The chapter argues that although this difference needs to be taken into account, it is not as great as it might appear because government support in enforcement was lacking in the provinces, just as it was in Italy.

The trading communities I describe in this book are reminiscent of the ones on Roman Delos, where there was a group of Italian settlers, as well as others from the eastern Mediterranean. Nicholas Rauh, in an extensive analysis, has argued that on Delos religious ties formed the foundation for mercantile organizations, ties that were closely associated with ethnic and geographical identity.[2] At first glance, then, the island of Delos seems to present the perfect material for a study of the kind undertaken in this book. However, there are some major objections. The commercial significance of Delos declined quickly after 88 BC, so the timeline for study is early in date and short in range. More important still is that Delos, a small island possessing a special status as an emporium, formed a world all its own. The foreign element was so visible there, and the footprint of immigrants so great, that Delos largely lost its Greek civic character: 'The social structure of the Delian community at this period [167–88 BC] was ... massively lop-sided, in the East quite unique and therefore totally atypical.'[3] Since I intend to construct an argument with a broader applicability, this aspect of the exceptional Delian social make-up is a serious limitation. Nonetheless, I think that much of what I am trying to argue is reflected in the Delian sources. The trading communities on the island shared many characteristics with the ones I have analyzed, and in the course of my discussion I will refer to them a number of times.

Of course, I am keenly aware that the Italian cities I choose to study instead are exceptional in their own right. Rome itself was the center of it

[2] Rauh (1993).
[3] Errington (1988) 145.

all and her shadow loomed large over Puteoli and, especially, Ostia. However, I do not think that the exceptional nature of these cities invalidates them for my purposes. More types of goods in greater volumes will have gone to Rome and its satellites than to most other places in the Empire, but in effect that only heightened the dynamic I think supported Roman trade, making it more visible. The biggest problem with selecting these cities for my discussion is the potential involvement of the central government in trade and shipping, most of all through the *annona*. But despite the *annona*'s importance, undoubtedly a sizable, if ultimately unknowable, percentage of business was private in nature. Steering away from government-controlled trade as much as possible, it is this private business I aim at in my discussion.

The chronological emphasis of my narrative is on the first two centuries AD, with important excursions into the time of the Republic where this is relevant to the argument (mostly in Chapter 5 but also in Chapter 1). The effect of the passage of time is discussed, and in fact forms an essential part of the argument in Chapter 1, but what I study is mainly how the Roman Empire functioned during a span of time that was arguably its most stable. In this period, Egypt—an important province for the imperial economy—had been added, the big conquests of Empire had decelerated markedly, and the Empire reached its maximum size. There was a more or less stable situation in the area around the Mediterranean, conducive to long-distance trade, which suits my goal of understanding how such trade operated.

A problem for the Roman historian, especially for the historian studying the Roman economy, is that data are often frustratingly hard to come by. Part of the solution in addressing that problem, adopted in this book, is to make a number of comparisons with other historical situations. By juxtaposing the Roman situation and another, better-documented one—arguing that the two were similar in key respects—gaps can be filled in, and elements that would otherwise have remained blurry can come into sharper focus. I should emphasize that the comparative methodology I employ is also micro-economic and not macro-economic in outlook, and the examples offered for comparison are not taken from other Empires, nor necessarily from trade situations within a Mediterranean or even a maritime setting. Instead, they are selected because they share three key characteristics: they are situations in which goods and information moved only slowly, where there was no central state that enforced contractual obligations, and where there is an abundance of source material to investigate how business took place under those conditions. This approach abstracts from considerations of time and place; California in the 1830s is as much worth considering as eleventh-century Tunisia. By presenting these examples—both for contrast and comparison—I intend to elucidate what in my view are the most important aspects of the institutional framework of Roman long-distance trade. Ultimately, though, what I offer is not definitive proof—an impossibility for much of Roman economic history—and a large part of my argument rests upon abstract economic and comparative analysis. I realize this approach might not appeal to everyone.

Comparative history is not, and has never been, much in vogue among ancient historians, although recent work by Walter Scheidel and Peter Bang deserves mention in this context.[4] The work of these scholars may signal a new trend, although it is still too early to tell if it will usher in real change affecting the whole field. The reluctance to engage in comparative history is perhaps understandable. In likening two historical societies, one runs the risk of not doing justice to the full complexity of at least one of them, which goes against the best instincts of the historian. Roman historians may be more reluctant to look for cross-historical similarities than historians of other time periods because of the scarcity of their sources. In many areas, the sources on the Roman Empire are so limited that it might well be argued we just cannot know if any given comparison is valid. The very reason to turn to comparisons in the first place in that sense furnishes an argument against doing so. Although I certainly acknowledge the concern, I do not think this should be seen as an insurmountable barrier. If the parameters are well-chosen, comparative history can, in my view, be completely legitimate, even for the poorly documented Roman economy. Although I will admit that comparative history is fraught with difficulties, I believe it is an intellectual exercise well worth the effort. It all depends on the questions we ask of the past. Peter Bang is his *Roman Bazaar* has summed things up succinctly: 'It is a widespread misperception that the individual characteristics of a particular culture are always to be considered paramount'. However, '[d]ifferences and similarities must be handled pragmatically. Whether to emphasise one or the other depends on our questions and the problems we examine'.[5] I wholeheartedly subscribe to this point of view.

[4] E.g. Scheidel (2009); Bang (2008).
[5] Bang (2008) 293.

Comparisons between Roman and medieval trade may be particularly charged. The field of ancient history may still be haunted by the ghost of Moses Finley who—famously—was adamantly opposed to any such attempts. Finley employed his formidable oratorical skill to denounce especially archaeologists evoking the image of medieval cities when describing ancient urban centers such as Tarsus: '... it seems commonly to be overlooked... that all ancient cities lacked the Guildhalls and Bourses which, next to the cathedrals, are to this day the architectural glories of the great medieval cities of Italy, France, Flanders, the Hansa towns, or England. Contrast the Athenian Agora with the Grande Place in Brussels'.[6] Some past attempts to incorporate the medieval economy in analyses of the ancient may admittedly have been unsatisfactory, although much more subtle and balanced forays in that direction have been made by Harry Pleket.[7] At all events, it is worth stressing here that the comparisons I am making are not aimed at ascertaining the position and importance of manufacture and commerce in ancient cities. I will also not attempt to assess the applicability of either the 'consumer' or the 'producer' city-model, 'ideal-type' categories that have formed a mainstay of the modern debate. Instead, I focus on personalized networks, access to information, and enforcement mechanisms.

In this context, Bang's work, already referred to above, deserves another mention. Some of the ideas presented there are similar to the ones found in this book, especially ideas on trade networks and personalized connections governing long-distance exchange. Like me, Bang stresses the limited role the state cared to play in enforcement, leading merchants to create their own social institutions to compensate for the lack of state control.[8] However, Bang's argument is drawn in broad outline employing a sweeping general theory. I deliberately attempt to be much more concrete and provide more detail. My approach, also visible in the kind of comparative history I engage in, is indicative of the different aim I have for this book.

Bang is interested not so much in details and micro-economics but in constructing a much larger macro-economic argument. He is therefore looking for another Empire, one close enough to the Roman to be a viable

---

[6] Finley (1973) 137. See also 195/196: Finley on the 'piazzale delle corporazioni' (cited below in Chapter 3).

[7] E.g. Moeller (1976) 72/73 comparing the wool production of Pompeii to that of medieval Florence. For a critical view of Moeller's analysis, see Jongman (1988). Pleket's use of medieval comparisons, e.g. Pleket (1984), (1990).

[8] See especially Bang (2008) Chapter 5 'Community: Cult, Courts, Credit and Collaboration in the Bazaar'. For some critical notes, see Chapter 3.

comparison in its entirety. The Indian Mughal state for him is a suitable candidate. This focus on the 'big picture' leads him explicitly to position his book in the debate on the Roman economy, dominated by the scholarly tribes of 'modernists' and 'primitivists'; or rather, he attempts to position his book *outside* that debate, striving to produce nothing short of a 'paradigm shift', a way out of the old-familiar primitivist-modernist dichotomy. This book has no such lofty aspirations. The questions it addresses are entirely of a practical nature, and the historical examples chosen for comparison are on a human, not an Empire-wide scale. The debate between 'modernists' and 'primitivists', inevitably alluded to here and there, is not explicitly engaged with. No history can claim to be entirely value-free, and for anyone familiar with the terms of the debate my own stance will probably be apparent. Nonetheless, the goal I set myself was not to provide ammunition for one or the other side. Instead, the goal I set myself was to answer concrete questions about the 'how' and 'why' of everyday Roman trade.

CHAPTER ONE

INTRA-COMMUNITY EXCHANGE AND THE USE OF LAW IN PUTEOLI

Legal Interaction and Personal Knowledge

On the first pages of Petronius' *Satyricon*—at least in its present, incomplete state—there is a story that encapsulates the main themes addressed in this book. Unfortunately, we possess only the second part of the story leading up to the *dénouement*; the part that contained the preceding events is lost. However, we can deduce that in an earlier adventure the two protagonists, Encolpius and Ascyltos, had hidden a number of gold coins in a cloak by stitching them into the seams, and had then somehow lost the precious garment to a farmer who was unaware of the treasure concealed in it. The early paragraphs of the *Satyricon* as we now have it tell us what happened next.

Encolpius and Ascyltos wander into a marketplace—the marketplace of the Italian harbor town of Puteoli, in all likelihood—and recognize both the man to whom they had lost their gold and the coveted piece of clothing that contains it.[1] The farmer has still not discovered the hidden money, and the two heroes see a chance of recovering their property and with it their fortune. Encolpius is delighted, and proposes to take the man to court. However, '... Ascyltos was afraid of the law: "Nobody knows us in this place," he said, "and nobody will believe what we say. I should certainly like to buy the thing, although it is ours, and we know it. It is better to get back our savings cheaply than to embark upon the perils of a lawsuit" '.[2] In the end, however, no purchase or lawsuit is necessary. Encolpius and Ascyltos get their cloak thrown back into their faces after a brawl ensues over another cloak they themselves had stolen.

---

[1] Petronius *Sat.* 12–15. Puteoli as the location of the *Satyricon*: D'Arms (1981) 105/106; Rose (1962) 402–405.

[2] Petronius *Sat.* 14, 1/2. 'Contra Ascyltos leges timebat et "Quis" aiebat "hoc loco nos novit, aut quis habebit dicentibus fidem? Mihi plane placet emere, quamvis nostrum sit, quod agnoscimus, et parvo aere recuperare potius thesaurum, quam in ambiguam litem descendere: Quid faciant leges, ubi sola pecunia regnat, aut ubi paupertas vincere nulla potest?" '. Tr.: M. Heseltine, Loeb (1969).

The relevance of this story is twofold. First, it seems to be taken for granted that in the Italian harbor city of the story, a lawsuit was the default way to argue over property, an element I will explore further in this chapter. Second, Encolpius and Ascyltos are clearly not native to the town they find themselves in. Worse: they do not know anyone there and no one knows them. For that reason litigating seems unwise to at least Ascyltos. In the story he continues to express his fear of the law with a rant (albeit in elegiac distichs) about corrupt judges and about the power of money: 'Of what avail are laws to be where money rules alone, and the poor suitor can never succeed?...' However, since the opposing litigant would have been a simple farmer, certainly no richer (consciously anyway) than the two protagonists, Ascyltos' anxiety must really have been caused by the fact that they were on unfamiliar terrain where they were an unknown entity. What makes this story so germane is that it points to the importance of personal knowledge about people in legal interaction, especially where people from different communities were involved. This second element has a wider bearing on the argument I will develop in Chapters 2 through 5, where I will discuss how inter-community exchange was conducted without government enforcement in private contracting, and without fast means of communication.

In this first chapter, however, I will begin by studying a situation where information availability was not a problem: the situation of intra-community exchange in the city of Puteoli. The discussion will address a seemingly puzzling element in the data-set, namely the propensity of the Puteolan trading community to follow the complicated and highly formal rules of the imperial legal system, despite the undoubtedly costly investments in learning this must have required. It is the dominance of this social convention we saw reflected in the story from the *Satyricon* related above. Though fictional, it seems to point to a social reality in this respect. The larger relevance of this chapter for the book as a whole is to show how within a small enough community a set of rules—no matter what their exact composition—can be dominant, forcing rule-conformant behavior even if there is no state mandate to do so. In my discussion I will also incorporate the mechanism of reputation in business, a topic I will explore further in the next chapters.

The choice of Puteoli is largely motivated by the available source material. Thanks to an extraordinary archaeological find, Puteoli is one of the few places in the Roman Empire for which we have sufficient evidence to reconstruct how local trade and finance operated. In this chapter I will be looking at such exchange on a micro-scale, focusing on the financial and business operations of one particular Puteolan banking venture. For my analysis I will use the documents from the so-called Sulpicii archive, a data-set I will introduce in greater detail below. I will start by investigating the socio-economic make-up of the people who produced the documents in the archive; I will then proceed to analyze how these people did business and how they solved their conflicts.

It will appear that the Puteolan group was a close-knit community in which reputation must have played a large role. However, it will also become clear that, despite the importance reputation must have had for this group, its members turned to the rules of the imperial legal system for much of their financial and business interactions. I will try to argue that this behavior can be explained by means of the concept of institutional 'path dependence', the theory that human institutions continue following the trajectory initially determined by historical circumstances. The 'path dependency' argument consists of three elements: the historical process of legal reception, the 'sunk' institutional capital of investments in information, and the outcomes the legal system produced. I will argue that in Puteoli these three elements in combination helped to maintain the Roman legal system in its role as the dominant social convention for economic exchange and dispute settlement.

The Murecine Tablets: Archive and Archaeology

In 1959 during road construction in the Agro Murecine just outside the walls of Pompeii, workmen discovered the remains of an ancient villa, about 600 meters south of the city.[3] In haste, an excavation was performed, but under pressure from the road contractors the archaeologists could uncover only a small part of the structure.[4] What they found were five elegantly decorated *triclinia* opening up onto an equally elegant little garden. In one of those *triclinia* they found a wicker basket containing a large collection of writing tablets. Wood is usually not preserved in Pompeii, and this find was therefore remarkable. What had helped conserve perishable materials in this villa—not just the tablets and the wicker

[3] Camodeca (1999) 11–14.

[4] For a comprehensive publication on the 1959 Agro Murecine excavations (including a discussion on the wall paintings in the *triclinia*), see Pagano (1983).

basket but also the latticework sliding doors of the *triclinia*—was the relatively wet condition of the soil.[5]

The villa was situated in a larger urban area just outside the walls of Pompeii, accessed through the Porta Stabia (one of the main city gates). This area once lined the bank of the Sarno River, and in all likelihood formed part of the river harbor.[6] The volcanic deposits from the eruption have changed the course of the river and have pushed out the ancient coastline, but in this relatively low-lying part outside Pompeii the high water table still makes the soil poor in oxygen. This fortunate circumstance had helped to seal and preserve the ancient wood.

Predictably, after almost 1900 years in an anoxic environment, the wooden tablets started to deteriorate quickly once they were exposed to the outside air. The immense importance of the find was obvious to the archaeologists, and they tried to preserve the tablets as best they could. Regrettably, attempts to seal a number of them in a paraffin and paraloid coating turned out to be disastrous; the tablets, still containing some moisture, 'sweated', and their wax covering flaked off, utterly destroying the writing.[7] Unable to stabilize the condition of the tablets, the archaeologists took photographs of them, and this set of (mostly) high-quality pictures now forms the basis for our knowledge of the tablets' content.[8] The collection as we now have it consists of 127 documents, although many are incomplete and some show no more than a name or a few words. They record various business transactions, mostly relating to loans, and as such they formed part of an archive apparently belonging to the banking house of the Sulpicii.

The nature of the building that sheltered the archive remains an open question. The arrangement of five *triclinia* opening up onto a garden is highly unusual; the southern end of the structure has never been exposed, but it could be that it is symmetrical and that the line of rooms is mirrored on the southern side. A house with a similar lay-out (a circle of *triclinia* around an open area) can be found also in Ostia. Inscriptions found there

[5] De Simone (2000) 49–51; Gröschler (1997) 23–27; Pagano (1983) 327/328.

[6] Pagano (1983) 332–334.

[7] De Simone (2000) 53/54; Camodeca (1999) 15; Gröschler (1997) 33/34; Pagano (1983) 329.

[8] See Camodeca (1999) 15–20. Unfortunately, some of the tablets were overlooked and not photographed, one of several reasons why early editions were unsatisfactory. The condition of the documents is now so poor that they are completely illegible with the naked eye. Using infra-red light, Camodeca was nonetheless able to distinguish and decipher parts of writing on the un-photographed surfaces.

make it almost certain it was a *collegium* building (probably of carpenters), and on the basis of that comparison it has been hypothesized that the Murecine structure too was the seat of a *collegium*.[9] However, recent excavations of the villa have found a bathing complex and an enormous kitchen attached to the *triclinia*-nucleus. Furthermore, archaeological explorations to the south of the building found no architecture there, only strata of silt. The suggestion has therefore been made that the central space bordered on the river, and that it was not enclosed but open towards the water. On the basis of these new insights, a recent interpretation is that the whole complex was a *hospitium* or *deversorium* welcoming travelers coming up the river with bathing and restaurant facilities.[10]

A large number of inscriptions from the villa—about ninety scratched on marble revetments stacked in the kitchen and two more scratched on the walls—show the letters 'SVL'.[11] Given also the presence of the archive, we can only conclude that the building belonged to the Sulpicii we encounter in the archive or to their descendants. Unfortunately, however, the archaeological data are not particularly helpful for our understanding of what is written in the tablets. Several circumstances disconnect them from their archaeological context. First of all, the villa was buried along with the rest of Pompeii during the eruption of Mount Vesuvius in 79 AD. However, the documents do not date from the period just prior to that event; they date from decades earlier, so far as we can tell from 26 AD to 61 AD.[12] In and of itself that does not mean they were void or invalid at the time they were buried, as is shown by another Pompeian discovery. In 1887, a set of writing tablets was found wrapped up in piece of cloth together with a large collection of silverware, a statue of Jupiter executed in bronze and silver, and three pair of gold earrings.[13] Whoever had packed those objects must have intended to take them with him (or in this case more likely: her) in an attempt to flee Pompeii. The bundle had been put down on a bench sometime during the eruption but was

---

[9] Bollmann (1998) 284–288, 368–371; Pagano (1983) 347–349.

[10] De Simone (2000) 70–75. Another recent interpretation of the building is that it was constructed to accommodate the Emperor Nero; Mastroroberto (2003).

[11] De Simone (2000) 65/66, 74.

[12] *TPSulp.*42 possibly dates to 26 AD. However, Wolf is not convinced by Camodeca's reading, and thinks *TPSulp.*66 (dating to 29 AD) is the oldest document; Wolf (2001) 79. The youngest document is *TPSulp.*91, dating to February 22nd, 61 AD.

[13] De Petra (1887); *FIRA* (1943) vol. 3, 291–294 nr. 91. See Meyer (2004) 140–142. The owner of the tablets was in all likelihood a certain Decidia Margaris, one of the protagonists of the documents.

then left there, perhaps after its owner had been killed or incapacitated or after the room in which it had been placed had become inaccessible. The documents' date is surprising; they are related to a fiduciary sale of slaves that had taken place in the year 61 AD. Amidst the turmoil and panic produced by the volcanic eruption, the owner still thought it worth the effort to pack them up along with precious silverware and jewelry. This chance find hints at just how important and valuable such documentation could be, even many years after a transaction had been concluded.

The documents in the Agro Murecine, on the other hand, were not fetched in an attempt to salvage them. Instead, they were left behind right where they were: in storage. By the year 79 AD probably all had lost their value as written evidence for concluded transactions, as is suggested not so much by their age as by another characteristic. Some of the tablets, linked together in 'booklets' of diptychs and triptychs, seem to have been disassembled in antiquity.[14] The majority of them are missing one or two tablets so that many documents are without their lists of witnesses, a state at least some were already in at the moment they were stored. This incompleteness would have rendered their value as evidence in a court setting zero, indicating that they were not being kept for business reasons. The room in which they had been placed further strengthens that notion; the *triclinia* of the Murecine building were being refurbished during the time of the eruption. The one in which the tablets were found was apparently used as a sort of general storage area containing building material and miscellaneous objects such as a part of a ship, oars, and an anchor—hardly a place for a current archive to be kept.[15] The fact that the latest legible document dates to 61 AD and that many documents had lost their value as written evidence by 79 AD are probably indicators that the banking venture had ceased to operate by the time Pompeii was destroyed.[16]

An even more important element disconnecting the documents from their archaeological context is that they refer to transactions that took place not in Pompeii, but for the most part in Puteoli on the other side of the Bay of Naples. Previously active on the other side of the Bay, the Sulpicii were seemingly in the process of relocating to Pompeii. Since

---

[14] Wolf (2001) 78/79; Camodeca (1999) 18/19. For a description of the Campanian diptychs and triptychs, see Meyer (2004) 127–132.

[15] Pagano (1983) 345/346, Camodeca (1999) 11–14.

[16] It is extremely tempting to connect the fact that the archive runs only to 61 AD to the earthquake that hit the Bay of Naples in 62 AD. However, I think it is safer not to make too much of the approximate coincidence of the two dates.

the villa was undergoing refurbishment, showing little sign of use or wear, this move was perhaps still ongoing when Vesuvius erupted. Given the state and age of the archive, the Sulpicii had by that time probably retired from the banking business. If indeed the villa in the Agro Murecine was a *deversorium* or the seat of a *collegium*, they may have changed metier sometime in the 60s or 70s AD. But why they brought the tablets with them to Pompeii from Puteoli is a mystery. A recent study of Pompeian graffiti shows a close and, it would seem, fairly warm relationship between the two Campanian cities.[17] Puteoli has to cede first place only to Nuceria as the town most frequently mentioned in these Pompeian scribbles. We could say that the documents are a further attestation of this close relationship, but even if true that still does not get us very far in explaining the location of the find.

Whatever the truth may be, it seems unlikely that the extant documents constitute all the archival material the Sulpicii-business produced between 26 AD and 61 AD. What ended up in the basket is therefore probably a deliberate selection brought over for specific reasons. It could be that the content of these particular documents was the determining factor. On the other hand, the disassembled state of many diptychs and triptychs could just as well indicate that reuse was the reason these tablets were saved; their physical state more than their content may have determined their survival. Unfortunately, we will always remain ignorant of the selection criteria.[18]

Intra-Community Exchange in Puteoli

The main protagonists of the tablets are three bankers: C. Sulpicius Faustus, C. Sulpicius Cinnamus, and C. Sulpicius Onirus.[19] We know from the archive that Cinnamus was the freedman of Faustus, while Faustus himself and Onirus seem to have been the sons of the freedman C. Sulpicius

---

[17] Benefiel (2004). See also Frederiksen (1984) 321 who stresses Campanian regional unity, and sees the Murecine tablets as a further confirmation of this unity: 'Pompeii, like Capua, Neapolis and Cumae, was part of a coherent social and economic whole with Puteoli at its centre…'

[18] On the nature of the Sulpicii archive and of Roman archives in general, see the extensive discussion in Gröschler (1997) 246–297.

[19] Camodeca (1999) 20–26. Possibly there were four Sulpicii, and the Faustus *maior* we see in three documents (*TPSulp.*22, 42 and 66) was a different person from the Faustus we see operating from March 34 AD onward (*TPSulp.*96). Wolf (2001) 80/81.

Heraclida.[20] Since Faustus appears in the tablets thirty-five years prior to Onirus' first mention, Onirus could also have been Faustus' son instead of his younger brother.

These freedmen of freedmen and sons of freedmen seem to have been running their financial operations independently; nothing indicates that a Puteolan or Campanian patron was involved in their activities. Insofar as Sulpicii are present in Campanian inscriptions they always appear to be people of quite humble social status.[21] It is possible that Faustus and his father Heraclida descended from the slave *familia* of C. Sulpicius Galba, member of a powerful senatorial family. In inscriptions from Minturnae (Latium), dating to late Republican times, slaves and a freedman of Sulpicii Galbae appear.[22] However, the C. Sulpicii we meet in the Murecine documents seem to have been operating independently; they had their own freedmen and slaves, and nothing indicates that the senatorial family from which they may once have originated was involved in their activities. Other sources, literary as well as epigraphic, had already made it likely that freedmen could conduct their business independently. In the tablets we now seem to have a confirmation of this suspicion.[23] As to the exact nature of the business of the Sulpicii, they were either moneylenders (*feneratores*) or true bankers who kept money on deposit and who specialized in auction sales (*coactores argentarii*). The evidence in the tablets does not point definitively in either one or the other direction, and the lively debate about the correct assessment of their activities is likely to continue.[24] Since for my purposes the matter is of little consequence, I will leave it aside here and simply refer to the Sulpicii as 'bankers'.[25]

What we have in the Murecine tablets are quite clearly the remnants of what once was an archive kept by the Sulpicii to record their financial operations. Two tablets, much larger in size than usual, were probably part of a ledger; they contain two entries in chronological order confirming that money had been paid out, possibly as loans, possibly as draw-downs

---

20 *Eph.Ep.* VIII 451. Camodeca (1999) 22/23 and fig. 4.

21 *CIL* X 2297, 2985/6, 2989; *Eph.Ep.* VIII 418. Possibly also (but of more uncertain origin), *CIL* X 2987, 2990/1, 2998. Camodeca (1999) 22, with nt. 48. However, see Dennison (1898) 394, nr. 54: C. Sulpici... / anus, pra[efectus?... / hic s[itus est].

22 Slaves: *CIL* I 2687, 2697; freedman: *CIL* I 2679. Camodeca (1999) 22.

23 See Garnsey (1981); D'Arms (1981) esp. ch. 5 and 6; Veyne (1961), esp. 224–231.

24 Verboven (2003a); Camodeca (2003) 74; Andreau (1999) 76–79; Andreau (1994) 49–55.

25 The Sulpicii as bankers, Harris (2006) 12; Camodeca (2003) 74; Gröschler (1997) 57–66.

on an account.[26] A number of documents are canceled; they have three big letters 'SOL' (for *solutum*, 'paid') scratched through the text; others are canceled by long diagonal lines. In both cases these marks are a sure sign that the documents were kept for the duration of the contracts, and then for some time afterward as records of completed transactions.[27] Two tablets show marks ('*tab*. XIII'; '*tab*. XVIII') that should in all likelihood be interpreted as archival markers; other documents are palimpsests showing traces of previous writing, in at least three cases with names that also appear in the later contracts.[28]

Reading the documents, it is hard to escape the impression that what we see reflected in them is the business of a relatively homogeneous socio-economic group. Of course, it is difficult to tell exactly how coherent this group was, but there are many indicators that give us valuable information about the socio-economic position of its members. First, many names seem to indicate freedman status: of the 249 people in the archive of whom we know the *cognomen*, 129 (51.8%) bear a Greek one; the great majority of Latin *cognomina* as well betray servile origin, e.g. Felix, Fortunatus, Primigenius.[29] Sometimes freedman status is explicitly stated, and in fact this is the case with one of the Sulpicii, Cinnamus, who identifies himself as a freedman of Faustus.[30] Given the abundance of freedman names, it is safe to say that what we are seeing is basically a freedman milieu, even if there are freeborn citizens in this social circle.

Second, the monetary sums in the documents provide us with an idea of the economic position of the community members. The documents are

---

26 *TPSulp*.94, 95. Camodeca thinks the payments were loans, Jones (2006) 65/66 proposes draw-downs. *TPSulp*.94 concerns an under-slave (*vicarius*) of a slave of the Emperor Claudius.

27 'SOL': *TPSulp*.54, 60, 61, 62, 65, 69; diagonal lines: *TPSulp*.43, 58, 82, 99, 108, 112. On the cancellation of *chirographa*, see Scaevola *Dig*. 2,14,47,1; Modestinus *Dig*. 22,3,24; Paulus *Dig*. 47,2,83,3.

28 Archival markers: *TPSulp*.90, 91; palimpsests: *TPSulp*.5, 10, 71, 75, 83, 85. *TPSulp*.10, a *vadimonium* between Cassius Serenus (and a Sulpicius?), was overwritten on a document that concerned a C. Sulpicius and likely the same Serenus. *TPSulp*.85's earlier text certainly concerned a Cinnamus, as did the later document. In the *scriptura prior* of *TPSulp*.92, the name of at least one of the same consuls appears (written upside down), as in the later contract.

29 Camodeca (1999) 28/29 (no figures are given for the number/percentage of Latin *cognomina* of servile origin). For a discussion on names as indicators of freedman status, see Andreau (1974) 140–155.

30 *TPSulp*.72, 74. *TPSulp*.111 may contain evidence on another freedman in the Sulpicii banking clan. Line 4 'Cinnami liberti' could mean either 'of the freedman Cinnamus' or 'of a freedman of Cinnamus'.

not all loans, and it is not even always clear what type of transaction they represent. It is therefore impossible to calculate a median loan-sum in the way we can for the Iucundus archive (where the median is 3,059 HS).[31] However, the sums in the Sulpicii archive do give us an indication of relative wealth. Amounts vary within a bandwidth of about 1,000 HS to 130,000 HS (although that latter amount seems to have been exceptionally large).[32] If that was the kind of money the Sulpicii and their associates moved around on any regular basis, then what we are witnessing are the transactions of a rather affluent community. Money like that fell far short of the stupendous riches of the senatorial and equestrian elite who had recourse to millions of *sestertii*. On the other hand, people who could command such sums were considerably wealthier than the average Roman, living at a level of maybe two or three times subsistence, say 300 HS a year.[33]

A further way of establishing the social make-up of the group of people in the tablets is to look at the frequency of patrons' involvement in the transactions of their freedman-clients. In some documents, imperial freedmen and slaves appear, and because of the involvement of the imperial court these relationships were, of course, of a different nature than the strictly intra-communal ones.[34] Confining the analysis to just that latter category, intra-communal freedman status is clear from a number of documents. In one instance, *TPSulp*.24, we see a patron claiming his legal right to a half-share of the inheritance of his deceased freedman.[35] In another, *TPSulp*.45, we see a borrower being helped out by his patron in securing a loan. *TPSulp*.48, an interesting but also difficult document, tries to arrange the business relationship between two groups of people: the

[31] This is the median of the 25 clearly legible loan-sums in the archive; the median of all 44 sums (not all securely legible) is higher: about 4,500 HS. Andreau (1974) 88–91.

[32] *TPSulp*.14, 56, 62, and (possibly) *TPSulp*. App.9 mention transactions for 1,000 HS. *TPSulp*.8, 61 and 110 mention smaller amounts, but the first two are for larger total transactions while the meaning of the last is unclear (perhaps it is a lease contract for publicly owned land or storage space). The reading of 130,000 HS in *TPSulp*.74 is not entirely certain. The next two largest sums would be 125,000 HS (*TPSulp*.49) and 94,000 HS (TPSulp.69). On the sums in the archive, see also Wolf (2001) 82/83.

[33] See Hopkins (1980) 117–119 for the calculation of 115 HS *per annum* as bare subsistence level. See also Jongman (1988) 195. For discussions on Roman income levels, see Bang (2008) 90/91; Jongman (2007); Temin (2006); Hopkins (2002) 197–203; Goldsmith (1984).

[34] Imperial freedmen: *TPSulp*.18 (but reading uncertain), 45, 51, 52 (all belonging to the same dossier), 89, 101, 119; imperial slaves: 67, 68 (same dossier), 94, 95 (same dossier), 49, 69.

[35] A patron-client relationship is not explicitly stated, but given the details of the document it is the only logical interpretation. See Camodeca (1999) 83; Wolf (2001) 89/99.

Sulpicii and their slaves on the one hand, and a certain C. Iulius Prudens and his slaves and freedman on the other. *TPSulp.*82 is a document written by a patron on behalf of his freedwoman. Documents like these show that patrons were regularly involved in the affairs of their freedmen.[36] However, perhaps, the best indicator of the involvement of a patron in a freedman's transaction—the direct mention of the relationship with the formula 'patron's *cognomen*' followed by '*l(ibertus)*'—occurs only four times, a somewhat surprising result given the overwhelming number of freedmen names.[37]

Freedman status and moderate wealth were common traits among the people in the Murecine tablets. In attempting to establish the socio-economic coherence of this group I think we can go further still. In the contracts and statements where we can read a location, this is almost always Puteoli (in seven cases it was either Capua, Volturnum, or Rome) indicating that the community had a strong local nature.[38] There are several *peregrini* attested, for example coming from Tyre, Alexandria, and Athens; of at least these people we know for certain that they had come from some place else (although they may have been sojourning in Puteoli).[39] It is possible that there are others in the documents who were not Puteolans but who are less easy to trace: out-of-towners with Roman citizen status, traveling through or on a short-term stay. Yet, it is reasonable to assume that a substantial number, if not the majority of the people we meet were closely associated with Puteoli; they either lived there (or close by) or they transacted business there on a regular basis.

The information we have both from the tablets and from other sources confirms this idea. A number of documents record the announcement of auction sales of assets belonging to defaulting debtors. Such announcements were always posted in or near the Puteolan forum, the place where the auctions were slated to take place.[40] In one instance (*TPSulp.*86), the insolvent debtor M. Egnatius Suavis, who had transferred six slaves as

---

[36] On the social and legal commitments of an ex-slave to his former master, see D'Arms (1981) 39–45.

[37] *TPSulp.*45, 53, 70, 103. Camodeca (1999) 27/28.

[38] Capua: *TPSulp.*12, 26 (possibly also 126); Volturnum: *TPSulp.*44; Rome: *TPSulp.*13–15, 19.

[39] *TPSulp.*4, 13 and 60, 61, respectively. Others: *TPSulp.*14, 49, 78, 80, 106. See further Chapter 2. On people from the East in Puteoli, and on Puteolan commercial relations with the West, see Dubois (1907) 83–111.

[40] *TPSulp.*83–88, 90–92. Announcements were usually posted in the Sextian portico or in the Caesonian *chalcidicum*. *TPSulp.*90–92 also announce that the auction will take place in that location.

security for a loan, had died before his slaves could be auctioned. He had no extant heirs, meaning that now not just the slaves but his whole patrimony would go up for public sale. The announcement asks his creditors and guarantors to come forward. The fact that an announcement of that sort was put up in the forum of Puteoli suggests that both Suavis and his business associates were local Puteolans, or at least frequent visitors.[41]

There is also evidence of another nature. In five cases, a contracting party or witness mentions the name of his *tribus*, the sole reason being, it seems, to emphasize freeborn status. The Falerna tribe—the local *tribus* freeborn Puteolans belonged to—is mentioned four times; the urban Collina is attested once.[42] The latter instance seems to betray some distant servile origin, even if M. Antonius M. f. Col. Maximus was freeborn himself. But the *gens* he belonged to occurs frequently in Puteolan inscriptions, and we have evidence for other assured Puteolans, magistrates of the colony, stating the Collina as their tribe.[43] Other epigraphic evidence providing prosopographical data to cross-reference the names in the archive further supports the idea of local ties. In *TPSulp.*70, for example, a Cn. Pompeius Blastus appears. He states that he is the freedman of Epirus who is known to us from an epitaph on a grave urn (now in its second life as a stoup in the Neapolitan chapel of S. Aspreno al Porto). The Julio-Claudian date of the urn in combination with the *gens* name Cn. Pompeius, a well-known Puteolan *gens*, and the unusual *cognomen* Epirus make the identification almost certain.[44] Along with Cn. Pompeius Blastus and Epirus, other names appear belonging to well-attested Puteolan *gentes* such as the Annii, the Cn. Polii, the Stlaccii, and the L. Faenii.[45]

Of these, the L. Faenii are known to have been involved in the lucrative trade in incense and perfume, products for which Puteoli was one of the

---

41 Written information was, of course, meant to spread partly by word-of-mouth, see Harris (1989) 34/35 with fig. 7: people reading a notice in Pompeii's forum.

42 Falerna: *TPSulp.*43, 44, 45, 52. Collina: *TPSulp.*50. The Falerna (and not the Palatina) as the Puteolan local *tribus*: Camodeca (1992) 161 and nt. 51; D'Arms (1974) 117. Interestingly, despite mention of the *tribus* Falerna, *TPSulp.*44 was drawn up not in Puteoli, but in Volturnum; Camodeca (1999) 27, 120.

43 See Camodeca (1992) 181; D'Arms (1981) 123, 138/139, and D'Arms (1975). In *TPSulp.*25 and 121, M. Antonii also appear.

44 Camodeca (1982b) 151–153 and Camodeca (1982a) 7.

45 Cn. Pompeii: *TPSulp.*23, 48 (maybe), 64, 70, 88; Annii: *TPSulp.*46, 53, 57, 121; Cn. Polii: 24, 46, 64, 110, 121; Stlaccii: *TPSulp.*21, 25, 115, 118, 122; L. Faenii: *TPSulp.*2, 3, 27, 61. See Camodeca (1996), esp. 106/107; Camodeca (1979) 17–34.

main trading centers.[46] This circumstance hints at yet another possible common characteristic of the community in the Sulpicii documents. Since Puteoli was the major port of call for merchant-ships to and from Rome, it seems likely that a fair number of community members were involved in trade with the imperial capital.[47] Two men, L. Marius Iucundus and C. Novius Eunus whom we see storing tons of Alexandrian wheat, were almost certainly grain traders.[48] Another indication for involvement in trade is a document in which a M. Caecilus Maximus declared that he owed money to C. Sulpicius Faustus from a profit ('quaestum') he had made; Maximus and Faustus, it appears, had entered into a *societas* in which Faustus provided the capital for Maximus' venture in return for part of the revenue.[49] The few people for whom we have occupational information outside of the tablets are indeed known to have been traders: M. Valerius Euphemus (a trader in Spanish goods), P. Attius Severus (a trader in Baetican oil or *garum*), and Cn. Cossutius Atimetus (a *paenularius*; producer of cloaks).[50] Ironically, the one person whose occupation we actually know from the documents seems to have been somewhat of an anomaly. L. Lucretius Firmus was a soldier of Cohort XIII; in the early 40s AD he was apparently involved in a lawsuit over damage done to him by a slave of his opponent. Suetonius tells us that the Emperor Claudius stationed cohorts as fire brigades in Ostia and Puteoli, and Firmus was perhaps a legionary in the Puteolan section.[51]

The people in the tablets appear to have been doing frequent business with one another. This is perhaps an unsurprising finding given the local nature of the community and the likely similarities in occupation and socio-economic position of its members. Several names occur in a number of documents, sometimes dating from years apart. Sex. Granius

[46] Camodeca (1992) 59/60, with nt. 70, 71; D'Arms (1981) 167/168. See also Frederiksen (1984) 329; Dubois (1907) 129/130.

[47] Puteoli as a center of trade: Dubois (1907) 64–83; D'Arms (1974).

[48] Iucundus: *TPSulp*.53, 79; Eunus: *TPSulp*.45, 51, 52, 67, 68. See also Camodeca (1994) 104–109.

[49] *TPSulp*.66. Unfortunately, the word following 'quaestum' can not be clearly read, so the source of this profit is unclear. Camodeca considers 'aeruginis'; *aerugo* (copper rust) was used as a green dyestuff and for medicinal purposes. Camodeca (2003) 86.

[50] Euphemus: *TPSulp*.58 and 89, *CIL* IV 9611, and Manacorda (1977) 130, fig. 1: N. 7920 (the Valerii seem to have been a local family, see *CIL* X 1814, M. Valerius Pudens, *duumvir* 161 AD); Severus: *TPSulp*.78, *CIL* XV 3642, 3644/5, 4748/9; Atimetus: *TPSulp*.120, *CIL* X 1945. For the Cossutii as a Puteolan family, see *CIL* X 1784, Cossutius Rufinus, decurion in 187 AD.

[51] *TPSulp*.12, 26. Suetonius *Claudius* 25,2. See Wolf (2001) 95, who thinks the date must thus be 43/44.

Numenius, for example, appears in two documents, one from the year 41 and the other from 49 AD; in the first he appears as the borrower, in the latter as the lender of a sum of money.[52] The name of M. Lollius Philippus occurs three times in documents dating from the years 45 and 48 AD; in the two instances from 45 he received and repaid a loan (likely the same), in the one from 48 a sum of money was paid in his name ('nomine').[53] C. Varius Cartus appears in a document dating from the year 41, and also in a document from the year 48 AD; in both cases he seems to have been embroiled in a lawsuit with the Sulpicii.[54] Other documents too point to repeat dealings. In several *vadimonia* (agreements to appear in court), the contested total sum consisted of two or three smaller ones, suggesting that sums for several transactions were being lumped together. So for example in *TPSulp.*1: C. Sulpicius Cinnamus intended to sue L. Marius Hermeros for three separate sums: 20,000 HS, 7,000 HS, and 1,000 HS. In all likelihood Cinnamus wished to resolve his dispute with Hermeros (perhaps a defaulting debtor with several outstanding debts) in one go, and therefore initiated a lawsuit for all three contracts between them.[55]

That the Sulpicii had long-standing business relationships with some of their clients is also clear from documents that mention accounts or long-term credit.[56] A document from 55 AD records an inquiry before a judge in which C. Sulpicius Cinnamus questioned his opponent C. Iulius Prudens. The questions were relevant, explained Cinnamus, for the future lawsuit over his (Cinnamus') credit. From another document we know that the Sulpicii and Prudens had been business partners for many years, the relationship dating back at least seven years to 48 AD.[57] Elsewhere in the archive we see a slave acting on behalf of his mistress Priscilla. He borrowed 4,000 HS for her, a sum he specified as being 'for the account of my mistress', stating that the loan came on top of a previous one of

---

[52] *TPSulp.*70, 55.

[53] *TPSulp.*54, 109 and 73. The date of *TPSulp.*107 can not be read, but the connection with *TPSulp.*54 (definitively dating to 45 AD) seems obvious. Camodeca (1999) 172 and (1992) 255–257 proposes Philippus was the freedman of Lollia Saturnina, who appears in TSulp.73, suggesting Saturnina was involved in both the transaction from 45 AD and the transaction from 48 AD.

[54] *TPSulp.*1 *bis*, 32. The date of the first document can also be 43 or 45 AD.

[55] Other *vadimonia* for separate sums: *TPSulp.*1 *bis* (possibly), 5, 7 (but probably a *sponsio tertiae partis*) and 8. For another explanation for the listing of several sums (partial guarantees), Camodeca (1992) 55.

[56] See Harris (2006) for a general discussion on the importance of credit money in the Roman economy.

[57] *TPSulp.*25 and 48.

20,000 HS.[58] The term 'account' ('rationem') and the mention of the previous loan both point to an open-ended and ongoing financial relationship between the Sulpicii and Priscilla. That accounts were being kept by the Sulpicii for some of their clients is also evident from *TPSulp.*60. A superscript reads 'for the account of Titinia Antracis' ('tabellae Titiniae Antracidis'), and the documents mentions sums 'paid out' ('expensos') and 'received' ('acceptos').[59] In yet another document, Publius Urvinus Zosimus declared to have received from C. Sulpicius Cinnamus 2,000 HS as a loan 'in addition to the 12,000 HS that I owe to him through my handwritten note on other tablets', once again suggesting an open-ended financial relationship.[60]

Commerce and Social Standing in Ancient Puteoli

Good repute as an honest trader is beneficial, if not crucial, in commercial life, and suspicions of misconduct can seriously strain business relationships. Reputation affects the way economic actors behave, and can have an effect also on how they solve their disputes. Merchants transacting a deal obviously want the transaction to work out for them they way they intended. They do not wish to be cheated, and would like their trading partner to deliver his side of the bargain without any fuss and without shirking his responsibilities. To govern their behavior they can invoke a legal system, a set of formal rules accompanied by institutionalized instruments to pressure a partner into compliance. But setting up such a law-based institution of exchange is costly; to codify a set of contractual laws and to install a judicial system with a court, judges, and enforcement mechanisms has a high fixed cost.[61] If such a system does not exist or only functions imperfectly, relying partly or wholly on reputation can be cheaper and more effective. If economic actors live in a small community in which everyone knows everyone, the importance of reputation is obvious enough. Cheating on your next-door neighbor with whom you contract on a regular basis is quite clearly not a wise business policy.

---

58 *TPSulp.*58: 'in rationem Priscillae dominae meae'.

59 *TPSulp.*61 and 62 belong to the same dossier. See also *TPSulp.*63–65 (also *nomina arcaria*).

60 *TPSulp.*57 'sestertia dua millia nummum, quae ei debeo per chirographum alis tabellis'.

61 High expenses are not the only problem in setting up a law-based system. Greif (2006) 311 and nt.1; Dixit (2004) 78–86.

Basing trade relations on the assumption that business partners will want to maintain a good name in order not to imperil future deals limits the need for formal contracts and for an institutionalized legal system.[62]

The city of Puteoli, though not one of the largest urban centers in the Empire, was no mere village.[63] Nonetheless, in the community of traders within this town, business relationships are likely to have been to a greater or lesser degree personal; traders probably knew one another well and probably met frequently. Cicero, in an anecdote he recounts to Atticus, gives an illustration of just how small a world Puteoli could be. The senator C. Sempronius Rufus, like Cicero on a stay in Puteoli, tried to avoid the Puteolan businessman Vestorius with whom he had some sort of financial disagreement. Since Cicero and Vestorius were close friends and often found together, Rufus also tried to avoid Cicero. His scheme did not work for long. Despite Rufus' best efforts, Cicero ran into him in the business district: 'How could I help seeing him when I walked through Puteoli bazaar? I said good morning to him there (he had some business on hand no doubt), and on a later occasion good-bye...'[64]

Given the apparently large degree of face-to-face interaction within the Puteolan trading community, information about business associates likely circulated freely, and acts of bad behavior such as shirking and cheating likely became common knowledge quickly. Reputation must, by implication, have played a crucial role in the city's economic life. Surely the members of the *gens* of the incense and perfume trading L. Faenii would rapidly have been out of business if they had not managed to maintain a reputation as honest traders. And by the same token, it seems unlikely that the Sulpicii themselves would have attracted funds and would have been entrusted with people's accounts if they had not enjoyed a name as upright bankers. Patron-client relationships will have increased the social pressure to uphold a good reputation; misdeeds of patrons would have reflected badly on their clients and vice-versa, and both had an interest in the good name and repute of their former slaves and masters.

There is indeed some tantalizing evidence in the tablets to support the idea that value was attached to a good business reputation. A lawsuit

[62] Posner (1997) 366; North (1990) 55. See also Ellickson's case-study of ranchers in Shasta County, CA. Ellickson (1991), esp. 230–239.

[63] An area of 100/120 ha, with a population size of 30,000/40,000 inhabitants, according to Camodeca (1977) 89/90.

[64] 'Qui potui non videre, cum per emporium Puteolanorum iter facerem? In quo illum agentem aliquid, credo, salutavi, post etiam iussu valere...' Cicero *Ad Att.* 5,2,2. Tr.: D.R. Shackleton Bailey, Loeb (1999). See D'Arms (1981) 48–55; Frederiksen (1984) 322.

between C. Sulpicius Cinnamus and Iulius Fortunatus, taking place in the year 49 AD, seems to have revolved around the question of whether or not Cinnamus had tarnished Fortunatus' good name.[65] Cinnamus had apparently been claiming that Fortunatus owed him 3,000 HS. Fortunatus, on the other hand, was of the opinion that no such debt existed, and that by making the claim Cinnamus was willfully discrediting him. He challenged Cinnamus to swear a legal oath to the effect that the claim was justified and that there was no malicious intent on Cinnamus' part. In another document, unfortunately poorly preserved, we may see the same Fortunatus up in arms again about his good name, this time possibly suing C. Sulpicius Faustus for insulting him.[66]

In the lawsuit between Cinnamus and Fortunatus, the litigating parties attempted to terminate legal proceedings by means of an oath on the formidable ensemble of 'Jupiter Optimus Maximus, and the divine power of the deified Augustus, and the *genius* of Tiberius Claudius Caesar Augustus'.[67] In another document, a guarantor declared: 'I acknowledge and have sworn by Jupiter and the divine power of the deified Augustus that I have, this year, stood surety on his behalf and on behalf of no one else'.[68] The swearing of oaths as an integral part of doing business has been extensively discussed by Nicholas Rauh in his analysis of trade on Roman Delos. He relied heavily on literary texts and did not discuss the documents just quoted, although they provide direct support for his thesis about the importance of this practice. Rauh sees this behavior largely in a spiritual light: 'With so little in the way of genuine security, Roman ancient merchants... clung to the securities and guarantees that religion alone could provide'.[69] My own interpretation of the value of oaths in business is different though, and has more to do with social

[65] *TPSulp*.28/29. I here follow Wolf's and not Camodeca's explanation of the documents. Wolf makes the case for an alleged violation of the *iniuria* edict (Ulpianus *Dig*. 47,10,15,25) as the central issue of this lawsuit. Wolf (2001) 102–107.

[66] *TPSulp*.116. Possibly a dispute over *convicium facere*: Ulpianus *Dig*. 47,10,15,2–14. Because of the poor preservation of the document, it is not entirely clear who is suing whom.

[67] *TPSulp*.29: 'per Iove[m Optimum Maximum et numen divi] / Augusti et G[enium Tiberii Claudi Caesaris Augusti...]'. Wolf (2001) 106/107 opts for the emendation 'Augusti et [deos penates...]'. Other oaths in the Murecine tablets: *TPSulp*.63, 117, but esp. 54, 68.

[68] *TPSulp*.54: 'fateor autem et iuravi per Iovem et numen divi Augusti me hoc anno pro eodem nulli ali fide mea esse iussisse'. Probably an allusion to the *Lex Cornelia*, see Gaius *Inst*. 3,124.

[69] Rauh (1993) 129–188; citation on 188.

standing than with mental support. In my view, benefits will have been quite tangible.

We must, of course, take into account that swearing oaths with overt religious (not to mention political) overtones, like the ones cited above, may in and of itself have been a psychological deterrent against misbehavior. But solemn declarations like these also provide evidence, if indirectly, for the value of good reputation in the Puteolan trading community. The imperial cult, including worship of the *genius* and *numen* of living and deceased Emperors, was by the mid-first century AD much a part of the Roman religious landscape.[70] It would seem that making someone swear a public oath in such a fashion—an oath that appealed to shared beliefs and values—would only have been effective in a community where reputation mattered and where people would have known about, and frowned upon, a violation.

Nonetheless, this relatively indirect evidence for the importance of a good name is all we have to go on. Direct references to reputation are wholly absent in the tablets, and transactions explicitly based on mutual confidence in professional commercial repute are conspicuously lacking. In fact, what is most striking about the Murecine documents, both in language and composition, is their highly formal tone and their painstaking legalism. The rules of Roman law are followed with great care and in the minutest detail, and the legal framework as we know it from the *Digest* and other legal sources is mirrored in the documents to a high degree. That this practice reflects a conscious desire to bring the content of contracts in line with the overarching imperial legal system is most evident from documents where the edict of the curule aediles is mentioned. In *TPSulp.*43, a seller guarantees that the slave he is selling is not a fugitive or one prone to running away and that the sale is also covered by 'the other provisions in the edict of the curule aediles of this year, which are written and included ... in keeping with the formula in the way that is customary'.[71]

For Joseph Wolf it is exactly this element which constitutes the principal gain from the archive; the documents provide 'irrefutable proof that

[70] Price (1984); Beard, North and Price (1998) vol. 1, 184–186, 206–210. In *Aug.* 98, Suetonius mentions how Augustus, sailing past Puteoli, was greeted as divine savior by the crew of an Alexandrian ship.

[71] 'et cetera in edicto aedilium curulium, quae huiusque anni scripta conprehensaque sunt, ... ex formula, ita uti adsolet'. Similar language is used in *TPSulp.*42 and in (badly preserved) *TPSulp.*44. For a discussion on the difficulties the reading of *TPSulp.*43 poses, Wolf (2001) 112/113.

Roman civil law, in all its complexity and in the way Roman jurisprudence had developed it, thoroughly obtained in everyday life.'[72] That is a major gain indeed. The tablets may do more than any other single set of epigraphic data so far available to support the idea that, to cite the same author again, 'Roman law was not a bloodless structure of norms without reality-value'.[73] But in light of the socio-economic make-up of the Puteolan community that produced this material, the question is: why did this relatively close-knit community use a rigid and highly formal way of doing business and of solving conflicts?[74]

The determination to use formal contracts drawn up in the state's legal jargon, even with regular business partners (for years sometimes), is remarkable. And, be it noted, even when things apparently got personal and someone's reputation was at stake, formal legal means were employed to address the situation. In the business coalition of the medieval Jewish 'Maghribi traders', which I will discuss in greater detail in Chapter 3, we posses a counterexample. The Maghribis, a group bound together by ties of religion and origin, explicitly and repeatedly referred to good repute as a guiding principle in business, making it clear how concern for reputation affected their decisions. Though this can be an efficacious and cost-effective strategy within a close-knit group, it is apparently not the solution the Puteolan community adopted.

Of course, this would all become less puzzling if we assume that much trade was wholly informal. After all, the archive as we have it is incomplete and, more importantly, it is likely that records were kept only of formal contracts, while informal contracts were not recorded and only concluded orally. Such informal and unrecorded business no doubt did exist, although by its very nature it is invisible to us. But all the same, the community in its socio-economic composition must have been coherent

[72] Wolf (2001) 131: 'Der Hauptgewinn ist indessen der unwiderlegliche Nachweis, daß das römische Privatrecht in seiner ganzen Komplexität, wie die römische Jurisprudenz sie entwickelt hat, durchaus im Alltag galt'.

[73] Wolf (2001) 98: '...die Rechtsordnung, wie sie sich in den gelehrten Schriften der römischen Jurisprudenz darstellt, [war] kein blutleeres Normengerüst ohne Wirklichkeitsgehalt'.

[74] Compare the 'close-knit community' of ranchers in Shasta County, CA (studied by Robert Ellickson) where members relied on the extralegal means of appealing to reputation ('truthful negative gossip') in order to solve conflicts over trespassing cattle; Ellickson (1991) 57/58, 232/233. See also Levinson (2003) 374/375, 'Smaller, close-knit groups whose members interact frequently tend to rely less on formal contracts and more on informal social norms to regulate behavior'.

enough for reputation to have played a much larger role in contracting and dispute settlement than we see reflected in the archive.

At this point in the discussion, other personalized ways of exchange need to be mentioned. The social dynamics of good repute should, I think, be distinguished from two other forms of personalized economic interaction that have received a fair bit of attention from ancient historians, namely those of *amicitia* and patronage.[75] Trade and business on the basis of *clientela* and 'friendships' (relationships containing a mutually understood reciprocal element, that is) have been put forward by scholars of both 'modernist' and 'primitivist' leanings to support their case. The idea that the Roman imperial elite was involved in trade at arm's length through clients and freedmen was famously argued by John D'Arms. But although this hypothesis is not implausible, hard evidence remains elusive. Besides, D'Arms suggestion that the more wealthy and important freedmen—people like the Sulpicii—were financially independent of patrons creates difficulties for this argument, as Peter Garnsey has noted.[76]

A more recent work of a different persuasion deals even more extensively with the impact of *amicitia* and patronage on economic conditions.[77] As the author, Koenraad Verboven, is acutely aware, the literary evidence on which he mainly relies is heavily skewed towards the imperial and provincial elite. In his preface he cautions: '... readers should be warned that the behavioural patterns studied in this book are those of the political, social and economic elite and their entourage, which are not necessarily the same as those of the "common" people.' This admonition notwithstanding, he seems to be assuming that what was true for the upper crust must have held true also for the rest of society: 'Regardless of what the ancient economy was truly like it cannot be denied that Greeks and Romans did not perceive the forces of the market economy as the determining factor

---

[75] See e.g. Yakobson (1999) esp. 65–111; the collection of articles in Wallace-Hadrill (ed.) (1989); Brunt (1988) 351–442; Saller (1982).

[76] D'Arms (1981). Garnsey (1984). In this context, I should not omit to mention Bang's suggestion that the terms of this debate are simply wrong. Bang (2008) 283 observes that: '[In Indian studies] most scholars have been keen to downplay the extent of involvement by the vast households of the political elite in commercial activities. They prefer to portray it as a marginal phenomenon precisely in order to assert the vitality, strength and potential modernity of the traders of pre-colonial India.... The contrast... is a product of different historiographical traditions'.

[77] Verboven (2002) studies mainly Republican material, but the arguments are said to apply to the early Empire as well: Verboven (2002) 10.

in their lives. Their "mental map" of the world focused on family, friends, and citizens, not on businessmen, firms, employees and markets.'[78]

I confess to having some doubts about the first part of that statement—whether applied to the political and social elite or to 'common' people, for that matter—but what concerns me here is the latter part. With regard to Romans' (leaving aside Greeks') 'mental map', if indeed *amicitia* and *clientela* were all-important in business, it is simply not visible in the Murecine documents. All that can be said with confidence is that patrons, to be sure, were at times involved in the affairs of their freedmen. But nothing in the documents betrays the kind of *amicitia* relations that someone like Cicero entertained with his friends and sundry acquaintances, and nothing indicates that *officia*, despite the enormous number of freedmen names, dominated business relations.[79] Instead, we witness a highly formal and legalistic way of economic interaction.

In addition, it was inherent to the nature of *clientela* and *amicitia* that only as an extreme measure did one take an *amicus*, a patron, or a client to court for debts; such a step was almost certain to damage the relationship beyond repair.[80] In this light, it is striking that no fewer than one third of the documents in the Murecine archive are related to litigation. Of course, we do not know the circumstances that gave the archive its present shape. Litigation is precisely what tends to get documented, and litigated cases are therefore likely to be overrepresented. Nonetheless, the Sulpicii and their associates did clearly not hesitate to sue for debts, and in fact seem to have done so as a matter of course. On the face of it, this behavior tells against the idea of predominating *amicitia* and *clientela* ties.[81]

Instead of explicitly basing transactions on personal rapport and reputation, economic actors employed the language of formal contractual law. There was a significant hurdle to be overcome in conducting business in this way. If businessmen commonly relied on the relatively intricate rules of the legal system, they had to acquire a working knowledge of those rules. A possible explanation for their willingness to do so might be their wish for a higher level of security where larger amounts of money were involved. Contracts for smaller amounts would have been entered into

[78] Verboven (2002) 11, 15.

[79] On Cicero's *amicitia* relations, see Verboven (2002) 63–67; Brunt (1988) 351–381; Saller (1982) 15–17.

[80] Saller (1982) 121. Like Verboven, Saller mainly limits his analysis to the role of patronage and *amicitia* in upper-class social circles.

[81] Ties of that nature may, in general, have been far less influential than often supposed. See Yakobson (1999) esp. 65–111; Brunt (1988) 382–442.

informally, while transactions for larger sums would have been drawn up in writing using Roman law. That solution seems logical but the problem with that approach is twofold. First, it does not bring us a great deal further since it is impossible to know where we should draw the line. The purchase on credit of a loaf of bread in a bakery was likely not written down in a legal contract, but the Iucundus tablets show us that loans for much smaller sums than the ones in the Sulpicii archive were regularly so recorded.[82] Second, and much more important, we may think it no more than natural that people who transacted for large sums of money would have wanted the safety of legal contracts, even if they knew one another well. However, this idea presupposes that using Roman law did indeed involve increased security, begging the question as to why.

Before discussing the reasons that may have induced economic actors to follow the formal rules of the law, I think it should be noted that this practice was not limited to the banking house of the Sulpicii, or even to Puteoli for that matter. There are contracts in which no Sulpicii appear, and although they will have had an interest in these affairs in some indirect way, it shows that transacting with the use of Roman law was not confined to dealings with them and was being practiced on a wider scale.[83] I also call to mind L. Lucretius Firmus, the soldier of Cohort XIII. For the damage he was claiming from L. Aelius Valentinus he entered into a lawsuit, which shows that this was done also by people outside the business community.[84] In Petronius' *Satyricon*—contemporary with the Murecine tablets—we find the story told at the beginning of this chapter where Encolpius and Ascyltos contemplate going to court to address a wrong they think was done to them. On a wider Campanian scale we have the supporting evidence of the Pompeian tablets of Iucundus as well as the Herculanean tablets containing, respectively, receipts for transactions at auction sales and, among many other things, documents referring to lawsuits over status.[85] In other words, in the world of the Sulpicii, using the

[82] The median sum in the (clearly legible) Iucundus tablets is 3,059 HS: Andreau (1974) 90. Of course, this is still 27 times annual subsistence level.

[83] Due to the poor preservation of many manuscripts, it is often difficult to tell if the Sulpicii were directly involved or not. Of the following sixteen documents we can read enough to tell that they were not: *TPSulp.*12, 15, 26, 43, 45, 51 (although C. Sulpicius Faustus appears in the list of witnesses), 52, 55, 60 (but see 61, 62), 64, 70, 71, 78, 80, 99, 106 (Camodeca excludes the reading 'C. Sulpicius' in line 1).

[84] *TPSulp.*12, 26. Of course, L. Aelius Valentinus may conceivably have been a Puteolan trader but he was not the one who initiated the lawsuit.

[85] Pompeian tablets: K. Zangemeister, *CIL* IV *Suppl.*1, 3340: 1–155; Herculanean tablets: V. Arangio-Ruiz and G. Pugliese Carratelli *La parola del passato* (1946–1961) 1:373–385,

rules of the law seems to have been a widely accepted way of arranging business and of solving conflicts. How had Roman law become the default institution, and why did it persist in this role?

Path Dependence: 'History Matters'

Roman law gave rules for how to behave in certain situations: in what specific form to draw up contracts, how to make legally binding promises, and how to incorporate provisions for payment. It also gave rules for how to act in case of non-compliance or violation of agreements: how to advertise auction sales after a debtor defaulted, how to initiate a lawsuit, and how to appoint a judge. These rules, together making up the Roman legal framework, formed an institution that was exogenous to all players in the Puteolan community; no individual could unilaterally have changed the rules or have chosen to follow only some but not others. That did, however, not mean the legal system was a 'package deal' that could either be adopted wholesale or not at all. In theory, players could have chosen to follow complementary or divergent rules of their own devising, provided everyone else did so too.[86] It is important to underscore that the decision of the members of the Puteolan business community to apply Roman law was, at least theoretically, a free choice; the rules could freely be ignored since their use was not prescribed by the state, nor was deviating from them state-penalized. That means that the decision to follow them must have been endogenous; it must have stemmed from internal motivations of economic actors, showing that they had an incentive to do so or, conversely, that they had an incentive not to deviate.

Legalistic and juristic thinking was, of course, deeply rooted in Roman society. By the time of the early Empire it had a long history, a history that can be traced back all the way to the time of the Twelve Tables.[87] Roman law formed part of Roman culture and traditions in many ways. Although fundamentally secular it had some obvious historical connections to

3:165–184, 8:455–463, 9:54–74, 10:448–477, 16:66–73. Camodeca is working on a new edition (including so far unpublished texts); Camodeca (2003) 92–95. It seems we have much to look forward to.

[86] That a particular set of rules, whatever its exact composition, would be followed had to be 'common knowledge'. See Lewis (1969) 52–60.

[87] See e.g. Cornell (1995) 272–292; Wieacker (1988) 287–309; Watson (1975).

religious practices.[88] Access to the legal system was one of the privileges of being a Roman citizen, and *commercium* and *conubium* (the rights of making contracts and of concluding marriages under Roman law) were desired by, and granted to, Latin communities during the Early Republic.[89] The most famous instance of a Roman citizen invoking his legal rights is no doubt St Paul, reminding the centurion and tribune who tied him up and were about to flog him that he was a citizen, and a citizen by birth at that.[90] The Roman state had used formal legal contracts in its dealings with the publicans from at least the time of the second Punic War.[91] Roman law, in short, formed part of 'Romanness' and of Rome's cultural and ideological heritage.[92] The story of how legal development was intertwined with Roman history from the earliest times has often been told, and it would be superfluous to repeat it here.[93] But although giving an exhaustive account of the law's history is not necessary for my purposes, I will spend a few words on its historical development. I think that this element provides the key to understanding its role as the default system in Puteoli.

Starting in the fourth-century BC, Campania—including the ancient Greek city of Dicaearchia (the later Puteoli) at the time still a fairly insignificant place—witnessed the spreading influence of Rome. In its conquest of the Italian peninsula, Rome attempted to establish 'working arrangements' with newly created or incorporated cities in matters of municipal administration.[94] Roman magistrates (*praefecti iure dicundo*) were sent out to Campanian towns that either were too small to maintain their own judicial system or that voluntarily accepted the jurisdiction of the prefects. The power of the *praefectura* was not great though and 'a good deal must still have depended on the wishes of the litigants

[88] Meyer (2004) 44–63; Beard, North and Price (1998) vol. 1, 24, 181. See also Watson (1992).

[89] Sherwin-White (1973) 32–34.

[90] *Acts* 22, 25–29. But see also Cicero II *Verres* 5,158–170.

[91] The fundamental book on *publicani* is still Badian (1972); more recently Malmendier (2002) esp. 65–91. Malmendier points out that the contracts between the state and the *publicani* were different from ordinary contracts under civil law, giving the state much more leverage than it would otherwise have had.

[92] On 'imperial ideology', see Ando (2000). See esp. 73–130 for the legal communication between the Roman government and the inhabitants of the Empire.

[93] E.g. Wieacker (1988), esp. 236 ff.; Kunkel (1968); Kaser (1949). See also Watson (1992); Frier (1985).

[94] Frederiksen (1984) 264–280 (quotation 268); Sherwin-White (1973) 39–47; Dubois (1907) 24–27.

and the circumstances'.[95] In 194 BC Dicaearchia received 300 Roman colonists, which probably meant it was withdrawn from the *praefectura* and received its own local magistrates.[96] An inscription dating to 105 BC, in which Puteolan *duoviri* are first attested, shows that these magistrates held powers equal to those of the prefects, making it unlikely that the two political offices coexisted.[97] From the inscription we further learn that the Puteolan constitution was typical for a Roman *colonia*; apart from the two annual *duoviri* there was a board of ex-magistrates that functioned as an advisory body.

The legal system that spread to Puteoli, first through the *praefecti iure dicundo* and then through local magistrates, was based on the praetorian edict which, in the fourth and third centuries BC, was still in an early stage of development. Rome's further conquest and expansion into the Hellenistic world with its more developed commercial organization slowly transformed and refined it.[98] A period of rapid and profound change for Rome's legal system was the time of the late Republic. According to Bruce Frier's extensive analysis, three factors had a crucial impact: the enfranchisement of the Italian allies, the rise in commerce and personal wealth from imperialism, and the instability of the political structure in the late Republic.[99] The increase in the size of the Roman citizen body, which enlarged and socially diversified the 'litigating class', increased the caseload for the courts, putting pressure on the judicial system. The courts, unable to bureaucratize, responded by relying more on jurists as external specialists; the necessity for greater speed and efficiency in handling cases lent authority to their expert opinions. In addition, political issues threatened to intrude in private suits, a dynamic that endangered the wealth of many in the Roman socio-political elite, a class enjoying a manifold increase in fortune through Rome's imperial expansion. The demand for more legal security created a force that would separate civil law more clearly from political and politicized affairs, leading to an 'ideology of

95 Frederiksen (1984) 269.

96 Livy 34,42,5/6. Frederiksen (1984) 269, 319.

97 *CIL* X 1781. See Pulice (1977) 30/31, 38–42. See also Frederiksen (1984) plate 12; Tran tam Tinh (1972) 3–6 and plates 37, 38.

98 Wieacker (1988) 346–351.

99 Frier (1985), esp. 276–282.

autonomous private law', a process that enhanced the acceptance of the legal system.[100]

A recent book by Elizabeth Meyer has drawn attention to another element of legal reception, namely the practice of writing in an archaic and formulaic style in wax tablets, which provided authority and legitimacy to acts both religious and secular.[101] Order—in Roman public as well as private life—had from days of old been created and preserved through the methodical observance of ceremonial, in some cases involving the use of *tabulae* (for example by the augurs and the pontifex maximus).[102] For Polybius it was exactly this peculiarly Roman element of solemnity and religiosity in public as well as private matters that bound the Roman state together; it kept the fickle masses in check and assured the honest behavior of Roman public officials. The authority assigned to tablets, Meyer argues, thus rested on venerable tradition and on the power of belief. This power surrounded legal documents too, in the case of *chirographa* supplemented by the expression of personal *fides*; a written statement in close conformity to the praetor's edict conveyed trust.[103] The prestige of citizenship, consisting also of the capacity to act as a witness, added to the efficacy of writing on wax tablets. Only Roman citizens were acknowledged as official *testes* to contracts, and being denied the privilege of witnessing was seen as dishonoring.[104] The desire to employ legal tablets in order to lend authority to acts, Meyer asserts, had the result that the Romans had effectively created written contracts, despite the fact that the jurists continued to adhere to the strict view that contracts were concluded orally and that writing was subsidiary.[105] Interestingly enough, Meyer notes that the involvement of the Roman government (or even the jurists) was minimal in all of this and that the use of legal *tabulae* stemmed from

---

[100] Frier (1985) 281. This ideology 'though ultimately impotent in the face of revolutionary movements such as those that produced the proscriptions of 43, was nonetheless powerful in more normal circumstances...'

[101] Meyer (2004), esp. Chapters 2–5.

[102] Polybius 6,56,6–15. Early Roman use of *tabulae*: Meyer (2004) 24–36. See also Harris (1989) 153/154. Harris is, on the whole, much more skeptical about the use of writing in early Roman history than Meyer.

[103] Meyer (2004) 36–43, 148–151.

[104] The Twelve Tables already contained a provision about declaring someone *intestabilis* (cited by Aulus Gellius *NA* 15,13,11). See Meyer (2004) 159.

[105] See Meyer (2004) 39/40, 115–120, 253–265.

the endogenous motivation of practitioners to give 'visible indicators of *fides*'.[106]

I am sympathetic to Meyer's argument, even if her analysis seems imprecise at times. For one thing, she seems deliberately to be conflating the use of Roman law and the use of wax tablets, two things that overlapped but were not the same exactly. Roman law was a system that provided social rules for economic interaction and dispute settlement, and as such we see it reflected in tablets. However, the tablets are not to be equated with the system for which they are evidence.[107] But despite Meyer's somewhat narrow focus on *tabulae* I think she is right in arguing that tradition and history provide a key part of the explanation for practitioners' use of the law, and I agree with her ultimate conclusions that '... Roman law initially drew its authority from outside government and outside itself, from the wider world of belief in which it was embedded', '... the more ways in which legal acts followed widely accepted, formalized techniques ... the more likely their users were to believe in their efficacy and, therefore, the more believable and efficacious legal practice in general would be.'[108]

Meyer's conclusions fit rather neatly with the idea of 'path dependence', although she does not frame her argument in those terms. Path dependence was made famous by Paul David's inquiry into the economics of the QWERTY keyboard. This keyboard was designed to avoid the common problem of 'jamming' in nineteenth-century typewriters, but at the price of making it inferior in typing efficiency. David explained how it could persist as the default standard—even after the mechanical problem

[106] Meyer (2004) 163. The *Senatusconsultum Neronianum* of 61 AD, a measure against forgery, is a rare instance of state interference; Suetonius *Nero* 17.

[107] And on a related note, I am not as convinced as Meyer that the Roman jurists' insistence that contracts were in principle concluded orally can be dismissed as a stubborn refusal on their part to face up to reality. For juristic writing in this sense, see e.g. Gaius *Inst.* 3,92/93; Gaius *Dig.* 44,7,1,13–15; Modestinus *Dig.* 44,7,52,2; Ulpianus *Dig.* 45,1,1,*pr.*; Venonius *Dig.* 45,1,137,*pr.*; Ulpianus *Dig.* 46,4,8,3.

[108] Meyer (2004) 294/295. Meyer describes the efficacy of the law as a 'manifestation of social consensus'; a better term would, I think, be 'social convention'. See Lewis (1969) 58: 'A regularity *R* in the behavior of members of a population *P* when they are agents in a recurrent situation *S* is a *convention* if and only if it is true that, and it is common knowledge in *P* that, in any instance of *S* among members of *P*,

(1) everyone conforms to *R*;
(2) everyone expects everyone else to conform to *R*;
(3) everyone prefers to conform to *R* on condition that the others do, since *S* is a coordination problem and uniform conformity to *R* is a coordination equilibrium in *S*'.

of 'jamming' had been solved—through its sheer embeddedness.[109] However, the application of path dependence as a theory is not limited to the introduction of new technology or to the problem of market failure. It can be used as a broader theory to study institutional dynamics as, indeed, David himself would later argue.[110] As such, put in somewhat oversimplified terms, it propounds the rather intuitive notion that human actions and behavior are the product of past actions and behavior.[111]

Applied to Roman law it can be described as follows: beliefs and perceptions about the legal system were reinforced each time conformity with these beliefs and perceptions followed anew. Players' shared historical experience created precedents leading to consistent mutual expectations about future conduct. The combined power of culture and history made Roman law part of players' cognitive mindset, and the more established it became the harder it became for individuals to deviate from it. As an institution it thus generated further institution-conformant behavior. 'And so it goes—we're here because we're here because we're here because we're here.'[112] This is what Meyer shows. There is, for example, no reason why for the Sulpicii a personal letter would intrinsically have expressed less *fides* than a formal legal statement. But because this was the established social convention, repeating the precedent had a higher chance of eliciting further convention-conformant behavior so that it actually *was* a more effective course of action.

Roman law as a 'carrier of history' was shaped by its past and as such exerted an influence over the future. The factors that had been instrumental in its development—such as the traditional authority ascribed to wax tablets and the events of the late Republic—had set it on a path to becoming the default institution. The people in the Sulpicii archive were, in that sense, indeed completely 'free' in applying whatever rules they wanted in drawing up their contracts and settling their disputes. But their behavior was directed by past events and by 'circumstances in which neither they nor their interests figured'.[113]

---

109 David (1985).

110 David (1994). Path dependence not primarily about market failure; David (2001) esp. 21–24.

111 Intuitive maybe, but not accepted by many neoclassical and neo-institutional economists who favor a teleological approach; David (1994) 206–208, 216; (2001) 32.

112 Lewis (1969) 41/42. See also David (1994) 209/210.

113 David (1984) 333.

Path Dependence: 'Sunk' Organizational Capital

An aspect of legal development that Meyer does not take into account, although it complements her argument about the propelling force of culture and history, is the aspect of the investments in information and learning the law demanded. In order to participate and conform to established behavioral patterns, players needed knowledge. That knowledge had to be broken down, processed, and applied to specific problems if it was to be of any use to individuals. The community as a collective could acquire and retain more expertise than single individuals could, but in order to put it to good use a 'code' for coordinating information had to be followed by all.[114] The collective investments involved both in acquiring expertise and in learning the 'code' for channeling and processing information were 'sunk' costs that together constituted a form of accumulated institutional capital. These costs directed further investments in the same direction. Future learning would take place more easily along the path the organization had taken, creating a bias against information that did not fit in; it would not be learned or incorporated as efficiently as information that *did* fit in. The investments the institution had required in the past thus molded individual conduct, pushing future investment further along the previously followed route.

If all of this sounds terribly abstract, it can be made concrete with the Murecine documents in which traces of the 'sunk' capital of the Roman legal institution are detectable. Knowledge about the correct rules and their application had to be acquired and coordinated. With whom did this knowledge reside and by whom was it processed? The answer to that question should, I think, be: for everyday transactions, most of all by the actual 'consumers' of the legal system like the Sulpicii, but to a certain degree also by a group of legal experts, especially for matters to do with litigation. To start with the latter category, magistrates and judges charged with supervising lawsuits and with pronouncing verdicts were generally not legal specialists. In exercising their duties, they needed professional advice.[115] We would, therefore, expect to see lawyers operating in court. Their names are never mentioned in the tablets and their professional counsel is never alluded to. Yet, we see lawyers' efforts in the work they left behind; their hand is visible most of all in the mistakes they made.

---

[114] David (1994) 212–215. See also Greif (2006) 187–216.
[115] Kaser (1996) 192–194.

Scribal errors and corrections abound in the documents. Because the texts were written on wax surfaces, mistakes could be erased with the blunt end of the stylus.[116] But in a few interesting cases, mistakes were not corrected in that way but crossed out. Two corrections show the experts' thinking and interpreting work as they listened to the litigating parties and tried to translate what they heard into the proper legal language. In *TPSulp.*29, for example, both copies of the text show part of the phrase 'against good morals' ('adversus bonos mores'), and in both cases it is crossed out. The phrase is part of the edict-formula on which the rest of the text is modeled.[117] The conflict seemed to match the provisions of that edict most closely, so the legal expert who fashioned the document initially wrote down the whole formula. However, thinking things over, one assumes, or perhaps listening more closely to the quarreling parties, he realized that he did not actually need the 'adversus bonos mores' clause and therefore decided to delete it again.[118] A similar example is presented by *TPSulp.*25. In court before the magistrate, the professional jurist who had to interpret what he heard and had to turn it into the correct legal formulas wrote the sentence 'C. Iulius Prudens responded that the slaves Hyginus and Hermes, object of the suit, are his and under his control'.[119] This follows the formula that seemed most appropriate to the case at hand. But having written down the full regular form, the legal scribe realized that the phrase 'under his control' ('suaque im potestate') was not actually applicable, so he crossed it out again.[120]

But professional legal experts seem occasionally also to have been employed in private business. In *TPSulp.*48, we have a document that is unusual and extremely complicated. It attempts in a novel and ingenious

[116] Sometimes the mistake was not erased properly and can still be read, so in e.g. *TPSulp.*23: 'II[[m]]virum'. Not all mistakes were detected and then corrected though, see e.g. *TPSulp.*28: 'se' repeated by mistake but not canceled.

[117] Ulpianus *Dig.* 47,10,15,2.

[118] Wolf thinks it is the special edict of Ulpianus *Dig.* 47,10,15,25 that is being referred to rather than the generic edict of Ulpianus *Dig.* 47,10,15,2 (*contra* Camodeca). The fact that the words 'adversus bonos mores' are canceled out certainly points in that direction; moreover, the examples given by Ulpianus (*Dig.* 47,10,15,31–33) seem relevant to the activities of the Sulpicii. Wolf (2001) 102–107.

[119] 'C. Iulius Prudens respondit homines Hyginum et Hermen quibus de agitur suos [[suaque im potestate]] esse'. The sentence is clearly modeled on a damage clause (see the *Digest* chapter Ulpianus *Dig.* 9,4,21). Note that only the 'inner' text (the only text that provided legal evidence) is corrected.

[120] Manthe (1981) 159/160 suggests it was Prudens himself who deleted the phrase, but it seems more likely to me that during the phase before the magistrate the document was only handled by a scribe.

way to circumvent the impossibility of direct agency under Roman law, though it does so using two standard legal tools: a 'mandate' and a 'stipulation'. The intention of the document was clearly to settle for the foreseeable future (no time-limit is incorporated) the legal relationship between multiple people (not limited to a fixed number) of different status (patron, client, and slave), and to do all of that in one fell swoop; within the strictures of Roman law a difficult, if not impossible task. Perhaps unsurprisingly, the solution falls short of being completely legally sound, although fathoming what is actually wrong with it is a bit of a brain teaser.[121] The document sought, in convoluted language, to find a tailor-made solution to a singular problem. Since there was no example to work from or standard form to follow, it is unique in its legal content. But even if the person who composed the document tried to stretch the possibilities of the law a bit too far, clearly it was someone with great expertise and ingenuity. It seems, in short, most likely that we here have the work of a local professional lawyer.[122]

In *TPSulp.*48, the uniqueness of the document is an indicator that it was drawn up with professional assistance. However, apart from this remarkable example, evidence for lawyers in private business is rather meager. None of the other documents is quite as out of the ordinary, and many follow standardized patterns repetitiously. Four documents, though fairly undistinguished in form, may show some further evidence. Of the grain trader C. Novius Eunus we have four *chirographa* written in Eunus' own hand, dated between 37 and 39 AD.[123] Though Eunus, to judge from his handwriting, was a proficient writer, he made many phonetic mistakes and had great trouble spelling. He wrote 'que' for 'quae', 'puplicis' for 'publicis', 'recete' for 'recte' and once wrote 'ets' before correcting it to 'est'. Most tellingly, he seems to have been confused as to the correct legal language, in one instance initially writing 'dico' but then deleting it and replacing it

[121] See the extensive discussion in Wolf (1993) who concludes (91) 'Die Lösing ist . . . mißglückt; ihre Swächen sind eklatant'. The document's legal shortcomings are hard to understand, though, and would, in my view, not have been obvious to ordinary businessmen. Apparently they were not obvious even to all legal specialists.

[122] In this sense, certainly, Camodeca (2003) 76 (*TPSulp.*48 is 'frutto della giurisprudenza cautelare locale . . .') and Wolf (1993) 91 (*TPSulp.*48 'gibt unmittelbar Einblick in die Kautelarpraxis').

[123] *TPSulp.*51, 52, 67, 68. Eunus' profession is not stated, but since he had several tons of Alexandrian wheat and other foodstuffs in storage it can be assumed he was involved in the grain trade.

with 'fateor'.[124] It is speculative, but Eunus' mistakes, especially the latter one, may be a sign that he received some help writing the formulas.

But even if this interpretation of Eunus' *chirographa* is right, it does not mean—indeed it is extremely unlikely—that he had to rely on a jurist to understand what rights and obligations would ensue from the deals he struck. He may have required some aid with the exact formulaic language, but as a professional grain trader will not have needed anyone to tell him what writing and signing his contracts entailed. This brings me to the important topic of players' acquaintance with the legal system. Since economic actors used formal legal contracts frequently, they must have had a working knowledge of the most important rules. The legal system as a whole was extensive, and it would have been far from necessary for non-specialists like merchants to know all of it; yet the core part, most pertinent to their trade, must have been familiar to them.

In the Puteolan community Eunus belonged to, not only knowledge of the core rules will have been widespread but also knowledge of the knowledge of those rules. An individual member will have known the rules, but will also have had reason to believe that other members knew the rules who, in their turn, will have had reason to believe that others had reason to believe that they knew the rules, and so on. Put differently, the rules will have been 'common knowledge'.[125] The incentive to learn them was clear enough; because formal contracts were ubiquitous in business, knowing the law was an invaluable asset or perhaps even a necessity in economic life. In the story of Trimalchio's dinner party, almost certainly set in Puteoli, the clothes-dealer Echion says as much while talking about his son's education. He relates that he had bought the boy some law-books to prepare him for running the family business: 'I want him to have a smack of the law in order to manage the property'.[126] For a professional grain trader like Eunus, familiarity with the rules pertaining to his business must have been imperative. All this is quite commonsensical, but

[124] All examples from *TPSulp.*51, 52. See Adams (1990) for a discussion of Eunus' many and varied spelling errors. NB, *TP.*15 = *TPSulp.*51; *TP.*16 = *TPSulp.*52; *TP.*17 = *TPSulp.*67; *TP.*18 = *TPSulp.*68. Flobert speculates on an Oscan influence to explain the 'dico' / 'fateor' mistake, Flobert (1995) 150.

[125] See Lewis (1969) 52–60.

[126] '…volo illum ad domusionem aliquid de iure gustare'. Petronius *Sat.* 46,7. Tr.: M. Heseltine, Loeb (1975). Echion, described as a 'centonarius', is either a clothes-dealer or (less likely in this setting) a fireman or a supplier of fire-fighting equipment; Smith (1982) 113/114.

what concrete clues are there in the Sulpicii archive for players' knowledge of the legal system?

Given the nature of the data, the evidence has to be indirect, but C. Sulpicius Cinnamus' documents provide a good starting point. Three tablets, dating between 45 and 51 AD, show his handwriting.[127] He could evidently write for himself, and was involved in contracts and legal affairs so often (his name appears in about fifty of all hundred-and-twenty-seven documents) that it seems unlikely he ever needed much, if any, professional assistance. Another document also provides indirect hints at practitioners' knowledge of things legal. From *TPSulp.*27 it appears that L. Faenius Eumenes and C. Sulpicius Faustus, while battling it out in court, had sent representatives (*cognitores*, in all probability business associates)[128] to Rome to continue the suit there.[129] Apparently, the matter was of great importance to them, and it seems rather unlikely that they were sending men without any legal know-how whatsoever as representatives to litigate on their behalf in the imperial capital before the urban praetor. Better evidence still for a community-wide acquaintance with the rules comes from the contracts for the sale of slaves in which the curule edict is mentioned. The succinct and casual way in which the edict is referred to presupposes a familiarity with its content, making elaboration unnecessary: '... duly to pay double the sum, in keeping with the formula, in the way that is customary...'[130]

For some freedmen in the Puteolan business community, learning may have started at an early stage—that is to say, in their former life as slaves—and the ability to draw up contracts in accordance with the demands of the law may have been the primary reason that they learned how to read and write.[131] Making himself useful writing contracts was certainly one of the tasks of the slave Nardus who, in a lease agreement dating from 40 AD, wrote: 'I, Nardus, slave of Publius Annius Seleucus, have written in the presence and on the order of Publius Annius Seleucus my master, because

[127] *TPSulp.*109 probably dating from 45 AD, *TPSulp.*73 from 48 AD and *TPSulp.*69 from 51 AD. See Camodeca (1999) 40.

[128] One of the representatives (L. Faenius Sporus) is without much doubt either a freedman or a fellow freedman of L. Faenius Eumenes whom he is representing.

[129] In *TPSulp.*27 Eumenes and Faustus, incidentally, agree to terminate the suit, and try to solve the problem of the *vadimonium* their representatives had meanwhile concluded.

[130] *TPSulp.*42–44: '... duplam pecuniam ex formula, ita uti adsolet... recte dari...'

[131] The social circle of the Sulpicii and their associates was conceivably one that had attained 'craftsman's literacy', Harris (1989) 7/8, 13. See also Camodeca (1999) 40.

he claims not to know letters...'[132] Likewise with the slave Diognetus: 'I, Diognetus, slave of C. Novius Cypaerus, have written, on the order and in the presence of my master Cypaerus...'[133] It is, in my view, hardly fanciful to suppose that in this world of freedmen and freedmen of freedmen, many had started out as former 'secretary' and business-assistant slaves, employed, like Nardus and Diognetus, in writing contracts for their merchant masters. In fact, this may well have been the case with C. Sulpicius Cinnamus, freedman of C. Sulpicius Faustus.[134]

Learning may have occurred through daily practice and self-schooling, or else maybe through formal instruction with the clear intention that the acquired knowledge be used in business. Education requires time, effort, and money, so if the intended purpose was clear this would have structured learning habits. Petronius' clothes-dealer Echion, in his musings about the value of culture and learning, surely displayed a predisposition toward a certain type of schooling, desiring that his son learn something useful: 'He has dipped quite deep enough into literature. If he is restless, I mean to make him learn a trade, as a barber or an auctioneer, or at least a barrister, something that he can carry to the grave with him'.[135] Echion is here talking about his son; masters paying for the education of their slaves will all the more have wanted to invest in something directly practical that promised to yield some returns.[136] Knowledge of the law, about this Echion is quite clear, qualified in this respect: 'That stuff has bread in it'.[137]

---

[132] *TPSulp.*46: 'Nardus Publii Anni Seleuci servus scripsi coram et iussu Publii Anni Seleuci domini mei quod is negaret se litteras scire...'

[133] *TPSulp.*45: 'Diognetus C. Novi Cupaeri servus scripsi iusu Cupaeri domini mei cora ipsum...' Cypaerus was not stated as being illiterate, but illiteracy must have been the reason why a slave was writing for him; he was physically present and, since he instructed the slave, was legally bound by the contract.

[134] *TPSulp.*72, 74. Faustus does not seem to have been illiterate though. On the relationship between Faustus and Cinnamus, see Camodeca (2003) 75/76.

[135] 'nam litteris satis inquinatus est. quod si resilierit, destinavi illum artificium docere, aut tonstrinum aut praeconem aut certe causidicum, quod illi auferre non possit nisi Orcus'. Petronius *Sat.* 46,7. Tr.: M. Heseltine, Loeb (1975). Echion first lists two lowly professions, and then adds 'aut certe causidicum'. These words 'added on as if to refer to a second best, become comic only on the assumption that *causidici* in general were no more impecunious than the average barrister today'. Smith (1982) 124. Given Petronius' intended audience, a large part of the fun was also, I would suggest, that barristers were less looked down upon by the elite than were barbers and auctioneers.

[136] Indeed, having received an education in the *artes ingenuae* while a slave seems to have been something to boast about, *CIL* XI 4866, 7856. See Veyne (1961) 219, with nt. 5.

[137] 'Habet haec res panem.' Petronius *Sat.* 46,7. On the basis of Trimalchio's own life-story (esp. *Sat.* 29,4), it is all too easy to think of masters as only interested in teaching their slaves things like bookkeeping and calculation.

To summarize, different people between them shared legal knowledge. On the one hand, there were the experts who had made the legal system their profession and who operated mainly in court; on the other, there were the 'consumers' of the law who needed a good working understanding of the rules in order to function in trade and finance. Professional jurists and practitioners together formed a network that collectively retained and relayed information, a network that assured the application of the law in opportune ways both in court and in daily practice. This web of knowledge was a valuable, but also a durable form of capital; self-enforcing, hard to replace or transform, and—because of the many 'irreversible investments' it had required—creating a bias against alternatives.[138]

Path Dependence: Satisfactory Outcomes

But despite the barrier against change that the 'sunk' capital of investments in learning had created, the legal system had by and large to produce satisfactory outcomes in order to remain a self-enforcing social convention. If it failed to do so, behavioral changes would eventually have come about. Generally speaking, once a convention is well-established, individual actors—no matter how dissatisfied—have no incentive to go against the grain and invest in alternatives.[139] A discontented individual, or group of individuals, would have had to sacrifice an unknown amount of resources in an attempt to make people follow new and thus far uninstitutionalized behavior, a possibly costly undertaking with uncertain payoffs. Apart from 'sunk' costs making people averse to change, there is also a psychological aspect to consider: 'institutionalized behavior and the associated outcomes lead to reinforcing norms, senses of entitlements, identities, self-images, thinking patterns, and ideologies.'[140] Deviating from established group conduct, in other words, is emotionally taxing and socially awkward, and convincing others to follow suit can be a daunting task. But still, if too many players are dissatisfied, change will ultimately occur. This can happen gradually, but because pressure has to build up to

---

[138] David (1994) 212.

[139] That is to say, as long as a general (Nash) equilibrium holds in the system. See David's comments on the use and abuse of the term 'lock in', and on the problem of imperfect information, making a coordination equilibrium in a decentralized process difficult to overturn; David (2001) 25–28. See also David (1994) 213–215; Lewis (1969) 8–24.

[140] Greif (2006) 181. See also 190–194.

overturn an established equilibrium, major changes can also happen suddenly and precipitously, and seemingly without warning.[141]

Since the Sulpicii documents span a period of only three decades, we can not conclude on the basis of that sample alone that the continued use of Roman law means there always was a stable equilibrium. But another and more fruitful approach is possible: we can try to establish how outcomes were reached and how that would have affected players' perception of the system. It is in litigation that we see the clearest indicators that the system must have been perceived as functioning adequately. From the many documents to do with lawsuits it would seem that the Sulpicii and their business partners were a rather litigious lot. This in itself can be taken as a sign that to initiate a lawsuit, or at least threatening to do so, usually produced the intended result: settlements of disputes that were regarded as satisfactory.[142] The procedure of a Roman lawsuit in its separate phases made it inherently conducive to producing outcomes that were acceptable to the litigants. A civil trial took place in two stages: a first stage before a magistrate (in which the litigants had to agree exactly what they were litigating about) and a second phase before a judge (in which the actual verdict would be pronounced). Unfortunately, we do not know for even a single lawsuit in the Sulpicii archive how it was ultimately settled. But there is ample evidence regardless that on the whole settlements must have been satisfactory to disputants.

In the phase before the magistrate there was a surprisingly large amount of consensual action. A civil trial started with a summons (*in ius vocatio*), which was done on a party's private initiative without the intervention of a state official. A defendant could either immediately follow the plaintiff to the magistrate or, if the timing was inconvenient or he felt unprepared, could send a representative to arrange a meeting on his behalf at a more suitable time. If a defendant and a plaintiff appeared in court but were unable to finish proceedings (for example because evidence had to be produced or witnesses called) they drew up a *vadimonium*,

---

141 The established equilibrium slowly erodes away until the institution is no longer self-enforcing, and a shift leads to a new equilibrium. Greif (2006) 168–170; David (1994) 215.

142 There is here, obviously, a certain paradox; after a dispute settlement in which one party loses and the other wins, the losing side will almost invariably feel dissatisfied. See for example the dedicatory inscriptions from Roman Delos, set up to arbiters in praise of their δικαιοσύνη by one particular party rather than by the community as a whole. 'This suggests that the arbitration in question resulted in a conclusion not satisfactory to everyone'; Rauh (1993) 15. However, such dissatisfaction does not necessarily preclude the losing side from accepting the legal system *qua* system as basically fair and sound.

an agreement to appear in court again at a later date.[143] A mutually agreed-upon penalty-clause assured that the defendant would turn up as promised.[144] A *vadimonium* was a private contract, but it was made under the supervision of the magistrate. The latter did not intervene unless the parties did not obey the rules, for example if the plaintiff demanded a penalty exceeding the legal maximum. The magistrate also intervened if the litigants were unable to agree on a date. In that case, he ruled that the trial would recommence at the day after the next (*intertium dare*). This procedure could be repeated as often as was necessary to conclude the first phase of the trial.

Several documents in the archive provide evidence for this procedure: *vadimonia*, (private contracts to reappear and resume a trial), *testationes sistendi* (documents in which a plaintiff declares he had showed up as agreed but his adversary had not), and *intertia* (documents testifying to an intervention by the magistrate, summoning the bickering parties, unable to agree on when to reappear, to return in two days).[145] The archive contains sixteen *vadimonia*—the largest single category of documents in the archive—and it would seem that agreements were usually reached consensually. The point of a lawsuit's first part before a magistrate was for litigants to conclude a 'litigation agreement' (*litis contestatio*), a contract primarily civil in nature, describing what exactly the trial would encompass.[146] The Murecine tablets demonstrate that often it was by way of making one or more private contracts in the form of *vadimonia* that they reached this stage. A good example of what must have been common practice is provided by *TPSulp.*2, 3, and 27 showing evidence for a string of such contracts: two *vadimonia* (one from June and one from July of the year 48 AD) followed by a document drawn up in September of the same year from which we learn that the disputants had nominated representatives who, in their turn, had agreed on yet a third *vadimonium*.[147]

---

143 I here follow the sensible interpretation of Ernest Metzger (2005) and (1997) who disagrees with the so far dominant view of Wolf (1985), which is also the one followed by Camodeca (1999) 49. In Wolf's and Camodeca's view, a *vadimonium* (designed to complement *in ius vocatio*) was completely extra-judicial.

144 Inclusion of a penalty-clause was not imposed by the magistrate, and was left to the litigants' discretion, a sign of the private nature of *vadimonia*. See Metzger (2005) 66–73.

145 *Vadimonia*: *TPSulp.*1–15; *testationes sistendi: TPSulp.*16–21; *intertia: TPSulp.*32, 33.

146 Kaser (1996) 69–81, esp. 77.

147 *TPSulp.*2, 3, 27. No *litis contestatio* was ever concluded in this case though; from *TPSulp.*27 we learn that the litigants decided to settle their dispute, and annulled the *vadimonium* made by their representatives.

In the proceedings *in iure*, there was only a cursory supervision of the magistrate, who would interfere mainly to break a possible deadlock. Part of the 'litigation agreement' was the appointment of a judge, and in this matter too litigants were expected initially to try to reach an agreement of their own accord. In 35 AD, A. Castricius Celer declared that he had made such an agreement with C. Sulpicius Faustus in a lawsuit that encompassed a seemingly wide array of issues, namely 'the affairs, accounts, disagreements, claims, complaints, and legal actions that exist between me and him, and that exist and did exist between him and A. Castricius Isochrysus'.[148] The judge, Celer and Faustus agreed, would be a certain A. Titinius Anthus *maior*. A penalty clause was added to ensure that Anthus would indeed be able to perform his future task; Celer promised to Faustus that neither he nor his heir would prevent Anthus from being judge 'with wrongful intent' ('dolo malo').[149] Exactly what that was supposed to mean is anyone's guess. But whatever Faustus had in mind in demanding the promise, he evidently wanted to preempt any form of obstruction on Celer's part. The sum due in case of violation was commensurate with the wide range and high number of issues to be resolved: no less than 100,000 HS.

What is interesting—and instructive—about the choice for Anthus as judge is that his name seems strongly to suggest he was a freedman. Freedmen could not be included in the official list of judges (the *album iudicium selectorum*) from which parties could choose. Thanks to the discovery in Spain in 1981 of bronze plates, dating to the time of Domitian and containing the municipal statute of the ancient town of Irni, we know that under that charter parties could select someone from outside the list.[150] The agreement between Faustus and Celer renders it all but certain that in the first half of the first century AD, a similar law obtained in Puteoli.[151] The *Lex Irnitana* reveals that mutual agreement on a judge was the ordinary procedure; the magistrate had to investigate if there were any

[148] *TPSulp.*22: 'de rebus [rationib]us controversis actionibus [petitionibus] persecutionibusque, quae [sunt] inter me et eum quaeque [inter eum et] A(ulum) Castricium [Is] ochry[sum…] sunt fuerunt'. Isochrysus is probably involved in this lawsuit only posthumously: *TPSulp.*23, 24.

[149] Wolf (2001) 97/98 disagrees with the reading 'dolo malo' but proposes an interpretation with a similar gist.

[150] Kaser (1996) 192–194. The evidence from the *Lex Irnitana* confirmed what had long been suspected about the *album*. Gonzalez and Crawford (1986) 176/177, Ch. 86 (Latin text), tr.: 196.

[151] See Wolf (2001) 96–98; Camodeca (1999) 78.

objections, but for the rest had to respect the litigants' choice. Only if the parties could not agree on an appointment would the elaborate back-up system under supervision of the magistrate (in which parties took turns rejecting proposed judges) be used; if one of the litigants refused to cooperate altogether, the magistrate would force matters forward by appointing the person the opposing litigant proposed.[152]

In the dispute between Celer and Faustus, such intervention was apparently unnecessary; they managed to reach an agreement bilaterally. Although their contract is the only explicit attestation in the archive of a mutual appointment of a judge, other tablets as well indicate that parties had come to an agreement on this point. In two documents we read 'L. Cocceius Anthus is said to be judge', 'Q. Laberius Cerdo *maior* is said to be judge'.[153] In another dispute where a *litis contestatio* had already been made, the litigants decided to drop official court proceedings altogether and to appoint an arbiter instead, a certain M. Barbatius Epaphroditus.[154] Note that, just like A. Titinius Anthus *maior*, these men were without much doubt of freedman status and hence not chosen from the official *album*.

The combined evidence from both the Sulpicii archive and the Spanish bronze plates has given us a wealth of new information about the Roman civil trial. What is most surprising about the procedure—and what, through the new discoveries, is now clearer than ever—is the strong element of inter-party consensus, both in the phase before the magistrate and in the second phase before the judge. An official played a critical role, but that role was mostly confined to helping out when an agreement could not be reached and negotiations threatened to stall. Another striking element of Roman litigation, an element long known but now understood in much greater detail, is the appointment of laymen judges. In the Sulpicii archive the men appointed to the task of arbiter in civil suits seem often to have been, as their freedmen names indicate, the social peers of the litigants. Both of these elements enhanced the chances that outcomes could be reached that were satisfactory to disputants.

152 *Lex Irnitana* Ch. 87 (Latin text), Gonzalez and Crawford (1986) 177 (tr.: 196/197). See Metzger (1997) 62/63.

153 *TPSulp*.32, 33. The phrase 'is said to be' ('diceretur') indicates that the documents were witnessed; Metzger (2005) 149, nt. 53. Cf. *TPSulp*.31 where the *duumvir* appoints a judge. *TPSulp*.31 was, in all likelihood, a *sponsio tertiae partis* which by its nature was not a mutual agreement but a way for a creditor of unilaterally putting pressure on a debtor who was delaying payment.

154 *TPSulp*.34, 35, 36.

The idea that the procedure of inter-party negotiation on the 'litigation agreement' and on the appointment of judges contributed to creating a basis for social acceptance had already been clearly expressed by Bruce Frier. In his lucid study of late Republican legal development he points out that '... the late Republican judicial system is strongly characterized by its efforts to handle almost all private lawsuits through a consensual model of procedure akin to domestic arbitration'.[155] Frier also took into consideration that Roman judges were only required to pronounce a bare verdict without having to give a motivation for their ruling, a verdict against which usually no appeal was possible. Although this system had 'obvious drawbacks' it provided speedy certainty while precluding the development of 'judge-made law'. This, Frier concludes, 'permitted the widespread participation of untrained laymen in the judicial process, thus avoiding a specialized judiciary while retaining a broader social legitimacy for the decision-making process'.[156]

This brings us back to the history of the legal system. The direction the institution had taken in the past had resulted in a strong element of negotiation and consensus in litigation. This element increased the chances that players would be satisfied with the results the institution produced, which in turn increased the chances that they would continue to display behavior in conformity with already institutionalized rules.

Conclusion

The members of the community we see in the Murecine tablets were overwhelmingly of freedman status, were comfortably off, and lived and worked in or around Puteoli. Many of them were active for years and did frequent intra-community business. As a result, they must often have possessed detailed information about one another's behavior, trustworthiness, and creditworthiness. However, instead of conducting business in an informal way, such as through personal letters, economic actors in this community regularly chose to draw up formal contracts, following the rules of the imperial legal system. To settle their disputes, they frequently litigated bilaterally in court.

Without a doubt, not all economic interaction within this community was governed by formal law, and there must have been numerous

---

155 Frier (1985) 243.

156 Frier (1985) 230.

non-legal 'do's' and 'don'ts' that were commonly understood and regularly complied with. But although informal rules and codes will have been important, members of the community relied much on formal law in their intra-community business. Because the Roman government did not penalize deviating from the rules of the imperial legal system, the observed behavior must have stemmed from endogenous incentives. To explain the conduct of the people in the Murecine tablets I have argued that it was in essence path dependent.

In the Murecine documents we have only a 'snapshot' encompassing a few decades, but although evidence for previous centuries is lacking, it is likely that in Puteoli there was a slow but steady adoption of Roman law. Historical circumstances had set the use of formal law, and with it an individualistic form of economic interaction, directly on a path to becoming the default system. In order to conform to established behavioral patterns, individual players had to invest in knowledge, which further cemented the use of Roman law; the 'sunk' costs of players' investments constituted a form of institutional capital, making them averse to change and directing their learning habits along the previously taken road. Changes would ultimately have occurred if the legal institution had failed to produce satisfactory outcomes, but I argued that the strong element of inter-party consensus in litigation led to outcomes that, on the whole, must have been perceived as satisfactory. Court proceedings required that the disputants negotiate on a litigation agreement and on the appointment of a judge. The men chosen to be judges were not aloof professionals but laymen who could be (and often were) the litigants' social peers. These important elements of participation by litigants in the judicial process and selection of community members as arbiters helped to legitimize verdicts, and ensured the social acceptability and efficacy of the legal institution.

CHAPTER TWO

INTER-COMMUNITY EXCHANGE AND THE ROLE OF TRADING STATIONS IN PUTEOLI

Intra- and Inter-Community Trade

The vast majority of people in the Murecine tablets appear to have been local Puteolans. However, Puteoli was a harbor that facilitated not just local but Empire-wide trade and was, at least before the harbor of Ostia was built, the main point of access for foodstuffs and other goods to Rome.[1] This community will therefore also have interacted frequently with outsiders; with non-locals hailing from different—and often distant—parts of the Empire. The Murecine evidence confirms the status of Puteoli as an emporium of Mediterranean importance. In some tablets people figure who were unmistakably outsiders; their names suggest a foreign origin, and usually it is explicitly stated that they belonged to another community.[2] If Puteolan traders relied on Roman law in their *intra*-community dealings, how did they conduct their *inter*-community business? Such business presented several practical problems. The two most important ones were no doubt that, first, acquiring adequate trading information and, second, enforcing contracts became increasingly difficult with growing distance.

A Puteolan merchant involved in a long-distance transaction, the purchase of a load of grain say, could face a considerable time gap between the *quid* and the *quo*; he would perform his obligation, knowing that he would have to wait for performance of the matching part of the deal. As an illustration of the sort of time lags involved, it seems even under favorable conditions to have taken approximately nine days to get from Puteoli to Alexandria.[3] Given the prevailing northwesterly winds in the eastern Mediterranean, the return trip would take even longer, perhaps fifteen to

---

[1] At the same time, Dubois' (1907) argument that the development of Ostia's harbor led to a sharp decline in the commercial importance of Puteoli is outdated: D'Arms (1974); Camodeca (1994) 113.

[2] See Dubois (1907) esp. 64–117; Frederiksen (1984) 319–349.

[3] Pliny *NH* 19,3, journey of Valerius Marianus, 'lenissimo flatu'. Pliny apparently considered this an exceptionally fast run. Casson (1971) 282/283.

twenty days.[4] In the absence of combustion engines, that journey can be considered relatively quick, but in this time-period all sorts of things could go wrong. Apart from the dangers of shipwreck and delays there was the risk that a business partner might, unintentionally or deliberately, fail to meet his obligations under the contract. The larger the distance and the longer the time lag, the less control could be exercised over what a business partner might do. Overseas shipping was not the only segment of the economy encountering this problem. In banking for example, the activity of the Sulpicii, a separation between the *quid* and the *quo* was intrinsic to the business; a sum of money, once lent out, would only be repaid with interest after a certain amount of time had lapsed.[5] This made banking risky when conducted locally, but all the more so where it involved maritime loans and transactions with partners overseas. As for the Sulpicii, the fact that *peregrini* appear in their archive shows that they were engaged in providing credit to people from different communities; there is also some tentative evidence that they were involved in maritime loans.[6]

A separation in both time and distance between the conclusion of a deal and its contractual fulfillment led to uncertainty on the part of the merchant awaiting payment or delivery; his partner might deliver unsatisfactory goods or services, making the investment a partial or even a total loss. Absent reliable personal identification like passports, the risks of impersonal exchange were incalculable. A merchant could lie about his identity, for instance claiming to be from Ephesus while in reality being a native of Miletus, effectively making enforcement impossible. As a corollary, wholly impersonal contractual transactions over long distances must have been virtually non-existent. But even for the more or less personalized transactions that *were* possible the lack of fast means of communication meant that much desired information about the past conduct and

---

[4] Rougé (1966) 101 reasons that the trip would have taken approximately 15 to 20 days since it seems to have taken that long to get from Caesarea to Rome, or from Lampsacus to Hydruntum. Average numbers are, of course, hard to give, and much depended on specific climatic conditions and on the season. For winds and climate, see Casson (1971) 270–273; Rougé (1966) 31–35.

[5] Interest is mentioned in none of the contracts from the Sulpicii archive, but it seems unlikely that loans were interest-free. The most probable explanation is that the rent was withheld at the moment the loan-sum was paid out. That means that less money was actually paid out than the nominal sum of the loan we see in the contracts. Verboven (2003b); Camodeca (1999) 133/134.

[6] *TPSulp.*61, 62 show that the Sulpicii were involved in providing credit to *peregrini*. *TPSulp.* 78 and *TPSulp.* 80 (see further below) might indicate involvement in maritime loans.

trustworthiness of non-local business partners was hard to obtain, compounding the problem of how to calculate risks.[7]

It might be argued that the gravity of these risks was mitigated by the fact that the Empire had a central government and a centralized legal system that comprehended the provinces (where it was administered by governors).[8] This is true. But how much good did that do an individual merchant? Should we imagine a trader from Puteoli, harmed financially by a business partner from, say, Ephesus, winning a judgment against his adversary *in absentia* and then writing a letter to the governor of Asia, requesting him to put the verdict into effect? Given the hands-off attitude of the Roman civil authorities towards legal enforcement, that scenario seems out of the question.[9]

Of course, the problems outlined above did not negatively affect all Mediterranean commercial traffic. An itinerant trader could load goods on a ship and sail off in search of markets in a more or less *ad hoc* fashion, peddling his wares and receiving payment at once on sale. With this type of trade, information was still useful but imperfect information did not impede business. With spot sales, enforcing contracts was also not a concern. Peregrine Horden and Nicholas Purcell have persuasively argued how trade like this—'*cabotage*' with ships staying close to the coast, sailing relatively short distances between harbors—connected many smaller and larger trading centers.[10] However, maritime *cabotage* did not constitute all commercial activity in the Roman Mediterranean; its complement was overseas trade based on contractual obligations such as we see it in the Murecine documents. Note that I am here not contrasting large-scale 'high commerce' with small-scale *cabotage* (as Horden and Purcell do) but contrasting trade involving a gap between the *quid* and the *quo* with spot sales involving simultaneous delivery and payment. The distinction I am making creates categories that probably had much overlap with those of Horden and Purcell, but the difference in emphasis is important. My point is that for Roman merchants to engage in inter-community contractual trade some sort of mechanism to facilitate risk-reduction must have been

---

7 Slow transportation and communication: Duncan-Jones (1990) 7–29; Casson (1971) 281–296; Rougé (1966) 99–105.

8 On this topic, see e.g. Kaser (1971) 214–221; Crook (1967) 85–87; Von Lübtow (1955) 654–659. See also below Chapter 5.

9 See Kaser (1996) 131–148, 383–407, 623–630 for a historical overview of the technicalities and procedures of enforcement under the Roman judicial system.

10 Horden and Purcell (2000) esp. 133–152.

in operation. The question of how this mechanism might have functioned is the subject of this chapter.

Inter-Community Exchange and the Debate on the Roman Economy

The Roman economy, generally speaking, cannot have been characterized by long-distance markets supported by completely impersonal exchange. The institutional framework of legal enforcement through state-provided force, necessary for such exchange, was just non-existent. Surprisingly, this institutional deficit has received little to no attention in the extensive literature on the Roman economy. The issue has usually been overlooked or, if acknowledged, underestimated. In fact, the absence of government enforcement in Roman litigation has not received much attention in general. John Kelly addressed the issue directly, but was more interested in class and social inequality than in overseas trade and commerce. Peter Garnsey would later take up the subject as well, formulating a view similar to Kelly's, though a much more balanced and nuanced one. Recently, Peter Bang correctly identified the problem, and to him goes the credit of putting the importance of social ties and networks on the scholarly agenda. But although he is interested in the world of commerce, he does not distinguish between intra- and inter-community trade, nor does he attempt to give a detailed answer to the question of what Roman private enforcement mechanisms might have looked like.[11]

Scholars have, on the whole, adopted two approaches to the problem that lack of state enforcement hampered overseas contractual exchange: either to ignore it altogether or to attempt to solve it indirectly by invoking the importance of dependent labor. A salient example of the first approach is presented by an article of Jeremy Paterson. Writing on the organization of trade, he comments: 'The jurists' language reflects what may be dubbed "mature mercantilism" or, perhaps better, "mature commercialism"—that is, that the deals envisaged are objective and impersonal between individuals who have no necessary connection with each other, other than that created by the contract of sale itself'.[12] An example of the second

[11] Kelly (1966), esp. 1–30; Garnsey (1970) 187–194 and 204/205; Bang (2008) esp. 189, 262–268. For some critical remarks on Bang's idea of the 'bazaar', see Chapter 3 below.

[12] Paterson (1998) 154. See also Kessler and Temin (2007) 321: 'Rome had a sophisticated legal framework that could enforce judgements, ... against agents who were found to be untrustworthy'.

approach is provided by David Johnston: '... communications being slow, there was a real restriction on how many contracts any individual could enter into in how many geographically dispersed locations. That difficulty was solved by relying on slaves or dependent children ... For a business of any great scale, it is improbable that a paterfamilias would have, or would have adopted, sufficient children to run it. Accordingly, slaves would play the major part.'[13]

Johnston's discussion is mainly concerned with the impossibility of direct agency under Roman law. That technical legal problem has enthralled Romanists and Roman historians alike, and has been studied exhaustively.[14] However, in my view it is a bit of a red herring.[15] In overseas shipping 'the vital question for anyone entering into a transaction with [dependants]' was not, I maintain, 'how far their master could be held responsible for their actions ...'[16] Instead, the vital question was, *tout court*, if the contract was deemed enforceable and, depending on the answer, whether it should be entered into yes or no. None of this is to deny that arranging principal-agent relations was important, and undoubtedly concluding transactions through slaves (or freedmen), sometimes as overseas agents, did regularly take place. The *Digest* explicitly refers to this practice, and in the Murecine tablets we repeatedly witness slaves acting on behalf of their masters (although in some cases this was clearly because the latter were unable to write).[17] But was this really the way in which the difficulties of information and enforcement constraints were met?

The problem of enforcing contracts in the absence of a state-controlled enforcement system is a central one that cannot be ignored if the nature

[13] Johnston (1997) 56. For a similar example, see Aubert (1994); in a discussion on trade in clay artifacts, it is, e.g., (212) simply stated that '[manufacturers] could rely on their own agents, slaves or freedmen, or deal with independent tradesmen, *mercatores* or *negotiatores*'. Aubert does not consider the question of how contracts were enforced, or who was monitoring agents' behavior.

[14] Apart from Johnston (1997), see e.g. Aubert (1994) 40–116; Verboven (2002) 227–274. See also Kaser (1971) 260–267; Crook (1967) 241–243; Bang (2008) 276–280.

[15] And as a small aside here: it may not be wise to read too much into an isolated example, but *TPSulp*.48 seems to suggest that agency relations were in practice treated more loosely than one would imagine reading the jurists.

[16] Morley (2007) 67.

[17] Gaius *Dig*. 40,9,10. See also Ulpianus *Dig*. 5,1,19,3; Paulus *Dig*. 40,2,22. Slaves acting for their masters, *TPSulp*.45, 46, (but 46 certainly, and 45 almost certainly, because of illiteracy), 48, 49, 51, 52, 56 (an interesting case: 'colonorum coloniae Puteolanae servus arcarius'), 58, 67, 68, 69, 71, 72, 73, 74, 78, 89, 94, 95, 97, 98 (illiteracy), 110, 112, 114 (see 56), 115, 116.

of Roman trade is to be understood. The solution given so far in the literature—a preponderant use of dependent labor in the form of children, slaves, and freedmen—is in itself inadequate to explain how merchants conducted long-distance trade operations. There are some objections to the idea of a relatively secondary importance. For one thing, the demographic regime made using children as agents highly impractical.[18] Furthermore, the evidence discussed in the previous chapter suggests that patron-client relationships played only a fairly modest role in business; they were at least not all-important in Puteoli. The essential reason, however, why this is simply an unsatisfactory solution is that relying on dependants did not really address the problems posed by long-distance exchange. Slaves and (dependent) children were in the power of their *patresfamilias*, and freedmen were (or could be) obligated towards their patrons. But in and of itself that did not make them reliable. They could be sent overseas as agents and, in that capacity, monitor transactions. But who was monitoring the agents? And quite apart from that question, why would a merchant trust a representative—whether an independent or someone's son, slave, or freedman—any more than he would trust the distant principal? The agent, too, could cheat or fail to meet contractual obligations. For a comprehensive model of agency, we need to be looking beyond dependent labor.

Inter-City Trade in Twelfth- and Thirteenth-Century Florence

The problems of imperfect information and enforcement I have just outlined were not unique to the Roman world and were, in fact, common in the pre-industrial past. Because traders in time periods different from the Roman were confronted with similar difficulties, the question of how they solved them is pertinent. I will offer one well-documented example for comparison, namely medieval Florence, an important mercantile center with a wide geographical reach. Roman cities, like Florence in the twelfth and thirteenth centuries, had a fair amount of leverage in matters of local administration and governance. Of course, they were far removed from

[18] Many fathers will have died before their sons were old enough to be employed as agents. Saller (1994) 229 concludes that perhaps about one-third of Roman children would have lost their fathers before reaching puberty, another third before age 25. Scheidel (2001) 26 cautions against the use of model life-tables, but concedes that they are 'good to think with'.

being independent city-states, but they were also not being controlled directly from Rome, instead being governed in large measure by a decurional class of local elites.[19] Another similarity between Roman cities and medieval Florence is to be found in legal enforcement; in both, this was in essence a matter of state-endorsed self-help.[20] Because both Roman and medieval Florentine traders also faced the same limitations of a preindustrial economy (slow information and transportation), a more sustained comparison is useful.

The data from municipal charters, treaties, contracts, court documents, and letters suggest that in the twelfth and thirteenth centuries an important form of Mediterranean inter-community exchange was based on collective punishment of a member of one community for misbehavior towards a member of another. A trader from a particular city would be compelled by his own community to compensate for the costs of any misdeeds committed against a foreign trader. If the city to which the defaulting merchant belonged failed to correct the alleged transgression, an inter-city dispute would arise; this could lead to a boycott by the aggrieved city and could ultimately end in a cessation of all trade between the two. There were significant exceptions in the form of individual grants of exemption, but the essence of the arrangement was collective responsibility of all members of a community; a community as an entity was required to remedy the misbehavior of any one of its members, and if that requirement was not met, the community as an entity would be held accountable for any debts.[21]

The evidence from the city of Florence shows that after a complaint was lodged, the city magistrates would call the accused merchant to account and, if they found him guilty, would try to make him compensate for the damage he had caused. Failure to appear or to comply entitled the magistrates to search for, confiscate, and sell the offender's property in order to fulfill his obligations for him. The city statutes also show that

---

[19] See, e.g., Jones (1940) esp. 170–191 for the cities in the East; Woolf (1998) esp. 29–40 for cities in Gaul.

[20] See Kaser (1996) 131–148, 383–407, 623–630 for the historical development of enforcement under Roman law. Throughout the Roman period a plaintiff had, basically, to take care of enforcing verdicts himself. The Florentine solution was retaliation with state approval. The Florentine authorities could (and in some cases were legally required to) provide assistance to the individual to whom a right of retaliation had been granted. However, even with the aid of state-power, the procedure remained essentially a matter of self-help; Del Vecchio and Casanova (1894) 189–191. See also Nippel (1995) 113–119 for a general comparative discussion.

[21] Greif (2006) 328–345 discusses the evidence and secondary literature.

the serious step of expulsion from the community could be used as an additional threat.[22] This system had a preventative effect in that the risk of community punishment deterred traders from cheating, which in turn reduced the chances of retaliatory measures.[23] The system not only functioned between Florence and its Italian trading partners; it also operated between Florence and communities in England, France, and Germany, which were the foci of important Florentine commercial activity. Although by the fifteenth century the system's importance had greatly diminished, the King of England took retaliatory steps against the city as late as 1448.[24] The frequency of trade conflicts and their potentially disastrous effects could be limited by means of bilateral diplomatic treaties, laying out procedures to prevent a chain of boycotts and reprisals spiraling out of control. Florence had made many such treaties governing relations, not only with big and important urban centers like Pisa and Bologna but also with many smaller and less powerful towns.[25]

However, trade conflicts between Florence and other mercantile cities did periodically break out. An example of what must have been a fairly typical, albeit dangerously far progressed conflict is presented by a case from 1239. On October 8th of that year the Florentine count Rodolfo di Capraia filed a request with the Podestà (civil authority) of Florence.[26] He asked for authorization to seize goods or money from the town of Pisa, or else from individual Pisan citizens, for a total value of 4,000 lira.[27] In an earlier attempt to settle this dispute, which involved Rodolfo and two Pisan natives, it had been decided through arbitration that Rodolfo could

[22] We know about the procedure in some detail through the treatise 'Discorso intorno al governo di Firenze dal 1280–1292'; Santini (1886) 166; Del Vecchio and Casanova (1894) 248/249. See also Greif (2006) 330.

[23] Cities could grant retaliation for claims based on loss of money or goods, damage to goods, tax extortion, and personal detention, but not for personal injury and murder. A document dating from 1235 regarding the murder of a Florentine citizen by two citizens from Volterra confirms that murder cases were not governed by the inter-city retaliatory system. Santini (1886) 170–176.

[24] Arias (1901) 170–176; Del Vecchio and Casanova (1894) 84, 87/88. See also Greif (2006) 338–345.

[25] Treaties were drafted between Florence and e.g. Bologna (1203 and 1216), Faenza (1204), Prato (1212), Pisa (1214), Perugia (1218), Volterra (1224), S. Gimignano (1225) and Città di Castello (1232). See Arias (1901) esp. 15–31; Del Vecchio and Casanova (1894) 69–71; Santini (1886) 167.

[26] Santini (1886) 166.

[27] In practice this meant seizing Pisan goods that were still on Florentine soil. If that did not satisfy the debt, an opportunity had to be awaited to intercept Pisan goods in transit through Florence. Del Vecchio and Casanova (1894) 190/191.

indeed rightfully claim this sum. Despite the fact that Pisan dignitaries had cooperated in the arbitration procedure, and despite the fact that two Florentine noblemen had been sent over to Pisa to request payment, no money had yet changed hands. For reasons unknown to us, the Comune di Pisa had been unwilling or unable to force its citizens into compliance, meaning it now faced retaliatory measures. An interesting detail is that Rodolfo, along with his claim for the 4,000 lira, filed an additional request for the seizure of Pisan goods worth 800 lira in compensation for the theft at sea of a number of horses. It appears that one of the Pisans involved in the dispute had plotted this scheme, a sign that a retaliatory cycle (if probably private in nature in this case) had already begun. At any rate, the Florentine Podestà granted Rodolfo's requests, including the one for the stolen horses, on the proviso that he follow proper procedures, meaning that he was to present everything he would cart off and was to deliver a public account of his actions.[28]

In this example, things had apparently gone quite seriously awry, with the result that Pisa and Florence came close to an all-out inter-city trade conflict. The disagreement, however, was still being governed by mutually understood rules; Pisa and Florence followed a step-by-step procedure in which both individual citizens and the civil authorities knew what the consequences and effects of their actions would be. In that sense, retaliation was 'a calculated response aimed at providing proper incentives and fostering exchange rather than an act of revenge'.[29]

Individual Legal Responsibility; The Murecine Tablets

What can we learn from the evidence on transactions between Puteolans and outsiders in the Murecine tablets? What does it tell us about the way inter-community exchange took place, and how does it compare to the Florentine example?

Without much doubt the group of outsiders in Puteoli consisted of two categories: people from elsewhere with Roman citizen status and non-Roman citizens (*peregrini*). The latter are easily recognizable, and determining their status is a straightforward matter, but identifying the former is more problematic. It is unlikely that *peregrini* were the only

[28] For a comprehensive description of the Florentine *rappresaglia* procedure, see Del Vecchio and Casanova (1894) 97–246, esp. 191–194.

[29] Greif (2006) 333.

outside-contacts in Puteoli, and presumably there are Roman citizens among the people in the tablets who were not native Puteolans. However, given the dearth of prosopographical evidence it is hard if not impossible to prove for any given individual that this was indeed the case.[30] I have therefore decided to disregard all Roman citizen names for my analysis and to focus only on the data that unequivocally point to peregrine status.

Eight tablets contain evidence for *peregrini*, and usually we can ascertain where they had come from.[31] The first thing that is striking about the contracts in which *peregrini* appear is the extent to which they employed Roman legal constructions, following the formulaic standards evident from the other tablets. In both format and content, there is little difference between a document concluded between Roman citizens and one concluded between a citizen and a *peregrinus*. Of course, in contracts made by non-citizens some modifications were necessary in the formulas, the most common one being that *peregrini* promised to perform contractual obligations by *fidepromissio* (a promise in good faith) instead of by the standard Roman way of *sponsio* (an official legal pledge).[32] But despite this difference it is clear that contracts were intentionally made almost identical to the standard ones under Roman law, and the legal outcome of the documents was, to all intents and purposes, similar if not the same. Compare, for example, two *vadimonia* (private agreements to appear in court), one made between two citizens and the other between a citizen and a *peregrinus*. In both cases, the plaintiff is a local Puteolan (Cinnamus, one of the three bankers in the archive). The men making the commitment to appear are the defendants in the coming suit; the first is a citizen and almost certainly a Puteolan local,[33] the second is a man from

---

[30] One can speculate about, for example, P. Attius Severus, a trader in Baetican oil or *garum* (*TPSulp.*78, *CIL* XV 3642, 3644/5, 4748–9). But the fact that he traded in Spanish products does not necessarily mean that he was an immigrant in Puteoli. Cf. M. Valerius Euphemus, also a trader in Spanish goods: *TPSulp.*58 and 89; *CIL* IV 9611 (the *CIL* edition has Euphileti, but this should probably be corrected to read Euphemi; Manacorda (1977) 130, fig. 1: N. 7920). The Valerii seem to have been a local Puteolan clan: *CIL* X 1814, M. Valerius Pudens as *duumvir* in 161 AD.

[31] *TPSulp.*4 (Tyre); *TPSulp.*13 and 14 (Alexandria); *TPSulp.*60 and 61 (Melos and Athens); *TPSulp.*78 (Ceramus); *TPSulp.*106 (Sidon); *TPSulp.*49 (illegible). Also, but more tentative, *TPSulp.*80, discussed at the end of this chapter.

[32] A *fidepromissio* was considered to be *ius gentium*, and could hence be used by Roman citizens and *peregrini* alike. Gaius *Inst.* 1,1; 3,93. See Kaser (1971) 661–663 on the three types (similar in many respects) of legal promise (*sponsio*, *fidepromissio* and *fideiussio*).

[33] Several L. Marii appear in the Sulpicii archive (*TPSulp.*1, 53, 79, 83, 84), as do M. Marii (*TPSulp.*53).

Syria. The similarity of these documents in both practical detail and legal effect is remarkable:

> Commitment to appear made by Lucius Marius Florus for the Ides of next January, at Puteoli in the Forum in front of the Hordionian altar of Augustus at the third hour; Gaius Sulpicius Cinnamus stipulated that he be paid HS 840 and HS 660; Lucius Marius Florus officially pledged...[34]

> Commitment to appear made by Zenon the Tyrian, freedman of Zenobus, for the third day before the Ides of next June, at Puteoli in the Forum in front of the Hordionian altar of Augustus at the third hour; Gaius Sulpicius Cinnamus asked to be paid in good faith HS 1,200; Zenon the Tyrian, freedman of Zenobus promised in good faith...[35]

Such contracts with *peregrini* are especially significant because their mere existence demonstrates that in Puteoli foreign defendants litigated in the same way as locals did. In the previous chapter we have seen how in Puteoli the court was the default arena for dispute settlement. In these documents we now see how a local and a non-citizen outsider would advance in the judicial process exactly as two locals would. The social conventions governing economic interaction and dispute settlement clearly included people from other communities, who were expected to conform to them.

Part of 'the law of all nations' (*ius gentium*), and thus without modification open to all non-citizens, were the rules on 'mandate' (*mandatum*). In a document from January 11th, 49 AD, a certain Purgias (unfortunately the document is too damaged for his place of origin to be legible) gave a mandate to C. Sulpicius Cinnamus.[36] He did this by means of a *chirographum*, a personal legal statement written in the first person: 'I, Purgias, son of Alexander, from... have written that I asked and mandated C. Sulpicius Cinnamus to...'[37] The rest of the sentence is, alas, illegible, but this phrase renders it certain that Cinnamus was asked to perform some sort of service on Purgias' behalf. It may be that the transaction involved

---

[34] *TPSulp.*8: '[V]adimonium factum L(ucio) Mario Floro in idus Ian(uarias) primas Puteolis in foro ante aram Augusti Hordionianam hora tertia; HS DCCCXL et HS DCLX dari stipulatus est C(aius) Sulpicius Cinnamus, spopondit L(ucius) Marius Fl[o]rus....' The day is January 13th, year illegible.

[35] *TPSulp.*4: '[Vadimoniu]m fac[tu]m [Zenoni] Zenobi l(iberto) [T]yri[o] [in] III idus Iunias primas, [P]uteolis in foro [an]te ara[m] A[u]gusti Hordionianam hora tertia; [H]S ∞ CC da[r]i fide r[o]gavit C(aius) Sul[picius] Cinnamus f[ide promi]sit Zenon Zenob[i] l(ibertus) Tyrius....' The date is June 9th, 52 AD.

[36] *TPSulp.*49. *Mandatum*, see Kaser (1971) 577–580.

[37] 'Purgias Alexandrini f(ilius) [...]us scripsi me rogasse C(aium) Sulpicium Cinna[mum eique ma]ndasse [u]t[i...]'. See *TPSulp.*48 for the same phrase.

the transfer of a fiduciary pledge, it may be that African and Italian grain was involved, but all of this is speculative.[38] In any event, we here again see a Puteolan and a *peregrinus* using the basic rules of Roman law in a way that would not have been different if it had involved two locals. The format, language, and legal constructions—a mandate given by writing a *chirographum*—were all standard under the Roman legal system.

Although the home community of the peregrine party is always indicated, and mention of a native city seems to have served as an identity marker, nothing in the documents suggests that cities or groups of merchants were being held liable for the contracts of individuals. This can be seen indirectly in the documents pertaining to litigation. C. Sulpicius Cinnamus, while suing Zenon, freedman of Zenobus, and equally while suing Trupho, son of Potamon, seems not to have expected, respectively, the business communities of Tyre and Alexandria to have served as a default security for the defendants in any way.[39] Zenon and Trupho were being sued on an individual basis, without any apparent involvement of their business factions or native cities.[40]

Similarly, in the loans documented in the account-books of *peregrini* in the Sulpicii archive we find strong supporting evidence for the notion that in Puteoli, non-citizen outsiders were held liable individually under the rules of Roman law without involvement of their home communities. In three tablets from 42/43 AD documenting loans and sureties we witness Euplia, a woman from the Greek island of Melos, borrowing money from Puteolan creditors.[41] In all three cases her tutor Epichares, an Athenian

---

[38] Camodeca thinks the words 'africum ita[l]um' are geographic indicators, not personal names. The word 'pro' followed by a sum of money, he considers, can refer to a fiduciary pledge (analogous to *TPSulp.*85).

[39] *TPSulp.*4 (Tyrian); *TPSulp.*13, 14 (Alexandrian). The latter two documents probably belong to the same lawsuit. The year can not be read, but must be later than 44 AD. Camodeca (1999) 66. Note how both *TPSulp.*13 and 14 are *vadimonia* to appear not in Puteoli but in Rome in the Forum of Augustus. The reason is unclear, but since this lawsuit involves the Puteolan bankers it is likely to have concerned a transaction that had originally taken place in Puteoli, not Rome.

[40] In this context it is also worth mentioning one document from the Iucundus tablets: *CIL* IV Suppl. I, nr. 100. It is a receipt for money paid to Ptolemeus, son of Masyllus, from Alexandria, the seller of a batch of linen at an auction sale. Ptolemeus was almost certainly a professional linen trader. However, as far as we can tell no Alexandrians appear in the witness list. See Andreau (1974) 289/290, 323.

[41] *TPSulp.*60, 61, 62. On these *nomina arcaria* in the archive, see Camodeca (1999) 151/152 and 156/157; Wolf (2001) 119–124.

citizen, stood surety for her, using the legal instrument of *fideiussio*.[42] Clearly Euplia did not need a fellow Melian to serve as her guarantor; having a fellow community member as a sponsor was evidently not required by either law or convention. And if things were to go wrong and she were to default on her payments, the Melian community would not be held to account. Nor, for that matter, would the city of Athens. Instead, Epichares, an individual Athenian, would be expected to repay the debt on the basis of his personal guarantee.

A similar, though more complex case is presented by a document dating to the 11th of April, 38 AD, containing a contract for a maritime insurance. P. Attius Severus contracted with the shipper Menelaos from Ceramus (in the province of Asia) for the insurance of cargo. Menelaos promised to repay 1,000 *denarii* 'in accordance with the shipping agreement' ('ἀποδώσω ἀκολούθως τῇ ναυλωτικῇ'), that is to say: he would either deliver the goods entrusted to him or he would reimburse Severus for the estimated value of the load in case of loss of cargo. The document is written in Greek and has a strong Hellenistic legal flavor. However, a statement written in Latin, and following a standard Roman legal formula, is added to the contract. It contains a pledge by a third party, M. Barbatius Celer, who promised the cargo owner Severus to be Menelaos' guarantor.[43] The content of the text therefore constitutes somewhat of a Roman-Hellenistic legal crossover.

We do not know if Severus—in all likelihood to be identified with the Severus known from painted signs on amphorae who traded in Baetican oil or *garum*—was a Spaniard or a Puteolan. Attius is a well-attested *gens* name in Puteolan inscriptions, but a C. Attius Severus is also recorded in a Baetican inscription, probably dating to 31 AD.[44] However, the guarantor M. Barbatius Celer was, judging by his name, almost certainly a Puteolan. Another M. Barbatius was appointed arbiter in a dispute that took place in the 50s AD, and as I have argued in the previous chapter it were

42 See Gaius *Inst.* 1,193 on tutors of peregrine women. On the basis of that passage, Camodeca speculates on a wife-husband, or a mother-son relationship between Euplia and Epichares; Camodeca (1999) 156/157. *Fideiussio* open to non-citizens, see Kaser (1971) 663.

43 *TPSulp.*78. The interpretation of the document as a maritime insurance is the one favored by Camodeca, who points out that 'ναυλωτικῇ' always means 'shipping contract' in Egyptian papyri; Camodeca (1999) 178/179 with nt. 34. Another possibility is to interpret it as a maritime loan (*pecunia traiecticia*); Ankum (1978), esp. 163–169. See also Groschler (1997) 160–162. Jones (2006) 115/116 suggests an advance of funds for the payment of harbor dues (*portoria*).

44 Attii in Puteoli: *CIL* X 2120, 2121, 2122, 2123; C. Attius Severus in Baetica: A. Merlin, *AE* (1955) 12 nr. 21. Severus on amphora stamps: *CIL* XV 3642, 3644/5, 4748–9.

precisely local men—and social peers—who were selected for this kind of task. Self-evidently, the community of Ceramus as such was in no way considered to be a factor in this contract. It was in the first place Menelaos and, if he failed to perform his contractual obligations, an individual Puteolan who would be held responsible.

Finally, there is the interesting but unfortunately poorly preserved document concerning a ship that had probably sailed to Puteoli from the Syrian city of Sidon.[45] The vessel is described in some detail, and we learn its tonnage (18,000 *modii*),[46] its name ('Notus'),[47] and the fact that it had a *parasemum*, a characteristic sculpture or painting on the starboard side of the prow. Two men—most likely the shipowner and the captain, presumably both from Sidon although the origin of just one can be distinguished—seem to have been engaged in a dispute with someone whose name can only be read as Gaius.[48] It is impossible to reconstruct the exact events from the mutilated text, but it is clear that it concerned the sale at auction of either the foreign ship or its cargo, or both. The document seems to reflect the local Puteolan tax collector in a hierarchy of creditors claiming first rights to the proceeds of the sale.[49] Perhaps the cause of the conflict was the culpable loss of goods, but it is also possible that there was some sort of evasion of harbor dues or embezzlement of goods involved; the clearly distinguishable word 'avertisset' seems to point in that direction.[50] At any rate, the document shows that in the execution of verdicts too, people from other communities were held accountable on an individual basis. It was not the city of Sidon or its business community in

---

[45] *TPSulp*.106. The year is 57 AD, the day, somewhat surprisingly, December 22nd. A day that late in the year fell well outside the regular sailing season. Maybe this is an indication that the conflict had been dragging on for some months.

[46] The ship's capacity can, assuming a *modius* equalled 6.74 kilograms (calculation is the mid-point for Italian wheat, based on Pliny *NH* 18, 66), have been about 120 tons; Duncan Jones (1982) 370. If that calculation is approximately correct, it would have been a fairly regular ship in size. See Rougé (1975) 83–87; Casson (1971) 170–173.

[47] A ship's name, hitherto not attested. See Casson (1971) 359/360.

[48] Camodeca reads 'C(aius) S[...]s' but excludes the reading 'C. Sulpicius' for lack of space. Camodeca (1999) 217. We do, therefore, not see the Sulpicii involved in auction sales here. This matter, centering mainly on the interpretation of *TPSulp*.82, has been at the heart of the discussion about the nature of the Sulpicii's activities. See Verboven (2003a).

[49] Legible are the word 'protopraxia' ('the first claim on a debtor's resources' [OLD]) and the phrase 'iure ipso et consuetudine sibi esset', which would fit well with the interpretation of a public official, such as a tax collector, demanding payment; Camodeca (1999) 219.

[50] A word that in the *Digest* often connotes fraudulent acts or stealing: Ulpianus *Dig.* 14,4,7,3; Alfenus *Dig.* 19,2,31; Ulpianus *Dig.* 47,4,1,13; Ulpianus *Dig.* 47,20,3,1.

general at which the execution sale was aimed; the property or merchandise of two foreign individuals was the object of the auction.

Scanty as the evidence may be, taken in the aggregate it shows that in Puteoli there was a strong element of individuality in contracting. This was true both for transactions between native Puteolans and for the interactions between locals and outsiders. *Peregrini* employed constructions in their contracts that strongly resembled those of Roman law. The element of individual contracting with individual legal responsibility and bilateral litigation—part and parcel of the Roman system—was equally adopted by them. From the evidence discussed so far, it would seem that the trade mechanism in Puteoli was fundamentally law-based. Yet—and here, of course, is the rub—this cannot have been the whole story. The law could quite simply not be relied upon completely because the Roman state did not use its coercive powers to enforce contracts. The data from the Sulpicii tablets thus present us with a conundrum: on the one hand we know that legal enforcement was not a government task; on the other we find no support for the solution adopted in medieval Florence of formalized community responsibility and group retaliation.

A Micro-Economic Model of Inter-Community Exchange

For merchants engaged in inter-community trade, there are two ways of dealing with the problem of opportunistic behavior: either an attempt *ex ante* to gather information on someone's past behavior so as to determine the likelihood that he will cheat again in the future or an attempt to punish *ex post* any misbehavior that may have occurred. In a situation with imperfect information and an imperfectly functioning legal system, *ex post* punishment cannot take the form of relying on state institutions, while *ex ante* investigations are time-consuming and costly. This is not to say that no inter-community long-distance transactions can be concluded in such a situation; two traders can build up a bilateral relationship in which both deem it in their best interest to remain loyal. If they interact repeatedly, and realize that the long-term payoffs of staying honest outweigh the immediate benefits of cheating, it is possible that both adopt a cooperation strategy.[51] This result can be described as a cooperation

[51] Posner (2000) 15–18. See also Mahoney and Sanchirico (2003).

outcome in a game with repeated prisoner's dilemma, and it might be argued that it formed the basis of many Roman trade relations.

But the problem with this form of exchange is that at some point, one side may unilaterally decide to deviate when he considers the relationship no longer valuable.[52] Moreover, given the finite life-span of the two players, the repeated game they are involved in also has a finite (if not fixed) time horizon. According to the iron logic of game theory, this would make the game unravel all the way down from the last interaction. Cooperation is a possibility, but only under strict conditions.[53] In addition, other than the two 'prisoners' of the classic game-theoretic dilemma, two traders involved in a game with repeated prisoner's dilemma have, apart from 'play, deviate' and 'play, cooperate', the third option of not playing at all. In practice this means that the risk of being cheated will lead many players in a two-stage game (in which they can opt not to enter) to choose the option 'do not play' so that many potentially viable and mutually beneficial relationships will never be established in the first place.[54]

To counter these game-theoretic problems, third-party enforcement is necessary. In the absence of state coercion, group-regulation must play a crucial role. If players operate in a group with restricted membership and with replacement of leaving members, the group as such has an infinite (or rather: an indefinite) life-span. The fact that the individual members have finite life-spans is now less of a concern, and cooperation and group-solidarity can result.[55] Cooperation depends on voluntary informal information flows and a self-enforcing equilibrium. In practice, therefore, groups must not be too big, for if they grow beyond a certain size they cannot rely on self-governance anymore and need external control—like that of a government—themselves.[56]

For outsiders, punishing a group as a collective can be both cost-effective and efficacious.[57] A group under continuous threat of communal punishment will try to regulate the behavior of its members, ensuring as much as possible that individuals toe the line and that wrongdoers receive a

---

[52] This can be the result of an exogenous shift in circumstances affecting only one player, circumstances the other player cannot influence nor predict.

[53] A cooperation strategy can result in a finite horizon game if agents have an amount of irrationality, and if the game has more than one Nash equilibrium; Cremer (1986) 34. See also Dixit (2004) 16; Benoit and Krishna (1985).

[54] See Dixit (2004) 19 for an analysis of a two-stage game with prisoner's dilemma.

[55] Cremer (1986). See also Posner (1996) 137–144.

[56] Dixit (2004) 59–76.

[57] Levinson (2003).

penalty. Because of the usually high quality information flows within a closed group, the penalty can be 'tailored' and can range from the relatively mild (e.g. withholding esteem) to the very harsh (e.g. expulsion from the group, a sanction that is particularly effective if membership provides a valuable service).[58] In the medieval example, communal punishment took the form of civil authorities, such as the Florentine Podestà or the Comune di Pisa, forcing defaulters to fulfill their obligations, doing that for them if necessary. Communal action formed the strength of that system.[59] But since the Murecine documents do not support such a model for the interactions in Puteoli, we have to look further to complement the theory.

Another way to facilitate inter-community exchange is to have a number of foreign settlers live permanently in another society.[60] The reputation of such a foreign group, based on its collective past behavior, conditions the current behavior of its members; their individual incentives and actions are affected by how the group is perceived by their host environment.[61] Once a group of foreign residents has built up a good collective standing, the members have a vested interest in maintaining it. Equally, a period of misbehavior gives the collective a bad name, and can lead to future misbehavior. Opportunistic agents, by engaging in misconduct, increasingly have an incentive to continue cheating; the more they cheat, the more widely information about their bad conduct will be disseminated. After having been corrupt a certain number of times, cheating is expected behavior, and their business partners will adapt their strategy accordingly. If that happens, agents stand to lose more than to gain by behaving honestly and are thus 'locked-in' into being corrupt.[62]

Opportunistic agents' bad behavior affects the whole group for the worse, the degree to which depending on the precision of information

---

58 Levinson (2003) 378–385; Ellickson (1991) 214–219. See also Dixit (2004) 61 (players do not necessarily adopt a 'grim-trigger' strategy) and Greif (1989), Greif (2006) 58–91 on the Maghribi traders' coalition.

59 Greif (2006) 326: 'The credible threat to have a defaulting borrower punished by his own community is at the crux of the community responsibility system'.

60 See Greif (2006) 213–216; Clay (1997); Langum (1987); Curtin (1984).

61 Tirole (1996) 1/2. This is a result of imperfectly observed individual past behavior: 'If past individual behaviour was fully unobserved, members of the group would have no incentive to sustain their own reputation and therefore the group would always be expected to behave badly. Conversely, the collective reputation would play no role if individual behaviours were perfectly observed. Imperfect observability of individual behaviour thus underlies the phenomenon of collective reputation'.

62 Tirole (1996) 7–9.

about individual conduct. If information is imperfect, business partners will make decisions based more on the reputation of the group. Since they will expect a higher level of corruption once opportunistic agents have started cheating, the other agents, even the ones who had remained honest in the past, have less of an incentive to continue their good conduct. This effect can remain in force in subsequent generations. If corruption is the dominant strategy when new agents enter the group, the level of mistrust they encounter with their outside business partners will undermine their incentive to behave honestly.[63] If and when that happens, rebuilding a good name can, at worst, be impossible, and, at best, be a long and arduous process. Only if information about individual conduct is relatively precise can the group return to a steady-state of low corruption relatively quickly. This too, however, will take time and effort. It requires that suspicion be phased-out to reestablish the trust the group enjoyed earlier, which depends on circumstances such as the level of confidence partners require and the turnover rate of agents.

The members of a well-regarded foreign group, knowing that their native business partners base their decisions partly on group reputation, will be concerned about losing the precious asset of their collective good name. Good repute, once established, is delicate and can only be maintained if all members avoid being 'locked-in' into a situation of corruption. For this reason, the group will monitor the behavior of agents as much as possible and will exercise great caution in allowing new members in.[64] Business partners in the host community can rely on newcomers in a group that has always enjoyed a good name being relatively reliable, even if they have little or no *ex ante* information on them.

At this point it is, I think, helpful to give a historical example, not a medieval but a more recent one this time. A workable model, different from thirteenth-century Florence and comparable to what I think happened in Puteoli, is presented by American traders living in Mexican California during the first half of the nineteenth century.[65] The legal system in this part of Mexico under supervision of the *alcalde*,[66] a locally elected, unpaid, layman judicial officer, was in essence based on arbitration

[63] Tirole (1996) 9–12.

[64] Tirole (1996) 15–18. In Tirole's model, there is no screening of workers at the hiring stage. For the value of informal screening mechanisms, see e.g. Saloner (1985).

[65] See Greif (2006) 213–216 and, esp., Clay (1997).

[66] The institution of the *alcalde* (derived from the Arabic word 'al-qadi', 'the judge') dates back to the time of the Arab conquest of Spain. It was incorporated into the Spanish legal system, and subsequently exported to the Spanish colonies. Langum (1987) 30/31.

procedures.[67] The system lacked government enforcement, and compliance relied on social control and adherence to customary behavioral conduct.[68] U.S. merchants interested in trading for hides, tallow, furs, horses, and lumber, products in which California was rich, were faced with the difficulty of not having access to this local social control mechanism. Because there was also no government enforcement, they had trouble establishing the credit relations necessary for their trade. The solution that emerged was integration of U.S. traders into Mexican communities, where they married into local families, converted to Catholicism, became Mexican citizens, spoke Spanish, and raised their children as the locals did. Because they made these investments in order to integrate, the institutions of social control now extended also to them.[69] American merchants in the U.S., in their trade and credit relations with Mexicans, made use of these 'Mexicanized' expatriates and their local connections. A reputation mechanism ensured that they could trust them to be honest; an agent who cheated would damage his reputation and thereby his economic prospects. This mechanism was an effective tool because of the investments the expatriates had made in settling in foreign communities.

I present this nineteenth-century example because it has been studied from a micro-economic perspective closely attuned to the one I take in this book. As such, it highlights the elements I, too, will focus on: the role of reputation and social control mechanisms in contract enforcement. However, the case of the 'Mexicanized' U.S. traders is by no means unique in its solution to the problems posed by long-distance inter-community trade, and there are many other examples known from world history, from trade in precolonial Sub-Saharan Africa, to pre-Columbian trade in the Americas, to European Indian Ocean trade in the seventeenth century. Philip Curtin explored these 'trade diasporas' in detail from an economic anthropology perspective and summarized the phenomenon as follows: 'Commercial specialists would remove themselves physically from their home community and go to live as aliens in another town, usually not a fringe town, but a town important in the life of the host community. There, the stranger merchants could settle down and learn the language, the customs, and the cultural ways of their hosts. They could then serve as cross-cultural brokers, helping and encouraging trade between the

67 Langum (1987) 97–104.
68 Clay (1997) 504–507; Langum (1987) 114–116.
69 Clay (1997) 514–519.

host society and people of their own origin who moved along the trade routes'.[70]

I argue that traders in Puteoli for their inter-community transactions relied on exactly such cross-cultural brokers. Small 'colonies' of foreign settlers in the city served the dual function of forming part of Puteolan society—being concerned with their collective reputation and therefore conforming to local conventions—while at the same time remaining separate groups with their own internal group-monitoring mechanisms. I will try to show that trading stations of foreign merchants in effect served as *ex ante* safeguards against dishonest behavior from agents.

The Tyrian Trading Station

In 174 AD, an inscription was set up in Puteoli by the resident Tyrians, containing both a letter they had written to their city-council and the council's reply. Although it is silent on many issues we would most desperately like to have been informed about, it is nevertheless an instructive document. I will discuss it in considerable detail and will therefore offer the translated text here almost in full, despite its length.[71]

> Letter written to the city of Tyre, the sacred, inviolable, and autonomous metropolis of Phoenicia and of other cities, and mistress of a fleet. To the chief magistrates, council, and people of their sovereign native city, from the (Tyrians) resident in Puteoli, greeting.
>
> By the grace of the gods and the good fortune of our lord the Emperor [= Marcus Aurelius] there is many a station in Puteoli, as most of you know, and ours excels the others both in adornment and in size. In the past this was cared for by the Tyrians resident in Puteoli, who were numerous and wealthy; but now this care has devolved on us, who are few in number, and since we pay the expenses for the sacrifices and services to our ancestral gods consecrated here in temples, we do not have the means to pay the station's annual rent of 250 *denarii*, especially as the expenses of the Puteoli

[70] Curtin (1984) 2. See also Berdan (1989) 101/102. There are also examples from the Near East and the Mediterranean. Apart from the cases discussed by Curtin (1984) see Heichelheim (1958) 222–249; Noonan (2011).

[71] *OGIS*, 595 (= *IG* XIV 830 = *IGRR*, I, 421). On this inscription, see Sosin (1999); Tran tam Tinh (1972) 153–156; La Piana (1927) 256–258; Mommsen (1913) 8–13; Dubois (1907) 83–97; Cantarelli (1900) 126; Waltzing vol. 3 (1899) 441–443. See also D'Arms (1974) 105; Frederiksen (1984) 330.

> Ox-Sacrifice Games have in addition been imposed on us.[72] We therefore beg you to provide for the station's continued existence. And it will continue if you make the 250 *denarii* paid annually for rent your concern; for the remaining expenses, including those incurred to refurbish the station for the sacred festival-days for our lord the Emperor,[73] we set down to our own account, so as not to burden the city [i.e. Tyre]. And we remind you that the station here—unlike the one in the capital, Rome—derives no income either from shipowners or from merchants. We therefore appeal to you and beg you to make provision for this unfortunate circumstance.
>
> Written in Puteoli, July 23, in the consulship of Gallus and Flaccus Cornelianus.[74]

The inscription continues with an extract from the minutes of the Tyrian city-council, where the request was read, followed by the council's decision: the Tyrian station in Rome was to pay the rent of the Puteolan branch, as it had done in the past.

> From the minutes of the council meeting, held 21 Dios, in the year 300 [= December 8th, 174 AD], under chairmanship of C. Valerius Callicrates, son of Pausanias, president.
>
> A letter from the Tyrian station-operators[75] was read, a letter delivered by one of them, Laches ... [Lines 23–31 repeat, in indirect speech, the letter cited above.] After this reading, Philocles, son of Diodorus, said: "The station-operators in Rome have always had as their custom to pay, from what they themselves receive, 250 *denarii* to the ones in Puteoli. The station-operators in Puteoli now wish that this (custom) be observed for their sake; if the Tyrians in Rome no longer want to grant them (the money), they wish to take charge of both stations themselves on the same condition."[76] The (councilors) proclaimed approval: "Philocles has spoken well; what the Tyrians in Puteoli wish is just. It has always been thus, let it be so now. It is to the benefit of the city [i.e. Tyre]; let the custom be preserved".

---

72 'τὸν ἀγῶνα τὸν ἐν Ποτιόλοις τῆς βουθουσίας'. Nothing further is known about this festival. Mommsen thinks these were games in honor of Hadrian, introduced by Antoninus Pius; Mommsen (1913) 12 nt. 6, but cf. W. Dittenberger, *OGIS*, 595 nt. 7.

73 'τὰς ἱερὰς ἡμέρας τοῦ κυρίου αὐτοκράτορος'. Without much doubt, this refers to the Emperor's birthday and day of ascension to the throne. W. Dittenberger, *OGIS*, 595 nt. 10; Mommsen (1913) 12.

74 Lines 1–19, translation (with modifications), Lewis and Reinhold (1990) 110.

75 My translation of the word 'στατιωναρίων'. Line 22.

76 'ἐπὶ τῇ αὐτῇ αἱρέσ(ε)ι', (line 35) probably meaning that the Tyrians in Puteoli proposed to manage both stations from the income derived by the Roman branch.

> A written message[77] was read—a message brought by Laches, son of Primogeneia[78] and by Agathopous, his son, of the Tyrian station-operators of the Tyrian station in the Augustan colony of Puteoli—in which they declared that our fatherland provides for two stations: one in the capital, Rome...[79]

The various editors of this inscription have interpreted the lease-sum differently, reading it as representing either 250 *denarii*, as I have given it here, or 100,000 *denarii*. I will return to this issue shortly and explain why I think 250 *denarii* must be the correct reading. But apart from the size of the lease-sum, a number of other things are unclear in this inscription. The Tyrians resident in Puteoli assert that their station had in the past been paid for by their own community; they make no mention of payments by the Roman station-operators. They do, however, point out that their Roman counterparts received an income from shipowners and merchants (probably from charging fees) while they did not,[80] and request that the city of Tyre take over the annual rent. Only from the second part of the text do we learn that the station in Rome used to subsidize the one in Puteoli by paying for its lease. Philocles in his speech, and his fellow council-members in their response, did not discuss the option of the city of Tyre furnishing the money, despite the fact that this was actually the request before them. Instead, the discussion makes it seem as if the Tyrians in Puteoli proposed to restore the previous situation with the Roman station forwarding part of its earnings, a proposal that was not put forward, at least not in the letter we have. Perhaps the written message, mentioned at the point where the text breaks off, contained a request to that effect. Presumably that message presented pertinent additional information, seeing how it was read aloud in the meeting of the city-council. But if it

[77] 'πιττάκιον', (line 38): writing (wax) tablets, G. Kaibel *IGRR*, I, 421 nt. 8; W. Dittenberger *OGIS*, 595 nt. 33.

[78] The inscription reads 'ὑπὸ Λάχητος Πρειμογενείας' (line 38/39). Some sort of mistake seems to have been made here, see W. Dittenberger *OGIS*, 595 nt. 35; Mommsen (1913) 10 nt. 5: '[v]ielleicht der Name des Vaters des Laches, den der tyrische Schreiber corrumpiert haben mag'.

[79] Given here is my translation of lines 20–23 and 31–41. The text breaks off in the middle of line 41.

[80] The Puteolan station-operators reminded the city-council (line 16/17) that 'οὐδεμία πρόσοδος γείνεται οὔτε παρὰ ναυκλήρων οὔτε παρὰ ἐμπόρων τῇ ἐνθάδε στατίωνι ὡς ἐν τῇ <βασιδι> βασιλίδι Ῥώμῃ'.

did propose to continue the custom of subsidy payments, it is unclear why it was not cited in the first part of the text.[81]

Charles Dubois, attempting to clarify the murky sequence of events, interpreted the inscription as follows. At some point in the past, the Puteolan station-operators were numerous and wealthy enough to pay for their own expenses. When trade shifted northward with the construction of the Tiber docks and then with the harbor of Ostia, the Puteolan station started to be in decline vis-à-vis the (newly established?) one in Rome. At some point the financial situation became so dire that the Roman station, now the more important of the two, had to begin subsidizing the Puteolan one. The latter, however, continued its slide into desuetude. In the end, practically all shipowners and merchants passed Puteoli by and sailed directly for Rome. Ultimately, the Roman station-operators, no longer inclined to pay for a moribund branch, stopped their payments. This prompted the Puteolan Tyrians to complain to their city-council which, in response, ruled that the Roman Tyrians should continue to pay the subsidy, and 'thus ended this mini-civil war.'[82] Important in Dubois' interpretation is that he reads the figure in the inscription as 100,000 *denarii*, arguing that this is a confirmation of the strongly reduced financial circumstances of the Puteolan station-operators. Besides, he reasons, if the sum had been 250 *denarii*, why would they have bothered their city-council with such a petty affair?[83]

I am not convinced Dubois' interpretation is correct, most of all because it relies heavily on a presumed severe decline of Puteoli and its role in Mediterranean trade. John D'Arms has made a compelling attempt to defuse that idea, arguing that even if one accepts the inscription as evidence that the Tyrian station had fallen on hard times, it does not automatically follow that Puteoli had generally. Apart from this inscription there is, he emphasizes, really not much evidence for a universal

[81] For an ingenious attempt to explain the inscription, see Sosin (1999). Sosin argues that the councilor Philocles, far from agreeing, contradicted the version of events given in the official request to the council. In response, he made a 'bid for the hostile takeover of the Puteolan *statio*'. This reading fails to convince me. It seems to me extremely unlikely that the Tyrian station-operators would have erected a public inscription containing invective against them, and portraying them in a negative light.

[82] Dubois (1907) 94–97. 'Ainsi se termina cette petite guerre civile' (97). See also La Piana (1927) 256–258.

[83] Dubois (1907) 89–92, followed by La Piana (1927) 258 nt. 21.

downturn.[84] He follows Dubois in interpreting the figure in the inscription as representing 100,000 *denarii*, but from this reading he reaches the exact opposite conclusion: if a lease-sum of that magnitude was still being received by the city as late as the third quarter of the second century AD, then the local economy can not have been in terribly bad shape. Whether the sum represents 250 or 100,000 *denarii* is relevant to the argument I will develop. Since, furthermore, the data from the Sulpicii archive shed new light on this matter, it is worth discussing here.

What figure the signs on the stone represent depends on whether one reads them as Greek or as Roman numerals.[85] The most obvious argument to see them as Greek numbers is of course that the rest of the inscription is in Greek; for that reason alone seeing them as Roman would be illogical.[86] The wish of Dubois and D'Arms nonetheless to interpret them as such seems to derive mainly from the fact that a much higher sum suits their general, if diametrically opposed, theses. However, I think that the information from the inscription in combination with the evidence from the Sulpicii tablets shows that 100,000 *denarii* (or even Richard Duncan-Jones' 25,000 *denarii*) is much too high to be a credible lease-sum.[87]

The inscription says that the building excelled the other stations in embellishment ('κόσμῳ') and that it needed to be renovated for the festival-days of the Emperor. The word 'στατίων' borrowed from the Latin *statio*—as can be see in its treatment as a feminine and not a masculine noun ('τις ἄλλη στατίων')—suggests that the building referred to was on the scale of a private dwelling or a *collegium* building, not a warehouse.[88] The impression one gets from this information is that the structure was a modestly-sized but attractive-looking (though perhaps a bit dilapidated) clubhouse.[89]

---

[84] D'Arms (1974).

[85] In the latter case it would be '(denarium) c(entum milia) n(ummum)'. This was Mommsen's suggestion; Mommsen (1913) 9 with Dessau's nt. 2; Dubois (1907) 92; Sosin (1999) 279–281.

[86] Dessau, commenting '[e]s ist unmöglich, in dieser griechischen Inschrift die Ziffern, so wie Mommsen es getan hat, lateinisch zu verstehen', proposes 250 *denarii* as the correct reading; Mommsen (1913) 13 nt. 1. W. Dittenberger ('δηναρίων διακοσίων πεντήκοντα') *OGIS*, 595 nt. 23; G. Kaibel ('δηναρίων σν'') *IGRR*, I, 421.

[87] Duncan-Jones (1982) 210, 236 (nr. 1187), interpreting the numerals as Greek, reads the figure as 25,000 *denarii*. On this interpretation see Sosin (1999) 279 notes 6 and 7.

[88] *Stationes* as domestic structures: Pliny the younger *Ep.* 1,13,2; 2,9,5. *Stationes* as *collegium* buildings: Suetonius *Nero* 37; Pliny the elder *NH* 16,236. See Dittenberger, *OGIS*, 595 nt. 4; Cantarelli (1900).

[89] On the architecture of *scholae* see Bollmann (1998) 58–126. A colonnaded structure located in the western part of Puteoli has, on the basis of two inscriptions found nearby,

Thanks to the Sulpicii archive, we now have at least some idea of lease prices in Puteoli. In a document dating from March 13th, 40 AD, a grain stall was leased for a monthly rent of 100 HS to store 13,000 *modii* (87.5 metric tons) of Alexandrian wheat. That load would have taken up a space of about 112 cubic meters.[90] On the basis of this information, and assuming that prices had remained more or less stable in Puteoli, an annual rent of 250 *denarii* (or about 83 HS a month) seems entirely realistic for the Tyrian building.[91] In a strict analogy, that amount would have rented a space of roughly 93 m^3, that is to say one commodious room, or perhaps two smaller ones, a space perfectly adequate for communal activities such as business meetings or other professional gatherings. As we shall see in Chapters 3 and 4, a station of that size is also completely in line with the archaeological evidence on *stationes* on the 'piazzale delle corporazioni' in Ostia and on the Sacra Via in Rome.

But if, nonetheless, one opted for reading the figure in the inscription as 25,000 *denarii* or 100,000 *denarii*, then the Murecine evidence suggests it would have been a building big enough to hold about 1,083,333 *modii* of wheat (circa 7,291 metric tons, or 9,338 m^3), or even more than 4,333,333 *modii* of wheat (circa 29,163 metric tons, or 37,353 m^3) respectively. That Tyrian merchants, not known for trade in bulky commodities like grain but renowned most of all as suppliers of high-value goods like purple-dye, would permanently have been maintaining such gargantuan storage facilities seems improbable, to say the least.[92] And even if they did need to deposit goods on occasion, the lease contracts in the Sulpicii archive

both regarding Tyre and Tyrian divinities, been interpreted as the Tyrian station (*CIL* X 1601 [= *IG* XIV *add. et corrig.* 842a] and *IGRR*, I, 420 [= *OGIS*, 594]); Gialanella and Sampaolo (1980/1981) 150–152 (with a drawing, fig. 11).

[90] *TPSulp.*46. At a weight of 6.73 kg. per *modius* of Alexandrian wheat, and at a capacity of 8.62 liters per *modius*. Duncan-Jones (1982) 370/371.

[91] Of course, it might be argued that prices had risen, and that 25,000 *denarii* or 100,000 *denarii* should be preferred because of inflation. The inscription falls exactly in the period (160s–190s AD) in which Dominic Rathbone observed a doubling of price bands in the Egyptian data. That effect can not explain a price increase this large though. Rather, it would seem that the information from the inscription, in combination with the Sulpicii tablet, shows that the phenomenon observed in Egypt did not affect lease prices in second-century AD Puteoli. Rathbone (1996). See also Duncan-Jones (1982) 7–11.

[92] E.g. Strabo 16,2,23; Pliny *NH* 9,135–139. There was an industry around purple-dye (and dyestuff in general) in Puteoli; Pliny *NH* 35,45; Puteolan *purpurarii: CIL* X 540, 1952. See Dubois (1907) 127–129.

demonstrate that storerooms could be rented on an *ad hoc* basis and did not have to be kept year-round.[93]

If the annual lease price was indeed 250 *denarii*, that leaves us with Dubois' objection that such a trivial sum was not worth complaining about; a few cuts in the station's cultural budget, he argues, would surely have sufficed to pay that amount. I think that argument is misguided for several reasons. First, a sum of 1,000 HS—about 8.7 times subsistence level or maybe three times the real annual income of the average Roman—should not be underestimated.[94] After all, the Tyrians were, as they themselves pointed out, a group that did not receive fees from traders. With the Roman station's subsidy gone, they now faced the prospect of having to pay the rent out of their own pocket. Second, it is impossible to be sure, but in a petition of the sort the Tyrians sent to their city-council there may well have been some rhetoric involved, and the financial hardship of the station may not have been as great as alleged.[95] Paying 1,000 HS in rent may have been painful, but may equally not have been the burden imperiling the station's very existence it is made out to be.

An alternative explanation to Dubois' would be that the Puteolan Tyrians simply had an ax to grind with their colleagues in Rome, colleagues who after many years of forwarding a share of their proceeds had unilaterally decided to discontinue that practice.[96] This explanation would reduce the power of Dubois' argument that the Puteolan station-operators could have coughed up 250 *denarii* if they absolutely would have wanted to. But whatever the truth may have been, the really interesting question—and a question that Dubois does not pose—is not so much why they troubled their city-council with this matter, but why they chose to set up an elaborate (and no doubt expensive) inscription to commemorate it.

Here, we should first consider at whom the message might have been aimed. We do not know where the marble slab with the text originally stood, but it would seem that a lengthy inscription like this one, mentioning the municipal affairs of a provincial city, would have been set up in a public space somewhere, perhaps in the Tyrian quarter; we know that

---

[93] Apart from *TPSulp*.46, see also *TPSulp*.45, although in that document the monthly rent of 1 HS was clearly a symbolic sum. Other lease contracts: *TPSulp*.110 (possible lease of a *horreum* or a *fullonica*), *TPSulp*.47 ('locationes hortor(um)').

[94] Subsistence level: Hopkins (1980) 117–119; Jongman (1988) 195. Real Roman incomes: Jongman (2007); Temin (2006); Hopkins (2002) 197–203; Goldsmith (1984).

[95] But cf. Sosin (1999) who argues that the station's existence was on the line.

[96] Dubois does briefly mention that interpretation. He summarily rejects it though; Dubois (1907) 92 nt. 2.

a *pagus Tyrianus* existed in Puteoli from a still unpublished inscription.[97] We could postulate that the choice for Greek is a sign of a restricted intended readership. However, Greek remained the dominant official language in inscriptions in nearby Neapolis well into the third century AD. In Puteoli as well it was still an influential language in public inscriptions in imperial times; it is, in this respect, surely significant that the town where the *Cena Trimalchionis* is set (almost certainly Puteoli) is referred to as a *Graeca urbs* in the *Satyricon* (*Sat.* 81,3).[98] On the assumption, then, that the inscription was on public display somewhere and that its content could be widely understood, why would the Tyrians want the Puteolans to know about an affair that was, all things considered, a domestic Tyrian squabble over money?

To answer that question, we should try to establish what it was exactly that the station-operators were supposed to be doing in Puteoli. If they did not manage or oversee storerooms, what service were they providing? A few things seem beyond discussion. First of all, there can, I think, be little doubt about the commercial nature of the station. The sister (or perhaps better: mother) branch in Rome received an income from merchants and shipowners, and the Puteolan building's rent used to be paid with part of those earnings. The two stations were evidently closely associated, and it would seem that both were basically in the same business; a business that had something to do with commerce and shipping.[99] Second, there is no question that the station-operators were more or less permanent residents. They called themselves 'the ones living in Puteoli' ('οἱ ἐν Ποτιόλοις κατοικοῦντες') and had obviously settled overseas for a long stay, possibly for life.

One other thing can, I think, be established with a reasonable amount of certainty. It would seem that Tyre did not maintain a station in Puteoli at the behest of the Puteolan civil authorities. It is not clear from the inscription whether the structure belonged to a private individual or whether it was publicly owned, although the latter seems more likely.

---

97 The inscription was apparently 'reperta Puteolis in S. Euphemia', which does not tell us much about its original location; Mommsen (1913) 10. The inscription related to the *pagus Tyrianus* is mentioned by Camodeca (1982a) 27.

98 Kaimio (1979) 70–73. On the location of the *Cena Trimalchionis*, see Rose (1962).

99 Dubois (1907) 86 rejects the interpretation put forward by Kaibel and Mommsen, according to which 'στατίων' meant a seating area provided by the Puteolans to the Tyrians, so that the latter could comfortably watch public festivals in the forum. Dubois' interpretation seems better to explain the mention of merchants and shipowners. See also Cantarelli (1900) 128–130.

From a Suetonius passage it can be inferred that it was not allowed for private individuals to lease space as *stationes* to foreign cities, at least not in Rome; Nero put the patrician Salvidienus Orfitus to death because he had done exactly that: '[he] was charged with having let to certain states as headquarters ('ad stationem') three shops which formed part of his house near the Forum'.[100] Note, incidentally, that from this story one gets the impression that *stationes* were fairly modest spaces. But in any case, if indeed the building was public property then the 250 *denarii* in annual rent were presumably a welcome addition to the local Puteolan treasury. But it would seem that the city was otherwise perfectly indifferent as to whether or not the Tyrians had a station there. The station-operators, at least, do not mention a requirement of any sort, and do not claim that without a communal building they would be in violation of municipal regulations.

The station was, in that sense, different from the medieval *fondachi* of cities like Genoa, Venice, and Pisa in the Orient, or of the Turks or the Germans in Venice. The Italian archaeologist Luigi Cantarelli first made that comparison, specifically taking the Venetian *fondaco dei Tedeschi* as an example. This idea, followed in some of the later literature, is based largely on the assumption that the Tyrian building comprised a large amount of storage space and that, therefore, the lease-sum was high and the revenue for the city of Puteoli great.[101] As I have argued above, I think that assumption is implausible. But an even more forceful reason to see the two as fundamentally different is that in Venice, German merchants were compelled by the government to lodge and work in the—Venetian controlled and run—*fondaco*. The Venetians, wanting to scrutinize and regulate the foreign merchants' dealings as much as possible, even went so far as to implement a curfew, locking the building at night and only unlocking it again at daybreak. The *fondaco* was intended first and foremost to house itinerant traders, and it was precisely Germans in more

---

[100] Suetonius *Nero* 37,1. 'Salividieno Orfito obiectum est quod tabernas tres de domo sua circa Forum civitatibus ad stationem locasset'. Tr.: J.C. Rolfe, Loeb (1979 [1914]). See Dubois (1907) 93 and nt. 3. It can legitimately be asked if this rule (if indeed it existed) was strictly observed though. Suetonius mentions Orfitus' case as an example of the capricious way in which Nero put people to death on the basis of futile accusations.

[101] Cantarelli (1900) 131–134; Dubois (1907) 93; La Piana (1927) 259, nt. 22. The *fondaco dei Tedeschi* (until recently Venice's main post office, now to be transformed into a department store) is a large building indeed: it counts three floors, 76 rooms for occupation, and 25 storage vaults. The present structure, built in 1508, is a rebuilding of an earlier one, destroyed by fire in 1505. On the *fondaco*, see Constable (2003) 315–328.

long-term residence—artisans, bakers, and tradesmen—who were considered exempt from living there.[102] In short, the medieval example, characterized by strict regulations and a desire for control, does not seem applicable to the Roman situation.

Tyrian Agents as a Trading 'Bridge'

The central argument put forward here is that the station functioned as a bridge between Puteolan businessmen on the one hand and their Tyrian trading partners on the other. Cantarelli's *fondaco*-comparison, though less suitable than he suggested, already introduced basically that idea over a hundred years ago. Nonetheless, it seems no one has ever considered the micro-economic intricacies of such a bridge-function. As a result, analyses have so far remained rather hazy on the question of what purpose the *statio* served.[103] It is my contention here that it served to overcome the constraints of imperfect information and an imperfectly functioning legal system.

Puteolan traders in their dealings with alien business partners relied on formal legal contracts, yet the government did not use its coercive power to enforce those contracts. To solve the riddle of how these things can be reconciled I think we need to be looking at group reputation. In the case of the Tyrian station, both Puteolan merchants and their business partners overseas could trust Tyrian agents to be loyal because the agents lived permanently in Puteoli and operated in a group with restricted membership.[104] In settling in Puteoli, the 'colony' of agents had made investments both socially and materially, that is to say: they had a social position in the local community and they probably had goods that could be affected by an execution sale. If they had really settled for the long term they will, in all likelihood, often also have had families.[105] Their social position, in other

---

[102] Constable (2003) 318, 324.

[103] Cantarelli (1900); Dubois (1907) 85–93; Pârvan (1909) 114/115; La Piana (1927) 256–260; D'Arms (1974) 105. Cantarelli and Dubois thought the station-operators' task consisted at least in part in receiving merchandise and keeping it in storage.

[104] Of course, we do not know how membership was organized, but from the fact that the Tyrians lived permanently in Puteoli it can be inferred that membership was relatively 'closed'. A Tyrian only passing through would not have been considered a member. Only a Tyrian with the intention of settling permanently in Puteoli and associating himself with the station would have received membership.

[105] Evidence for Tyrian families, epigraphic or otherwise, there is none, but see the epitaph set up in Puteoli by a native of Caesarea to his daughter who had died, age twelve:

words, will have resembled the one of the 'Mexicanized' U.S. traders who had invested in settling in Mexican California.[106] The economic benefits that accrued from enjoying good collective standing provided incentives to individual group members to behave honestly and to submit to legal procedures. The motivation to uphold a collective good name worked on an exogenous level (peer pressure) but crucially also on an endogenous level.[107] Opportunistic behavior and failure to comply with social conventions would give an individual, but also the group as a collective, a bad name as untrustworthy and non-compliant. Agents could therefore be trusted to follow conventions—which included cooperating in litigation and respecting the word of the court—just as native traders would. A Puteolan merchant doing business with a principal in Tyre through a local Tyrian agent could thus effectively hold the agent responsible if he felt he was being wronged.

This social mechanism equally had the result that Tyrian businessmen could have greater faith in their overseas agents; they knew that there would be internal monitoring by the group within which the agent operated. The group would not want a Tyrian principal to level suspicions of misconduct against any of its members for fear that this might damage its collective good name. To prevent such accusations, it would be monitoring individual behavior. It is possible that there were forms of communal punishment, although these will likely have been informal. Imaginably, too serious an allegation might ultimately have jeopardized an agent's station-membership.[108] But the efficacy of a system of collective reputation relied on prevention rather than correction. It was an *ex ante* rather than an *ex post* mechanism that yet did not require extensive information about, and costly investigations into, past individual conduct.

In their capacity as permanent residents, the Tyrians could also serve as a liaison for fellow-community members passing through Puteoli. Because they were a culturally and religiously distinctive group, other Tyrians were able to prove their identity and affiliation by associating themselves with

---

CIL X 1985. Other inscriptions providing evidence for the family-life of alien residents: *IG* XIV 837, 840; *CIL* X 1970 (discussed further below).

[106] Greif (2006) 215.

[107] See Tirole (1996) who provides an extensive analysis of the impact of group reputation on individual incentives and behavior.

[108] Ostracism is the ultimate punishment, but because of good information availability within a closed group, the group can adapt punishments according to the threat level that the 'bad' member poses to the collective. Levinson (2003) 378–385; Ellickson (1991) 214–219.

them.[109] The group as a collective will have been careful in allowing non-station members to do this for fear that a corrupt or non-conformant compatriot would do damage to what they as an immigrant community had built up. Here, information about individual reliability was crucial. But because the station-operators had ties to a larger Tyrian network, such information was easier to obtain for them than it was for native Puteolans.[110] If and when they allowed a captain or merchant to associate himself with their station, local businessmen could feel relatively secure that the newly introduced individual was reliable as a trading partner. This is as close as traders in the Roman world could get to 'impersonal' exchange with a separation between the *quid* and the *quo*: community affiliation taking precedence over individual identity.

Unfortunately, the Tyrian station-operators do not give us any direct information about their activities or about the purpose of their station. Admittedly, therefore, all of this has to remain speculative to a degree. But when the details of the inscription are evaluated with this hypothesis in mind, a lot makes good sense. Clearly the Tyrians lived permanently in Puteoli, but just as clearly they remained a separate unit preserving a distinctive cultural identity. Not only did they have a communal building but they also maintained the cults of their ancestral deities, consecrated locally in Puteolan temples.[111] In the opening sentences of their letter they express their allegiance to Tyre, calling the city 'the sacred, inviolable, and autonomous metropolis' and addressing its officials as 'the chief magistrates, council, and people of their sovereign native city'.[112] At the same

---

[109] Compare Greif's analysis of the medieval Champagne fairs at which merchants were organized in communities. 'These arrangements enabled a trader to establish his communal and personal identity in interactions with merchants who did not know him personally. Living in the quarters of a particular community represented a way of demonstrating one's communal identity.' Greif (2006) 334.

[110] On the basis of an inscription mentioning a Syrian deity from Sarepta (*IGRR*, I, 420 [= *OGIS*, 594]) Dubois speculated that Sareptan traders could perhaps also make use of the Puteolan station. Supporting that idea is the way in which the Tyrians refer to Tyre (lines 2/3): 'μητροπόλεως Φοινείκης καὶ ἄλλων πόλεων'; Dubois (1907) 161. However, Torrey (1948/1949) 45–49 interpreted the inscription as evidence for Sareptan exiles moving to Puteoli, bringing their god with them.

[111] Tyrian deities in Puteoli: *CIL* X 1601 (= *IG* XIV *add. et corrig.* 842a), and *IGRR*, I, 420 (= *OGIS*, 594). See Visonà (1985/1986); Tran tam Tinh (1972) 152/153, 156–158; Torrey (1948/1949) 45–49; Dubois (1907) 157–161, 358.

[112] 'τῆς ἱερᾶς καὶ ἀσύλου καὶ αὐτονόμου μητροπόλεως Φοινείκης', 'ἄρχουσι βουλῇ δήμῳ καὶ τῆς κυρίας πατρίδος'. Lines 2/3. Tyre initially remained nominally independent under the Empire (but see Cassius Dio 54,7,6). It had the right to mint its own coins until the end of the reign of Nero, continuing thereafter to mint 'pseudo-independent' coinage (i.e. without the name or image of the Emperor). It received the status of colony with *ius italicum*

time, they are careful to demonstrate their loyalty to Roman imperial power, in the same breath, as it were, adding 'by the grace of the gods and the good fortune of our lord the Emperor'.[113] Further down they also mention how they would, at their own expense, renovate their station in honor of the sacred festival-days of Marcus Aurelius.

They show their close and friendly relations with their host city, mentioning how they were paying for the Puteolan local festival of the Ox-Sacrifice Games.[114] But equally they display their good standing in, and importance to, Tyre. Their request, they note, was discussed by their city-council, indicating how they and their station were taken seriously at the highest level of municipal politics. They present as fact not only that the council was aware of their existence but also that it was familiar with the general situation in Puteoli: 'there is many a station ... as most of you know'.[115] In the additional message they state that the city of Tyre 'provides for two stations', having made sure to mention that this practice had a long tradition.[116] Their main request seems to have been that the city itself take over the annual rent. Even if they never expected the request to be granted, it at least suggested to readers of the inscription that the option was real. Finally, the city-council's reaction, as presented in the text, contains as its key elements that the petition was justified and—more important still—that maintaining the station was to the benefit of Tyre.[117] In relating these things, the station-operators hinted at how much they were valued by Tyrian officialdom, which helped to endorse their official status and underscored their reliability as a group.

The gist of the letter to the city-council is quoted twice in the inscription—once in direct and once in indirect speech—including the remarks about the Ox-Sacrifice Games and about refurbishing the station for the festival in honor of the Emperor. To clarify the events that led up to the petition, there was no need to do this, and the repetition demonstrates how much the Tyrians wanted to highlight these elements. Herein lies,

---

around the end of the second century AD. See Ulpianus on his native city: *Dig*. 50,15,1.*pr*. See Rey-Coquais (1978) 50 (with nt. 76), 56.

[113] 'διὰ τοὺς θεοὺς καὶ τὴν τοῦ κυρίου ἡμῶν αὐτοκράτορος τύχην'. Line 5.

[114] The inscription suggests that this was not a voluntary step: 'μάλιστα ἧ καὶ τὰ ἀναλώματα εἰς τὸν ἀγῶνα τὸν ἐν Ποτιόλοις τῆς βουθουσίας ἡμεῖν προσετέθη'. Lines 11/12. Maybe this refers to a system of liturgies.

[115] 'εἰ καί τις ἄλλη στατίων ἐστὶν ἐν Ποτιόλοις (ὡ)ς οἱ πλείους ὑμῶν ἴσασι'. Lines 5/6.

[116] 'ἐδήλουν παρέχειν τὴν ἡμετέραν πατρίδα στατίωνας δύο'. Lines 40/41. But see W. Dittenberger's thoughts on the grammatical construction of the sentence (unclear because it breaks off) and the place of 'παρέχειν' in it. *OGIS*, 595 nt. 37.

[117] 'δίκαια ἀξιῶσι οἱ ἐν Ποτιόλοις', 'τοῦτο τῇ πόλει συμφέρει'. Lines 36/37.

I would suggest, an important clue as to why the inscription was set up, despite the fact that it concerned an affair that was of no intrinsic interest to the Puteolan public. It expressed the separate corporate identity of the Tyrians as well as their involvement in Puteolan public life; it conveyed their loyalty to their native as well as to their adopted city. Throughout, it shows concern for a collective good name. In other words, we here see the station-operators confirming or reconfirming that they performed the 'bridge' function I think they were supposed to perform.

The social position of the Tyrian station-operators resembles the one of the 'Mexicanized' U.S. traders in Mexican California in its essential attributes: a small 'colony' of merchants migrated to a different community for the long term, assimilating to their new environment while at the same time remaining different and separate. It does not conform completely to that model though. We do not know to what extent the Tyrians integrated into their new environment, but they certainly did not assimilate as much as the U.S. expatriates. They continued to appeal to their own political institutions and continued to worship their own gods. In a certain sense, they even 'advertised' their separateness from the Puteolan community by publishing the letter to their city-council. To a degree, however, this is what one would expect from a community that served as a 'trading bridge': 'Without barriers of some kind, the traders from abroad would likely disappear through assimilation into the host society within a generation or so; their capacity to act as cross-cultural brokers would then come to an end. Diaspora merchants needed contact with their hosts, but they also needed to keep their distance and enough of their original culture to serve as brokers for the traveling merchants from the original homeland'.[118]

But although the Tyrians maintained some of their differences, in things legal they adhered to local customs, just as the U.S. expatriates did. In one tablet from the Sulpicii archive, quoted above, we witness a Tyrian making an agreement with the Puteolan banker C. Sulpicius Cinnamus to appear in court.[119] Establishing the relationship between this document and the Tyrian *statio* is not entirely straightforward. The problem is that the document was drawn up in 52 AD while the *statio*-inscription dates to 174 AD. We can infer from the inscription that the Tyrian station had by that time been in use for quite a while, but can not know for certain

118 Curtin (1984) 38.

119 *TPSulp*.4, cited above: Zenon, freedman of Zenobus, from Tyre concluding a *vadimonium* with C. Sulpicius Cinnamus.

if it already existed as early as 52 AD. That it was in operation at that date is plausible enough though. Tyrians had a long history of establishing trading 'colonies' in cities overseas, a history stretching back as far as the ninth century BC.[120] In Roman times, they maintained a trading colony on Delos, as evidenced by a second-century BC inscription from the island.[121] No mention of this Delian community is made in the Puteolan inscription, but because Delos had been in slow decline as an emporium ever since the first Mithridatic War, the Tyrian κοινόν there likely did not exist anymore by 174 AD. But however that may have been, the Murecine tablet shows that by the mid-first century AD, Tyrians were conforming to legal conventions in Puteoli, confirming that already by that date a mechanism existed through which local social control was extended to them.

Overseas Agency as a General System of Exchange in Puteoli

The Tyrians did not form the only immigrant community in Puteoli, and we possess much more evidence on the presence of other small 'colonies' in the city. In at least some cases these will also have been trading stations. After all, the Tyrians mention in the letter to their city-council that 'there is many a station in Puteoli', which can only refer to those of other communities.[122]

Evidence for other Syrians in the city is provided by an inscription dating to the reign of Antoninus Pius, set up by the priests of Jupiter Damascenus. The mention of a college of priests implies that the cult was well-established, although there are only two known Puteolan inscriptions referring to it.[123] More extensive information on a Syrian 'colony' is presented by the inscription set up by a group of worshippers of Jupiter Heliopolitanus; Berytus is explicitly stated as their native city. They were Puteolan residents ('qui Puteolis consistunt'), and dedicated their inscription to the Emperor Trajan, giving a full list of his honorary titles.[124] Once

---

120 Under the ninth-century king Ithobaal I, Tyre established trading colonies at Auza (Libya) and at Botrys (Lebanon). Later ninth- and seventh-century BC examples include colonies at Cition (Cyprus) and Memphis (Egypt). Noonan (2011) 183–187.

121 *I.Délos* 1519 (153/152 BC) (see also *I.Délos* 2612). See Rauh (1993) 28/29, 45, 298; Roussel (1916) 89/90.

122 'τις ἄλλη στατίων ἐστὶν ἐν Ποτιόλοις'. Lines 5/6. Much of the material concerning overseas traders in Puteoli is discussed by Dubois (1907) 83–117 and by Pârvan (1909) 107–116.

123 *CIL* X 1576 (= *ILS* 4326); *CIL* X 1575 ('Iussu I.O.M.D.'). Dubois (1907) 157; Waltzing vol. 3 (1899) 433 nr. 1658; Tran tam Tinh (1972) 135, 151/152 and fig. 74, 75.

124 *CIL* X 1634 (= *ILS* 300), datable to 116 AD. Waltzing vol. 3 (1899) 435 nr. 1667.

more we see a group of outsiders living in Puteoli, worshipping foreign gods, pledging allegiance to imperial power. Of course, we can not know for certain if this religious community consisted of people who lived in Puteoli for commercial purposes, but in light of the Tyrian inscription it seems most likely, especially since we know that, as the Tyrians, Berytians had had experience with overseas trading organizations from an early date; a Berytian association ('κοινόν') possessing a communal building is well-attested on second-century BC Delos.[125]

We have a second Puteolan inscription from a group of people worshipping Jupiter Heliopolitanus[126] organized in what is described as a *corpus*.[127] No place of origin is given, but it seems a safe assumption that we see the same people from Berytus here.[128] Their organization controlled a sizable necropolis of seven *iugera* (17,626 square meters) with a cistern and *tabernae* that seems to have served not only as a resting-place for the dead but also as a gathering-place for the living.[129] Its use was restricted to members, and only those could enter through its gates and had access to its streets 'who will have continued doing nothing against the law and statute of the *corpus*'.[130] Mention of these internal regulations provides interesting evidence on a group-regulation mechanism enforced by a penalty (exclusion from the communal funerary space), based on social control.

Another group of people from the East, Nabataeans, were also present in Puteoli.[131] A particularly important inscription discloses the existence

---

125 *I.Délos* 1520, 1772–1774, 1777–1782, 1791, (1795?). See Rauh (1993) 28/29, 45, 113; Roussel (1916) 90–92.

126 This cult was apparently well-established in Puteoli. We have an inscription mentioning a temple of Heliopolitanus (*ILS* 4289 = Dennison [1898] 374 nr. 2), and two others mentioning priests of the cult (*Eph. Ep.* 8, 359 and *CIL* X 1578 [= *ILS* 4290]). See Steuernagel (2004) 245; Tran tam Tinh (1972) 131–133; 147–149, fig. 71/72; Dubois (1907) 97/98, 156–161.

127 *CIL* X 1579 (= *ILS* 4291), no date. Tran tam Tinh (1972) 149/150, fig. 73; Peterson (1919) 146–149; La Piana (1927) 312/313; Waltzing vol. 3 (1899) 433/434, nrs. 1659/1660.

128 The cult of Jupiter Heliopolitanus was widespread in the East, and had a special significance for the Roman settlers in Berytus. Beard, North and Price (1998) vol. 1, 283, 334. See Lenormant (1876) on the votive statue dedicated to Heliopolitanus by an ex-soldier from Berytus, found in Nîmes; Ronzevalle (1901) on such a statue dedicated by two Roman citizens, found in Deir el-Qala'a.

129 1 *iugerum* = 2,518 m^2; Duncan-Jones (1982) 371. 'Tabernis' in the inscription does clearly not mean 'shops' (since only *corpus*-members were allowed access to them) but funerary buildings 'pour les *refrigeria* ou repas funèbres en l'honneur du mort'. Tran tam Tinh (1972) 150. See also Dubois (1907) 97, nt. 2.

130 'Atque ita is accessus iusq(ue) esto per ianuas itineraque eius agri qui nihil adversus legem et conventionem eius corporis facere perseveraverint.' Transcription: Tran tam Tinh (1972) 149. See also Waltzing I (1895) 336.

131 I discuss the Nabataeans in Puteoli, and the Mediterranean more generally, in greater detail in Terpstra (2013).

of a Nabataean temple in the city—almost certainly dedicated to Dushara, the Nabataean chief deity—built around 54 BC; the inscription commemorates the renovation of the structure in 5 AD by men with Nabataean names.[132] In 11 AD—a commemorative plaque says—Zaidu and Abdelge offered two camels to Dushara (whether this meant actual live animals or votive images is unclear).[133] In addition, an altar, three bases, and several marble revetments were discovered, bearing the words 'Dusari' or 'Dusari sacrum'.[134] That the community-members maintaining the temple were Nabataeans living in Puteoli, not just people traveling through, is suggested by a Puteolan grave stele marking the final resting place of Tholomiaos, son of Thaimallos, from Petra, died age thirty-three. Tholomaios, so his epitaph says, was 'also known as Maximus' ('ὁ καὶ Μάξιμος'). The Roman nickname of this very foreign individual strongly suggests ties to the Puteolan community.[135]

The Nabataeans were involved as middlemen in the movement of goods from Arabia, India, and China (incense, spices, and silk) to the Roman Empire.[136] Given Nabataean mercantile activity, it seems highly likely that the community in Puteoli served as agents. They may have had ties with the gens Annia, engaged in trade with Sicily, Egypt, Delos, and Arabia, although no definite proof of such connections exists.[137] Although the literary sources are silent on the Nabataean community in Puteoli, Strabo provides us with a most interesting bit of information on the mirrored situation. His friend, the philosopher Athenodorus of Tarsus, had visited Petra and '...said that he found both many Romans and many other foreigners living there, and that he saw that the foreigners often engaged in lawsuits, both with one another and with the natives...'[138] Apparently, the domestic Nabataean mechanism of social control included the

---

[132] Steuernagel (2004) 46, 247; Lacerenza (1988/1989); Tran tam Tinh (1972) 127–131; Peterson (1919) 151/152; Dubois (1907) 161/162.

[133] Tran tam Tinh (1972) 141–144, nrs. S.1, S.2 (= *CIS* II,1, 158 and 157), both in Aramaic only and therefore obviously intended strictly for internal use.

[134] See Terpstra (2013) appendix for a full list of the epigraphic evidence.

[135] *IG* XIV 842a.

[136] Terpstra (2013); Zayadine (2007).

[137] The Annii are attested in inscriptions in the East, and there is also the story of a freedman of Annius Plocamus in Pliny *NH* 6,84. De Romanis (1996) 247–250; Lacerenza (1988/1989) 122; Camodeca (1979) 23–30. Annii in Puteolan inscriptions: *CIL* X 1782, 1784; in the Murecine archive: *TPSulp.*46, 53, 57, 121.

[138] '... εὑρεῖν γὰρ ἐπιδημοῦντας ἔφη πολλοὺς μὲν Ῥωμαίων, πολλοὺς δὲ καὶ τῶν ἄλλων ξένων· τοὺς μὲν οὖν ξένους ὁρᾶν κρινομένους πολλάκις καὶ πρὸς ἀλλήλους καὶ πρὸς τοὺς ἐπιχωρίους, ...', Strabo 16,4,21. Tr. (with small alteration): H.L. Jones, Loeb (1930). See De Romanis (1996) 165/166.

Romans residing in Petra to the extent that they could litigate with the local population. The same was true, I surmise, for the Nabataeans living in Puteoli.

Evidence for groups of people from the East is not limited to people from Syria and Arabia. One Puteolan public monument should not go without mention here, although its use for my purposes is not entirely straightforward. It is a statue base honoring Tiberius for his help to the cities in Asia that were struck by two disastrous earthquakes in 17 and 23 AD.[139] The marble pedestal displays a relief of fourteen human figures—representing the afflicted cities indicated with their names—running around all four sides; the front is inscribed with an honorific inscription by the Augustales to Tiberius.[140] A similar monument is believed to have stood in the Forum Iulium in Rome, and the Puteolan version is, if not an exact copy then probably a close adaptation.[141] The events that led to the creation of the monument are clear enough, but why it was dedicated not by the Greek communities themselves but by the Augustales is open to question. Dubois thinks this was because the religious body of the Augustales was made up for the most part of people from Asia Minor.[142] That may or may not have been true. But an alternative explanation would be that the Greeks had requested the Augustales to consecrate the monument on their behalf. After all, the imperial cult was the Augustales' province, and it may have been that putting up such an elaborate base and statue that so conspicuously honored an Emperor had to be run through them.[143] But either way, it seems almost certain that it was ultimately Greeks from the stricken cities who were expressing their gratitude with the monument. It would seem that its placement in Puteoli would be inexplicable without assuming there were communities of at least some of the places named and depicted on the base present there. This seems to be corroborated by an epitaph set up by a native of Ephesus (one of the cities mentioned on

---

[139] Tacitus *Ann.* 2,47; 4,13; Seneca *Quaest. Nat.* 6,1,13; Pliny *NH.* 2,86; Strabo 12,8,18; Cassius Dio 57,17.

[140] *CIL* X 1624. For an extensive description of the statue base, with illustrations, see Jahn (1851) 119–151 with plates 1–4. See also, Peterson (1919) 123/124; Dubois (1907) 104/105 and fig. 1–3.

[141] C. Morselli ([in: Steinby II] 1995) 300; Platner and Ashby (1929) 226/227. The Puteolan monument is probably a smaller, simplified version of the Roman original, depicted on Tiberian coinage; Jahn (1851) 122–126 and fig. II B. See also Chapter 4.

[142] Dubois (1907) 105; 146–148. See also Peterson (1919) 123–131.

[143] But cf. *CIL* X 1634 (= *ILS* 300), mentioned above, where citizens from Berytus are seen honoring the Emperor Trajan without any apparent involvement of the Augustales.

the base) to his freedman, and by another grave inscription for a woman named Stactia, also an Ephesian.[144]

That there were communities from Asia Minor and Greece in Puteoli seems further to be confirmed by two monuments, almost certainly also copies or adaptations of originals placed elsewhere.[145] The first is an inscription set up by the city of Cibyra. Due to the mutilation of the stone it is unknown to whom or what exactly it was dedicated, but 'Hellas' is a possibility. The Cibyrians mention that they were old friends of the Romans and that they had received high honors from the Emperor Hadrian.[146] Dubois suggested that the placement of this copy in Puteoli (the original may have stood in Athens or in Cibyra itself) should be explained by the intense interest the Greek 'expatriates' took in all things concerning their native city. However, I think that rather than some sort of expression of homesickness this is more likely yet another example of an immigrant community in Puteoli, wanting to highlight its good relations with its Roman hosts. A similar reasoning should, in my view, be adopted to explain the Puteolan monument dating to the Antonine age, showing two caryatids and a seated woman carved in relief, dedicated to (for certain in this case) 'Hellas' ('τῇ Ἑλλάδι').[147]

Some scattered grave inscriptions show us a rare glimpse of the personal life of Greeks from Asia Minor, living in Puteoli. From four epitaphs we know of a community from the city of Corycus; in one of them we see three generations represented in the male line: a grandfather, Hygeinos, dedicated a grave monument 'to his dearest grandson' ('υἱωνῷ γλυκυτάτῳ') Diodotos, son of Menodotos. Two of the four texts mention that the deceased was a shipowner (*nauklêros*), so a connection between this community and trade is highly likely.[148] A community from Nicomedia seems also to have been present. Two inscriptions provide evidence for women and family life: one is an epitaph from a husband to his young Nicomedian wife (died age fifteen), a second an epitaph from a brother to his sister.[149] A third inscription was set up in Nicomedia and was dedicated to Deios, son of Deios: 'lived twenty-eight years, died in Puteoli. Farewell'.[150] It may

144 *IG* XIV 847; *CIL* X 1616.

145 Dubois (1907) 106–109.

146 *OGIS* 497 (= *IGRR* 418).

147 Dubois (1907) 108/109 with fig. 4.

148 Hygeinos to his grandson: *IG* XIV 840; *naukleroi*: *IG* XIV 841, 854; Corycus also: *IG* XIV 848.

149 *IG* XIV 837; *CIL* X 1970.

150 *CIG* 3780. 'Δεῖος Δείου ζήσας ἔτη κη', τελευτήσας ἐν Ποτιώλοις. Χαῖρε'.

have been put up by a mourning family member who had stayed behind when Deios left to go live overseas. To judge from two further epitaphs, one dedicated by a patron to his freedman, another by a certain Callistos to his friend Hermes, other Greek communities may have included one from Perge (Pamphylia) and one from Athens.[151]

The commercial activity in Puteoli focused more on the East than on the West, and communities of traders from the western Mediterranean are less visible in our sources. However, there is conclusive epigraphic, archaeological, as well as literary evidence for trade connections with the West. The pottery shards from Puteolan-made ceramics found in Narbonensis and Spain, for example, bear witness to this.[152] We know, furthermore, that Q. Capito Probatus—in his epitaph somewhat pleonastically described as a 'marine shipmaster', 'naviclario (*sic*) marino'—had in his lifetime been a member of the Augustales in Puteoli, as well as of those in Lugdunum.[153] Another Puteolan Augustalis was patron of the bargemen of the Arar (Saône) River.[154]

Strabo tells us that large merchant ships sailed from Baetica to Puteoli in great number.[155] Although there seems to be no direct epigraphic evidence for Spanish settlers, there is the entertaining tale told by Aelian about a giant octopus that had made a habit of raiding the Puteolan storage space of Iberian traders at night. The animal, Aelian recounts, used to slip into the building through the sewers, break the storage vessels it found there with its tentacles, and eat its fill on their content of salted fish, leaving the Spaniards dumbfounded as to what was going on.[156] Regardless of what one thinks of the anecdote about the mischievous octopus, although nothing is said explicitly about Baetican residents, the story strongly suggests that in Aelian's time a community of such people did (still) exist in Puteoli. That the reverse was true and that there were Puteolan communities in Baetica is, at least, made more than likely by the

---

151 *IG* XIV 838, 842.

152 Pottery from the workshop of Numerius Naevius Ilarus (Puteoli: *CIL* X 8056; 17, 56, 97, 142, 149, 165, 229, 286, 337, 365, 385) has been found in Tarragona (*CIL* II 4970; 190, 226, 405). Pottery from other Puteolan workshops too (*CIL* X 8056; 130–132, 273, 367) has been found in Nîmes (*CIL* XII 5686; 696) and Tarragona (*CIL* II 4970; 475, 525). Dubois (1907) 121.

153 *CIL* XIII 1942.

154 *CIL* XIII 1960. Text heavily emendated.

155 Strabo 3,2,6 speaks of 'Turdetania' (i.e. Baetica: Strabo 3,1,6).

156 Aelian *Nat. Anim.* 13,6. Aelian's 'Iberians' were probably Baeticans; many communities on the Baetican coast had specialized in producing salted fish; Strabo 3,1,8; 3,4,2. See also Dubois (1907) 111 with nt. 1.

inscription where we witness a certain L. Iunius—he is explicitly identified as a native Puteolan—as Augustalis in the Baetican town of Suel (modern Fuengirola).[157]

Evidence for Africans in Puteoli is provided by three inscriptions mentioning the cult of Venus Caelestis, a goddess who, although of Phoenician origin, had probably reached Puteoli via North Africa. In pre-Roman Carthage she had been known as Tanit, in Roman times to become Juno Caelestis or Caelestis Augusta. In Italy, however, she was associated mostly with Venus. From at least the Severan era Caelestis had a dedicated temple in Puteoli, a sanctuary that must have been extraordinarily richly decked out given the epigraphic references to *ex votos* ('munera') in silver, gold, and precious stone. At the consecration ceremony, the new building was offered to Caelestis for the well-being of Caracalla and his mother Julia Domna. Apparently the members of the religious community (people from Carthage living in Puteoli?) intended to demonstrate their loyalty to the imperial dynasty, perhaps recognizing an opportunity to associate themselves with Julia by emphasizing the Phoenician roots of their goddess. However that may be, in Puteoli Caelestis had certainly already been venerated well before the Severans. In October 134 AD, she had received the religious offer of the 'taurobolium' (a bull sacrifice). Since the inscription states this was a renewed offer we know the cult's ritual activity in Puteoli dates back to an even earlier time. On December 2nd, 144 AD, the same priest who had performed the 'taurobolium' in 134 AD consecrated a private sanctuary ('thalame' of Rhea? Attis? Atargatis?) on behalf of a certain Hosidia Afra whose name betrays her African origin; she was perhaps one of the Caelestis faithful.[158]

To conclude this chapter, I will return to the Sulpicii archive once more. With regard to inter-community exchange, one tablet is of particular interest. It is a peculiar document that stands apart from the rest if only because it is written in the form of a letter. So far it has, to my mind unrightfully, not received much attention. Unfortunately, it is poorly legible but I think it nonetheless illustrates how the concept of stationing overseas trading communities in Puteoli functioned. In translation it reads:

[157] *CIL* II 1944.

[158] *CIL* X 1596, 1597, 1598; A. de Franciscis, *N.d.sc.* 8 (1954) 283–286. Tran tam Tinh (1972) 137–140, 159–163; Steuernagel (2004) 53, 245. See also the 'numen caeleste' in Ostia (Chapter 3).

> Theophilus to brother[159] Aphrodisius, blessing. From the ship the Octa, you will receive six medium-sized amphorae of wine, and seventy-seven of vinegar; sixteen Sicilian jars[160] of honey, and ten of m[...], one amphora of grape syrup, one amphora of s[...], ...[161]

This seems to be a rare example of a bill of lading from the Roman world, the only one, to my knowledge, to have survived on a wax tablet.[162] Although the bottom-half is lost and the text is damaged, it gives us a lot of good information. It plainly concerns a transaction with a time gap between the *quid* and the *quo*, visible in the future tense 'you will receive' ('accipies').[163] Furthermore, because these men were not citizens and do also not seem to have been slaves, they were likely *peregrini*.[164] From the text it would seem that they were not in the same location. Without much doubt this location was Puteoli for Aphrodisius. The place where the document was signed and where the shipment was made—information now unfortunately lost—would have revealed from where Theophilus was sending the goods. Although no foreign city is mentioned, we may witness a long-distance transaction here. However, the fact that this document was kept in the archive of the Sulpicii suggests that members of the Puteolan community, most likely in the shape of the Sulpicii themselves, were also somehow involved.

---

159 *Frater*, someone of equal social standing; Camodeca (1999) 184; 'colleague', Bove (2006) 22 nt. 1.

160 'amphoras vini sematas' ('medium-sized amphorae') is somewhat mysterious; Camodeca: 'mezze amfore'. 'urnalia' ('jars'): containers with a capacity of ½ amphora (*OCD*, Camodeca [1999] 184).

161 *TPSulp.*80. 'Theophilus Aphrodisio fratri sal(utem). Accipies de nave Octa amphoras vini sematas VI, aceti LXXVII, urn[a]lia sicula XVI mellis (?), X m[---], am[ph]or(am) I defriti, a[mp]hora(m) I s[---] VE[-2/3-]+o+m [·]+[---]+N[-2/3-] suis. -----'; Camodeca (1999) 47/48.

162 Rougé claims there are many on papyrus, but the only example he gives (*P.Mich.* 468, early second century AD) is not really a bill of lading but a personal letter from a son to his father. The son, who served in the army, listed some goods he had received, and other goods he had sent back. Rougé (1966) 368 with nt. 4.

163 I remain unconvinced by Lucio Bove's (2006) attempt to interpret this document as a mandate given by Theophilus to Aphrodisius for the collection of goods. For one thing, the text does not use the language of *mandatum* (cf. *TPSulp.*48, 49). Interpreting it as a bill of lading, as Camodeca does, makes more sense to me. Cf., e.g., this medieval bill of lading from 1369 AD: '... Gentlemen: I am transmitting to you, in the name of God and of salvation, by the ship captained by En Lois Frexinet, who is the bearer of the present, 27 large sacks of wool, of which 23 are white and 3 black, and one of which is one part white and two parts black....' Lopez and Raymond (2001) 245/246.

164 Were these two men really *peregrini*? Both Camodeca (1999) and Bove (2006) think so. The hypothesis that they were slaves can not be ruled out, but it seems strange that in that case their master(s) were not identified.

My interpretation of this document, tentative admittedly, is as follows. A peregrine merchant, Theophilus, sent merchandise to his local Puteolan agent Aphrodisius who was a compatriot of his, and a settler in Puteoli just like the Tyrian station-operators. Aphrodisius was expected either to resell the goods locally or to reship them to another location (imaginable is Rome).[165] Given the unquestionably large amount of overseas commercial activity in Puteoli, a transaction like this one must have been fairly commonplace.[166] Assuming, as seems probable, that Puteolan merchants or financiers were involved, the shipment might have been financed with borrowed money or have occurred on the basis of a previous contract of sale. We see here the type of transaction that, because of information constraints and imperfect legal enforcement, entailed high risks; a contract that involved a separation in both space and time. With such transactions, a Puteolan trader and a business partner on the other side of the shipping lane could try to build up a bilateral relationship based on trust and loyalty (the two-stage game with repeated prisoners' dilemma I discussed earlier). But a better way to reduce the risks to a workable level was to operate through local agents with a stake in the local community. I think that is what we see in action here, and I have tried to argue that this was common practice in Puteoli.

Conclusion

Roman merchants faced two fundamental problems in conducting overseas trade: information could be obtained only with great difficulty, and the government did not provide any physical assistance in enforcing contracts. Insofar as scholars have addressed these issues, they have suggested that the problems of long-distance trade were solved by using dependent labor. I have argued that this answer is unsatisfactory for the simple reason that dependent agents too needed monitoring.

During the twelfth and thirteenth centuries, Mediterranean trade was also hampered by imperfect information and imperfect legal enforcement. In a prominent solution adopted between Florence and its business

[165] The quantities involved are fairly small, even containing single amphorae (although a total of 111 vessels are mentioned, which is still a large amount). Given the mercantile activities of the people in the archive, I would suggest that what we see here is a transaction for commercial purposes.

[166] Puteoli as a commercial center, Dubois (1907) 64–117; Frederiksen (1984) 319–349; Camodeca (1994).

partners during this time period, the civil authorities of a particular city were expected to force their wayward members to comply with court decisions. On failure to do so, a reprisal in the form of a trade boycott of the one community against the other would follow. This system of communal punishment and retaliation underpinned commercial relations and facilitated inter-city trade.

However, nothing in the Murecine documents indicates that such communal arrangements played a role in Puteolan business. From the documents it is apparent that non-citizen outsiders in Puteoli used Roman law both in contracting and in litigation, where necessary in a somewhat modified form. They contracted on an individual basis and litigated on an individual basis, just as local Puteolans did. As an alternative historical model, I presented the case of the U.S. traders who integrated into local communities in Mexican California during the first half of the nineteenth century. I argued that the system of inter-community exchange in Puteoli functioned in a similar way.

Enforcement in Puteoli depended on social control and on obedience to social rules and conventions. To have the force of those conventions apply also to merchants from overseas, a number of them would settle in the city for the long term. Because these groups of outsiders were living permanently in Puteoli, their members could, at least for purposes of trade, be seen as forming part of the local business community. However, they were still recognizable as a foreign element, and the group reputation they enjoyed provided incentives, both exogenous and endogenous, to behave honestly. This solution had the effect that native businessmen could trust the foreign settlers to adhere to the local conventions governing contracting and litigation. Group reputation and group monitoring also had the effect that the distant principals could trust their overseas agents to be loyal. Finally, the integrated immigrant merchants could serve as local contacts for itinerant traders and shippers from their hometowns.

CHAPTER THREE

COALITIONS OF FOREIGN MERCHANTS AND SHIPOWNERS IN OSTIA

The Maghribis' Coalition and Medieval Trade

In the year 1040 AD, Abu 'l-Faraj Jacob Ibn ʿAllān, a merchant based in Fustat (Egypt), accused his former agent Yaḥyā al-Majjānī, based in Al-Mahdiyya (Tunisia), of misconduct. Yaḥyā, he alleged, had incorrectly stated the profits from certain sales and withheld the difference.[1] Word of the accusations spread quickly, prompting Yaḥyā, evidently in alarm, to write to his new local Fustat business partner Abu 'l-Khayr. Claiming to be innocent and complaining bitterly about the effect the allegations had had on his business, he wrote: '...I am harassed on every side... I was accused of things of which I had no knowledge and with which I had nothing to do and which I did not commit... people became agitated and hostile to me and whoever owed [me] anything conspired to keep it from me.'[2] Imploring his business partner to help him clear his name in Fustat, he continued: 'Please, brother, meet all these people; keep an eye on what is going on and report back to me with every courier coming here. Likewise, assure them under oath, in my name, that I have nothing to do with any of their claims and don't know anything about them...'[3]

The Tunisian agent Yaḥyā and the Egyptian traders from Fustat belonged to the 'Maghribis', a business community consisting of middle-class Jewish traders. Originating from the Abbasid caliphate centered in Baghdad, they emigrated from their place of origin to North Africa (mainly Tunisia the 'West', 'Maghrib', of the Muslim world, hence their name) during the first half of the tenth century AD.[4] From Tunisia, at that time under the control of the trade-friendly Fatimid caliphate, some of them emigrated to (Fatimid-controlled) Egypt, Palestine, Sicily, and even further to Spain.

---

[1] Goitein (1973) 95–107. See Greif (2006) 77, nt. 53; Greif (1989) 870. See also Greif (2012) 452–454; Goldberg (2012).

[2] Tr.: Goitein (1973) 104/105. The letter actually reads: '...whoever owed *the old man* anything...' Yaḥyā alludes to his recently deceased father whose business he inherited.

[3] Yaḥyā continues: '...except for a claim concerning a transaction made many years ago', casting at least some doubt on his trustworthiness and sincerity.

[4] Greif (2006) 60/61, 77/78; Greif (2012) 457; Greif (1989) 860–862. See also Goitein (1973) 3–21.

Their trade network ultimately stretched all over the Mediterranean and the Levant.[5] Although the Maghribis and their descendants were, after their move westwards, incorporated into the larger Jewish communities in North Africa and around the Mediterranean, they preserved a strong sense of group-identity. By a stroke of luck a fair number of their letters survive. In this correspondence they refer to themselves as 'our people' or 'our friends, the Maghribis'.[6] It is impossible to determine how large their numbers were in the eleventh century but we do know that they were not trivial; in 175 documents, 330 different names appear.[7] Avner Greif has studied these letters to investigate the way in which the trading operations of the Maghribis functioned. The question he tried to answer was: how were the Maghribis able to overcome the problem that neither the anonymous market nor the medieval legal system helped them establish the overseas relations they needed for their trading ventures?[8]

Because of their shared cultural and historical background, the Maghribis—though not a religious-ethnic entity separate from the Jewish population at large—were a distinct group. The members of this community only used other members as overseas agents in conducting long-distance trade.[9] If an agent cheated, the whole community would know about it fairly quickly by virtue of the business correspondence that went to and fro on a regular basis between all Maghribi traders. If found out, a cheating agent would be ostracized. The unwritten rule to which all members adhered was that no deals were to be made anymore with an agent who had proven to be unreliable. This arrangement, Greif asserts, was financially beneficial to all members; the profits of only dealing with other members were greater than the potential benefits of starting agency relationships with outsiders.[10]

This system of voluntary cooperation could only work as long as three criteria were true. First, there had to be no established date for its termination; second, information about cheating had to be shared; third, the reaction to cheating had to be uniform. Only under these conditions could such a system remain in equilibrium; no cooperation strategy would

[5] Goitein I (1967) 209–217; Goitein (1973) 23–25; Gil (1983).

[6] Greif (2006) 78; Greif (1989) 862. For examples, see Gil (1983) 121, line 12; Goitein (1973) 32, nr. 1, F.

[7] Greif (2006) 61.

[8] Greif (1989) 857/858, 865/866. Greif's analysis has been challenged by Edwards and Ogilvie (2008). For Greif's reply, see Greif (2008) and Greif (2012).

[9] Greif (2006) 59.

[10] Greif (2006) 81–83; Greif (1989) 859.

have emerged if, in game-theoretic terms, the players had known from the outset the 'game' was finite, and if imperfect information sharing had undermined the threat of the ostracism penalty. Frequent communication among members of the community ensured that the behavior of all members was 'common knowledge'.[11] Because information about cheating was passed along with the regular mail, such information was virtually cost-free. This made monitoring cheap, and made the threat of ostracism real.[12] As for the time horizon of the 'game', any misdeeds of traders or agents were held against their sons, brothers, or even other, more distant relatives.[13] Traders did therefore not acquire license to start cheating in their old age. Reputation retained its value throughout a trader's lifetime and transcended the generations.

From the letters that have come down to us it appears that this coalition was remarkably effective.[14] The desire to maintain a good name was so strong that it could induce traders to honor their contracts, even if this was not in their immediate financial interests. This can be seen in a letter from Māzar, Sicily, written in 1059 AD.[15] The writer, we learn, had made a deal selling two loads of flax in Tunisia before the opening of the official trading season. The sale had fetched an average price of thirteen dinars per load, but when the season officially opened and trading ships started arriving, the price of flax dropped sharply to eight dinars a load. The customers refused to pay and, so the seller writes, 'there erupted a fierce controversy between us and them'. Eventually, however, the buyers agreed to pay anyway, solely for fear of damaging their good name. The seller, clearly relieved and pleased with the outcome, commented: 'if not for the prestige... we would not have received anything from them'.[16]

New or unfamiliar members were allowed access to the coalition only with great caution, and only after tests of the wider network to check the newcomer's reliability. This is illustrated by a letter from the 1060s, sent by a trader in Alexandria to a merchant in Fustat, in which the appearance of an unfamiliar third party is discussed. The new arrival came carrying

---

[11] On 'common knowledge', see Lewis (1969) 52–60. See also Chapter 1.

[12] Greif (2006) 83.

[13] Greif (2006) 73, 83. For an example of sons becoming traders, see Goitein (1973) 60. See also Goitein (1973) 95–107: the embattled trading agent Yaḥyā (mentioned above) who is held responsible not only for his own actions but also for those of his father.

[14] Of the many Maghribi letters fewer than 5% contain allegations of misconduct. Greif (2006) 63; Greif (1989) 864 with note 33.

[15] Gil (1983) 113–126 with plates 3a, 3b. See especially lines 21–27.

[16] Tr.: Gil (1983) 124/125. See Greif (2006) 68; Greif (1989) 870.

several letters confirming his trustworthiness. He was treated with circumspection nonetheless: 'Please inform [Abū Zikrī] that a Jew from al-Mahdiya called Nissīm b. 'Aṭiya has arrived from Māzar in Sicily. He is a partner of Ḥassūn b. Isḥāq and has brought with him lead, olive oil, and some textiles. He has delivered several letters to me from Ḥassūn which strongly urge me to take care of this man.... I asked [the new arrival] whether there was much cargo on the ships for our colleagues and he said: "There is no cargo for all of you, but only for one of you." I asked him if they carried any cargo for Isḥāq b. Khalaf, and he said: "No." I had him swear to this effect... If (notwithstanding), any goods should arrive, I will write about this to Ḥassūn in Māzar. Please inform him of this.'[17]

Although the eleventh-century legal framework functioned too imperfectly to support the trade operations of the Maghribis, this did not mean they never made use of established courts of law.[18] Instances where they resorted to bilateral litigation can certainly be found in their correspondence, and in fact in the example of Ibn 'Allān and Yaḥyā I started out with, the accusations of the former were made before a Jewish court. However, the efficacy of such courts was ultimately underpinned by a multilateral reputation mechanism. Fellow traders often served as lay judges, while legal experts were often also businessmen. Because these courts were often composed of community members who knew one another, they served as venues to make misconduct public, thus contributing to the force of the reputation mechanism and the ostracism penalty.[19] Of course, to be able to label someone a cheater and ostracize him the Maghribis needed agreed-upon rules to determine what exactly constituted 'cheating'. A set of cultural behavioral rules (the 'merchants' law') was known to all and served as a sort of default contract; non-compliance with this code was regarded as misbehavior, while conformity was rewarded with good repute.[20] However, this code was not a codification: 'The Maghribis' code of conduct was a social norm, a rule that is neither promulgated by

[17] Cited and discussed by Udovitch (1977) 76.

[18] Greif (2006) 63/64; Greif (1989) 865/866.

[19] Greif (2012) 461–463. Goldberg (2012) 32 insists that 'threats to reputation were occasionally used by Geniza merchants to help prevent cheating, but only as a very minor plank laid on top of an important framework of market and legal institutions'. But what determined the efficacy of those legal (not to mention market) institutions? With imperfect enforcement, was this ultimately not reputation also? This is a point Greif explicitly makes; Greif (2012) 467: 'The Maghribis did not establish agency relations in the shadow of the law but used the court in the shadow of multilateral reputation'.

[20] Greif (2006) 70/71. Unfortunately, very little is known about the content of the 'merchants' law'.

an official source, such as a court or a legislator, nor enforced by the threat of legal sanctions but is nevertheless regularly complied with'.[21]

The Maghribis' coalition continued to function until the Muslim rulers in the West forced them to end their international trading ventures. With this change, their motivation for social interaction disappeared, their business operation ceased to function, and they assimilated into the larger Jewish community, leaving only their letters as a testimony to their coalition.[22]

Comparing the Maghribis and Trade Networks in the Roman Empire

In the argument I have developed so far, I have not discussed much how trading coalitions operated internally, focusing mostly on their interaction with the outside world as collectives. This omission needs to be addressed because the effect of social control I described in Chapter 2 did not extend far enough to include all members of foreign trading coalitions; the force of this mechanism did not include itinerant traders. Foreign merchants who did business in Puteoli but were not long-term residents there did not form part of the Puteolan community, unlike their colleagues who had taken the step of settling in the city. Local social mores and local reputation did therefore not have much controlling power over them. How was their behavior regulated?

In the following, I will make a comparison, proposing that trading coalitions in the Roman Empire, like the Maghribis' coalition in the eleventh century, relied on information-sharing to control their members' behavior. I will try to argue that a parallel can be drawn particularly with regard to the ostracism penalty, which enabled networks stretching over large distances to function. The reason I think this is a valid comparison is that Roman trade networks, despite notable differences, were in one essential aspect comparable to the Maghribis' coalition: at the heart of both lay a sense of shared identity. In the case of the Maghribi traders, group identity was determined by history and ethnicity, paired with a common religion. Within the Roman networks, the emphasis was first and foremost on geographical provenance. The religious aspect was less pronounced, although the situation on Roman Delos should receive another mention in this context; trading coalitions on the island commonly centered on a

21 Greif (2006) 59, paraphrasing Posner (1997) 365.

22 Greif (2006) 84.

specific cult.[23] But apart from that particular example, as we have seen in Chapter 2, and will see again in this one, religion was certainly a factor in the coherence of many business coalitions, worship of particular gods being intimately intertwined with geographical origin.

In the previous chapter I suggested that agents who had settled overseas maintained *stationes* in part to serve the needs of itinerant merchants and shipowners from their home communities, providing them with a place to identify themselves as natives of a particular city. In what follows I will elaborate on this element of my theory. Unfortunately, source material for large-scale trade operations of a quality even approaching the medieval letters is lacking for the Roman period. I will therefore have to rely on indirect evidence, in combination with the the Maghribi comparison and the cumulative argument as I developed it in the first two chapters.

The Ostian Material Evidence: the 'Piazzale delle Corporazioni'

Like Puteoli, the important harbor-town of Ostia provides valuable information on the commercial organizations of foreign shipmasters and traders. A key piece of material evidence takes the shape of a sizable building, a structure in the literature commonly dubbed the 'piazzale delle corporazioni'. In the 'piazzale', discovered and excavated about a century ago, we possess an exceedingly rich source, archaeological, visual, as well as epigraphic in nature. For my purposes, all these different strands combine.

The 'piazzale' is a curious space with no real equivalent anywhere in the Roman world. It has played a minor role in the modernist-primitivist debate on the Roman economy, its significance for the organization of Roman trade being the bone of contention. Moses Finely commented disdainfully '... there were no ... Guildhalls, no Cloth Halls, and further no Bourses, no Exchanges. Occasional attempts to discover them are desperately pathetic, as ... in the so-called "Piazzale delle Corporazioni" of Ostia, a typically exuberant archaeologists' name for a building with an uncertain function, that was at most a commercial office building with cell-like rooms'.[24] The role of the 'piazzale' in the debate continues to this day. To underscore this point it suffices to refer to recent work by Peter Bang on the one hand and David Kessler and Peter Temin on the other.[25]

---

23 Rauh (1993); Roussel (1916) 199–280.

24 Finley (1973) 195/196.

25 Bang (2008) 250–253; Kessler and Temin (2007) 329.

It would be hard to find scholars more divergent in their views on the Roman economy, yet Bang as well as Kessler and Temin have turned to the 'piazzale' to support their case. Of the two resulting discussions, Kessler and Temin's more insightfully highlights the important aspects of the structure (on which more below). But both discussions treat the 'piazzale' only cursorily, and neither incorporates the archaeological data or the building's architectural history. I, too, intend to use the structure as evidence to support my broader argument. Since we are dealing with a source from material culture and since, moreover, the building is rather exceptional, I think a careful consideration of the physical evidence is warranted.

The 'piazzale' (see fig. 1) can briefly be described as follows: it consists of a U-shaped double colonnade that is connected to Ostia's theater on its southern end and that centers on a large unroofed space. The square in the middle of the portico, adorned with a temple, seems to have been a garden area; it was not paved over, and traces of a travertine ridge to drain rainfall as well as vases to collect the water were found by the original excavator, Guido Calza.[26] The colonnade is divided into sixty-one small rooms all opening up onto the central square. The pavement in front of these rooms is decorated with floor mosaics in black and white tesserae, just under half of them still extant; it is primarily through these that we know of overseas trading coalitions operating in Ostia.[27]

Archaeological data reveal that the 'piazzale' was constructed in three main stages. The original edifice is early Augustan in date, and undoubtedly contemporary with the theater with which it forms a single architectural unit.[28] In the mid-first century AD it was subsequently restructured in a second phase which split the U-shaped portico, originally consisting of only a single nave, by adding a row of columns down the middle throughout its length. The structure in its present form is the result of rebuilding in yet a third phase which, according to the latest excavation results, should be dated to the time of Hadrian. With this Hadrianic renovation, the main entrance through the northern wall, consisting of twelve

---

26 Calza (1915) 184.

27 *CIL* XIV Suppl. 4549; Calza (1915) esp. 187–189; Meiggs (1973) plates xxii, xxiii, xxv a/c; Becatti (1961) 64–85. See also La Piana (1927) 261–264.

28 Battistelli and Greco (2002) 395–405; Bollmann (1998) 298–300; Pohl (1978) 185/186, 214; Meiggs (1973) 284/285.

piers of tufa blocks, was closed off, limiting access to the narrow passages on the opposite end, left and right of the theater.[29]

The relationship between this phase and the temple in the center of the garden is not certain. Based on its brickwork and brick stamps, the temple is commonly thought to have been constructed in Domitianic times. However, it is oriented south towards the theater and has its back turned towards the blocked northern entrance, suggesting it postdates the Hadrianic restructuring. Unfortunately, the building sequence is still unclear in this respect. It is possible that the temple is indeed Domitianic, and that the northern entrance was already closed in Flavian times.[30]

We no longer know to what deity the sanctuary was dedicated. Ceres has been proposed as its occupant, but this is based solely on circumstantial evidence. Another hypothesis, based on scattered epigraphic finds and a comparison with Rome's Theatrum Balbi, attributes it to the cult of Vulcan. In my view, the most credible suggestion put forward so far in the literature is that it served the imperial cult.[31] We have already seen foreign traders displaying allegiance to the Emperor and the imperial family in Puteoli, and will see this phenomenon again in Rome. Given the universality of Emperor worship, interpreting the building as a place for the imperial cult also solves the problem of having to assign a single deity to a temple visited by a multiplicity of diverse foreign groups.

The stalls along the colonnade are roughly square in shape, about 4.20 meters wide and 4.50 meters deep.[32] Visible now between most of them are the remains of masonry dividing walls, but these bear every sign of being an architectural afterthought. No traces of earlier walls are in evidence, and it would seem that originally the spaces were separated by wooden instead of stone partitions.[33] The Hadrianic reconstruction created new

---

[29] Battistelli and Greco (2002) 406–416. The fourth phase they identify seems only to have affected the theater, not the 'piazzale'. Based in large part on the dedicatory inscription *CIL* XIV 114 with *CIL* XIV Suppl. Nr. 114, p. 613, Calza (1915) 180–186 held that the third phase was late Antonine in date. Pohl (1978) 185–193, 214 revised Calza's interpretation.

[30] Temple Domitianic in date: Van der Meer (2009) 169; Meiggs (1973) 65/66; 285/286. If correct then the blocking of the main entrance likely also dates to that time: Battistelli and Greco (2002) 412/413, 415 nt. 52.

[31] Temple dedicated to Ceres: R. Lanciani, *N.d.sc.* (1881) 114; Calza (1915) 183 with nt. 1. Temple dedicated to Vulcan: Coarelli (1997) 223–225, (Coarelli's hypothesis is based on epigraphic finds, discussed in Pellegrino [1986]). Temple dedicated to Emperors: Van der Meer (2009). On temple and 'piazzale' see also Steuernagel (2004) 76/77, 198–202.

[32] See Pohl (1978) 187 with nt. 18, and fig. 1.

[33] Becatti (1961) 64; Calza (1915) 182/183. Pohl dates the brick partitions to the third century AD; Pohl (1978) 193.

floor space, and as a result the number of small rooms increased from fifty to sixty-one. Whether or not a need to enlarge the area available for business was the reason for blocking the main entrance, as Calza proposed, its effect was certainly to render the entire 'piazzale' quite private. By blocking the large monumental entrance-way through the northern façade the 'piazzale' attained the appearance of an essentially closed-off space. Especially in its final manifestation it must therefore have possessed an intimate atmosphere.

There has been much debate about the use and purpose of the 'piazzale', both before and after the Hadrianic rebuilding. One puzzling element is immediately apparent: the odd architectural alignment of entertainment and commercial areas, divided only by a wall but without a transitional spatial barrier in-between. The conjunction and the contemporaneity of the two sections indicate that initially the colonnade did not have a commercial purpose and was designed to be part of the theater. This interpretation was suggested from early on by Calza, and has found universal acceptance. Supporting this idea is the passage in which Vitruvius advised that a theater should have a portico behind the *scaena* to provide shelter for the spectators during rain-intermissions.[34]

The archaeologist Ingrid Pohl has argued that the portico always retained this function, even its in final shape. The stalls, she argues, were probably awarded to groups of spectators as civic honors in return for financing theatrical productions and, perhaps, minor building repairs. However, this hypothesis seems improbable for a number of reasons. For starters, it is not consistent with the relatively low quality of many of the mosaics. Furthermore, although less than half of the floor decoration is preserved, rendering inferences tricky, the balance of evidence is tilted heavily towards groups of *navicularii* from Africa. This makes one wonder: if these people had honorary stalls in the colonnade, why overwhelmingly they and not others? One could, incidentally, also legitimately ask whether foreign shippers who traveled for their livelihood could really be so intimately involved in the goings-on in the Ostian theater.

There is, moreover, the fact that a spot was occupied by the *restiones* and the *stuppatores* (rope makers, flax workers, and caulkers) people who most decidedly were not high in the social pecking order.[35] A similar

[34] Battistelli and Greco (2002) 395–405; Pohl (1978) 215/216. See also Calza (1915) 189; Paschetto (1912) 283/284. The Vitruvius passage is 5.9.1.

[35] On the *stuppatores* and their Ostian guild, see Hermansen (1982); Bollmann (1998) 278–282; Waltzing vol. 4 (1900) 44 nr. 140.

reasoning can be adopted for the tanners and merchants in hides ('corpus pellion(um)').[36] Yet another group without a particularly elevated social status were the people operating barges between Ostia and Rome ('codicari').[37] It seems doubtful whether alien shipmasters and people involved in menial labor (even if they were likely the employers and not the ones actually handling tanning tanks, flax, and tar) would have been paid such conspicuous tribute in a public space. Given the nature of their trade, the presence of the craftsmen can, I think, better be explained by the constant need to repair the hulls, sails, and rigging of ships. The *stuppatores, restiones, pelliones* (who may have sewed sails), and of course the *codicarii* can all plausibly be linked to seafaring and maritime transport. Their presence alongside a large number of shippers' associations makes it much more likely that the slots on the 'piazzale' were not rewards for public benefactions but the product of people in the same or in supporting businesses, conveniently concentrating their activities.

If it is as good as certain that the colonnade of the 'piazzale' was originally part of the theater, and just as good as certain it was converted into something else at some point in time, it remains uncertain when exactly this transformation occurred. Some tentative evidence can be found in the four mosaics of an older series discovered at a depth of about thirty centimeters below the present floor surface.[38] These representations, postdating the Claudian, but predating the final Hadrianic phase of the building, bear no reference to foreign mercantile organizations. The *restiones* and *stuppatores*, however, seem already to have been present on the 'piazzale' at the earlier date; one of the older mosaics displays the letters 'S.R.', together with depictions of the tools and raw material used in rope-making.[39] Maybe their continued presence indicates that already before the final rebuilding there was some connection between this space and shipping activities. Given the shortage of evidence, though, I am here entering the realm of speculation. The most that can be said is that the

[36] *CIL* XIV Suppl. 4549, nr. 2; Becatti (1961) 65, nr. 84; Meiggs (1973) 286. See also Waltzing vol. 4 (1900) 36 nr. 113.

[37] *CIL* XIV Suppl. 4549, nr. 43. *Codicarii*, see Meiggs (1973) 293–296; Waltzing vol. 4 (1900) 10/11 nr. 21.

[38] Battistelli and Greco (2002) 412/413; Calza (1915) 188/189 nrs. 52, 53, 57, 58; Calza, *N.d.sc.* (1914) 72/73; A. Pasqui, *N.d.sc.* 98/99. Pohl notes that the correct numbers are actually 51, 52, 56, 57 (the shift by one number in the older literature may be due to a misprint); Pohl (1978) 190, nt. 26.

[39] *CIL* XIV Suppl. 4549, nrs. 1, 58; Calza (1915) 187, 189 nrs. 1, 58; Calza, *N.d.sc.* (1914) 72/73; Becatti (1961) 65, nr. 83; 84/85, nr. 137. See also Hermansen (1982) 125.

older mosaic may point at a more gradual change in use, rather than a drastic break.

Whatever the truth may have been in that matter, the portico was most likely used for commercial purposes from the Hadrianic building-phase onwards. The youngest mosaics are hard to date, but were probably put in place, at least in part, during the third reconstruction.[40] Additional evidence has come to light, confirming that by that time the space had been converted and was used by coalitions of foreign shippers. A triangular marble slab found in the eastern section of the colonnade—on stylistic grounds dated to the reign of Hadrian—bears the words 'naviculari Africani'. It may once have stood over the doorway of one of the stalls.[41]

In line with the theory of the 'piazzale' as a place connected to commerce and shipping are the marble pedestals with honorary inscriptions from the area, thought once to have lined the colonnade. Sixteen inscribed pedestals are known to us, three of which were unearthed on the 'piazzale' itself. Twelve more were discovered in a wall of the theater (where, between 385–389 AD, they had been reused as building blocks), and one was found southeast of the theater where (also in the fourth century) it had been re-erected with a new inscription on its reverse side. In 1911 during reconstruction work, the blocks that were reused in the theater wall were extracted and put up in the 'piazzale', where they can still be seen today along with the pedestals actually found there.[42] These blocks of marble, many containing dedications to public officials and magistrates of private associations, almost certainly originally bore statues of the honorees. The Ostian city-council was apparently the civic body to decide on placement of such objects; many inscriptions contain the abbreviation 'L(ocus) d(atus) d(ecreto) d(ecurionum) p(ublice)'. So far as we can tell, the dedications all date from the mid-second to the mid-third century AD.

The inscriptions betray a unmistakable relation to trade and guilds, and to riverine and maritime shipping. The food supply of Rome also plays a prominent role; a number of procurators of the *annona* are among the honorees.[43] An example of that last category is the dedication to Q. Petronius Melior who, apart from procurator of the *annona*, was 'assistant to

---

[40] Becatti dated the mosaics to the late second century, but he wrote before it was known that the last major building phase was Hadrianic, not Antonine in date; Becatti (1961) 64. Battistelli and Greco (2002) 414/415, 418/419; Pohl (1978) 192, 214.

[41] Bloch (1953) 285, nr. 44; Meiggs (1973) 285.

[42] Van der Meer (2009) 172/173; Paschetto (1912) 330–338. See also Meiggs (1973) 432.

[43] The *procurator annonae* was a subordinate of the *praefectus annonae*. On the administration of Ostia and Portus, see Bruun (2002); Lo Cascio (2002).

the curator of the Tiber riverbank and sewers' ('adiutori curatoris alvei Tiberis et cloacarum').[44] He was honored by the 'guild of the Ostian grain measurers' ('corpus me(n)sor(um) frum(entariorum) Ost(iensium)'). A 'guild of helpers of the Ostian grain measurers' ('corp(oris) mensor(um) frum(entariorum) adiutorum Ostiensium'), supposedly a subdivision of some sort, is also known from the 'piazzale'. Sometime at the end of the second century, its members honored a certain Q. Aeronius Antiochus who functioned as their *quinquennalis*.[45] The pedestal was set up by Antiochus' wife Aninia Anthis, although the spot had been allocated by the city-council. Two more honorary inscriptions were set up to honor procurators of the *annona*, one bears a dedication made by the guild of grain merchants, a second contains yet another dedication made by the 'guild of helpers of the Ostian grain measurers'.[46]

Of that last inscription, honoring Q. Acilius Fuscus, a close parallel is known from Thibursicum Bure (in the province of Africa Proconsularis), like its Ostian counterpart dating to the late second century AD. Fuscus was honored by the citizens of Thibursicum Bure as their patron, and since he belonged to the tribe Papiria he may have originated from Africa himself.[47] Another African connection is provided by a statue base erected in the 'piazzale' by (among others) the African shipmasters to M. Iunius Faustus, an Ostian *duumvir* and grain merchant.[48]

The statues and honorary inscriptions that ornamented the 'piazzale' were not all for men involved in the grain trade or long-distance shipping though. One inscription, dating to 147 AD, was set up for C. Veturius Testius Amandus, a Roman knight. He was patron and protector of the five guilds of Ostian ferrymen (*lenuncularii*, people who operated ferries and tugboats on the Tiber), and *quinquennalis* of the guild of bargemen (*codicarii*).[49] Two other inscriptions contain dedications to officials of guilds of local craftsmen, and have nothing whatsoever to do with riverine or maritime trade and transport. C. Iulius Tyrannus was *magister quinquennalis* of the *collegium* of builders in the 160s AD. Between the years 200–204 AD, M. Licinius Privatus held that same position, later to become

---

44 *CIL* XIV 172; G. Fiorelli, *N.d.sc.* (1880) 475–477.

45 *CIL* XIV 4140; R. Lanciani, *N.d.sc.* (1886) 57; Royden (1988) 105, nr. 95. On the subdivision of the *mensores frumentarii* in different types, see Royden (1988) 51–53.

46 *CIL* XIV 154, 161; G. Fiorelli, *N.d.sc.* (1880) 470–472.

47 *CIL* VIII 1439. Cébeillac-Gervasoni (1994) 53.

48 *CIL* XIV 4142. Sardinian shipmasters are also among the dedicators. More below.

49 *CIL* XIV 4144; R. Lanciani, *N.d.sc.* (1886) 56/57; Royden (1988) 104, nr. 93. On *lenuncularii* and *codicarii*, see Meiggs (1973) 296–298.

quaestor and *quinquennalis* of the Ostian bakers' association.[50] Overall, though, the relation to long-distance shipping and the grain trade in the dedications is pronounced.

One much-discussed question has therefore been if foreign shipmasters, many involved in transporting grain, assembled in the 'piazzale' as a result of government coercion. Calza first suggested this idea, seeing the 'military style' line of uniform rooms as a sign of an imperial bureaucracy intending to keep tight command over the *annona*.[51] His analysis was followed widely in the subsequent literature, but Russell Meiggs has noted that it is not compatible with what we now believe the relation between trade and government to have been. Besides, as mentioned above, the authority to erect honorary statues in the 'piazzale' was given not by the procurator of the *annona* but by the local city-council, suggesting the imperial administration did not directly control it.[52] It is conceivable, as another contributor to this debate has argued, that the imperial civil service somehow employed the commercial officials of private associations in managing Ostia and its port.[53] Though not implausible, and definitely more in line with modern thinking about Roman administration than Calza's, firm evidence for this theory is lacking.

Be that as it may, the notion of the 'piazzale' as a place that served solely the government's program of the *annona* is not consistent with the evidence. Undeniably, grain shippers had a considerable presence there, but evidence exists also for shippers transporting other cargo than grain; the 'wood shippers' ('naviculariorum lignariorum') did not even carry foodstuffs (although they may have been employed by the government to supply the imperial baths with fuel).[54] There is also the circumstance that large ports important for the *annona* are absent—possibly due to

50 *CIL* XIV 370, 374; G. Fiorelli, *N.d.sc.* (1880) 472–474; Royden (1988) 66, nr. 6; 70, nr. 17. On *fabri tignuarii*, see Meiggs (1973) 319–321.

51 Calza (1915) 191–196.

52 Meiggs (1973) 283–286.

53 Houston (1980) esp. 163–166. See also Lo Cascio (2002). Lo Cascio (103) speculates that the predominance of African *navicularii* on the 'piazzale' resulted from the effects of the Antonine Plague in Egypt, leading the imperial administration to attempt to secure a regular supply of grain from North Africa.

54 *CIL* XIV Suppl. 4549, nr. 3; Becatti (1961) 65, nr. 85, plate clxxv. Obtaining the massive amounts of fuel the imperial baths demanded was apparently becoming somewhat of a problem in the third and fourth centuries AD. Direct government intervention was needed. In 364 AD, for example, the Emperors Valens and Valentinianus informed the governor of Africa that they were continuing the long-held privileges of the African *navicularii* who brought wood to the city; *Codex Theodosianus* 13,5,10. See Meiggs (1982) 258/259. In *P.Mich.* inv. 5760a l. 22 we see a shipment of pine wood from Side to Egypt 'for our lord

loss of evidence, admittedly—as well as ports included that as far as we know were not particularly significant.[55] Besides, inscriptions attest to the existence of an Ostian *forum vinarium* (probably located a few hundred meters west of the 'piazzale') where presumably most of the wine merchants will have congregated.[56] The concept of a space devoted to one or more specific types of trade is, in other words, perfectly compatible with private business, and does certainly not in itself imply it was a government-run venue.

What purpose the stalls on the 'piazzale' served exactly is a difficult question, and a detailed answer will not be attempted here. Yet, some crucial aspects of how these rooms were used can be established based on what both the architecture and the epigraphy have to tell us. Increasing the floor space in the colonnade by closing the original entrance may or may not have been the objective of the Hadrianic rebuilding. But either way, blocking the monumental entrance clearly was not felt to be an impediment to whatever character the renewed 'piazzale' was supposed to acquire. It would therefore seem that it did not serve the purpose of a sort of market square where one would wander into more or less at random. In addition, nothing suggests that the rooms around the portico were ever used for retail. Roman shops, especially in Italy, have a characteristic architectural appearance, and are easily recognizable as such. Examples can, in fact, readily be found in Ostia itself.[57] The rooms on the 'piazzale' are different, and do not resemble that type of building at all.

To establish use and function, one can push the architectural evidence a bit further still. After the main entrance was closed off, the portico became a rather secluded place; to reach it, knowledge of even how to find and enter it was necessary. Given the nature of that structural design it seems logical that only specific groups of people went there for clearly defined reasons of business. This interpretation is strengthened by the abbreviations

the Emperor' ('τῷ κυρίῳ Καίσαρι'), although this was probably construction material. See Heilporn (2000) 558 22D.

55 Some major ports, like Hippo Regius, Rusicade, and Hadrumetum, are absent, while unimportant ones, like Hippo Diarrhytus, are represented. See Houston (1980) 165 with nt. 74.

56 On the location of the 'forum vinarium' see Coarelli (1996). See also Meiggs (1973) 275/276, 288.

57 Ostian shops, see Meiggs (1973) 272–274, with plates viii b and xv b; Packer (1967) 84–86.

in the mosaics. To the uninitiated visitor, announcements such as 'M.C.', 'S.C.F', or 'S.N.F.C.C' were not going to be terribly meaningful.[58]

The floor mosaics on the pavement in front of the rooms are in many ways our best indicator of what purpose the 'piazzale' served in its final phase. In their choice of subject matter they refer above all to seafaring and harbor activities. Nautical themes such as lighthouses, fish, leaping dolphins, Nereids, and ships with billowing sails recur over and over.[59] References to the grain trade are frequent as well; grain measures and ears of grain form another recurrent theme.[60] But there are also unmistakable allusions to trade in other goods. So, for example, a depiction of a large amphora flanked by two palm trees, of freighters loaded with amphorae, and of a man (a stevedore, undoubtedly) aboard a ship, carrying an amphora on his shoulders.[61]

The maritime themes and the references to the grain trade in the floor decoration are scarcely surprising given Ostia's position as Rome's main harbor. Harder to explain are representations of wild animals and, in the earlier phase of the pavement, depictions of what looks like hunting scenes.[62] Though a staple of Roman art in both painting and mosaics, pictures like these seem somewhat out of place in this context. Meiggs tentatively proposed they are references to the trade in African animals that supplied Rome's amphitheater with an assortment of fauna for the staging of *venationes*. Weighing against that view is that the animals depicted are mostly fairly ordinary: stags, a boar, and a bull. In the later mosaics there are also depictions of elephants though, which just might be a reference to trade in African wildlife.[63]

---

[58] *CIL* XIV Suppl. 4549, nrs. 58, 48, 38, 34; Becatti (1961) 77–85, nrs. 137, 122, 115, 112. Of course, there were also the mosaics (and presumably other forms of art) to help the illiterate or uninitiated visitor. But without preexisting knowledge of types of trade and the accompanying symbols and signs, it would still have been difficult to find any particular group of traders.

[59] Calza (1915) 187/188, nrs. 3, 9, 10, 11, 18, 19, 21, 22, 23, 26, 27, 32, 35–36, 45, 46, 47, 48, 49, 50, 51, 52, 53 (previous floor level), 54, 55.

[60] Calza (1915) 187/188, nrs. 5, 7, 10, 17, 21, 22, 33, 53, 55, 56.

[61] Calza (1915) 188, nrs. 25, 48, 52; Becatti (1961) plates clxxiii, clxxxii, clxxxi.

[62] Calza (1915) 188, nrs. 28, 52, 57; Becatti (1961) 69–84, nrs. 95, 128, 136, plates xciii, ci, lxxxi. The latter two, part of an earlier series of mosaics, may be an indication that the decorative themes changed over time, though too few of the older mosaics can be studied to be certain.

[63] Meiggs (1973) 287. In this sense also Becatti (1961) 65. Meiggs suggests the picture of an elephant in the Sabratha mosaic is a reference to trade, not in wild animals, but in ivory.

This finally brings me to the epigraphic evidence for overseas trading coalitions represented on the 'piazzale'. Twelve are identifiable, the majority from African cities, namely: Misua, Hippo Diarrhytus, Sabratha, Gummi, Carthage, Sullecthum, and Colonia Iulia Curubis.[64] One mosaic is marked 'M.C.' which is commonly understood to stand for 'Mauretania Caesariensis'. If so, that would make it the only name on the 'piazzale' not of a city but of a whole province. Though differing from the general pattern, reading 'M.C.' that way is not necessarily problematic; none of the specified African cities were located in Mauretania (they were all, in fact, concentrated in Africa Proconsularis).[65] The city of Alexandria was also represented, as were Narbo in Gaul, and two Sardinian towns: Turris and Caralis. Tarraco in Spain, as well as another African city, Musluvium, may also have been present, but the reading of those names is uncertain.[66]

Crucial attributes of the stalls on the 'piazzale' are reminiscent of the trading stations in Puteoli. Mercantile groups from cities overseas organized and presented themselves in the Ostian stations along lines of geographical provenance. That way of operating coincides with the information we have from the Tyrian *statio*. Another parallel is the size of the rooms; they are all confined spaces, clearly not intended as storerooms for large quantities of merchandise. The building the Tyrians possessed in Puteoli was most likely of a comparable scale. If my calculations are correct, it seems to have been just over twice the size of one of the roughly twenty-square-meter booths on the 'piazzale'. The Suetonius passage quoted in Chapter 2 (*Nero* 37,1) and the archaeology of the *stationes* on the Sacra Via in Rome, discussed in Chapter 4, also suggest that *stationes* were usually relatively small spaces, on the size of a single large room or perhaps two or three smaller ones.

The identification of the stalls as *stationes*, akin to the Tyrian structure in Puteoli is further confirmed by the appearance of the word *statio* in the floor decoration. However, the use of this word both on the 'piazzale' and elsewhere in Ostian inscriptions presents somewhat of a

[64] *CIL* XIV Suppl. 4549, nrs. 10, 12, 14, 17, 18, 23, 34, 48; Becatti (1961) 68–80, nrs. 92, 94, 95, 98, 99, 105, 112, 122, plates clxxviii, clxxiii, xciii, clxxxv, clxxvii, clxxix, cxc. See also Noy (2000) 162/163.

[65] For another example of a *statio* of a whole province, see *CIL* VI 250 (*stationarius* of Noricum) discussed in Chapter 4.

[66] Alexandria: *CIL* XIV Suppl. 4549 nr. 40; Becatti (1961) 78/79 nr. 116. Narbo: *CIL* XIV Suppl. 4549 nr. 32; Becatti (1961) 77 nr. 110. Turris and Caralis: *CIL* XIV Suppl. 4549 nr. 19, 21; Becatti (1961) 71–73 nr. 100, 102. Tarraco and Musluvium: *CIL* XIV Suppl. 4549 nrs. 4, 11; Becatti (1961) 67–69 nrs. 86, 93.

problem. The word occurs for certain only once in the mosaics: 'stat(io) Sabratensium'.[67] On the assumption that all rooms were *stationes*, this scarcity is a bit surprising, especially given how much of the floor survives. Other occurrences may be hiding in abbreviations; one other room is marked 'S.N.F.C.C', another 'S.C.F'. The first abbreviation is taken to mean 'S(tatio) N(egotiatorum) F(rumentariorum) C(oloniae) C(urbitanae)', which is a plausible enough reading since the mosaic also has the words 'naviculari Curbitani'. The second, however, is read as 'S(tatio) C(orporis) F(rumentariorum)' which seems too generic to be of much use as an identity marker.[68] But even if both readings are accepted, that still leaves us with only three instances. There is no noticeable difference between the sixty-one rooms on the 'piazzale', and given the many similarities in, for example, the decorative themes it seems a bit fanciful to assume different use based on the presence or absence of a single word. The conclusion should probably be that '*statio*' could designate the room of a particular group of overseas traders, but was not a strict official label for that purpose.

In line with that idea is the circumstance that the word is seen in diverse use elsewhere in the Ostian epigraphic record. The office of the Gallic and Spanish export tax administration, for instance, was called the 'statio Anto[nini] Aug. n(ostri) XXXX G[alliarum] et Hispaniar[um]'.[69] An organization to do with the production of iron, seemingly under government management,[70] had a division in Ostia, witness a lead token stamped 'stat(ionis) ferr(ariarum) for(i) Os[t(iensis)]'.[71] Supervision of the Tiber and its embankments was the responsibility of the Tiber Authority, which had an office in Ostia: 'stationi alvei Tibe[r]i[s]'.[72] It would seem that in both Ostian business and official parlance '*statio*' was employed quite loosely, and could indicate any space used by a particular group of professionals.

---

67 *CIL* XIV Suppl. 4549, nr. 14; Becatti (1961) 69/70, nr. 95.

68 *CIL* XIV Suppl. 4549, nrs. 38, 34; Becatti (1961) 77/78, nrs. 115, 112.

69 *CIL* XIV Suppl. 4708. It is unclear to which Antonine Emperor the text refers. See Meiggs (1973) 279.

70 See *CIL* XIV Suppl. 4459, set up to T. Petronius Priscus who is described as 'procuratori Aug(usti) ferrariarum et annonae Ostis'); *CIL* XIV Suppl. 4326, set up by Hilarus, 'socior(um) vect(igalis) ferr(ariarum) ser(vus)'.

71 *CIL* XIV Suppl. p. 773, note to number 4326. See Meiggs (1973) 302.

72 *CIL* XIV Suppl. 5384. Ch. Bruun ([in: Steinby IV] 1999) 345; Meiggs (1973) 303. See also *CIL* XIV 172.

Although the word *statio* is found for certain only once in the 'piazzale' mosaics, the word *navicularii* in one form or other can securely be identified no fewer than thirteen times;[73] in eight (probably nine) cases it explicitly refers to people from overseas. The word 'traders' (*negotiantes*) also appears, but only three times. Once it refers to Sardinians ('navicul et negotiantes Karalitani'). Somewhat confusingly, in the other two cases the mosaics in front of adjacent stalls contain the exact same words: 'naviculari et negotiantes de suo'.[74] Obviously, this was too general a phrase to indicate any particular group (not to mention that there were two rooms with an identical sign), so we must almost certainly imagine some other form of decoration specifying what type of shipowner and merchant was represented there. Previously, I mentioned the marble pediment with the words 'naviculari Africani'. Although that sign itself is hardly specific, it is a reminder that we must be alert to the likelihood of one-time identifiers other than the mosaics—paintings, sculpture—that have now completely vanished.

The Role and Importance of Coalition-Membership

From the Puteolan inscription discussed at length in the previous chapter we can deduce that Tyrian shipowners and merchants (*nauklêroi* and *emporoi*) paid fees to their *statio* in Rome. Although the station-operators in Puteoli complained that they were not the ones collecting the fees, the same Tyrian shipowners and merchants who traded with Rome presumably also made use of the Puteolan branch. In Ostia, commercial networks seem to have been organized in an analogous fashion: itinerant members enjoyed the services of associated local institutions in a foreign city. The people who visited the 'piazzale' seem, by and large, not to have been settlers living permanently in Ostia. Of course, some of them, especially the *negotiantes*, may on occasion have stayed in the city for some weeks or months, or perhaps even longer. But the prevalence of the word *navicularii* in combination with the names of foreign cities indicates that by occupation they were principally traveling folk: shipmasters, captains,

---

[73] *CIL* XIV Suppl. 4549, nrs. 3, 4, 10, 11, 12, 15, 16, 17, 18, 19, 21, 23, 34; Becatti (1961) 65–78, nrs. 85, 86, 92, 93, 94, 96, 97, 98, 99, 100, 102, 105, 112.

[74] *CIL* XIV Suppl. 4549, nrs. 21, 15, 16.

itinerant traders and the like.[75] The decorative scheme of the mosaics (ships, lighthouses) agrees with that idea.

Whatever use these people made of the rooms at their disposal in Ostia, their shared communal spaces demonstrate that they organized themselves somehow and that they coordinated their business with the city. Just as in Puteoli, the pivotal element around which trading coalitions revolved was clearly geographical origin; origin functioned as the distinguishing marker for identity on a communal level.[76] Itinerant traders and shipowners who shuttled back and forth between their home communities and Ostia will, to a degree, have been aware of how they were regarded in the place they regularly sailed to. But their primary focus will have been on their standing within the origin-based network they formed a part of. This network consisted of, first, the principals in their home community, second, the colony of overseas settlers serving as their intermediaries, and, finally, their colleague-traders and captains. To stay in a network, members will have had to comply with its internal social mores. In this, I propose, the networks must have functioned not unlike the coalition of the Maghribi traders. Unfortunately, we do not posses any source material on their behavior. But the dearth of written data need not deter us. I took some time discussing the architecture and archaeology of the 'piazzale' because I think we can build a case based on the material evidence.

The Ostian 'piazzale' may have been unique, but what it represents is not. People from distant communities organized themselves there along lines of geographical provenance, just as they did in Puteoli. The stalls on the 'piazzale' provided traders from overseas with a designated spot where they would be able to identify themselves and confirm their group-allegiance. The mere fact that there was such a building is an indicator of how deeply embedded and institutionalized this origin-based mechanism was. From the building's existence it is obvious that it was not a short-term temporary arrangement. On the contrary, it evidently constituted an ongoing organizational framework of trade, in force from generation to generation.[77]

---

[75] For the meaning of the word *navicularius* as 'captain' or 'skipper', see e.g. Cicero *Ad Fam.* 16,9,4; *CIL* III 14165, nr. 8. See also Cicero II *Verres*. 2,137; 5,153; Tacitus *Ann.* 12,55.

[76] On group identity based on geographical origin of immigrant groups in Rome, see Noy (2000) 157–160; Ricci (2005) 51/52.

[77] For a theory of cooperation in ongoing organizations (old members leaving, new members being admitted), see Cremer (1986).

Though it is theoretically possible that shippers and merchants from overseas managed to operate in Ostia outside of the organizations created by people from their hometowns, it seems hard to imagine. As I tried to show in the previous chapter, in pre-industrial long-distance trade, inspiring trust in business partners was hard enough. So why would anyone have confidence in an isolated individual who, for whatever reason, was excluded from the recognized social and professional structure formed by the people from his native community? A foreign trader involved in *cabotage* of the kind described by Horden and Purcell could, of course, sell goods and receive payment without the support of an Ostian network.[78] But if he attempted to do business with delayed payment or delivery, could he still ignore the trading coalition from his native city (or do business if none existed)?

It seems equally hard to imagine how a shipowner or trader who did form part of a network but who had fallen out of favor because he was considered non-compliant or untrustworthy would have been tolerated for long in the Ostian business community. Information about individual conduct will have circulated freely between members of the trading networks. On the 'piazzale' people operated in close proximity to one another, and the intimate nature of the space suggests a high level of connectivity and information-sharing, both within groups and between groups—an aspect rightly emphasized by Kessler and Temin.[79] It would seem that no one with a damaged reputation would have been able to function adequately or perhaps at all in such an environment.

Information-sharing within the larger network will also have occurred. No evidence for this type of communication can, of course, be gleaned from the mosaics, but the letters quoted in the Tyrian inscription leave no doubt that the station-operators in Puteoli corresponded with their mother-city. Although in that particular case the circumstances seem to have been exceptional, the way things are explained in the letters makes clear that information in one way or other was exchanged fairly regularly.[80] The station-operators took it for granted that back home, the members of their city-council were familiar with the situation of both the *statio* in Puteoli and the one in Rome, as well as with the situation of the shippers

[78] Horden and Purcell (2000) esp. 137–143.

[79] Kessler and Temin (2007) 329.

[80] On the topic of information-exchange between groups overseas and their homeland, see Noy (2000) 157–160. Noy thinks mainly of written evidence; I suspect gossip and word-of-mouth played an equally, if not a more important role.

and merchants who made use of these *stationes*. None of this should come as any great surprise. To achieve the level of organization we see reflected in the Tyrian inscription and on the 'piazzale', a good deal of communication within networks was all but obligatory. Such communication allowed for individual background checks; the effect will have been similar to the vetting practices of the Maghribis.

Traders coming to Ostia from elsewhere in the Empire would not easily have been able to join another coalition because of their identity as people from a particular place. This put the coalitions in a position of immense power over individual members. In the words of the legal scholar Daryl Levinson (taking shippers' associations as an example): '[t]he ultimate sanction available to any group with control over its membership is expulsion or ostracism. Expelling deviant members may inflict tremendous disutility on the outcast while costing the group virtually nothing. In general, the severity of the expulsion sanction will depend on the value of the collective goods provided by the group relative to the value of extra-group alternatives.'[81]

In Ostia, coalition membership was without much doubt extremely useful to shippers and traders. It seems likely that, for instance, access to funds for commercial shipping ventures was arranged partly through trading coalitions, as seems to have happened within the *collegia* on Roman Delos.[82] If so, loss of good repute would have imperilled access to an important source of funding. But more importantly, as I explained above, it seems probable that for traders sailing to Ostia, successful long-term business involving regular time-gaps between the *quid* and the *quo* was simply not feasible without the support of the established networks. The desire traders will have felt to remain members in good standing of their respective coalitions will therefore have resulted in considerable psychological pressure to behave honestly or to make amends after a misstep. Where disagreements arose, this pressure will have led to a willingness to comply with the acknowledged rules of conflict-resolution. For internal conflicts, compliance would have meant submission to whatever type of rule—whether

[81] Levinson (2003) 385. See also Posner (1996) 142/143. On the shippers' associations (operating in the U.S. cotton industry) mentioned by Levinson, see Bernstein (2001) 1737/1738.

[82] Rauh (1993) 251–287. Note, though, how the evidence from the Sulpicii archive also seems to show that in Puteoli access to funds could cross the boundaries of geographical origin: *TPSulp*.60, 61, 62; *TPSulp*.78.

codified in a charter[83] or unwritten and informal—governed the network.[84] What the rules in any particular case prescribed exactly there is no way of knowing (even with the well-documented Maghribis we have only a dim notion of what their 'merchants' law' encompassed).[85] They may have differed from group to group, or maybe even within groups, depending on occupation, specialization, or type of cargo. A misbehaving trader or captain who refused to play according to the agreed-upon rules appropriate to the situation ran the serious risk of being cut-off from his coalition, forfeiting the support it offered. If the damage was irreparable, exclusion would effectively have ended his business, at least where his sailing to Ostia was concerned. The effect will have been similar to the ostracism penalty the Maghribis employed.

Like me, Peter Bang analyzes the Ostian evidence as part of a larger theoretical model of Roman trade, and his treatment is emblematic of the similarities between our ideas, but also of the differences. Bang also identifies the problems of pre-industrial trade and frames them in a way similar to mine: traders faced difficulties acquiring information, could move merchandise only slowly and precariously, and were not assisted by the state in contract enforcement.[86] These difficulties '... generate[d] distinct patterns of behaviour and g[a]ve rise to commercial strategies designed to cope with the many uncertainties'. Bang defines the mercantile world and the 'social universe' these constraints produced as a 'bazaar', a term borrowed from Clifford Geertz. In this usage, 'bazaar' does not refer to the kind of marketplace in spices and trinkets that tourists traveling in today's Middle East encounter. Instead, it describes a market institution with ubiquitous uncertainties, irregularities, and asymmetries in which one important strategy traders adopted was to operate through networks, social ties, and informal connections.[87]

As the previous discussion will have made clear, none of this I necessarily disagree with. However, I find Bang's description of the 'social universe'

---

[83] For an example of a group with a statute for internal use, see *CIL* X 1579 (the *corpus* of worshippers of Jupiter Heliopolitanus, likely from Beirut, discussed in the previous chapter).

[84] For a modern example of this phenomenon, see the case study by Bernstein (2001). The private legal system of the cotton industry in the U.S.'s 'Old South' '... has endured since the mid-1800's, surviving widespread social change, years of extreme price volatility, and substantial changes in the background public legal regime'; Bernstein (2001) 1725.

[85] Greif (2006) 70/71.

[86] Bang (2008) Chapters 3 and 5.

[87] Bang (2008) 197–201. Quotation on page 197.

of the bazaar problematic. My critique hinges on Bang's lack of distinction between intra- and inter-community trade, a distinction I expressly consider in this book. Bang does not separate the two, and treats all professional collaborations, partnerships, and *collegia* uniformly. His discussion encompasses bakers in Ephesus and weavers in Oxyrhynchus, as well as Sabrathan traders operating in Ostia and Palmyrene traders operating on the Persian Gulf.[88] But in the Roman world, local artisans did not face the same challenges as merchants and shippers involved in long-distance inter-community trade. The professional organizations of these disparate groups addressed different problems, reflecting the different needs and concerns of their members. Clarity is of the essence here, and treating all communal commercial life under the blanket heading of 'cooperation within the bazaar' risks missing key aspects of the evidence.

This lack of clarity is visible in Bang's treatment of the Ostian 'piazzale'. He recognizes that geographical provenance was important for the groups that traded there. However, he seems to miss the wider implication that provenance was the organizational linchpin for Roman overseas trading communities in general, even though this is supported by the string of Palmyrene stations in Arabia, Egypt, and Rome he also mentions.[89] Moreover, he ignores the fact that a permanent brick-and-mortar structure like the 'piazzale' suggests something quite different from the 'poor information, fragmented organisation and low standardisation' of the bazaar, and is instead indicative of a highly institutionalized mode of commerce.[90] In short, although Bang identifies the problem correctly and formulates the answer in the correct terms, his use of the bazaar as a uniform model ultimately leaves him too little room to differentiate within the Roman mercantile world. Somewhat paradoxically, the current work can therefore be seen as both an endorsement of, and a challenge to his ideas.

---

[88] Bang (2008), mainly Chapter 5. Examples cited on pages 248, 250, 253/254. On Palmyra and Palmyrenes operating overseas, see also Chapter 4 below.

[89] Bang (2008) 253 presents Lugdunum as a counter-example, but the quality of the evidence offered does not support his conclusion that in Lugdunum there were '*collegia* admitting practitioners of a particular line of trade... whatever their geographical or ethnic background'. We do not know where the wine merchants 'Lugud(uni) kanab(is) consist(entes)' (*CIL* XIII 1954) had come from, let alone whether they were multi-ethnic. As for the *utricularii*, they were all from Gaul (See Waltzing vol. 2 [1896] 176–182). They were, incidentally, not traders like the people on the 'piazzale' but likely muleteers (Deman [2002]; Liu [2009] 136/137), which underscores my point about differentiating within Roman trade.

[90] Bang (2008) 198.

Overseas Settlers in Ostia

Given the similarities between Puteoli and Ostia with regard to history and economic position—both Roman colonies from an early age, both major Italian port cities serving Rome—it is reasonable to assume that in Ostia too the Roman legal system was the default for intra-community exchange and conflict resolution.[91] I do not consider it too far-fetched to suppose that something similar to what we saw happening in the Sulpicii archive, where *vadimonia* were made between a Tyrian and a Puteolan, and between an Alexandrian and a Puteolan, happened in Ostia too. For the level of trust that such inter-community interaction required there had to be an element of local permanence; a number of foreign settlers had to live in the city, effectively becoming part of the local community.[92]

If the stalls around the 'piazzale' were *stationes* frequented by itinerant traders, they were really only useful if they were maintained by people who had settled in Ostia; small colonies of people from the same cities and regions as the traveling merchants had to serve as links to the Ostian business community. Only through the aid of such 'colonies' could itinerant merchants and shipowners prove their identity, and only through the mediation of such 'colonies' could they hope to be trusted by members of Ostian mercantile groups.

Some of the places and regions we encountered in the mosaics are mentioned also in inscriptions found both in Ostia and in the harbor area of Portus. An important example is the grave monument of L. Caelius Aprilis Valerianus, which he created for himself and his wife, and for his freedmen and freedwomen. He is described as a curator of Carthaginian ships, and must himself have come from Carthage, registered as he was in the Carthaginian Arnensis tribe.[93] Nothing further is really known about his responsibilities, but from other inscriptions we do know there were guilds of curators of shipping in Ostia, suggesting Valerianus held something of an official commercial post.[94] The mention of the curatorship

[91] Ostia as Rome's harbor: Meiggs (1973) esp. 278–298. Ostia's population size: Meiggs (1973) 532–534; Packer (1967) 83–86. Packer concludes that Ostia's population cannot have exceeded 27,000. On Puteoli (size, importance as a harbor city), see Frederiksen (1984) 317–358. See also D'Arms (1981) 121–148. On the administration of Puteoli and Ostia, see Houston (1980).

[92] *TPSulp.*4, 13, 14.

[93] *CIL* XIV Suppl. 4626; 'curator navium Cartha[g]'. Meiggs (1973) 214, 288; Noy (2000) 115.

[94] *CIL* XIV 363, 364 (with *CIL* XIV Suppl. p. 615, note to 363), 409, 4142. Waltzing vol. 4 (1900) 14, nr. 33. According to a theory put forward by George Houston, the imperial

on Valerianus' epitaph as his defining occupational characteristic implies Carthaginians could count on the full-time support of some sort of local Ostian organization. An honorary inscription to Hadrian may reveal another glimpse of this organization, although the dedicators ('domini navium Carthaginensium ex Africa') were more likely shipowners like the *navicularii* on the 'piazzale' than people taking care of Carthaginian ships once they had docked.[95]

Another example of an African city we find both in the mosaics and elsewhere is provided by the grave stele of P. Caesellius Felix, set up in Ostia by his wife; the inscription reveals that Felix had come from Sullecthum.[96] Yet another city in Africa, Hippo Regius, was probably home to P. Aufidius Fortis; he was a member of the city-council of that town. In the middle of the second century AD he rose to prominence in Ostia becoming a *duumvir*, patron of the grain measurers and merchants, patron of the divers, and a five-time *quaestor* of the local *aerarium*.[97] Though none of the 'piazzale'-mosaics has evidence for a booth of Hippo Regius, one of the inscriptions mentioning Fortis was found on the 'piazzale', while the other was found nearby, next to the theater. Given the find-location of the inscriptions and given Hippo's importance for the grain trade it seems likely it was once represented on the 'piazzale'. Valerius Veturius too had clearly come from Africa ('civis Afer colonicus'), although his hometown is not given in his epitaph.[98] Yet another African with a somewhat idiosyncratic career—he had been a member of the praetorian guard, a *decurio*, and a *duumvir* in Aelia Uluzibbira—had come to Ostia and was involved in the wine trade there: 'corporatus in templo fori vinari inportatorum negotiantium'.[99] In general terms, the prevalence of African cities in the mosaics is mirrored in the epigraphic record. As Meiggs observed '[t]he tribe Quirina, most widely spread of the tribes in Africa, is more common in Ostia than any other non-Ostian tribe'.[100] Many Africans apparently lived and worked in the city.

---

administration made use of these curators and other commercial officials to supplement the imperial civil service; Houston (1980) 163–166.

95 *CIL* XIV 99. The inscription was found in Portus.

96 *CIL* XIV 477.

97 *CIL* XIV 303; *CIL* XIV Suppl. 4620, 4621, 4622. See Meiggs (1973) 203/277; Paschetto (1912) 334.

98 *CIL* XIV 481.

99 *Epigraph.* 1 (1939) 37–40, fig. 6. Aelia Uluzibbira, a city otherwise unknown to us, was in all likelihood founded by Hadrian as a military colony.

100 Meiggs (1973) 215. The numerical strength of African immigrants is confirmed by recent onomastic studies, see Salomies (2002) 152/153; Cébeillac-Gervasoni (1994).

Sardinians are also present in an Ostian inscription, as they are in the mosaics: in 173 AD the 'domini navium Afrarum universarum item Sardorum' set up a statue in the 'piazzale delle corporazioni' to a patron of the curators of shipping.[101] As with the Carthaginian *domini* mentioned above, they were likely all shipowners, but the dedication shows the importance for such people of connections with local Ostian curators. Likewise, Egyptians and more specifically Alexandrians are mentioned. Two men with Egyptian names were enrolled in the shipbuilders' guild,[102] and then there are T. Flavius Apollonius and Aphrodisius, son of Arpocration, both from Alexandria.[103] From the grave inscription of the latter it appears that he lived in Ostia with his *familia*: his wife set up the grave marker for herself and her husband; also mentioned are a son and daughter, and freedmen and freedwomen. The shipmasters of the Alexandrian grain fleet collectively honored Commodus, while an inscription from the Severan era was set up by C. Valerius Serenus Xiphidus, manager of the whole Alexandrian fleet ('ὁ ἐπιμελητὴς παντὸς τοῦ Ἀλεξανδρείνου στόλου'). Xiphidus, perhaps a government employee, could have been recruited locally, but he was also the custodian of the temple of Serapis at Portus ('νεωκόρος τοῦ μεγάλου Σαράπιδος'), which makes him more likely a native Egyptian who had moved to Ostia.[104]

There were people from Gaul as well living in the city. A dedication was set up in Vienna, in Narbonese Gaul, by the sons of L. Maecius Maelo to commemorate their father; Maelo, the inscription says, had died in Ostia, age fifty.[105] A fellow Narbonese who had served as *sevir Augustales* in Aquae Sextiae had become president of the Ostian builders.[106] P. Claudius Abascantus had come to Ostia as a slave of the provincial council of the Three Gauls, late in the second century AD. Once freed, he established himself permanently overseas and became a proud member of the 'Dendrophori'; from other inscriptions we know he had two sons and a grandson in Ostia.[107] In the 'Isola Sacra', the harbor cemetery of Portus, we can find the graves, both Antonine in date, of two other men from

---

[101] *CIL* XIV 4142; R. Lanciani, *N.d.sc.* (1886) 56. See Meiggs (1973) 277, 288/289; Paschetto (1912) 336.

[102] *CIL* XIV 256, nrs. 148, 185.

[103] *CIL* XIV 478, and 479.

[104] *I.Porto* nrs. 2, 3.

[105] *CIL* XII 2211.

[106] *CIL* XIV 296.

[107] *CIL* XIV 324, 325, 326, 327, 328. See the reconstructed family tree in *CIL* XIV Suppl. p. 615, note to 326. See also Meiggs (1973) 215, 362.

Gaul, the first set up by slaves to their master, the second by a wife to her husband.[108]

Sardinians, Egyptians, Gauls, and, most of all, Africans are thus also to be found elsewhere in the Ostian epigraphic record, paralleling the evidence from the 'piazzale'. However, the record also in an important way corrects the picture that emerges from the mosaics, displaying a much greater geographical range in the provenance of settlers. Whether due to chance or other reasons, no images representing cities from Asia Minor, Greece, or Syria can be seen today on the 'piazzale'. Evidence for Spanish cities, with the possible exception of Tarraco, is also lacking. However, from several inscriptions we know of a whole host of people who had come to Ostia from these regions. The trader L. Numisius Agathemerus, in Ostia serving as a *sevir Augustalis*, had come from Hither Spain ('negotiatori ex Hispania citeriore'); M. Aemilius M. f. Malacitanus' cognomen shows him to have been a native of the Baetican city of Malaca; M. Caesius Maximus was born somewhat further away, in Aeminium in Lusitania.[109] His epitaph contains a bit of Romano-Hispanic folklore in the abbreviated funereal phrase, particularly popular in Spain in the second century AD, 'H(ic) S(itus) E(st), S(it) T(ibi) T(erra) L(evis)'.

A wide array of people from the East can also be found. M'. Silius Balbinus was still fairly close to home; he had served as a *quattuorvir* in Vicetia (modern Vicenza) and was, given his name, likely a native of that town. Around the time of the Emperor Augustus he set up a grave monument in Ostia to his wife.[110] His presence in the city should probably be explained by the mercantile activity of the regions around the northern Adriatic with Ostia. From several inscriptions (some still incompletely published) we know there was a *collegium* of shippers from the Adriatic Sea active in Ostia; just like the Carthaginians, they had curators there ('curator naviclarior maris Hadriat').[111] The commercial ties between Ostia and the Adriatic are borne out by the archaeological evidence, and it seems likely that

[108] Thylander (1952) 29, nr. A13 (Pict(onis) = Poitiers); 130, nr. A170 (Samus Samifilus, a Celtic name).

[109] *CIL* XIV 397; *CIL* XIV Suppl. 4778, 4822.

[110] Inscription pieced together and discussed in Cébeillac-Gervasoni and Zevi (1976) 608–611.

[111] This was the occupation of A. Caedicius Successus, also *sevir Augustalis* and *quinquennalis*. For the complete inscription (elsewhere incompletely published), see Cébeillac-Gervasoni and Zevi (1976) 611 nt. 2. See also D'Arms (1981) 176, nr. 19.

Balbinus was somehow involved in this trade.[112] Other men from the area may have included Q. Aeronius Antiochus a *quinquennalis* of the 'guild of helpers of the Ostian grain measurers', already mentioned above, for whom a statue was erected in the 'piazzale delle corporazioni'; his *nomen* (not otherwise attested in Ostia) indicates a Dalmatian origin. Another example is provided by Ti. Claudius Germuilia(nus?) whose *cognomen* seems derived from Germullius, a Dalmatian name attested in the town of Rider.[113]

Also from the East but from much further away were: Asclepiades, son of Simon, from Cnidus; Socrates, son of Astomachus, from Tralles, and Phileros from Miletus.[114] Aristida from Rhodes erected a grave monument in Ostia to his wife of almost forty years, to his son, and to his freedmen and freedwomen.[115] We know of a Phrygian buried in Ostia; a group of people from Gaza set up an inscription in nearby Portus to honor the Emperor Gordian.[116] A Syrian, Maros, had moved to Ostia from Seleucia; Gaionas, a fellow Syrian, erected a granite column in Portus, dedicated to Jupiter Heliopolitanus for the safety of the Emperors Marcus Aurelius and Commodus.[117]

That last inscription brings me to the topic of foreign religions in Ostia. In the evidence from Puteoli we saw people from overseas bringing their ancestral religious practices with them, and in Ostia something similar seems to have occurred. Egyptian deities were especially well-established; Isis and Serapis both had their own temple, and numerous terracotta statuettes and dedicatory inscriptions bear out the pervasiveness of their worship.[118] The connection between Ostia and the Alexandrian grain fleet naturally suggests itself to explain this phenomenon. However, given the general popularity of Egyptian cults in the Roman Empire, it is hard to say whether in Ostia they catered mostly to the spiritual needs of locals or of

---

[112] D'Arms (1981) 130/131; Cébeillac-Gervasoni and Zevi (1976) 610/611; see esp. 611 nt. 1 for the epigraphic evidence for the Ostian *collegium* of Adriatic shippers.

[113] Q. Aeronius Antiochus: *CIL* XIV 4140. Germuilianus/Germullius: *CIL* XIV 323 and *CIL* III 6411. See Salomies (2002) 153.

[114] *CIL* XIV 475, 480 (inscription in elegiac distichs); *IG* XIV 938.

[115] Thylander (1952) 39/40 nr. A27. Trajanic/Hadrianic in date.

[116] *IG* XIV 933; *IG* XIV 926. Steuernagel (2004) 248.

[117] Maros: *IG* XIV 934; Gaionas: *CIL* XIV 24 (= Thylander [1952] 370/371, nr. B297). Gaionas is better known from Roman inscriptions, and likely lived in Rome rather than in Ostia (see Chapter 4). Steuernagel (2004) 244/245; Meiggs (1973) 216, 388; Squarciapino (1962) 62/63; Taylor (1912) 77/78.

[118] Steuernagel (2004) 92–94; Meiggs (1973) 367–370; Squarciapino (1962) 19–36; Taylor (1912) 66–75.

Egyptian settlers. The fact that the dedicatory inscriptions in the Ostian Serapeum are mostly in Latin may be a sign that there it was primarily locals who practiced these rites. At the same time, inscriptions connected to the Serapeum in the harbor area of Portus are typically in Greek which, following the same logic, would indicate that here it was more likely Egyptians who worshipped their native gods.[119] A curious object may be relevant in this context. It is a large terracotta hanging lamp molded in the shape of a slender ship; on each side, five burners stick out as if they were oars. On the deck surface, three figures are shown, each framed by a columned sanctuary. They represent three deities: above ('aft') Harpocrates, Isis (much larger and in the prominent central position), and Serapis below ('fore'). The lamp may have been a votive offering reflecting the role of Egyptian gods—and of Isis in particular—as protectors of ships and sailors.[120] If this is not proof that Egyptian cults were practiced by Egyptians, it at least suggests that they were practiced by people involved in seaborne activities with Egypt.

Worship of Jupiter Dolichenus, a deity originating from Doliche in the Roman province of Syria, usually associated with the military, was apparently also perfectly respectable for civilians. A dedication was found, set up by a local bigwig, L. Plinius Nigrinus, a *quinquennalis* and probably the same man who was *duumvir* in the year 147 AD. An inscription containing a magical alphabet also belongs to this cult, which renders it almost certain that Dolichenus had a shrine or sanctuary somewhere in Ostia.[121] Evidence for a famous cult from Asia Minor is provided by a cylindrical marble fragment with a carved relief showing sphinxes, a dog, griffins, and what could be a temple; it is thought to be the *polos* crown of a statue of Ephesian Artemis.[122] Other examples of foreign gods include Jupiter Sabazius and a Rider God, both native to Thrace.[123] Yet another dedication was set up by P. Clodius Flavius, a *sevir Augustalis*, to a Sky God ('numen caeleste') perhaps to be identified with the Carthaginian

119 Steuernagel (2004) 212; Meiggs (1973) 368, 387; Squarciapino (1962) 24/25.

120 D. Vaglieri, *N.d.sc.* (1909) 118/119 n. 7 with fig. 2. Meiggs (1973) 370; Squarciapino (1962) 32; Taylor (1912) 71. In addition, Steuernagel (2004) 216–218 tentatively interprets an Ostian statue as representing 'Isis Pharia'.

121 Meiggs (1973) 375/376, 512; Bloch (1953) 242, nrs. 4 and 5. See also Steuernagel (2004) 244.

122 D. Vaglieri, *N.d.sc.* (1909) 234 n. 10 with fig. 2; Steuernagel (2004) 242.

123 *CIL* XIV Suppl. 4296; D. Vaglieri *N.d.sc.* (1912) 439/440 with fig. 3. Meiggs mentions a second, unpublished sculptural relief; Meiggs (1973) 376 with nt. 10. See also Squarciapino (1962) 67/68.

Caelestis.[124] Apparently, it had taken a bit of divine talking-to in a dream to persuade Flavius to honor this deity: 'somno monitus fecit'.

To return to the 'piazzale delle corporazioni' one final time, some evidence for the practice of foreign cults was found there as well, although it is hardly clear-cut. A small altar shows a seated female figure flanked by two griffins and with Mercury, easily recognizable with his characteristic hat and staff, standing beside her.[125] We no longer know to what cult this altar belonged, though it seems clear it was a religion from the eastern part of the Empire. If it was excavated in, or in close vicinity to, its original location it may have been used by a group of foreign shippers in the performance of their religious rites. If this was the case we have to assume shippers from the East frequented the 'piazzale' as well, although now the remaining floor mosaics contain no evidence for such people. More straightforward evidence, at least on the face of it, is provided by a statue found near the temple in the garden area that shows Serapis within a small shrine, seated on a throne.[126] With Alexandrians present in the 'piazzale', it is tempting to assume a connection.

Conclusion

Reputation within the Ostian community did not have the same behavior-controlling force for itinerant foreign merchants and shippers as for their compatriots who had settled in the city, and their behavior had to be regulated through different means. In this chapter, I argued that concerns for continued group membership in effect constituted those means.

The Ostian 'piazzale delle corporazioni', containing a large number of rooms used by coalitions of merchants and shipmasters from overseas, betrays a well-organized mechanism of inter-community trade. From the 'piazzale' evidence, it is clear that foreign trading coalitions formed a deeply embedded element of the commercial life of Ostia. These coalitions were so interwoven with the Ostian mercantile fabric that traders coming to the city were obligated to use them. No native trading partner

[124] *CIL* XIV Suppl. 4318. See Meiggs (1973) 376; Taylor (1912) 93. Meiggs, however, suggests both Sabazius and the Sky God were associated with the cult of Mithras; so also Squarciapino (1962) 65–67. For Venus Caelestis (for certain a Phoenician/Carthaginian goddess), see Chapter 2.

[125] G. Calza, *N.d.sc.* (1914) 289/290, with fig. 6, there interpreted as Cybele, wrongly according to Meiggs (1973) 377 with nt. 1.

[126] Steuernagel (2004) 227; Meiggs (1973) 368; Squarciapino (1962) 25.

would have trusted them if they stayed outside of the established foreign groups and if their business conduct was therefore not controlled by group-membership. Since geographical origin defined membership, networks had the definitive power to include and exclude. A shipper from city X would, given his origin, not easily have been able to join the network of city Y. If he wanted to stay in business in Ostia, he would therefore be forced to adhere to whatever internal rules governed city X's network. Since we lack written source material to study how Ostian networks functioned and how people behaved within them, I drew a comparison with a well-documented medieval example where the binding element of the trading coalition was also a sense of shared origin. The example of the Maghribis shows how such a coalition might deal with enforcement constraints; the solution was to rely on the threat of ostracism from the group.

As a qualifying remark to this conclusion, a one-on-one comparison between the Maghribis and the Roman coalitions should not be made. The Maghribi network consisted of traders scattered all over the Mediterranean and the Levant without a single geographical 'center of gravity', whereas the networks of merchants and shipmasters under the Roman Empire all looked to a native region or hometown. This meant that the nature of the networks differed, and that the way information circulated within them also diverged (if anything, the focus on a single native city in the Roman coalitions will have made information-sharing easier than in the medieval example). But despite this difference, the Maghribis' coalition is a useful comparison when studying Roman overseas trade. It shows how closed networks based on origin can overcome the problems of enforcement and information constraints in long-distance trade.

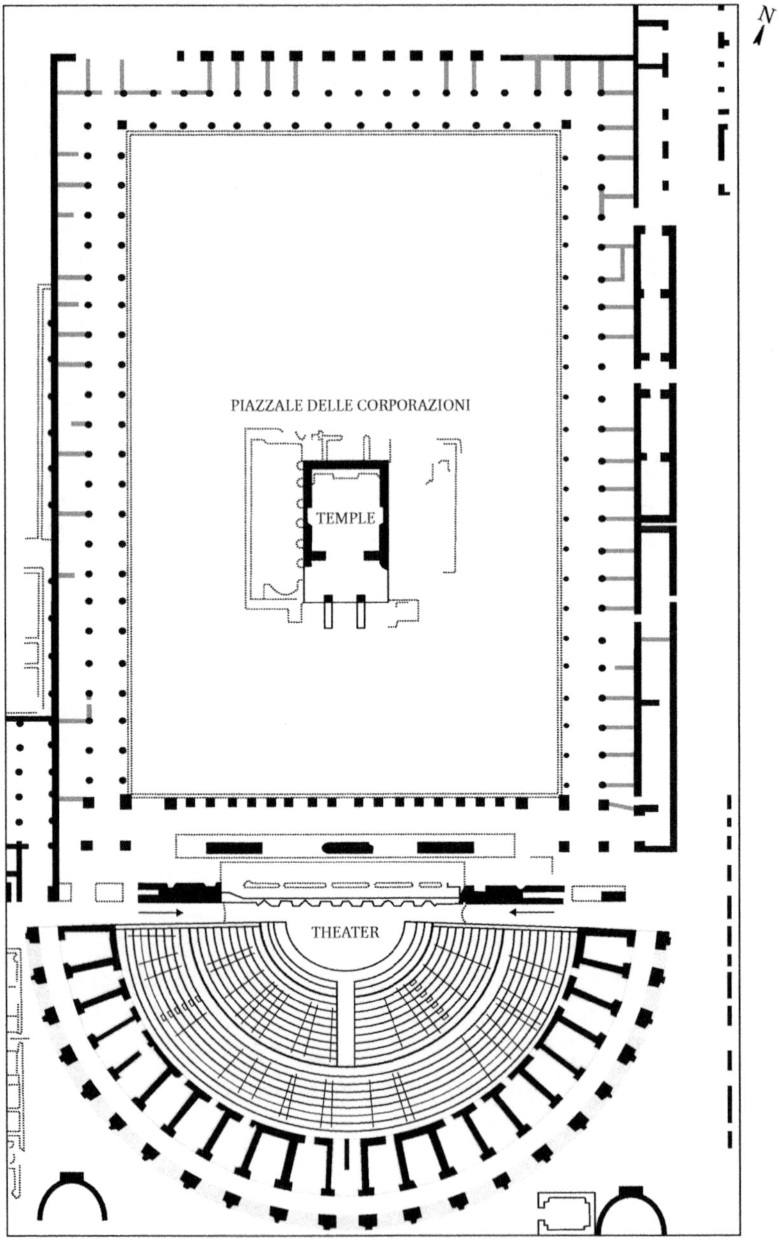

Figure 1. 'Piazzale delle corporazioni'.
Reproduced by permission from DER NEUE PAULY. Band 9. Or-Poi. Hubert Cancik and Helmuth Schneider. S. 99–100.

CHAPTER FOUR

INTER-COMMUNITY TRADE AND THE CITY OF ROME

Orbis in Urbe

Aelius Aristides' flowery style and fulsome praise make his speech 'To Rome' a problematic source, to say the least. Seen by generations of scholars as an eloquent celebration of the 'golden age' that was the second-century Empire, for modern Roman economic historians it now seems almost obligatory to accompany a quotation with eye-rolling and sighs about 'blatant flattery and undisguised hyperbole'.[1] Aristides is not to be taken at face-value, although I doubt anyone ever did, including his well-heeled audience. But no one would deny that Rome attracted massive amounts of goods from all over her Empire. Reflections on Aristides' rhetorical tricks aside, there must thus be at least a kernel of truth in his claims that:

> Here is brought from every land and sea all the crops of the seasons and the produce of each land, river, lake, as well as of the arts of the Greeks and barbarians, so that if someone should wish to view all these things, he must either see them by traveling over the whole world or be in this city.[2]

What interests me here are not macro-economic considerations on a 'tributary Empire' or on supposed flows of taxes and trade from periphery to center and back again. What interests me is the micro-economic mechanism that brought goods to Rome. The previous chapters contained discussions on the two towns that served as ports to the capital. Now it is time to look at the imperial city itself.

Based on the model I presented, the obvious step is to investigate evidence for provincial settlers in Rome. However, people flocked to the city for a wide variety of reasons, and the problem is to find the right evidence in the large data set. Rome counted many outsiders, as individuals and as groups, among its denizens; they were apparently so conspicuous that in

---

[1] Bang (2008) 290, with references to literature on Aristides.
[2] Aelius Aristides *Or.* 26,11. Tr.: Behr (1981) 75.

Athenaeus' 'The learned banqueters', a work of the late second century AD, we find this passage:

> [Athenaeus] refers to Rome as an international community. He also says that you would not be far from the mark if you call the city of Rome an epitome of the inhabited world, since you can see every single city settled in it, many of them in individual neighborhoods, for example golden Alexandria, lovely Antioch, gorgeous Nicomedia, and in addition the most radiant of all the cities ... Athens. One day would not be enough, if I tried to offer a complete list of the cities included in the count of the Romans' heavenly city; indeed, there are so many that all the days in a year would be required. The fact is that whole populations have settled there *en masse*, such as the Cappadocians, Scythians, Pontians, and many others.[3]

Even allowing for a good dose of exaggeration, provincials residing in Rome obviously comprised a large and miscellaneous group.[4] Discussing all the evidence would go far beyond the scope of this chapter. Besides, two works have appeared recently that deal specifically with that topic. They do an admirable job of highlighting all the aspects of immigrant life in Rome: peoples' reasons to move there, their first impressions of the city, their social position, religious practices, and problems in encountering xenophobia.[5] It is not my aim to cover all of these various aspects, nor will I incorporate every immigrant group ever identified into my discussion. Instead, I will test my model by looking for data on communities that fit the picture that emerged previously. The most important characteristics, as seen in the Puteolan and Ostian data, are outsiders involved in trade, settling locally, often maintaining a building, and often having local patrons and curators.

Another common characteristic is that settlers from overseas frequently worshipped their ancestral gods in local temples and shrines; in the previous chapters I have therefore incorporated the evidence on foreign cults. For Rome this is a potentially promising avenue of research; it was a city of great religious diversity, and although it must have been somewhat of a melting-pot, in religious matters little melting took place if Dionysius of Halicarnassus is to be believed:

---

[3] Athenaeus *Deipnosophistae* 1,20. Tr.: S.D. Olson, Loeb (2006). See Noy (2000) 31; La Piana (1927) 206.

[4] On the problems of demography and quantification, see Ricci (2005) 11–14; Noy (2000) 15–19.

[5] Ricci (2005) and Noy (2000).

> The most striking thing of all, in my view, is this: despite the influx into Rome of countless foreigners, who are under a firm obligation to worship their ancestral gods according to the customs of their homeland, the city has never officially emulated any of these foreign practices—as has been the case with many cities in the past;[6]

Although establishing a connection between the arrival of immigrants and the worship of foreign gods in Rome can be problematic—many native Roman inhabitants found new cults alluring, especially mystery cults such as Mithraism—it cannot be doubted that some groups from overseas brought their religious practices with them.[7] The remark by Dionysius would lead us to believe that, by and large, those religious communities remained separate and distinctive, both from one another and from their Roman environment.

All the different elements just mentioned—trade, communal buildings, ancestral religious rites—will form part of this chapter. In the process of discussing Roman *stationes*, I will also engage with the literature on the subject, which is wide-ranging but also often in disagreement. The older literature took all the evidence for *statio*-type institutions together, focusing on similarities rather than differences, an approach to which I am fundamentally sympathetic. More modern literature on the other hand tends to confine *stationes* to just two locations, often surmising a difference in two categories based on the difference in location.[8] On the whole, there seems to be no consensus on basic questions such as where in the city to locate them, how to define them, or how to interpret them. The suggestions put forward about what they were exactly are usually remarkably vague. Perhaps this is not surprising; the sources leave a lot to be desired. From the Puteolan inscription considered in detail in the second chapter, for example, we know for certain there was a Tyrian *statio* in Rome. From the information given we can, furthermore, deduce it must have been in operation for an extended period of time. Yet, from Rome itself not a shred of evidence remains whether it be literary, epigraphic,

---

[6] Dionysius of Halicarnassus, *Roman Antiquities* 2,19,3. Tr.: Beard, North and Price (1998) vol. 2 nr. 8.7a. The context is the introduction into Rome of the cult of Magna Mater.

[7] On membership of foreign cults in Rome, see Beard, North and Price (1998) vol. 1, 291–301; Noy (2000) 183–187; La Piana (1927) 282–320.

[8] Cantarelli (1900) and La Piana (1927) took all the evidence together. Moretti (1958) proposed a distinction in two locations, and in two types of *statio*. His ideas were followed by Richardson (1992), Ricci (2005) 57–60, and E. Papi and C. Lega ([in: Steinby IV] 1999) 349–352. Noy (2000) 160–164, however, seems hesitantly to have reverted to the earlier approach.

archaeological, or visual; a reminder of how limited and fragmentary our knowledge is.[9]

It therefore seems necessary to approach this problem with a general theory. I propose to see Roman *stationes* in the light of the sources, presented in Chapters 2 and 3. If my theory about long-distance trade networks is correct, we should expect to see this phenomenon in Rome too. Of course, there are some obvious methodological problems with transferring my hypothesis to Rome. Does it hold water also for the imperial capital, the heart of political and military power, a metropolis that positively dwarfed both Puteoli and Ostia in size? Not to make light of these caveats, my answer would ultimately be yes. Though Rome was exceptional in many ways, the constraints on business there were ultimately the same as in Puteoli and Ostia. Merchants involved in inter-community exchange had to find a way to deal with those constraints, just like their counterparts in the much smaller harbor cities. It therefore makes sense to look for the same dynamic in Rome that also operated in the two towns closely associated with the city.

Writing back in 1929, Samuel Platner and Thomas Ashby proposed Roman *stationes* had a commercial component, describing them as 'probably the headquarters of organised corporations of the inhabitants of foreign towns who were residing or doing business in Rome'.[10] In the following, I will try to argue that this viewpoint was essentially correct.

Stationes on the Forum Iulium

In a study of Roman *stationes*, the first problem that presents itself is where in the city to look for them. Most of the modern literature discusses only two locations: the row of vaulted spaces comprising the western side of the Forum of Caesar, and a collection of buildings along the Sacra Via. Briefly put, the Forum of Caesar is believed to have housed *stationes* because of a reference in Pliny the elder, while the Sacra Via is included because of a number of inscriptions discovered there. Although I am convinced that foreign *stationes* were not limited to these locations

[9] One inscription, once believed to refer to the Tyrian *statio*, almost certainly refers to the *statio* of Tiberias instead. See *IGUR* I 82; La Piana (1927) 260, nt 25; Pârvan (1909) 116; Cantarelli (1900) 126/127 nr. 10.

[10] Platner and Ashby (1929) 497.

and could be found elsewhere in the city, I will begin by discussing these two spots, which are included in all scholarly discussions on the subject.

To take the Pliny passage as a starting point, it reads: 'But there is another lotus tree in the precincts of Vulcan founded by Romulus from the tithe of his spoils of victory, which on the authority of Masurius is understood to be of the same age as the city. Its roots spread right across the Municipal Offices as far as the Forum of Caesar'.[11] Pliny, whose real interest in this exposition is trees, and not anything man-made, regrettably does not bother to describe or elaborate on the buildings he alludes to. He does not give details about location nor, for that matter, does he care to explain what the 'Municipal Offices' ('stationes municipiorum') were used for.

What site can Pliny have had in mind? The general area around the arch of Septimius Severus was once believed to have been the right location, but today the structures forming the western side of Caesar's Forum are seen as a more likely candidate. That can mean either the vaulted chambers opening up on the forum square or, connected to those at the back, the ones opening up at a higher level on the opposite side on the Clivus Argentarius (or possibly both) (see fig. 2).[12] Pliny's account does not give us much to go on, but one element in his narrative is helpful in this respect. He states that the roots of the tree ran *through* the *stationes to* the Forum, seemingly making a distinction between the two ('in forum usque Caesaris per stationes'). That description seems to fit better with the rooms giving access to the Clivus. Though structurally integrated into the forum-building, these higher-level rooms face outward instead of inward and as such are spatially detached from the inner square, communicating with a different part of the city in both orientation and elevation.[13]

Pliny is the sole author who employs the term 'stationes municipiorum', a term that is really not of much help in determining the purpose of these structures. Appian on the other hand, though silent on *stationes*, gives us an interesting bit of information on Caesar's Forum in general. He tells us that it was not planned for commercial activities: '[Caesar] laid out ground around the temple [i.e. of Venus Genetrix] which he

[11] Pliny *NH* 16,236. Tr.: H. Rackham, Loeb (1945).

[12] C. Lega ([in: Steinby IV] 1999) 350; Richardson (1992) 368; Moretti (1958) 114.

[13] The two sides, though oriented differently, are directly connected; two flights of stairs, one Augustan, the other Trajanic in date, run straight from the Forum up to the Clivus Argentarius. *Tabernae* and Trajanic rebuilding, C. Morselli ([in: Steiby II] 1995) 303–305; Ulrich (1993) 50, 70, 77–79; Lancaster (2000) 779–784.

intended to be a forum for the Roman people, not for buying and selling, but [as] a meeting-place for the transaction of public business, like the public squares of the Persians, where the people assemble to seek justice or to learn the laws'.[14] Because Appian emphasizes the non-commercial character of the forum and because the Curia Iulia is contiguous with the structure on its southeastern corner, it has been argued that it was built to accommodate senatorial business.[15] In line with this thinking, Pliny's 'stationes municipiorum' are often interpreted as political institutions, essentially a sort of 'embassies' to the Senate.[16]

A first objection to this view would be that not all spaces around or near the forum can logically be seen as connected to affairs of state. As I explained above, it may have been that the line of rooms opening up on the forum proper served 'public business', however defined, but it is to spaces separate from the central square that Pliny seems to allude. For the row of *tabernae* along the opposite side that do not interact directly with the forum, things are different. The name of the street to which they connect—'Clivus Argentarius'—is suggestive of mercantile activities in this area. The earliest known mention of this street only appears in medieval manuscripts.[17] However, if the double-aisled building prolonging the forum colonnade towards the northwest is indeed the 'Basilica Argentaria', as is commonly believed, it is likely that the name dates back to at least the early second century AD. The *argentarii* who worked in the 'Basilica', incidentally, were probably manufacturers of, or traders in, bronze and silver vessels, not people offering financial services.[18]

But much more important than the objection about the spatial relationship of *stationes* to the forum, about which we will never have any certainty, there are more fundamental problems with the theory of cities'

[14] Appian *BCiv.* 2,102. Tr.: H. White, Loeb (1913). First-century AD literary sources seem indeed to suggest that the Forum was used for lawsuits; Maiuro (2010) 193.

[15] See Ulrich (1993) for an interesting discussion on how the intended purpose my have changed over time. See also Maiuro (2010) who argues that the Forum Iulium from Augustus to Trajan was used for administrative, economic, and judicial activities associated with the imperial treasury.

[16] C. Lega ([in: Steinby IV] 1999) 351; Richardson (1992) 368. See also Moretti (1958) 115/116. The *stationes* of the *arcarii* attached to Trajan's Forum for certain served public affairs; Plutarch, *Fr.Vat.* 134. See Maiuro (2010) 194.

[17] C. Buzzetti and G. Pisani Sartorio ([in: Steinby I] 1993) 280; Platner and Ashby (1929) 121/122.

[18] C. Morselli ([in: Steinby I] 1993) 169/170; C. Morselli ([in: Steinby II] 1995) 304/305; Platner and Ashby (1929) 76. See also E. Papi ([in: Steinby V] 1999) 10–12; Ulrich (1993) 78. The colonnade was constructed sometime in the second century AD after the hillside into which Caesar's Forum was built was cleared away.

delegations permanently seated on the forum and transacting with the Senate. Note that, if Appian is a reliable guide to Caesar's designs, providing Rome with space for diplomatic or political business was not what the dictator envisioned while planning his forum; if anything, it was a place for law courts and legal education he had in mind. But even if the forum is seen as a space used, from its very conception or subsequently, to facilitate senatorial transactions, no one has ever been able to explain satisfactorily what the Senate's business with permanent provincial delegations was supposed to involve. Diplomatic missions from cities or provincial *concilia* sent over to Rome for specific appeals or petitions are, of course, a well-documented phenomenon, but these never acquired the character of permanent posts.[19] But even if this were the case, it opens up the question which cities would have been represented on the forum and on whose initiative they would have maintained diplomatic seats there. Did the municipalities themselves decide on this? Was it on request, or perhaps even on demand of the Senate? Did virtually every self-respecting city in the Empire maintain, or aspire to maintain such a delegation? If the answer is yes then the logistical problems of accommodating them all around the forum square must have been formidable. Interpreting the Roman *stationes* as political institutions raises more questions than it answers.

The information we have for activities of provincials in this quarter of Rome does little to support the interpretation of ambassadorial seats. A statue honoring Tiberius showing the Emperor seated and dressed in toga is known to have been erected in the forum by fourteen cities in Asia Minor, recipients of imperial largesse after the earthquakes of 17 and 23 AD.[20] A probable copy of the base that supported the statue, still extant, displaying the stricken cities personified and carved in relief was set up in Puteoli. The Puteolan monument, I argued in Chapter 2, can best be seen as an attempt to highlight or strengthen the good relations that settlers from the area were enjoying with their host city. The original in the heart of Rome, however, was presented by the Asian cities themselves out of gratitude for the financial help they received after the natural

[19] Deininger (1965) 161–169; Noy (2000) 100–106; Ricci (2005) 36–38. Some of the earliest acts taking place in the Forum Iulium were, in fact, related to provincials coming over for political business, see the inscription dating to 45 BC recording that the Cnidians took an oath there, *I.knidos* 33 A, line 2. See Maiuro (2010) 190.

[20] C. Morselli ([in: Steinby II] 1995) 300; Platner and Ashby (1929) 226/227. See also C. Lega ([in: Steinby IV] 1999) 351; Jahn (1851) 122–126 with plate II B (coin type showing the statue).

catastrophes.[21] It does not provide evidence for settlers from Asia, whether traders or ambassadors.

But things look different with the sizable statue-base set up by people from Sabratha ('Sabrathe[nses] ex Afr[ica]'), found on the Forum Iulium. It bears an inscription telling us that it was dedicated to the deified Sabina on December 13th, 138 AD.[22] An inscription on the left-hand side of the base gives the reason it was placed here; apparently this had happened on the order of the Emperor Hadrian, the specific location having been assigned by two men with the title of *curatores operum locorum publicorum*.[23] It has been hypothesized that the donation of the base (and the statue it no doubt supported) was a gesture of appreciation from Sabratha for certain privileges it had received during the reign of Hadrian, but if this was the case it is strange the inscription makes no mention of any of these benefits.[24] It seems equally strange that the city of Sabratha, expressing gratitude in an official context, would corporately identify itself as 'the Sabrathans from Africa'; the absence of any mention of the city as such or of any of its political institutions rather suggests it was a group of individuals who set up the base on their private initiative.[25]

Sabratha, it will be remembered, occupied a room on the 'piazzale delle corporazioni', not far away in Ostia. The room's floor mosaic echoes the use of the ethnic identifier 'Sabrathenses' on the Forum Iulium: 'stat(io) Sabratensium', here clearly meaning a group of people from the city, not the city itself. If indeed the base on the forum was a gift from the city's *statio*, either in Ostia or in Rome, the explanation may be a show of adher-

---

[21] Phlegon *Mirabilia* 13: ''Ἀπολλώνιος δὲ ὁ γραμματικὸς ἱστορεῖ ἐπὶ Τιβερίου Νέρωνος σεισμὸν γεγενῆσθαι καὶ πολλὰς καὶ ὀνομαστὰς πόλεις τῆς Ἀσίας ἄρδην ἀφανισθῆναι, ἃς ὕστερον ὁ Τιβέριος οἰκείᾳ δαπάνῃ πάλιν ἀνώρθωσεν. ἀνθ' ὧν κολοσσόν τε αὐτῷ κατασκευάσαντες ἀνέθεσαν παρὰ τῷ τῆς Ἀφροδίτης ἱερῷ, ὅ[ς] ἐστιν ἐν τῇ Ῥωμαίων ἀγορᾷ, καὶ τῶν πόλεων ἑκάστης ἐφεξῆς ἀνδριάντας παρέστησαν.' Maiuro (2010) 205/206 argues that the location was fitting because the office of the imperial treasury was nearby.

[22] *CIL* VI 40528 (= R. Cagnat and A. Merlin, *AE* [1934] 39/40, nr. 146).

[23] 'Iussu Imp(eratoris) Caesaris Traiani Hadriani Aug(usti), p(atris) p(atriae), locus adsignat(us) a Valerio Urbico et Aemilio Papo cur(atoribus) operum locor(um) public(orum)'. Offices probably created by Agustus, see Suetonius *Aug.* 37.

[24] See Alföldy's commentary to *CIL* VI 40528; C. Lega ([in: Steinby IV] 1999) 351.

[25] Honorary dedications (many to members of the imperial family) in Sabratha itself often use the term *Sabrathenes*, but with the word *publice* added: *IRT* 37, 44, 48, 50, 112, 113, 147, 148, 149. Other indications of Sabratha as a city include 'civitas Sabrathensis', 'splendidae col(oniae) Sabrat(hensis); in others, the *ordo*, sometimes in combination with the *populus* or *plebs*, is mentioned: *IRT* 101, 102, 103, 104, 111, 117, 126. See also *IRT* page 20/21. See further the dedication to Hadrian and Sabina by (probably) the 'colonia Iulia Augusta Pietas Catana' set up in Rome. Alföldy (1992) 147–154.

ence to imperial power (to the new ruler Antoninus Pius as it turned out; Hadrian had died five months prior to the dedication).

An inscription discovered in the Basilica Aemilia, so roughly midway between the Sacra Via and the Forum Iulium (fig. 2), also contains a dedication, this time to the patron-goddess of the city of Vienna in Gaul ('Numini deae Viennae'). So far, this is the only attestation of this deity, and nothing further is known about her. Local divinities carrying the name of the area or city under their tutelage are a fairly common phenomenon in the epigraphic record from Gaul though.[26] The inscription was set up by decree of the local councilors ('ex d(ecurionum) d(ecreto)') by M. Nigidius Paternus, a onetime *duumvir* ('II vira(lis)'). Paternus, though no longer in office as a magistrate, seems to have acted upon the direct instructions of his city-council, which is unusual. These circumstances have prompted speculation that the inscription was originally placed in a town somewhere outside of Rome, and was brought to the city only in the post-classical period.[27] However, I fail to see the logic of a former magistrate of an anonymous town somewhere in the surrounding area of Rome setting up a dedication to a Dea Vienna. It seems more likely to me that we witness the actions of a man (or maybe several men) from Vienna with some business or other in Rome itself. Unfortunately, we have no inkling what that business entailed. A diplomatic mission is one possibility, but if this was the case it would seem Paternus was on a temporary stay, having been sent over by the Viennese city-council for a specific purpose.

Yet another Latin inscription is, because of its possible relation to Pliny's 'stationes municipiorum', commonly treated with the evidence surrounding the Forum Iulium, although in truth nothing is actually known about its find-location.[28] It is dedicated to the *genius* of the people of Noricum ('genio Noricorum') by a certain L. Iulius Bassus who calls himself 'a station-operator of theirs' ('stationarius eorum').[29] Since Noricum is a province and not a city, a connection between Bassus and a provincial *concilium* has been conjectured, but without any good reason. As far as we know, representatives or officials of *concilia* were never called *stationarii*.[30] The word does, however, neatly echo the term that the Tyrians living in

[26] *CIL* VI 36835.

[27] G. Gatti, *N.d.sc.* (1899) 289/290. See C. Lega ([in: Steinby IV] 1999) 352.

[28] C. Lega ([in: Steinby IV] 1999) 351; Richardson (1992) 368; Moretti (1958) 113; Cantarelli (1900) 125.

[29] *CIL* VI 250 (= *CIL* VI 30723 = *ILS* 3675).

[30] Deininger (1965) 148–156.

Puteoli used to describe themselves: 'στατιωναρίων'. That seems to support the idea, put forward by some scholars, that the *statio* Bassus belonged to was connected to trade, more specifically the trade in iron ore, a commodity in which Noricum was particularly rich.[31]

The final piece of epigraphic evidence supposedly from this general area (allegedly the inscription was found somewhere near the so-called 'Tabularium') actually mentions a *statio*.[32] It is a dedication to 'Hercules Tiburtinus' ('[H]erculi Tiburtino'), presumably by an (—)ius Asinius Panaristus; at the end the word *statio* appears ('[i]demque statione[m]'). Other than that, it does not give us any information. The interpretation of this inscription is far from easy due mainly to its damaged state and dubious provenance. The suggestion that it was attached somehow to the statue of Hercules reported by Pliny the elder to have stood near the Rostra should, in my view, be rejected; that particular statue was brought to Rome from the East as war booty by L. Lucullus and bore no relation to Tibur whatsoever.[33] Furthermore, a sanctuary of Hercules is known to have existed in Tibur, and worship of the demigod is well-attested there.[34] A connection to the Tiburtine Hercules cult seems clear.

However, it may be that the mention of Hercules Tiburtinus is deceptive and that there is no connection whatsoever between the city of Tibur and the *statio* mentioned in the inscription. Conceivably, the inscription does not even refer to an organization of a city at all; as in Ostia the word *statio* is used variedly in public inscriptions (e.g. *statio alvei Tiberis, statio annonae, statio aquarum*).[35] It is also possible that it was originally set up in Tibur and brought to Rome only later; it has even been suggested that the excavation reports are unreliable, and that it was actually unearthed in Tibur in modern times.[36] Unless more of the inscription is recovered, all of this will have to remain uncertain.

---

[31] See C. Lega ([in: Steinby IV] 1999) 351; Cantarelli (1900) 132–134. Note though how the *OLD*, referring to Ulpianus *Dig.* 1,12,1,12 and Paulus *Dig.* 11,4,4, gives a different definition of *stationarius*: 'Belonging to a detachment (of soldiers on police or guard duties)'; see also *I.Eph.* VI, 2319.

[32] *CIL* VI 342 (= 30742, with add. pp. 3004, 3756), 'Repertum sub Tabulario'. See Moretti (1958) 114.

[33] Pliny *NH* 34.93. Pliny mentions a dedicatory inscription by L. Lucullus, 'in hac [statua] tres sunt tituli: L. Luculli imperatoris de manubiis, [...]'.

[34] See C. Lega ([in: Steinby IV] 1999) 351/352.

[35] See the entries by Ch. Bruun, F. Coarelli, P. Burgers, W. Eck, A. La Regina, all in: Steinby IV (1999) 345–349, 352/353.

[36] See H. Dessau's commentary to *CIL* XIV 3552; Cantarelli (1900) 125, nr. 4. C. Lega rejects the idea, following Ch. Hülsen; see Hülsen's commentary to *CIL* VI 30742; C. Lega ([in: Steinby IV] 1999) 351.

In sum, the evidence for *stationes* on the Forum Iulium is hardly very revealing. The literary sources are confined to Pliny's rather vague remark, the archaeological evidence consists solely of the forum's silent standing walls, and the scanty epigraphic evidence from the area, riddled with methodological problems, is not particularly illuminating either. The data from the Sacra Via, on the other hand, are much more abundant, more varied in nature, and much richer in detail.

Stationes on the Sacra Via

The second location where a concentration of *stationes* is thought to have stood is a stretch of land south of the Sacra Via, across from the 'Temple of Romulus' (see fig. 3). This zone is generally supposed to have accommodated another category of *statio*, namely the so-called 'stationes exterarum civitatum', a term coined in 1958 by Luigi Moretti to set them apart from the ones mentioned by Pliny. Moretti is not clear on their function. In his view they apparently did not really serve a practical end but were 'most of all an act of prestige, a statement of presence in the *Urbs, caput mundi*'.[37] His idea of distinguishing between two types of *statio* was widely accepted in the subsequent scholarly literature; in Eva Steinby's authoritative *Lexicon Topographicum Urbis Romae* the two are treated under separate entries. However, Emanuele Papi's entry for 'stationes exterarum civitatum' does not repeat Moretti's interpretation of status symbols but sees them as '...rooms with primarily a religious function intended to house, among others, the cults of the mother city; analogous purposes can be hypothesized for the Ostian building-complex of the "piazzale delle corporazioni"...'[38] From the previous chapter it will have become apparent that I do not subscribe to this proposed view of the 'piazzale'. As I will explain shortly, I also question both the validity of Moretti's distinction between two types of *statio* and his and Papi's interpretation of the *stationes* on the Sacra Via.

In the course of the nineteenth century the fragments of a number of inscriptions were found on both sides of the Sacra Via, all either mentioning a *statio* or otherwise containing evidence for activities of foreign

[37] '...soprattutto un atto di prestigio, una attestazione di presenza nell' Urbe, caput mundi'. Moretti (1958) 115/116. See also Moretti *IGUR* I 70–78, nrs. 78–93.

[38] '...ambienti con funzione prevalentemente religiosa, destinati a ospitare, tra gli altri, i culti delle città di origine; funzioni analoghe possono essere ipotizzate per il complesso del "Piazzale delle Corporazioni" di Ostia...'; E. Papi ([in: Steinby IV] 1999) 350.

immigrants. Up until recently, no one had ventured to link the epigraphic to the architectural data. This changed when the results of the large-scale excavations, conducted in this area between the 1880s and 1904, were finally published comprehensively in 1986. The excavations, which extended from the 'Temple of Romulus' to the church of S. Maria Nova, show that during the first three centuries AD the street underwent some major changes in appearance. The oldest surviving road surface, a narrow street constructed in basalt with sidewalks in travertine, was lined with buildings that can roughly be dated to Augustan times. The best preserved of these—*tabernae* constructed in *opus quadratum* with dividing walls in brick and travertine blocks—are built partly on top of older reticulate walls following the same outline; the corridors between them show the remains of floors in *opus spicatum*. Building techniques, material, as well as architecture point to structures for commercial use and storage, leading to the conclusion that at the time this stretch was 'an important commercial road'.[39]

A subsequent phase saw a dramatic transformation with the razing of all existing buildings and construction of long monumental porticoes, turning the street into a straight, wide (circa twenty meters) avenue. During the nineteenth-century excavations, the massive foundations of the southern portico were exposed; the northern portico is largely covered by the Basilica Nova, but excavations conducted in the 1930s have traced it underneath the floor of the building. It has long been believed that the monumentalized boulevard, postdating the fire of 64 AD, formed a vestibule to Nero's Domus Aurea, but more recently that notion has been thrown into doubt.[40] It may be that the porticoes were built, completely or in part, by the Flavians as an element of their new building program in the Colosseum-valley. No consensus exists on the question of what purpose these structures served. Both the walls on the southern side as the structures visible during the excavations in the Basilica Nova show rectangular rooms opening up onto internal courtyards; hypotheses range from commercial use to offices for imperial officials.[41]

---

39 Buranelli Le Pera and D'Elia (1986) 243/244, 247 ('Complesso C'), 251/252 with fig. 10 a/b; the road in this period is qualified as 'un importante asse commerciale'; 254–258 with fig. 23.

40 Buranelli Le Pera and D'Elia (1986) 244/245; 257–261; Platner and Ashby (1929) 458.

41 Platner and Ashby (1929) 423; Buranelli Le Pera and D'Elia (1986) 258–260; Richardson (1992) 314/315; C. Lega ([in: Steinby IV] 1999) 129/130. See also F. Coarelli ([in: Steinby IV] 1999) 227.

The next phase saw the gradual disappearance of the colonnades and the construction of a rather disorderly collection of edifices, narrowing the road again.[42] *Tabernae* reappeared on the southern side, and a somewhat mysterious semicircular building that could have been a modestly-sized fountain was put in place. On the opposite side, the Domitianic 'Horrea Piperataria'—a storehouse for pepper and spices from Egypt and Arabia—went up, incorporating and modifying the Neronian/Flavian colonnades.[43] The whole complex seems to have been destroyed by fire in 191 AD. Whatever else may have stood on the northern side (perhaps the rebuilt *horrea*), Maxentius' 'Temple of Romulus' and Basilica Nova subsequently obliterated it all; these buildings monumentalized this side of the road again, especially with the Constantinian southern entrance to the Basilica Nova, framed by four porphyry columns and with steps leading down into the Sacra Via. The final addition consisted of a small, late antique 'portichetto' built up against the Basilica, further narrowing the road.

This stretch of street, it would seem from the archaeology, was strongly connected to the sale and storage of goods from at least late Republican or Augustan times onward. The archaeological findings are in accordance with the literary and epigraphic evidence, also signaling that during the early Empire the road was a place for shops, apparently mostly selling upmarket wares. We possess a good number of inscriptions telling us that it was home to pearl dealers, goldsmiths, metal workers, gem engravers, and dealers in garlands and musical instruments. Propertius and Ovid seem to have regarded the Sacra Via as the place to turn for buying fancy gifts for their girlfriends.[44] The inscriptions all date roughly from the first century BC to the end of the first century AD, but so far none have been found postdating the early imperial period. This would seem to indicate that there was no continuity in use, at least not in type of warehouse and shop, when the Neronian/Flavian colonnades and then the spice warehouses of the 'Horrea Piperataria' were built. But although the sellers of jewelry may have left never to return, the evidence shows a large degree of continuity in use of the Sacra Via; from at least the early Empire to well into

[42] E. Papi ([in: Steinby IV] 1999) 349; Buranelli Le Pera and D'Elia (1986) 247–253, 261.

[43] M. Piranomonte ([in: Steinby III] 1996) 45/46; Platner and Ashby (1929) 262/263.

[44] Pearl dealers: *CIL* VI 9545–9549; goldsmiths/metal workers: *CIL* VI 9207, 9418, 9419; engravers: *CIL* VI 9221, 9239; dealers in garlands: *CIL* VI 9283, 9795; dealer in instruments: *CIL* VI 9935. Propertius 2,24,11–15; Ovid *Ars Am.* 2,265/266; *Amores* 1,8,99/100. See Platner and Ashby (1929) 459; F. Coarelli ([in: Steinby IV] 1999) 225.

late antiquity it had a predominantly commercial character, even with the monumentalizing architecture by Maxentius and Constantine on the northern side.

Several inscriptions in Greek of which the archaeological context is mostly secure and relatively precise confirm activities in this area of groups of people from overseas. They were found in and around a cluster of a dozen or so buildings, roughly dating to the late second century AD. These buildings have their back-walls partly built on the foundations of the monumental colonnade of the previous phase (fig. 3).[45] Their walls are constructed in *opus latericium* and *opus caementicium*, forming rooms of an uneven size, but all more or less comparable in floor surface to the booths on the Ostian 'piazzale delle corporazioni' (and likely the Tyrian *statio* in Puteoli). Both their appearance and their construction-sequence show that they were not designed as one unified structure.[46] They were built making use of previous architecture, over time getting rebuilt and adapted. Based on what is left we can tell the collection of structures was diverse in shape. Most rooms were rectangular; one had an apsidal back-wall. The best preserved room probably was roofed by a small cross-vault resting on four pillars at the corners; another further down the road consisted of a space sheathed in marble slabs, projecting from what was left of the Neronian/Flavian colonnade. Some at least seem to have had basements created by excavating below the street level. How tall they stood is hard to tell; given the variation in plans and architectural detail, it may well have differed considerably from room to room.

The cities mentioned in the inscriptions from this area are all concentrated in the East; all but one are located in Asia Minor. No fewer than three from Cilicia seem to have been present, the most important one, capital of the province, being Tarsus. The evidence for that city consists mainly of two inscriptions both discovered on the Sacra Via.[47] One, a

---

[45] Buranelli Le Pera and D'Elia (1986) 252 ('struttura H') with fig. 18 a/b; E. Papi ([in: Steinby IV] 1999) 349, with fig. 175/176. The identification is E. Papi's; Buranelli Le Pera and D'Elia do not mention *stationes*. E. Papi dates the buildings to the end of the second century AD; Buranelli Le Pera and D'Elia, however, seem to prefer a much later date, seeing the Basilica Nova, the 'Temple of Romulus' and the late antique 'portichetto' all as predating the *tabernae*. E. Papi's dating seems to me to fit better with the epigraphic record (see below).

[46] Cf. E. Papi who disagrees with Buranelli Le Pera and D'Elia 'La costruzione ... sembra rispondere a un progetto unitario anche se realizzato in tempi diversi ...'; E. Papi ([in: Steinby IV] 1999) 349.

[47] *IGUR* I 79, 80 (= *IG* XIV 1066a, 1066b). See Moretti (1958) 108, nr. 2; Cantarelli (1900) 125, nr. 6.

finely-carved marble lintel that can still be seen on the site today, has the city's name: 'of the people of Tarsus' ('Ταρσέων'). The second, a much lengthier but fairly damaged text, is written on a pedestal made from a reused block of marble (it has an older inscription in Latin on the horizontal surface where the statue would have stood). It is a dedication datable to the period mid-239 to mid-241 AD to the Emperor Gordian III by 'the first, greatest, and most beautiful metropolis' ('[ἡ πρώτη καὶ μεγίσ]τη καὶ καλλίστη μη[τρόπολις]'). The two pieces of stone bearing the inscriptions may have formed part of a small *aedicula*, with a pedestal and statue surrounded by a wall, and with the lintel over the doorway.[48] If this is correct, Tarsus should be read also in the second inscription otherwise only showing the word '[Ἰ]σαυρία[ς]' as a geographical pointer. A third inscription, find-location unknown, has the word 'Ἀλεξανδρε[ιανή]' which might refer to Tarsus as well, 'Alexandrianê' (after Alexander Severus) being one of its honorary titles.[49]

Another Cilician city that may have had a *statio* here is Anazarbus, although the evidence is indirect. One inscription found on the Sacra Via must once have been quite large but is now reduced to a fragment showing only a few letters. The word '—]αθεζομένη' should probably be read as 'προκαθεζομένη' ('leading' or 'presiding'), a title only known to have been used by Tarsus and Anazarbus.[50] The only other legible word is '—]σαρεια' likely to be completed as reading 'Καισαρείᾳ'. This epithet was regularly used by Anazarbus but never by Tarsus, so Anazarbus seems to be the city in question.

Yet a third Cilician city that left its mark in this area is Mopsuestia, in a remarkably well-preserved inscription dating from 140 AD.[51] Moretti questions if this inscription should be treated with the material from the Sacra Via. Not only was it found in 1499 on the opposite side of the road somewhere near the church of St Cosmas and Damian but it would also be the earliest from the area, considerably older than the rest all dating from Severan times or later. These objections need not be decisive though. The find-location is so close to the *tabernae* on the southern side of the Sacra Via that the stone, perhaps reused in some medieval building project, could easily have traveled that distance in the course of the centuries.

48 R. Lanciani, *Bull.Com.* 8 (1880) 80/81 has both Greek inscriptions and the older Latin one (Latin text also in: *CIL* VI 31128).

49 *IGUR* I 81. Anazarbus (see below) is another possibility.

50 *IGUR* I 78, and especially Moretti (1958) 106–108.

51 *IGUR* I 24.

There is also the possibility that it actually belongs to the area where it was discovered, meaning there were *stationes* on the northern side of the road as well, possibly predating the cluster on the southern side.

More problematic is the inscription's content; the city-council and the people's assembly, calling Mopsuestia a 'friend and ally of the Roman people', honor Antoninus Pius for his 'divine and solid administration of justice' in upholding the city's ancient rights.[52] These references to a judgment and city-rights seem to suggest that the Emperor had made some sort of official decision, perhaps arbitrating a dispute in Mopsuestia's favor. It is not unthinkable that such an inscription would have been attached to a *statio*. That said, it is definitely not evidence for a group of individuals in Rome acting on their private initiative (like the statue-base set up by the *Sabrathenses* on the Forum Iulium). Perhaps the most compelling reason for placing the inscription in this context is the evidence for the other two Cilician cities in the area.[53]

Leaving Mopsuestia out of the equation for the moment, it could be that specifically Tarsus and Anazarbus, with their buildings on the Sacra Via, had taken a competition over prestige and a 'battle over titles' to the capital.[54] But Cilician cities were not just interested in civic honors; economic interests are just as likely, if not more likely, to explain the presence of these towns. The *Expositio totius orbis*, a work of the mid-fourth century AD, mentions that Cilicia produced much wine, to the delight of other provinces.[55] Wine, however, is hardly the product mostly associated with the region; it is textile production that has left most traces in our sources. A woolen fabric by its generic name called 'cilicia' is already discussed by Varro who reflects on the origin of the word; Cicero also simply uses 'cilicia' to refer to cloth or rugs.[56] Dio Chrysostom discusses the social position of the lower classes in Tarsus who were called 'linen workers' ('λινουργοὺς'), apparently 'no small crowd' ('πλῆθος οὐκ ὀλίγον'); in

[52] 'Μοψουεστίας τῆς Κιλικίας... φίλης καὶ συμμάχου Ῥωμαίων ἡ βουλὴ καὶ ὁ δῆμος διὰ τῆς θείας αὐτοῦ δικαιοδοσίας βέβαια τηρήσαντος αὐτῇ τὰ ἐξ ἀρχῆς δίκαια'.

[53] E. Papi ([in: Steinby IV] 1999) 349 also hesitantly puts the inscription with the ones from the Sacra Via.

[54] Moretti (1958) 115/116: '... non è da sottovalutare... il continuarsi nell' Urbe, a pochi metri di distanza nella zona della via Sacra, della "guerra dei tituli" tra le due metropoli della Cilicia'.

[55] *Expositio* 39: 'Deinde iterum regio Ciliciae, quae faciens multum vinum laetificat et alias provincias,...' In *P.Mich.* inv. 5760a (second half of the second century AD?) l. 5–8 we indeed see ships from Cilicia transporting wine to Egypt. See Heilporn (2000) 351 5B.

[56] Varro *De re rustica* 2,11,12; Cicero *Verr.* 2,1,95. See Levick (2004) 194; Broughton (1938) 821–823.

Diocletian's 'Edict on Maximum Prices' Tarsus appears over and over as a source of linen shirts, tunics, bedding, hoods, and handkerchiefs.[57] An inscription from Anazarbus contains an honorary decree to the Emperor Hadrian by a guild of linen workers ('συντεχνία λινουργῶ[ν]').[58] Clemens of Alexandria, railing against various forms of indulgence, lamented the fact that people no longer bought linen only from Egypt but also from Judea and Cilicia, which suggests there was a whiff of luxury about these garments.[59]

But to return to the discussion on Roman *stationes*, much more information than the inscriptions discussed so far is provided by an inscription set up between 211 and 217 AD. It consists of two fragments both found on the northern side of the Sacra Via, one near the Temple of Antoninus Pius and Faustina, the other near the 'Temple of Romulus'. It is one of the most interesting and instructive inscriptions from the area, telling us that a woman named Galene had built a *statio* of the people of Tralles 'from the ground up and with its entire decoration, from her own expenses'.[60] It honors Caracalla for his liberality ('ἐκ τῆς... χάριτος'), a phrase that might have indicated financial help were it not contradicted by Galene's claim that she had paid for the building and all its decoration herself. Perhaps this is a reference to an imperial land-concession of the site, or perhaps it has to do with the honorific title of 'temple-warden' (*neôkoros*) which Tralles started using in Severan times (although it is disputed it was Caracalla who granted the honor).[61] It could also just be a polite bow to some perceived general well-wishing of the Emperor towards Tralles. There are some interesting parallels between this inscription and the one set up by the Tyrians in Puteoli. First of all, there is the word *statio*, in both cases a loan-word from Latin referring to an physical building. There is also talk of adornment of the structure, '*kosmos*', which seems to have been an essential part of the appearance both of the Trallian *statio* and the *stationes* in Puteoli ('our station excels the others in both size and adornment', the Tyrians boasted).

---

57 Dio Chrysostom 34,21–23. *Edict*, ch. 26, 27, 28; Lauffer (1971) 169–183. See Pleket (1984) 31/32.

58 *I.Anaz.* 3 (= *IGRR* III 896).

59 Clemens of Alexandria *Paed.* 2,10,115 (written circa 190 AD).

60 *IGUR* I 84 (= *IG* XIV 1079, 1064): 'τὴν στατίωνα... ἀπο θεμ[ε]λίων ἀνεγείρασα σὺν τῷ πα[ντὶ] [κ]όσμῳ ἐκ τῶν ἰδίων'. To Moretti goes the credit of combining the two fragments of the stone, greatly enhancing the informative value of the text. See also Cantarelli (1900) 125, nr. 5.

61 Burrell (2004) 130–132; Moretti (1958) 110/111.

Prior to the reign of Caracalla, Tralles apparently did not have a *statio* in Rome or at least not one in this location. It is intriguing that it was paid for by a single woman, and we would like to have known what connection Galene had to Rome and what she hoped to get out of her generous act. Unfortunately, we know next to nothing about her or about her capacity. She must have been a Trallian native since she devoted the inscription to her fatherland ('[τῇ ἑ]αυτῆς πατρίδι ἀνέθηκεν'). Moretti conjectured she was a member of a distinguished family in the city, although there is no real proof for this hypothesis.[62] Because of her sex she can not have been a magistrate; a priestess might have been a possibility but no priesthood is mentioned nor does the inscription in general have a religious connotation. A wealthy woman involved in commerce—trade in leather goods perhaps—is yet another option.[63] Women in business, as patrons of a guild or otherwise, was a not uncommon phenomenon in the Roman world. Eumachia of Pompeii comes to mind as a possible parallel, but also the women, some of them *peregrinae*, we saw making contracts in the Sulpicii archive.[64]

Also in western Asia Minor and possibly possessing a *statio* was the city of Sardis. An architectural fragment (part of an architrave) was found on the southern Sacra Via, showing only the word '[π]ρωτοχθό[νων]'.[65] Despite the limited information, the find makes it likely that Sardis had a building in this location since the epithet is only ever found in inscriptions referring to that city. Two other inscriptions on what could either be statue bases or altars (find-location of both unfortunately unknown) are dedications set up by imperial freedmen to Dea Cora ('Θεὰν Κόρην'), a local deity from Sardis.[66] They date to the second or third century AD, and demonstrate Sardian ancestral religious practices in Rome.

Two inscriptions that almost certainly concern the same city both bear the word *statio*. The city in question is Tiberias in Syria-Palestine, the only one in the evidence from this area not located in Asia Minor. A long marble architrave found near the Curia Iulia, although reused

---

[62] Moretti (1958) 110.

[63] Diocletian's 'Edict on Maximum Prices' mentions hides from Tralles: *Edict*, ch. 8, line 1, 3; Lauffer (1971) 126.

[64] On Eumachia, cf. Jongman (1988) 179–184. Women in the Sulpicii archive: *TPSulp.* 40, 58, 60, 61, 62, 63, 64, 71, 73, 82, 90, 91, 92, 93, 99, 105. In none of these cases is it certain that it concerns business deals, but involvement in trade of the community we see in the archive seems likely (see Chapter 1).

[65] *IGUR* I 85.

[66] *IGUR* I 86, 87. See Moretti (1958) 113.

there and not its original location, reads '*statio* of the people of Tiberias also known as the people of Claudiopolis' ('στατίων [Τιβε]ριέων τῶν καὶ Κλ[α]υδιοπολιτῶν'); it probably dates to the second century AD, and must be a dedication of someone whose name is now lost to his fatherland ('τῇ πατρίδι').[67] The lower half of a small female cult statue discovered on the Sacra Via, and also dating to the second (or perhaps third) century, is dedicated by an Ismenos from Tiberias 'to the *statio*' ('Ἰσμῆνος ... Τιβεριεὺς τῇ στατίωνι').[68] That this word refers to a building seems likely given that it was written on an architrave.

Finally, a number of inscriptions give only tentative information, but since most were discovered in the general area under discussion they are usually included in the list of possible *stationes*. I too will briefly mention them here, although their informative value is extremely limited. First, there is the statue base found in the Basilica Aemilia bearing an inscription in Greek telling us that it was set up by Aelius Poppaeus and Aelius Asclepiodotus to honor Heracles Alexicacos. Even if that dedication was made to an ancestral deity, which is not at all certain, it still does not allow us to know which city of Heraclea it refers to.[69] Then there are the two statue fragments, one found in the Atrium Vestae the other with unknown find-location, both possibly votive statues of female deities, protectors of foreign cities (the second shows the word 'πατρίδι[ι]').[70] Finally, there are three heavily damaged inscriptions, two found on the Sacra Via, one of unknown origin. The latter seems to be dedicated to a fatherland ('[τ]ῇ κυρίᾳ [π]ατρίδι'); the two from the Sacra Via seem to be dedications to Emperors.[71]

What does the evidence discussed so far tell us about the function of Roman *stationes*, and about the relationship between the cluster near the Forum Iulium and the one on the Sacra Via? Ultimately, Moretti's idea that the two groups represented two different types of *statio* rests on no other circumstance than that they were located in separate places; nothing in the archaeological, literary, or epigraphic evidence really supports

---

[67] *IGUR* I 82. The name of the city has also been read as '[Τυ]ρίων', i.e. referring to the *statio* mentioned by the Tyrians in Puteoli; '[Τιβε]ριέων' seems a more plausible reading though: Moretti (1958) 108/109 nr. 3; Cantarelli (1900) 126/127, nr. 10.

[68] *IGUR* I 83. Ismenos is the son of someone with a Semitic name, although it is not entirely clear how the patronym should be read. See also Cantarelli (1900) 126 nr. 9.

[69] *IGUR* I 88; Moretti (1958) 111/112. Heraclea Pontica, Heraclea Sebastopoli and Heraclea ad Salbacum are all possibilities.

[70] *IGUR* I 89, 90. Moretti (1958) 112/113.

[71] *IGUR* I 91, 92 (Septimius Severus?), 93 (Hadrian? Trajan?).

the notion that we are dealing with two distinct categories. Besides, a more logical alternative explanation can be devised to explain the different locations.

The literary and epigraphic evidence can be put in the following chronological order. Suetonius, recounting an episode that occurred late in the reign of Nero, tells us how the blue-blooded Salvidienus Orfitus was executed by the Emperor for letting out parts of his house around ('circa') an unspecified forum as *stationes* to certain cities.[72] Next comes Pliny writing about a decade after that supposed event, mentioning the roots of the lotus tree extending to the Forum of Caesar. Then there are the Latin inscriptions found in the general vicinity of Caesar's Forum, dating from the period mid-second to early third century AD.[73] Finally, there are the inscriptions found on the Sacra Via, all in Greek and all, so far as we can date them, belonging to the late second to the mid-third century AD.[74]

When presented in this way the following sequence of events can be imagined.[75] *Stationes* started out by being located mostly near the Forum of Caesar, where already in the 60s AD the available space was insufficient to accommodate all foreign groups. Consequently, they began to spread to random places such as the *tabernae* in the house of the hapless Orfitus. On the assumption that *stationes* were, and continued to be, located in the buildings along the western side of Caesar's Forum, the substantial Trajanic modifications to the structure must have exacerbated the problem of limited space. During the massive overhaul of the whole area with the construction of Trajan's Forum, a considerable section of the rooms opening up on the Clivus Argentarius was converted into a large elevated public latrine (a marvel of Roman engineering, by the way).[76] Wherever else the *stationes* may have gone in the intervening period, from the mid-

---

[72] Suetonius *Nero* 37,1 (see also Chapter 2). However, to conclude, as Richardson does, that space for *stationes* was 'jealously guarded' by the central government is to miss the point of the story; Richardson (1992) 368. Suetonius tells the story as an example of the mere pretexts Nero would use to get rid of people.

[73] *CIL* VI 250 (= 30723, with add. p. 3004, 3756) (third century AD?); *CIL* VI 342 (= 30742, with add. p. 3004, 3756) (second or third century AD); *CIL* VI 36835 (no date); *CIL* VI 40528 (= R. Cagnat and A. Merlin, *AE* [1934] 39/40, nr. 146) (138 AD).

[74] *IGUR* I 78 (post 207 AD); 79 (no date); 80 (239–241 AD); 83 (no date); 84 (211–217 AD); 85 (second or third century AD); 89 (second or third century AD); 92 (post 195 AD); 93 (no date). Most likely also *IGUR* I 24 (140 AD).

[75] In this sense essentially also Richardson who, unlike Steinby, does not award the 'stationes exterarum civitatum' their own entry; Richardson (1992) 368.

[76] Lancaster (2000) 779–784. Overhaul probably begun by Domitian; C. Morselli ([in: Steinby II] 1995) 305.

second century AD, if not earlier, they spilled over at least in part to the Sacra Via.

Our knowledge is far too patchy to attain any kind of certainty that this reconstruction is actually correct. Still, at first glance this reading of the evidence seems to me preferable to an analysis in which an artificial distinction in two types of *statio* is needed to explain the different locations. The term 'stationes exterarum civitatum', I would like to stress again, is an invention of modern scholarship and is found in no ancient source. There is, furthermore, little in the evidence to support the interpretation of these structures as status symbols or temples; they fit much better in their archaeological context if they are seen as commercial institutions. Supporting that view is the fact that we have already witnessed the clustering of *stationes* on the Ostian 'piazzale'. Another parallel with the 'piazzale', where many rooms were occupied by African cities from Africa Proconsularis, is that the geographical range of the towns found on the Sacra Via seems not to have been extensive; of the six identifiable cities, two were located in western Asia Minor and two more (or three if we include Mopsuestia) were located in Cilicia. As I argued in the previous chapter, clustering makes sense from a business perspective; information, whether as official correspondence or gossip, spreads more easily that way, increasing the volume of knowledge.[77]

In the following, I will discuss the evidence for a Roman building of yet a third city in western Asia Minor: Ephesus. As we shall see, the inscriptions referring to Tralles and Ephesus share some interesting parallels. If indeed *stationes* had a tendency to group together according to the geographical location of the mother cities, as they seem to have done in Ostia, the Ephesian building could have been located on or near the Sacra Via as well. Unfortunately, the sources do not allow us to know anything about its whereabouts.

Ephesians in Rome

Two pieces of marble forming part of the same long and rather plain looking lintel contain bits of a most interesting inscription. It is not clear when and where the one piece was discovered (it has meanwhile also disappeared again) but the other was found in 1592 when the new *confessio* was

[77] See Noy (2000) 164. Noy thinks exclusively in terms of *written* communication though.

dug underneath St Peter's Basilica. The prominent find-location—right in front of the papal altar—may make for an intriguing archaeological story, but unfortunately not one that is conducive to understanding the inscription; further excavations in this location are quite unlikely, and we will probably never know if the stone was *in situ* or was reused in some other building. In any event, the text of the two combined fragments is interesting enough to quote here in full:

> To the Emperor Caesar Titus Aelius Hadrian Antoninus Augustus Pius and Marcus Aurelius Caesar and to [—] of the Ephesians, the first and greatest metropolis of Asia and twice temple-warden of the Emperors; M. Ulpius Domesticus *periodonikês, paradoxos* and overseer of the baths of the Augusti [—] (erected a building?) to the shipowners and the merchants, from the ground up with all the decoration around it, and with the statues. In the consulship of Lucius Aelius Aurelius Commodus and Titus Sextius Lateranus on the 15th day before the Kalends of February (= January 18th, 154 AD)[78]

The text is lacunose—more so, in fact, than is apparent from my translation as I will explain presently—and it was once believed that 'στατίων' should be read where the letters '[—]ων' appear. However, it is now generally accepted that the word should be completed as reading '['Εφεσί]ων'.[79] The reason is twofold. First, there is the date of 154 AD combined with a description of a city that fits contemporary Ephesus ('first and greatest metropolis of Asia and twice temple-warden of the Emperors').[80] Then, there are the words '*periodonikês*', '*paradoxos*', and 'overseer of the baths of the Augusti' ('ἐπὶ βαλανείων Σεβαστῶν'), the titles and occupation of a person. The first two are athletic honors meaning, respectively, a victor in all four Panhellenic games and an 'outstanding champion', originally a contestant who had won at both wrestling and *pankration* on the same day; the third refers to an official attached to an imperial bathing complex. No personal name is preserved, but the description agrees so well

[78] *IGUR* I 26 (= *IG* XIV 1052 = *IGRR* I 147): '[Αὐτοκ]ράτορι Καίσαρι Τίτῳ Αἰλίῳ Ἀδριανῷ Ἀντωνείνῳ Σεβαστῷ Ε[ὐσεβ]εῖ καὶ Μάρκῳ Αὐρηλίῳ Καίσαρι καὶ τῷ [— Ἐφεσί]ων τῆς πρώτης καὶ μεγίστης μητροπόλεως τῆς [Ἀ]σίας καὶ δὶς νε<ω>κόρου τῶν Σεβαστῶν ναυκλήροις καὶ ἐ[μπόροις Μ. Οὔλπιος Δομεστικός — περιο]δονε<ί>κης παράδοξος καὶ ἐπὶ βαλανείων Σεβαστῶν [...]του ἐκ θεμελίων σὺν ἅπαντι τῷ περὶ αὐτὸν κόσμῳ καὶ τοῖς ἀγάλμ[ασιν —] ἐπ<ὶ> ὑπάτων Λουκίου Α[ἰ]λίου Αὐρηλίου Κομμόδου καὶ Τίτου Σεξτίου Λατερανοῦ πρὸ ιε' καλ(ανδῶν) Φεβ(ρουαρίων)'.

[79] Cantarelli (1900) 127 nr. 11; Moretti (1958) 114. See also Caldelli (1992); Noy (2000) 121, 160/161.

[80] Hadrian granted a second *neokoria* to Ephesus, probably in 131 AD; Burrell (2004) 66–70. The phrase also appears in *I.Eph.* IV, 1089 (see below).

with a certain M. Ulpius Domesticus that his name can be inserted with confidence.

Domesticus was an Ephesian native and a celebrated Greek athlete who, sometime in the first half of the second century AD, had moved to Rome where he became president of the athletes' guild. His memory in the capital is preserved through three inscriptions forming a small 'dossier'. They tell the story of how he had sent petitions to the Emperors Hadrian and Antoninus Pius requesting them to donate a patch of land for the athletes' guild headquarters, a structure intended to hold both the guild's cultic objects ('τὰ ἱερὰ') and its archives ('τὰ γράμματα'). In 134 AD, he had received a favorable answer from Hadrian, but the promise was made good only by Antoninus Pius in 143 AD after a second appeal. From these inscriptions, we know Domesticus had managed to climb to the position of overseer of an imperial bathing complex, almost certainly that of Trajan since Pius assigned a location near the *thermae Traiani* on the Esquiline Hill for the guild's headquarters.[81]

Since we have a dedication made by (almost certainly) Domesticus written on an architectural fragment, the question logically presents itself: do we here have part of the structure he had been petitioning for with Hadrian and Antoninus Pius? Although this is a tempting assumption, there is not much evidence to support it. The find-location of part of the lintel on the Vatican, on the opposite side of the river from the Baths of Trajan, may not mean all that much; the two locations are far removed, but medieval reuse of stone may still account for that circumstance. Much more important is that, the dedication to Antoninus Pius and Marcus Aurelius notwithstanding, Domesticus claims sole credit for erecting and beautifying the building. Surely Antoninus Pius' role in honoring his predecessor's promise would have deserved mention if this was indeed the long-desired athletes' headquarters? Furthermore, no reference to sports or athletics is made. The city of Ephesus, on the other hand, features prominently in the text, which also points in a different direction. From the petitions it seems that the athletes' headquarters was a place that welcomed sportsmen regardless of their native city; the athletes housed there are only defined as 'the ones devoted to Hercules' ('τῶν περὶ τὸν Ἡρακλέα ἀθλητῶν'). Finally, there is the reference to the *nauklêroi* and *emporoi*, who do not figure

[81] *IGUR* I 235, 236, 237 (also 238, mentioning Domesticus' son Firmus who succeeded his father as president). For the 'curia athletarum', see Platner and Ashby (1929) 142; Richardson (1992) 102; L. Chioffi ([in: Steinby I] 1993) 330, and especially Caldelli (1992). See also Eck (2009) 95/96.

anywhere in the inscriptions related to the petitions. The conclusion can only be that we are dealing with two separate structures, both of which materialized in Rome due to Domesticus' energetic efforts.[82]

The purpose of the athletes' headquarters is clear enough, but what function did the other building have? Equally interesting is the question of what could have motivated Domesticus to have it constructed. It seems reasonably clear that Ephesian shipmasters and merchants had some stake in the whole affair. The text on the lintel is too damaged and elliptical to be certain, but it seems a safe assumption that it was a structure intended for their use. In line with the theory I set forth in the first three chapters, I think it was a communal space in which they could identify themselves and show their group allegiance, which helped them to establish the requisite amount of trust for their business ventures. If that explanation is correct then why did Domesticus, of all people, see fit to donate such a building to them? This is a difficult question, and we can really only speculate about the answer.

No self-evident connection exists between, on the one hand, a retired athlete, president of the athletes' guild, overseer of an imperial bathing-complex and, on the other, Ephesian shipmasters and traders. The only logical hypothesis for an immediate relationship would be to suppose that the latter were somehow provisioning the baths and that it was the task of the *epi balaneiôn* to contract with them. Wood for stoking the furnaces comes to mind as a possible commodity; on the 'piazzale' in Ostia we have already encountered the 'wood shippers', who may have been in this business. However, Ephesus is not known to have been a city important in shipping fuel.[83] Besides, it is not clear how exactly the imperial baths were run, but it is reasonably certain that it was not part of the task of an *epi balaneiôn* to contract with shippers; he was charged most of all with overseeing places to do with sports and athletics.[84] For this task Domesticus was, of course, eminently suited. But even if he did deal with shippers and traders in the course of his official duties, it cannot have been

[82] This is also Moretti's conclusion, who therefore classifies the inscriptions under separate headings: *IGUR* I 26, and 235–238. Caldelli also thinks they are two different buildings, but both to do with sports, conjecturing that the one built in 154 AD was a *xystos*; Caldelli (1992) 77.

[83] Campania and North Africa seem to have played a dominant role, Meiggs (1982) 258/259; Caldelli (1992) 83. *P.Mich.* inv. 5760a l. 21/22 also provides evidence for the area around Side as a source of wood (probably for construction in that case), Heilporn (2000) 358, 22D.

[84] Caldelli (1992) 80–86.

part of his job to donate buildings to them. The structure that Domesticus built seems to have been a private bequest, and although the extant lines of the inscription do not tell us if he paid for it with his own money, it seems likely. The phrase 'from the ground up, and with all the decoration around it' ('ἐκ θεμελίων σὺν ἅπαντι τῷ περὶ αὐτὸν κόσμῳ') is a phrase we have seen before in the inscription related to the *statio* of the people of Tralles that Galene paid to have constructed on the Sacra Via. Quite a different reasoning should, in my view, be adopted to explain Domesticus' involvement.

Domesticus' career had been on the ascent ever since his days as a professional athlete. By the mid-second century AD he was an accomplished and probably fairly well-off man, influential still in Ephesus and well-known in the East in general. His name appears on a Spartan inscription from which we know he was made an honorary citizen of Antinoeia and of Athens. Two Ephesian inscriptions, one found in the harbor gymnasium, the other in the street leading down to the harbor, mention him and his titles; both were set up after he had already moved to Rome since they list his position as president of the athletes' guild and as *epi balaneiôn*.[85] In his capacity as a minor celebrity, known both in the Greek East and in the capital, he must have been an ideal patron for his fellow-Ephesians sailing to Rome. To have Domesticus associated with their organization must have been an asset to them; it added to their standing and respectability. From the evidence in Ostia we know Ostian guilds regularly elected patrons; some even had patrons of senatorial rank, which no doubt boosted their prestige.[86] As we shall see further below, African and Spanish oil merchants sailing to Rome also managed to attract men with splendid resumes as patrons.

If the idea that Domesticus acted as the Ephesian shipmasters' and traders' patron is correct, it would explain his bequest. However, just as with Galene from Tralles, it still leaves open the question of what exactly he would have received in return for his support. There is no way of knowing, but in the tit-for-tat world of Roman patronage the reward would likely have been ample. All of this can, of course, only be a hypothesis; nothing in the evidence is conclusive. However, I think it is a hypothesis well worth entertaining.

---

85 *IG* V 1669; *I.Eph.* IV 1089, 1155. See L. Moretti, *MemLinc* s.8, vol. 8 (1957) 162/163 nr. 844.

86 Meiggs (1973) 316.

Palmyrenes in Rome

We do not know where the Ephesians' building once stood, although a case could be made for the stretch along the Sacra Via discussed above. However, at this point I think it is worth posing the question if the focus on the heart of Rome and on just two locations is not too narrow. If there were two zones where *stationes* could be found, can there not have been more? In the following I will be discussing the evidence for a building of Palmyrenes in Rome, located in the southern part of the city. This evidence is almost exclusively religious in nature, and whether it actually relates to a Palmyrene *statio* is not a straightforward matter. However, because the general characteristics are similar to the evidence on *stationes* in Ostia and Puteoli, I will make the argument that the structure maintained by Palmyrenes in Rome was indeed a *statio* like those of other foreign groups.

In 1859 and 1860 a Roman garden lot called the 'Vigna Bonelli', situated on the western Tiber riverbank south of Porta Portese, was explored archaeologically. In antiquity this plot probably bordered on, or formed part of, the 'Horti Caesaris', a park bequeathed to the city by Julius Caesar.[87] Its park-like setting notwithstanding, this area close to the water was dominated by the Roman harbors; right across the river, connected by the Pons Sublicius, lay the so-called 'emporium', a vast complex formed by quays, wharves, and major warehouses stretching for about a kilometer along the Tiber. Further south, quays and harbor installations continued in a long and almost uninterrupted sequence on both sides of the river.[88]

The nineteenth-century excavations yielded a number of interesting objects, most related to Syrian cults.[89] The remains of a building also came to light. Regrettably, the archaeological notes on this structure are brief in the extreme. For fear of landslides, the trenches were filled back

---

[87] For a map, see Beard, North and Price (1998) vol. 1, xviii/xix map 2, nr. 14. Horti Caesaris, E. Papi ([in: Steinby III] 1996) 55/56; Platner and Ashby (1929) 265/266. See also, Visconti (1860) esp. 415–421.

[88] 'Emporium' (consisting in large part of the Porticus Aemilia and the Horrea Galbana), see C. Mocchegiani Carpano ([in: Steinby II] 1995) 221–223; F. Coarelli ([in: Steinby IV] 1999) 116/117; F. Coarelli ([in: Steinby III] 1996) 40–42. On the harbors, see M. Maischberger ([in: Steinby V] 1999) 71/72.

[89] An anomaly is a *krater* in black granite with Egyptian iconography. Visconti suggested it represents the Emperor Hadrian being initiated into Egyptian cults, proposing it was a gift of an Egyptian to the temple of Sol. Visconti (1860) 437–439, plate R3 a/b. The *krater* is not discussed by Richardson (1992) 365, or in the entry by J. Calzini Gysens ([in: Steinby IV] 1999) 334/335.

in quickly and the walls were only exposed for a short period of time, not allowing for extensive study. But despite its brevity, the excavation report contains some helpful details. Discovered was apparently a large and complex structure in brick and high quality *opus reticulatum*. It had multiple vaulted rooms, corridors, and porticoes; overall, the report comments, it resembled not a temple but a domestic structure (guided by the inscriptions from the area, a temple is no doubt what the excavators had expected to find).[90] Some bricks carried stamps that from their description in the report we can date to the year 135 AD. Two other brick stamps, published in *CIL*, are datable to the years just prior to 108 AD and the end of the first century AD. Another set of *bipedales* bricks were, judging by their stamps, manufactured in the second half of the first century AD, suggesting initial construction perhaps in the Flavian era.[91]

One of the inscriptions found in the area further elucidates the construction-history of the building. It is a dedication made in the year 102 AD by Iulius Anicetus, who declares that from his own money and with the permission of the attendants (*kalatores*) of the priests he had refurbished the structure and had enlarged it with a portico, which was apparently consecrated to the Sun God ('Sol').[92] The inscription substantiates the information from the brick stamps, telling us that when the temple was renovated in 102 AD it had already been standing for some time. It also confirms that by that date, the cult of Sol was well-established, since a college of priests and their attendants was attached to the sanctuary. It must have been institutions like this one that elicited the remark from the xenophobic protagonist of Juvenal's third Satire bemoaning, in an oft-quoted line, the 'Syrian Orontes since long pouring into the Tiber'.[93]

Yet another inscription that provides us with information on the appearance, as well as on the function of the building is a dedication to 'Deus Sol Victor' made by Q. Octavius Daphinus, a wine merchant ('negotia(n)s venarius') by trade.[94] Daphinus had, the text says, of his own expenses

---

[90] Visconti (1860) 422, 434–436; G. Gatti and L. Borsari, *N.d.sc.* (1887) 18/19. No dimensions or numbers of any kind are given. Visconti speculated that what he uncovered was not the temple proper, but rather its 'parti accessorie', by which he meant the 'triclias' mentioned in inscriptions (see further below).

[91] Visconti (1860) 422; *CIL* XV 1008 nr. 7, 1103 nr. 6, 792 nr. 11. See Chausson (1995) 663.

[92] *CIL* VI 31034 a, b (b = 2185): 'Iulius [A]nicetus [vo]to suscepto [---] primam porticu[m] [S]olis cum marmorib[us] [------] opere novo ampliat[o] [------]ntis inchoatis su[a] [pecuni]a a solo restituit permissu ka[l]atorum pontificu[m et] [fl]aminum'. See Chausson (1995) 664/665 nr. A; Borsari (1887) 93–95; G. Gatti and L. Borsari, *N.d.sc.* (1887) 18/19.

[93] 'iam pridem Syrus in Tiberim defluxit Orontes'; Juvenal *Sat.* 3,62.

[94] *CIL* VI 712. See Chausson (1995) 666/667 nr. B *bis*.

and with the authorization of the priests' attendants, built what is called a *triclia*.[95] That word without question here means 'banqueting hall'; in Palmyrene sanctuaries it is not uncommon to find one or more of such halls, serving social events like ceremonial meals, attached to the structure.[96] In the case of the temple of Sol there must have been several of them, as is made clear by an inscribed request by C. Iulius Anicetus—perhaps the same man who had the temple renovated in 102 AD—invoking the might of Sol and politely asking 'if no one would please write or scratch on the walls or on the banqueting halls' ('triclias').[97] We encounter C. Iulius Anicetus again in an inscription on a reused stone that was not discovered in the Vigna Bonelli with the other inscriptions, although its find-location in Trastevere in combination with its content render it all but certain it belongs to the same collection. The text tells us that Anicetus, having made a vow, had consecrated an altar to Sol.[98]

The inscriptions related to a Sun God discussed so far do not explicitly mention Palmyra, and some doubt as to whether they are actually related to a Palmyrene cult is justified.[99] The site later housed a sanctuary to Palmyrene deities, including the solar divinities Iarhibol and Malachbel, as is shown by inscriptions from the same Vigna Bonelli (presented below). In other Roman inscriptions that for certain pertain to the Palmyrene pantheon a god 'Sol' appears, confirming that Sol and Iarhibol/Malachbel were equated. Still, it could be that the location had previously been sacred to an indigenous Roman Sun God, and was later taken over by Palmyrenes precisely because of its religious significance. Worship of Sol was by no means a novelty in imperial Rome. According to the literary tradition it dated back to the regal period; a depiction of Sol is known from a coin-type dating to 217–215 BC.[100] However, there are two important circumstances that weigh against that reconstruction. First, Daphinus named his god 'Deus Sol Victor', a name close to 'Sol Invictus' who for certain was a Semitic and not a Roman god (it was 'Sol Invictus Elagabalus'

95 '... tricliam fec(it) a solo inpen[sa] sua permissu kalator(um) po[tific(um)] et flaminum ...'

96 Kaizer (2002) 220–229.

97 'C. Iulius Anicetus ex imperio Solis rogat ne quis velit parietes aut triclias inscribere aut scariphare', *CIL* VI 52 (= *ILS* 4335). See Chausson (1995) 665/666 nr. B. The phrase 'ex imperio Solis' might refer to a vow, or else perhaps to a dream.

98 *CIL* VI 709. See Chausson (1995) 667 nr. C.

99 Moretti (*IGUR* I 117–125) and Schneider (1987) exclude them from their discussion. Cf. Chausson (1995); Borsari (1887).

100 Savage (1940) 52; Beard, North and Price (1998) vol. 1, 33 fig. f.

whom the Syrian Emperor Elagabalus attempted to elevate to the position of supreme deity in 220 AD).[101] Moreover, there is the reference to the 'triclias' associated specifically with Semitic temples and cultic gathering places; for a parallel, see the building, discussed below, that Palmyrenes possessed in the city of Vologesias. It seems sound judgment, in short, to connect the inscriptions related to Sol to a structure built, maintained, and frequented by Palmyrenes.

The dossier of inscriptions thus continues with two bilingual texts in Latin and Greek, closely resembling each other.[102] Only one is known to have been found in the Vigna Bonelli but the other, find-location unknown, mirrors the first so closely that a relation is obvious. In both inscriptions the Latin and Greek versions do not have exactly the same content. The Latin texts in probably both cases began with a salutation to an unidentifiable Emperor, 'pro salute imp(eratoris) [Caes(aris)]', a phrase absent in the Greek texts. However, all texts record, with minor variations, that C. Licinius N(—) and Heliodorus Palmyrenus had built a shrine ('ναὸν', '[ae]dem') to the god Bel (in the Greek version of one inscription called 'Malachbel', in the other seemingly named 'the Palmyrene Bel'). Another bilingual inscription from the Vigna Bonelli, written in Greek and Palmyrene this time, is a dedication made by two men with unhellenized Semitic names, Maqqai and So'adu, to the Palmyrene ancestral gods ('Θεοῖς πατρῴοις') Bel, Iarhibol, and Aglibol.[103] Of the marble plaque carved in bas-relief on which the inscription is written, only the lower-left corner survives. It shows two pair of feet of male figures, presumably images of two deities. The upper-right corner of yet another plaque, or possibly the same plaque, shows the head of a female figure with the word 'Ἀστάρτη' written next to it.[104] In the two fragments combined we see four major Palmyrene deities represented: the celestial divinity Bel with the solar Iarhibol and the lunar Aglibol; the mother-god Astarte, meanwhile, is often associated with this male triad, mainly with Bel.

An altar with a complete Greek inscription, still from the Vigna Bonelli, was consecrated to yet another prominent member of the Palmyrene pantheon, Arsû. In the text the name is rendered as 'Ares' but this is largely

---

[101] See Beard, North and Price (1998) vol. 1, 259. See also Schneider (1987) 71, nt. 13.

[102] *IGUR* I 117 (= *CIL* VI 50 = *IG* XIV 969 = *IGRR* I 43 = *ILS* 4334); *IGUR* I 118 (= *CIL* VI 51 = *IG* XIV 970 = *IGRR* I 44). See Chausson (1995) 668/669 nrs. D, E; Schneider (1987) 70–72; Noy (2000) 243.

[103] *IGUR* I 120 (= *CIS* II 3904 = *IG* XIV 972 = *IGRR* I 46). See Chausson (1995) 669 nr. F; Schneider (1987) 73 with fig. 1.

[104] *IGUR* I 121. See Chausson (1995) 670 nr. F *bis*; Schneider (1987) 73/74 with fig. 2.

because of the phonetic resemblance; Arsû, often depicted as a cameleer, had a war-like quality but was mostly seen as the protector of desert caravans. For Palmyrenes he was therefore an important deity. In Palmyra he occupied one of the main temples, and in the Roman inscription the epithet 'ancestral' is applied to him ("Ἄρῃ θεῷ πατρῴῳ ἐπηκόῳ').[105] The dedication of the altar to Arsû is preceded by a wish of well-being to the Emperor Hadrian. The votary, L. Licinius Hermias, was in all likelihood a Palmyrene native; not only did he set up an altar to an ancestral god of Palmyra but the *nomen* Licinius is amply attested in the city (see also the C. Licinius N(—) mentioned above who, together with Heliodorus, had built a shrine to Bel).[106]

The last inscription from this find-location is written on an architrave-fragment. It mentions an Emperor who is not securely identifiable (Antoninus Pius?) and conceivably began with a wish for his well-being, analogous to the one on the altar to Arsû.[107] It further only mentions a Q. Iulius S(—) who presumably had the building erected of which the architrave formed an element. Unfortunately, we no longer know anything about this building other than that it was likely adorned somehow. The word 'decoration' ('[κό]ζμῳ') seems to appear in the inscription; the spelling with *zeta* could indicate a Syrian milieu. In this context, I should also not omit to mention an inscription that, though discovered far from the Vigna Bonelli, offers some evidence for a Palmyrene community in Rome. It is a second-century AD bilingual (Latin and Aramaic) grave stele found on the Via Appia commemorating Habibi, son of Annubath, from Palmyra.[108]

Many more inscriptions from Rome related to the worship of a Sun God, a Dea Syria, and other Semitic gods have been known since the fifteenth century but unfortunately their exact provenience is uncertain. Most belonged to the collection of Battista Giacomo Mattei, an avid collector of Roman inscriptions related to Semitic religions who owned land in Trastevere, south of Porta Portese. Given the location of his plot, there can be little doubt that a number of pieces from his collection were found

---

[105] *IGUR* I 122 (= *IG* XIV 962 = *IGRR* I 33). See Chausson (1995) 670 nr. G; Schneider (1987) 72 with nt. 20. On Arsû, see Starcky and Gawlikowski (1985) 102/103.

[106] Schneider (1987) 71/72.

[107] *IGUR* I 123 (= *IG* XIV 1035 = *IGRR* I 47): '[Καίσ]αρος Τίτου Αἰλίου Ἀδ[ριανοῦ]'. Note that in the transcription in *IGUR*, and in Chausson (1995) 671 nr. H, the word 'Αἰλίου' has accidentally been omitted.

[108] 'D.M. Habibi Annubathi f. Palmurenus'; *CIS* II 3905 (= *CIL* VI 19134). See Fabiani (1878).

in his own garden. Unfortunately, it is now impossible to tell how many or which ones. The inscriptions from the Mattei-collection should, in other words, be treated with a healthy dose of caution; in what follows I have singled out only the two that actually mention Palmyra.[109]

One of the finest pieces in the Mattei collection, now on display in the Capitoline Museums, is an altar with a somewhat mysterious iconography. On the front are carved an image of Sol, rays radiating from his head, on an eagle with outspread wings. The back has a cypress tree with a ribbon wound around its top, while a youth with a young goat on his shoulders is seen emerging from its branches. On the right-hand side is yet another image of the Sun God, this time mounting a chariot drawn by four griffins while a figure of Victory is in the act of crowning him with a palm wreath. The left-hand side shows a bust of Saturn, bearded and with his tunic drawn over his head, holding his characteristic sickle. The interpretation of the imagery is not easy, but a general consensus seems to have formed around seeing it as representing the departure of the rising sun conquering the darkness of night on its journey through the sky.[110]

The altar bears two inscriptions: one in Latin on the front and one in Palmyrene on the right-hand side.[111] The Latin text informs us that it was dedicated by Tiberius Claudius Felix, his wife Claudia Helpis, and their son Tiberius Alypus 'to the most sacred Sun' ('Soli sanctissimo'). The text in Palmyrene says: 'This is the altar which Tiberius Claudius Felix and the Palmyrenes offered to Malachbel and to the gods of Palmyra. To their gods. Peace'.[112] The fact that different names are given to the solar deity in the two inscriptions can be explained by interpreting the images on the front and on the right-hand side as representing two different manifestations of the Sun God. Malachbel in his chariot is the rising sun, while Sol on his eagle is the sun at its zenith, midway on its course through the skies. It is worth noting that we see the Latin name 'Sol' here in an unquestionably Semitic religious context, which strengthens the case for taking this altar

[109] Cf. Chausson who uses all inscriptions from the Mattei collection as evidence for the same sanctuary, arguing that Mattei ' "collectionnait" tout simplement les inscriptions que l'on trouvait dans un jardin lui appartenant'; Chausson (1995) 671/672 nt. 16. See also J. Calzini Gysens ([in: Steinby IV] 1999) 335; Savage (1940) 44 nt. 181.

[110] Schneider (1987) 74–78, with fig. 3–6. See also Savage (1940) 53, with plate 4, nrs. 1–4. Schneider emphasizes Malachbel's double role as god of the rising sun and as god of vegetation and agriculture.

[111] *CIL* VI 710 (= 30817 = *ILS* 4337 = *CIS* II 3903).

[112] I rely here on the translations given by Chausson (1995) 675 nr. N, and Noy (2000) 242/243.

and the inscriptions figuring Sol discussed earlier as belonging to one and the same Palmyrene cult.

That notion is strengthened further by the probable date of the altar. We cannot date it with any great precision by the content of the inscriptions, but its typology and the carving of its reliefs support the idea that it was manufactured in Flavian times or perhaps at the beginning of the second century.[113] If correct, that date would coincide with the archaeological information, most of all the information from the brick stamps found in the Vigna Bonelli; it could mean the altar was one of the oldest cultic objects in the Palmyrene temple. The inscriptions do not permit us to know whether this is true or not, but the Latin text does give us the precious bit of information that Felix and his family worked in the 'Horrea Galbana' ('Calbienses de co(horte) III'). These warehouses—founded probably by Ser. Sulpicius Galba, consul in 108 BC, and later renovated and enlarged by the Emperor Galba—were not only the earliest but also the most important ones in Rome. They stood right across the river from the Palmyrene temple in the harbor area of the 'emporium'. In and around the *horrea*, all sorts of goods changed hands; wine and oil arrived there in bulk, but we also know of a fishmonger, a merchant in marble, and a trader in woolen cloaks who had set up shop there.[114]

The second inscription appears on a carved marble plaque—about a meter in height, sixty-three centimeters in width—another choice piece from the Mattei collection, now also in the Capitoline Museums. The sculptural relief shows Malachbel holding hands with the lunar deity Aglibol.[115] The duo is represented standing upright and turning towards each other; Malachbel, on the left, is dressed in Syrian civilian garb while Aglibol, on the right, is holding a spear and is wearing a Roman-style cuirass; a crescent moon rises behind his shoulders. In the background between the two figures, a cypress tree is visible. A temple-like aedicula with pilasters and a tympanum frames the whole scene.

---

[113] Schneider (1987) 76. An alternative and, according to Schneider, less probable date is the early third century AD.

[114] The *horrea* staff were organized in *cohortes*, a word that in this case does not have a military connotation. Ancient sources on the commercial activities at the *horrea*: Horace *Carm.* 4,12,18 with Porphyrio ad loc.; *CIL* VI 9801, 33886, 33906, *CIL* XIV 20. On the *horrea* see especially Virlouvet (2006). See also 'Horrea Galbae/Galbana', F. Coarelli ([in: Steinby III] 1996) 40–42; Richardson (1992) 193; Platner and Ashby (1929) 261/262.

[115] See cover illustration. See also Schneider (1987) 82 fig. 13. The part showing the gods' interlocking hands is a later restoration; behind the handshake, and partly obscured by it, Malachbel is holding an object (a book scroll?) in his left hand (personal observations).

An inscription in Greek and Palmyrene identifying the divinities runs along the bottom of the tablet; the Greek version marks them 'gods of the fatherland' ('πατρῴοις θεοῖ[ς]').[116] The text in both cases states that the stone commemorates a dedication made by Iulius Aurelius Heliodorus from Palmyra; the Palmyrene text just gives his unromanized Semitic name: Iarhai. Apparently, he had presented Malachbel and Aglibol with a silver statue ('σίγνον ἀργυροῦν') and all its decoration, spelled 'κόζμῳ' in Greek (compare the architrave from the Vigna Bonelli), paid for with his own money. The objective of his generosity is also given: 'for the health of himself, his wife, and their children' ('ὑπὲρ σωτηρίας αὐτοῦ καὶ τ(ῆς) συμβίου καὶ τ(ῶν) τέκνων'). We can date the event quite precisely to February 236 AD, that is to say during the reign of the Emperor Maximinus. Since a commemorative plaque with a bilingual inscription was made to mark the occasion, it seems likely that both plaque and silver statue (a figure of Malachbel? Aglibol? Heliodorus himself?) were meant to be placed not in a private but in a (semi)public space. Given the cultic nature of the objects, the Palmyrene temple in Trastevere is a likely candidate. If correct, that would mean the temple was still standing and functioning as a communal building in at least 236 AD, some hundred-and-fifty years after it was originally built.[117]

It is beyond doubt that Palmyra played a role as a hub bringing products from China and India to the markets of the Roman Empire.[118] But although it seems likely that the Palmyrene building in Rome was a *statio* connected to these mercantile routes, in most accounts on *stationes* it is not included. The reason for this omission is probably that little information is available on the associates' occupation, and also that the emphasis in the epigraphy is heavily on religious and not on mercantile matters. However, a comparison with other Palmyrene trading stations does indeed suggest it was essentially a commercial institution.

Trading communities of Palmyrenes resident in foreign cities are a well-documented phenomenon; in the epigraphic record they can be traced east across the Tigris and Euphrates river-basin all the way to the Persian Gulf.[119] A good example and possible parallel to the Roman community

---

116 *IGUR* I 119 (= *IG* XIV 917 = *IGGR* I 45 = *CIS* II 3902). Chausson (1995) 677/678 nr. O.

117 Borsari (1887) 95 suggests the the temple area was abandoned and used as a funerary space after Aurelian built a new temple to the Sun God on the Quirinal.

118 Gawlikowski (1996); (see also the articles by Will and Stauffer in the same volume); Starcky and Gawlikowski (1985) 73–81; Matthews (1984) 164–170.

119 Gawlikowski (1996) 142–145 with a list of the epigraphic evidence and with a map.

is provided by the Palmyrenes living in Vologesias, a city on the Euphrates River south of Babylon. From an inscription, close in date to the one recording the addition of a *triclia* to the temple in Rome, we know that Palmyrenes resident in Vologesias possessed a similar building there. In 108 AD they erected a statue in Palmyra to honor their benefactor Aqqiah, son of Nuhrai, to thank him for building them a temple, a cultic fire-altar, and a roof for their ritual banqueting hall.[120] The structure in Vologesias too, in other words, seems to have consisted of a sanctuary and a communal space for social gatherings.

The fact that the Roman building facilitated both religious activities and other communal activities like dining may be the reason it seems to have been larger than the *stationes* we have seen so far. This might also be the reason it was not located prominently in the heart of the city. The rules concerning the *pomerium* dictated—nominally at least—that temples to foreign gods had to be situated outside Rome's sacred boundaries.[121] But whether or not this inference is correct, even though the word *statio* is never used in the Palmyrene inscriptions, the important elements are that Palmyrenes, at least some demonstrably involved in trading, storing, and moving goods, were organized to the degree that for generations they maintained a collective building in Rome. Differences in detail notwithstanding, this is a phenomenon, well-known from groups of traders in both Puteoli and Ostia. The location of the structure near the Roman harbor-area lends further support to the view that it served primarily a mercantile organization.[122]

Syrians in Rome

No single piece of evidence can positively be identified as belonging to a building in Rome used and maintained by specifically people from Tyre, although we know for a fact that there was one. However, apart from Palmyrenes there is abundant evidence for other Syrians in the city.

---

[120] *Inv.* IX 15 (= *CIS* II 3917). See Starcky and Gawlikowski (1985) 75/76; I rely here on their discussion of the Palmyrene text; the extant Greek version has only two lines and does not give this information. For the Palmyrene trading community in Vologesias, see also Matthews (1984) 166–168; Gawlikowski (1996) 142 nr. 14; Bang (2008) 253–259.

[121] This rule seems to have existed throughout Republican times, but it was certainly reinforced by Augustus; Beard, North and Price (1998) vol. 1, 180. The idea that the boundaries of the *pomerium* explained the temple's location was already proposed by Visconti (1860) 431.

[122] In that sense also Schneider (1987) 69/70.

The Damasceni and the Seleucenses, for instance, honored the consul M. Licinius Crassus Frugi around 14 BC, probably as their patron. About two decades later the Seleucenses erected what seems to have been a monument to the imperial family.[123] These honorific dedications were donated by the cities themselves, though, and are not necessarily evidence for Syrians resident in Rome. Cultic structures provide better evidence in that respect.

Syrian deities are attested in a number of locations in the city. Jupiter Dolichenus for instance, whose worship originated in Doliche in northern Syria, had several shrines or sanctuaries. Many of Dolichenus' followers were found among the military—the cult was widespread in the Rhine-Danube frontier zone—and unsurprisingly two of his Roman shrines have military contexts: one was situated in or near the barracks of the imperial cavalry guard, the other, close-by on the Esquiline Hill, was used by soldiers of the watch. His temple on the Aventine Hill however, probably the best documented temple of Dolichenus in the Roman world, apparently attracted an exclusively civilian audience; it is not known if the cult was open only to Syrians, but the lists of initiates do show a large number of men with Greek and Semitic names.[124] Multi-ethnic or not, the dedications certainly suggest that the adherents formed a 'tightly knit group, with a complex hierarchy'.[125]

In Trastevere two smaller sanctuaries of Dolichenus also existed. One near the Ponte Cestio consisted of a marble altar, still visible in the 1500s but long since vanished, dedicated to 'Jupiter Dolichenus the best and greatest', 'Iovi O(ptimo) M(aximo) Dolicheno'. Other epigraphic discoveries confirm that the area around the altar was a cultic center of sorts.[126] The other sanctuary must have been located a bit further south near the church of S. Maria dell'Orto, where a travertine base was unearthed, also dedicated to Jupiter Dolichenus. Other inscriptions found in the area employ terms that suggest a building ('porticus', 'cella', 'culina', 'maceria')

---

[123] Alföldy (1992) 77–93; *CIL* VI 40313. Monuments probably set up in the 'Porticus ad Nationes' (to be identified with both the 'Porticus Lentulorum' and the 'Hecatostylum'; F. Coarelli ([in: Steinby IV] 1999) 138/139; S. Orlandi ([in: Steinby IV] 1999) 125/126; F. Coarelli ([in: Steinby III] 1996) 9/10.

[124] *CIL* VI 366, 406–413, 30758–30761.

[125] Beard, North and Price (1998) vol. 1, 275, 294, 301 with map 2 nrs. 7, 8, 12. See also Noy (2000) 244/245; the entries by L. Chioffi and P. Chini ([in: Steinby III] 1996) 133/134; Platner and Ashby (1929) 292; La Piana (1927) 313/314.

[126] Altar: *CIL* VI 418, (with notes on p. 3005, 3756). Other finds: *CIL* VI 116, 117, (with notes on p. 3003, 3755); *CIL* VI 1118; *CIL* VI 10117, (with note on p. 3906). See L. Chioffi ([in: Steinby III] 1996) 132.

indicating that in this case too the base may have belonged to a fairly substantial religious center.[127] Both locations are in the general vicinity of the temple to the Palmyrene gods, and this quarter of the city (the Augustan *Regio* XIV) seems to have borne a noticeable stamp of Syrian religions. Given the geographic and socio-economic position of this sector of Rome—'Transtiberim', likely always outside the *pomerium*, close to the harbors, known for its heavy immigrant influence—this characteristic is not all that surprising.[128]

A much more elaborate affair than the shrines down below in Trastevere was the temple to an array of Syrian gods, halfway up the Janiculum Hill. Excavations conducted on the site between 1906–09 and 1981–82 showed it went through a number of distinct architectural phases. Faint traces of an enclosure or building dating to the latter half of the first century AD may represent the temple's earliest manifestation, although next to nothing is known about this phase. An intricately carved altar, dedicated to Zeus Ceraunius by a certain Artemis from Cyprus and possibly connected to the earliest building, might suggests the temple was associated with Syrian cults already at this date. Two other alters found at the site, one dedicated to Hadad Libaneotes the other to Jupiter Maleciabrudes, both show a connection to the Lebanon (Iabruda being the name of a town in the Antilebanon).[129]

Much more substantial remains turned up of a structure, similar in outline and orientation to the previous one, built in the 170s AD. Based on the epigraphic evidence it would seem that this temple, a modestly sized building but adorned with exquisite decoration, was dedicated exclusively to Jupiter Heliopolitanus.[130] However, Heliopolitanus—like Jupiter Maleciabrudes, Hadad Libaneotes, and (to a lesser degree) Zeus Ceraunius—has an unmistakable relation to the Lebanon and more specifically to Berytus. A group of Berytian settlers, it will be remembered, worshipped Jupiter Heliopolitanus in Puteoli. Federico de Romanis has, in my view

---

[127] Base: *CIL* VI 415. Other inscriptions: *CIL* VI 75, 881, 2219, 2220. See L. Chioffi ([in: Steinby III] 1996) 134/135.

[128] M. Maischberger ([in: Steinby V] 1999) 77–83. See also Savage (1940). One *pomerium cippus* (*CIL* VI 31538c) was found in Trastevere under the church of S. Cecilia. However, it was reused there, and was not in its original position.

[129] *CIL* VI 36802 (= *IGUR* I 111), 36803 (= *IGUR* I 110), 36792. See Calzini Gysens (1996) 264–269; Savage (1940) 50. The dedication to Zeus Ceraunius includes a dedication to the 'Phorrine Nymphs', showing the site was tied to Roman tradition, and was also sacred to indigenous Roman spirits; see Beard, North and Price (1998) vol. 1, 283.

[130] *CIL* VI 420 (= 30764 = 36749 = *IGUR* I 166), 423, 36791, 36793. See J. Calzini Gysens ([in: Steinby III] 1996) 138.

convincingly, argued that the Roman building should therefore not be seen as chronologically housing a succession of Syrian deities but should throughout this phase be seen as a place of worship for people from Berytus.[131] If so, colonists from that city for centuries maintained a cultic place in Rome for all the gods from their area, a situation that lasted at least until the reign of Gordian III (242–244).

Interestingly, the temple's vicissitudes form a close reflection of Rome's religious development. The building was destroyed sometime in the mid-fourth century (likely in consequence of the imperial edicts of 341 AD by Constans and Constantius II, banning pagan rites) but re-erected shortly after, probably during the reign of Julian ('the Apostate') when the religious climate was more favorable again to non-Christian cults. Julian's reign and religious reform being but short-lived, the temple was abandoned soon after (during the last third of the fourth century) apparently in great haste and suffering violence; its walls were torn down and covered over with earth. Unfortunately, it is unclear what deities were venerated in the temple during this short final period. No inscriptions from this last phase remain, and the cultic objects that came to light (many still *in situ* due to the rapid abandonment and destruction) show a large degree of religious syncretism, incorporating elements from mystery cults, Dionysiastic rites, and Egyptian religion. Part of a human skull buried beneath the floor of the eastern *cella* may even betray illegal human sacrifice.[132]

A direct link can be established between the Roman sanctuary and the town of Ostia. In Portus, the Ostian harbor area, a certain Gaionas had set up a dedication to Heliopolitanus for the safety of the Emperors Marcus Aurelius and Commodus (see Chapter 3). The very same Gaionas was a prominent contributor to the temple in Rome. He is known from five Roman inscriptions, four of which are associated with the temple; the fifth is his epitaph. In 176 AD he donated a marble table (in the fourth-century structure reused as a threshold) as a gift 'for the safety and return and victory' of Marcus Aurelius and Commodus.[133] Ten years later he set up a marble column dedicated to Heliopolitanus and to Commodus;

---

[131] De Romanis (2008). Zeus Ceraunius was not a Berytian deity; his cult, though attested in Syria, was mainly to be found in Cition, Cyprus. However, De Romanis argues that the strong maritime ties between Cition and Berytus explain the Ceraunius dedication.

[132] J. Calzini Gysens ([in: Steinby III] 1996) 139–143; Savage (1940) 47–49; Platner and Ashby (1929) 294–296; La Piana (1927) 314–317. Cf. Ch.J. Goddard ([in: La Regina II] 2004) 278–284 who argues that the building in its last phase was a Serapeum.

[133] *CIL* VI 36793 'pro salute et reditu et victoria imperatorum'.

a limestone column without a precise date bears a similar dedication.[134] In his epitaph, Gaionas describes himself as '*cistiber*', a title of which he was evidently proud since he flaunted it also in the other three inscriptions.[135] Finally, a somewhat mysterious marble slab with a hole in the middle and bearing a cryptic inscription was a gift from Gaionas 'so that it might supply sacrifice to the gods'.[136] The hole has been variously interpreted as either intended to hold a water spout or a ring for tying a sacrificial animal.

Gaionas, without much doubt of Syrian origin, had moved to Italy permanently, settling either in Ostia or more likely in Rome where he seems to have been well-integrated. The meaning of his title of *cistiber* is debated, although probably it denoted a minor office involving responsibilities for night-time security and fire patrol.[137] But whatever its precise significance, it was probably a sort of honorary title and not Gaionas' actual profession. It is often assumed that he was a merchant, but although this is an attractive hypothesis there is no way for us to know for certain.[138] The honorary column to the Emperors he set up in Portus could well be an sign that he had some business down in the harbors, but if he did, the accompanying inscription does not tell us of what nature.

The Western Provinces and Africa

As in Puteoli and Ostia, so in Rome associations of traders from the West are far less visible in our sources. However, traces of such organizations are definitely to be found in the epigraphic material. I will conclude this chapter with a quick survey of the evidence.

From one inscription we learn of an organization of Baetican oil traders operating in Rome: 'negotiatores oleari ex Baetica'. In the mid-second century they honored their patron whose impressive career included the

---

[134] *IGUR* I 166 (= *CIL* VI 420 = 30764 = 36749); Duthoy and Frel (1996) 294 (not previously published).

[135] *IGUR* III 1157 (= *CIL* VI 32316).

[136] *IGUR* I 109 (= *CIL* VI 36804), 'Δεσμὸς ὅπως κρατερὸς θῦμα θεοῖς παρέχοι ὃν δὴ Γαιωνᾶς δειπνοκρίτης ἔθετο'. See Noy (2000) 241 nr. 3; Savage (1940) 36/37.

[137] The other possibility is to read *cistiber* as *cistifer*; a bearer of a *cista* in religious rites. See Beard, North and Price (1998) vol. 1, 292; Moretti's note to *IGUR* I 166; Savage (1940) 37 with note 104.

[138] See Noy (2000) 240–242 who rightly signals (note 303, referring to Duthoy and Frel [1996] 293) that claims about Gaionas such as 'a Heliopolitan, whose family was well established at Rome for at least one generation' are unfounded.

prefecture of the *annona* and the prefecture of Egypt.[139] The Baetican oil merchant L. Marius Phoebus—in all likelihood the same man who appears in the '*tituli* β' amphorae stamps from Monte Testaccio, dating from the mid-second century AD—may have been a member.[140] Phoebus was, according to his grave stele, also attached as a clerk to an office of the imperial government.[141] The text of his epitaph only gives 'Baetica' as his place of origin ('mercatori olei Hispani ex provincia Baetica'). We have already seen such a reference, alluding not to a city but to a whole province as a marker of geographical identity, in the inscription by the *stationarius* from Noricum, and probably also in the room used by people from M(auretania) C(aesariensis) on the Ostian 'piazzale'. This practice is especially common in inscriptions from the Spanish peninsula, which almost as a rule mention a region or province ('Hispania', 'Lusitania', 'Baetica') frequently, but by no means always, followed by a town or city.[142]

An inscription that does refer to a Spanish city was set up by an association of traders from Malaca: 'corpus negotiantium Malacitanorum'.[143] Since Malaca was located in the province of Baetica and since the inscription probably also dates to the mid-second century, the conclusion can only be that the Baetican oil merchants and the Malacitani employed their activities alongside each other. This could mean that there was some flexibility in organizational composition and that traders sometimes operated in larger 'umbrella' associations, while also being organized in smaller ones according to their respective hometowns. Alternatively, the type of trade determined organizational adherence; conceivably the Malacitani traded in different goods than the Baetican oil merchants. A prominent official ('quinqennalis corporis') of this organization, P. Clodius Athenio, was himself a merchant in salted provisions ('negotians salsarius'), and the entire organization which he presided over may have been involved

139 *CIL* VI 1625b. Panciera (1980) 243/244; Waltzing vol. 4 (1900) 35 nr. 106. Though unconnected to trade, the Spanish towns honoring the senator L. Aelius Lamia as their patron around 22 BC perhaps also deserve mention in this context. Alföldy (1992) 113–123.

140 Phoebus alone: *CIL* XV 3943–3948. Phoebus with others: *CIL* XV 3949–3959. See Panciera (1980) 245.

141 *CIL* VI 1935. Phoebus' title as a clerk: 'viatori tribunicio decuriae maioris'. Compare the inscription discussed by Panciera (1980) 242, 245: 'viatori apparitor[i] Augustor[um] diffusori [olear(io)] ex Baetica'. Because of Phoebus' duties as a clerk, Noy rules him out as a native Baetican. Noy (2000) 269 nt. 41. However the words 'ex provincia Baetica' in Phoebus' epitaph seem most logically to refer to Phoebus himself, not to 'olei Hispani'.

142 Noy (2000) 209/210 has a list of the Roman evidence.

143 *CIL* VI 9677. See Noy (2000) 208; La Piana (1927) 264; Waltzing vol. 2 (1896) 108, vol. 4 (1900) 33/34 nr. 98.

in the trade in salt or pickled products; Malaca, according to Strabo, had big installations for salting fish.[144]

The organization of Baetican oil traders had a local curator in Rome, a certain C. Sentius Regulianus, a Roman knight.[145] We have already encountered curators of shipping—of Carthaginian ships and of ships sailing on the Adriatic Sea—in the evidence from Ostia; the *collegium* from the Adriatic, in fact, had a curator in Rome as well.[146] Although we do not know what the tasks of these curators were, it seems logical they were charged somehow with providing local facilities for foreign ships and for their crews and cargo. That Regulianus was somehow supposed to handle the oil the Baetican merchants brought in is suggested by his title of *diffusor olearius*. No consensus exists on what that term means in general, but in this particular context it most likely denotes a distributor who repackaged the oil into smaller containers.[147]

The only extant inscription from Rome mentioning a group of African traders is the honorary inscription which the African grain and oil merchants, 'mercatores frumentari et oleari Afrari', set up to C. Iunius Flavianus.[148] Flavianus seems to have had no ties whatsoever to Africa; if anything, he was strongly associated with Gaul and Spain. The list of his former positions includes the procuratorship of the provinces of Lugdunensis and Aquitanica, the procuratorship of Hispania citerior, and the procuratorship of the Alpes maritimae. However, he was also (or had been) prefect of the *annona*, which may explain the Africans' dedication. It is noteworthy that the group that set up the inscription comprised a large number of people: all the African grain traders and all the African oil merchants. This seems far too large a group to have been a viable mercantile organization, able to manage its membership and exercise control over the behavior of its members. It seems more likely that in this instance the Africans cooperated solely for the purpose of donating an

---

[144] Strabo 3,4,2 '... Μάλακα ... ταριχείας ἔχει μεγάλας'.

[145] *CIL* VI 29722.

[146] *CIL* VI 9682: 'L. Scribonio Ianuario negotianti vinario item naviculario cur(atori) corporis maris Hadriatici'. See Waltzing vol. 4 (1900) 34 nr. 103.

[147] The *OLD* describes a *diffusor* as 'one who draws off (into smaller vessels), a "bottler"'. Another interpretation sees *diffusor* as essentially equivalent to *mercator* and *negotiator*, but that seems an unlikely meaning at least in this case because Regulianus is in the same inscription also described as a *negotiator*; there seems here to be a difference between the two terms. See Panciera (1980) 241–243. The recent discovery in Seville of an honorary inscription to a 'diffusori olei ad annon[am]' has led to a novel theory holding that a *diffusor* was a high official supplying the imperial *annona*. See Étienne (2003).

[148] *CIL* VI 1620.

honorary inscription, similar to the inscription set up by 'all the African and the Sardinian shipmasters' found in Ostia.[149] This could be seen as a sign of the organizational flexibility and cooperation in larger 'umbrella' organizations I mentioned earlier. A hint of this flexibility was also visible in the pediment with the words 'naviculari Africani' found on the Ostian 'piazzale', a space that also accommodated many smaller groups from African cities.[150]

Conclusion

People came to Rome for all sorts of reasons: the opportunities of a political career attracted some, others were brought over willy-nilly as slaves, others still arrived as soldiers or as envoys. But although it is impossible to quantify how many, undoubtedly a good number came over for reasons of trade. Focusing on that segment of Rome's foreign inhabitants, I tested my hypothesis, built on the Puteolan and Ostian evidence, that intercommunity exchange operated through provenance-based networks.

Two main locations in Rome are generally thought to have housed communal structures used by foreign immigrants: the Forum Iulium and the Sacra Via. I argued that the hypothesis of the *stationes municipiorum* on the Forum Iulium as diplomatic posts is unfounded; more likely they were mercantile institutions. The second location along the Sacra Via provides much more substantial evidence. I argued that, seen in their archaeological context, the buildings there are best seen as mercantile stations rather than temples or status symbols. Although they are often treated as a separate species of *statio*, different from the ones on the Forum Iulium, the evidence does not support that view; the modern label of 'stationes exterarum civitatum', by implication, does not have any use or justification.

Structures maintained in Rome by provincials are usually designated with the term *statio* in the scholarly literature, a practice which, for reasons of clarity and convenience, I have largely followed. However, although the word *statio* is significant, I have focused not on that word but on broader institutional similarities. Arguing that *stationes* could be found elsewhere in the city as well, I have shown that the Roman evidence shares the basic characteristics with the data discussed in the previous two chapters: groups of traders from distant communities organized themselves along

149 'domini navium Afrarum universarum item Sardorum', *CIL* XIV 4142. See Chapter 3.
150 Bloch (1953) 285, nr. 44.

lines of geographical provenance; some of their members settled in Rome. These groups had ties locally: they had local patrons and local curators; at least a number of them maintained a communal building, sometimes with a religious function. Despite the differences between the metropolis of Rome on the one hand and the harbor towns of Puteoli and Ostia on the other, in this respect the picture that emerged is fundamentally the same in all three cases.

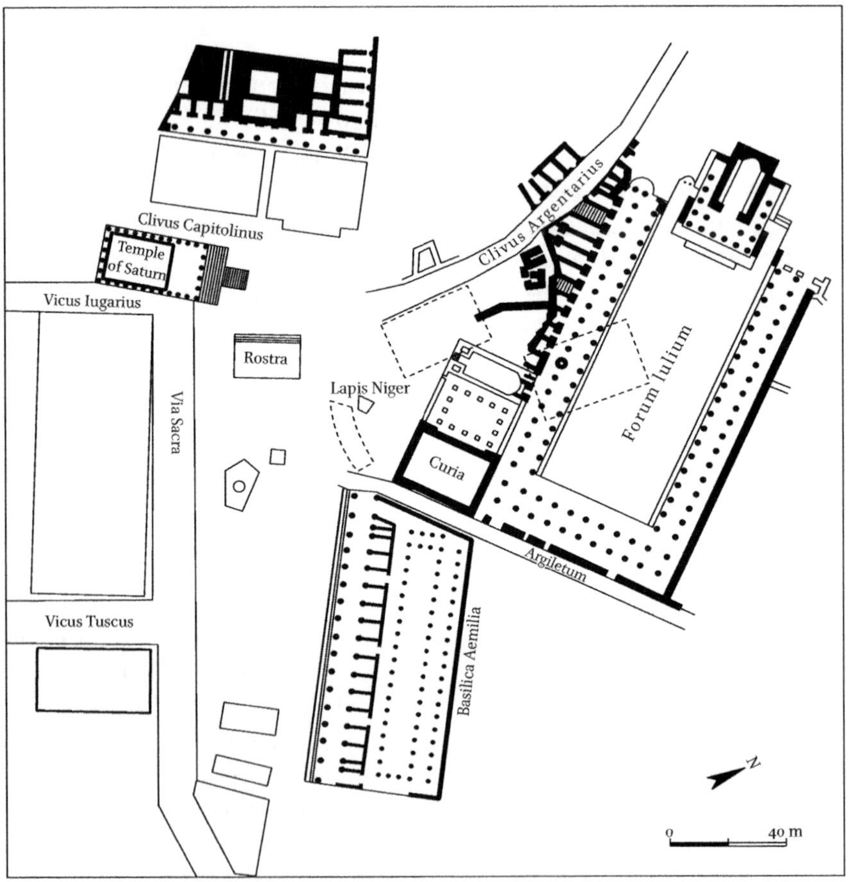

Figure 2. Forum Iulium and Clivus Argentarius.
Reproduced by permission from DER NEUE PAULY. Band 4. Epo-Gro.
Hubert Cancik and Helmuth Schneider. S. 605–606.

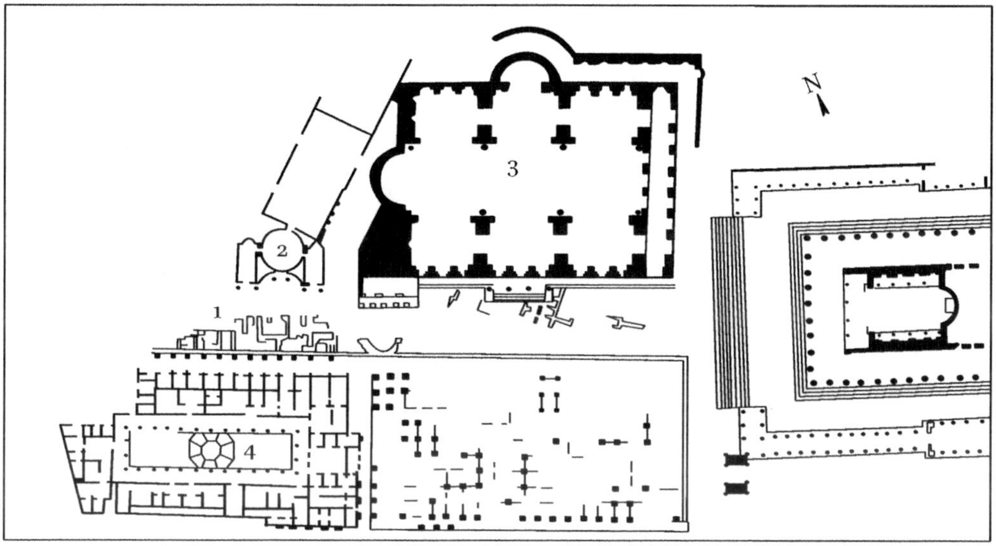

Figure 3. Nr. 1: *Stationes* on the Sacra Via, 2: 'Temple of Romulus', 3: Basilica Nova, 4: Atrium Vestae.
Reproduced by permission from DER NEUE PAULY. Band 12/2. Ven-Z. Nachträge. Hubert Cancik and Helmuth Schneider. S. 1153–1154.

CHAPTER FIVE

ROMAN TRADERS IN THE PROVINCE OF ASIA

The Roman East as a Case-Study

Of all Verres' enormities, Cicero inveighed, one was surely the worst: that he had condemned a Roman citizen to the Syracusan stone quarries and, after the man briefly escaped, had him flogged in public and then crucified. This abominable treatment of a citizen, Cicero went on, counted as an offense not just against one man but against the sanctity of citizenship itself and hence against the whole Roman citizen body. To underscore his point he added: 'Poor men of humble birth sail across the seas to shores they have never seen before, where they find themselves among strangers, and cannot always have acquaintances to vouch for them. Yet such trust have they in the single fact of their citizenship that they count on being safe, not only where they find our magistrates, ... and not only among their own countrymen ...: no wherever they find themselves, they feel confident that this one fact will be their defence'.[1]

Cicero's accusation here, obviously, was that Verres as governor of Sicily had betrayed the trust Romans overseas should rightfully have in the protective powers of their legal status. However, did Roman merchants of low social station really regularly set sail for the horizon, counting on their legal status to protect them from all harm, even on the most alien of shores? Perhaps we have to allow for some exaggeration here. But more interesting than Cicero's rhetorical figures is his mention of Roman magistrates and communities of Roman citizens overseas; more interesting still is his implicit assumption that shippers did indeed usually have 'acquaintances to vouch for them'.

[1] The story of the maltreated citizen Publius Gavius: Cicero II *Verres* 5,158–170; citation 167: 'Homines tenues, obscuro loco nati, navigant, adeunt ad ea loca quae numquam antea viderunt, ubi neque noti esse iis quo venerunt, neque semper cum cognitoribus esse possunt. Hac una tamen fiducia civitatis non modo apud nostros magistratus, ... neque apud cives solum Romanos, ... fore se tutos arbitrantur, sed quocumque venerint hanc sibi rem preasidio sperant futuram'. Tr.: L.H.G. Greenwood, Loeb (1935). N.B.: Greenwood translates 'have acquaintances *with them* to vouch for them', but the passage makes more logical sense this way. See also Bang (2008) 239–241.

In this chapter I will be addressing a question that naturally follows from the discussions in the previous ones, namely: were there Roman trading communities in cities overseas, comparable to those of provincials in Italian cities (the mirrored situation, that is, from the one looked at so far)? If immigrants came to Puteoli, Ostia, and Rome as part of provenance-based trade networks, were Romans living abroad for the same reason? A treatment that spans the entire Empire is not feasible in one chapter, so I will have to limit myself to a case-study.

In its heyday as an emporium, Roman Delos housed a large Italian community, and despite the problems I outlined in my introduction, for this particular study the island might still seem a well-suited subject. However, settlers of Italian origin were so numerous there that they outnumbered any remaining resident Delians and probably also the resident Athenians.[2] Because I am looking for Romans integrating into local communities overseas, gaining trust there for purposes of trade, this imbalance between the Italian and the original Greek population makes Delos a less than ideal case-study even for this chapter.

The territory I have selected instead is the province of Asia, in particular the area around the cities of Ephesus, Tralles, and Apamea. A number of reasons motivate this choice. First of all, there is a relative abundance of evidence on Asia in general. We possess many helpful literary texts on the province and its governance, for example through the correspondence of Cicero with his brother Quintus. The area also has been, and even continues to be, somewhat of an epigraphic treasure trove. In 1976, for instance, a lengthy inscription was discovered in Ephesus that has greatly enhanced our understanding of key aspects (economic, geographical, as well as historical) of the creation of the province. This 'Customs law of Asia', as it is now mostly referred to, was set up in Ephesus in 62 AD, and consists of a chronological aggregate of laws going back almost two centuries.[3]

Second, the route between Ephesus and Apamea was of major mercantile significance. Ephesus was one of the most important harbors in the Empire, and seaborne trade played a critical role in the city's economy, a situation that predated the arrival of the Romans.[4] Despite the continuous problem of silting the Ephesian harbor experienced, it seems that

---

[2] See Rauh (1993) and esp. Errington (1988) 144/145. See also Roussel (1916) 75–84.

[3] Recently published with revised text and extensive commentary by Cottier and Crawford (2008). More below.

[4] Strabo 14,1,24. Already in the mid-second century BC, King Attalus II Philadelphos (159–138 BC) had his engineers renovate the port facilities.

from at least the days of Strabo, if not earlier, it formed the city's main source of revenue. The 'Customs law of Asia' places the city in a list of seaports where harbor dues were levied. The paragraph that gives the list contains the oldest laws dating to 120s BC, the time just after the annexation of the area as a province by Rome.[5] This early taxation indicates that Ephesus saw a large volume of goods move through its port already at the time of its incorporation into the Empire. The city apparently continued to be an important harbor throughout imperial times. In Diocletian's 'Edict on Maximum Prices' the sea-route from Nicomedia to Ephesus is included, suggesting it saw much traffic (which may also have to do with the increased political importance of Nicomedia under the Tetrarchy); the shipping lane from Alexandria to Ephesus is also listed.[6]

As to the nature of the goods that passed through Ephesus: although much about the organization of the Roman slave trade remains murky to us, literary sources as well as the epigraphic record suggest that Ephesus started playing a role as a hub in this trade. An inscription from about 42/43 AD, for example, honors a now anonymous man, possibly C. Sallustius Crispus Passienus, a Roman consul; the dedicators were slave traders.[7] In an inscription from some fifty years later, a high Roman official, Tib. Claudius Secundus, is also honored as a benefactor by the 'association of Ephesians who do business in the slave market' ('civitas Ephesiorum qui in statario negotiantur').[8] But apart from slaves, a wide variety of other merchandise moved through the city. If there is anything to the suggestion that the author of *Revelation* was closely affiliated with Ephesus, and that *Rev.* 18:12/13 was inspired by the goods he saw in transit there, the passage may show us a glimpse of the richness and diversity of that trade.[9]

Going east from Ephesus, a road ran along the Maeander River continuing into the interior all the way to Apamea (hugging the central Anatolian

---

[5] Cottier and Crawford (2008) 35/36, line 22–26, §9; commentary 110–112.

[6] *Edict*, ch. 37, line 8, 39 (also line 20: from the diocese of Oriens to Ephesus); Lauffer (1971) 201/202. See also Levick (2004) 185. The number of ships sailing to the city probably declined surprisingly early. Archaeological explorations uncovered part of the harbor's southern quayside and a jetty sticking out at a right angle to the quay. A late antique house, dated to around 400 AD, appeared to have been built at the junction of the quay and the jetty, effectively blocking access in all directions. Already by that time, if not earlier, a major part of the Ephesian harbor had silted up, and had become inoperable. See Zabehlicky (1995).

[7] *I.Eph.* III, 3025. See Harris (1980) 127, 130.

[8] *I.Eph.* III, 646. Secundus was an official with a variety of duties; he is described as 'viatori tribunicio', 'accenso velato', and 'lictori curiato'.

[9] Zabehlicky (1995) 212/213.

plateau), passing through Tralles (see fig. 4).[10] In Roman times this was one of the main overland trade arteries to the East, and the cities on the road were important links on this commercial route. The first place of note traveling eastward from Ephesus to Apamea is Magnesia on the Maeander, some twenty kilometers inland. I will briefly include the evidence from this city, mostly because there is some indication that a Puteolan *gens* was active there. Tralles is situated some twenty-five kilometers further inland still from Magnesia, on a fork in the road where one branch led east to Apamea, the other south to the Lycian coast via Alabanda and Stratonicea. Because of its location at a junction, it was an important station on the road.[11]

Decidedly of greater commercial importance, however, was the next big city, Apamea. Dio Chrysostom, in a speech delivered there, stressed the city's commercial ties with both East and West: '...you stand as a bulwark in front of Phrygia and Lydia and Caria besides; and there are other tribes around you whose members are more numerous,...and for them all your city constitutes a market and a place of meeting.'[12] Several ancient authors refer to Apamea as 'ἡ Κιβωτός' ('chest'), and the legend 'κιβωτοί' is found on Hadrianic coins from the city (also bearing a representation of five chests). Apamea probably earned this moniker because of its commercial importance and because of the large number of goods—packed in chests—that moved through the city.[13] Strabo, for sure, described Apamea as a great emporium of Asia, ranking second only to Ephesus. He gives the precious bit of information that goods from Italy found their way there, calling the city 'a common entrepôt for the merchandise from both Italy and Greece'.[14]

---

[10] Mitchell (1999) 19–21 (with map); Wilson (1966) 122–124 (with map). See Strabo 14,2,29 for a description of the road-network in western Asia.

[11] Tralles, an old city founded before Hellenistic times, flourished under the Pergamene Kings who built a royal residence there. In the first century BC it was a 'centre of wealth and culture'. Magie (1950) 129/130. In 26 AD, Tiberius passed it over as too insignificant for the construction of a temple though; Tacitus *Ann.* 4,55. See Broughton (1938) 723/724.

[12] Dio Chrysostom *Or.* 35,14. Tr.: J.W. Cohoon and H. Lamar Crosby, Loeb (1940). 'τῆς τε Φρυγίας προκάθησθε καὶ Λυδίας, ἔτι δὲ Καρίας, ἄλλα τε ἔθνη περιοικεῖ πολυανδρότατα,...καὶ τούτοις ἅπασιν ἀγορὰν ὑμεῖς καὶ ξύνοδον παρέχεσθε τὴν αὑτῶν πόλιν'. See also Wilson (1966) 137, 140.

[13] Apamea named Cibotos: Strabo 12,6,4; 12,8,13; Ptolemy 5,2,25; Pliny *NH* 5,106. An alternative explanation for the name is that it refers to a legend according to which Mt. Celanae should be identified with Mt. Ararat, where the biblical Ark rested after the flood. See Magie (1950) 983/984.

[14] Strabo 12,8,15. Tr.: H.L. Jones, Loeb (1928). 'αὕτη γὰρ καὶ τῶν ἀπὸ τῆς Ἰταλίας καὶ τῆς Ἑλλάδος ὑποδοχεῖον κοινόν ἐστιν'. See Wilson (1966) 124, 131–133; Broughton (1938) 860–864; Levick (2004) 184.

Looking for organizations of Roman merchants along this route seems a logical choice based on all of this evidence. In the case of Ephesus and Tralles, there is the added reason that we have encountered them before. We have seen Ephesus in Puteoli where it was one of the cities mentioned on the statue-base honoring Tiberius, and in Rome where Ephesian traders seem to have had a *statio*, courtesy of their expatriate city-member Domesticus. The city of Tralles too had a *statio* in Rome on the Sacra Via, donated by the Trallian lady Galene. We know, therefore, that the Ephesians and Trallians were familiar with the concept of maintaining *stationes*.

The main question addressed in this chapter is: was a comparable Roman phenomenon to be found in Asia? That many Romans moved east is not in doubt. We know that the last two centuries BC especially saw a large movement of Romans in that direction, and this migratory process has been extensively studied. Much of the evidence is epigraphic in nature, but our literary sources as well leave little question that in the early first century BC there were large numbers of Roman civilians living in the East. The ancient authors may have greatly inflated the number of Romans slain during the Mithridatic War for rhetorical effect (no fewer than 150,000, according to Plutarch), but such rhetoric could only work if it was grounded at least partly in fact.[15] That many of these people went eastward for reasons of trade can be seen in the way they presented themselves in inscriptions; they referred to their communities as, in Latin, 'Italici...' or 'cives Romani qui... negotiantur' or, in Greek, 'οἱ πραγματευόμενοι Ῥωμαῖοι'.[16] In line with that aspect of the evidence, I will try to argue that Roman trade organizations similar to the trading coalitions I have discussed in the previous chapters did indeed exist in Asia.

However, in this chapter I will also be highlighting an important difference. By the time the province of Asia was created, Rome was the unquestionably mightiest state in the Mediterranean, an aspect not to be ignored when studying the social position of Roman settlers. As part of her imperial agenda Rome sent over officials who were, among other things, charged with administering the law. This meant Roman law, a system alien to the Greco-Hellenistic world, which points to a key difference with the Italian

---

15 Plutarch *Sulla* 24,4. Valerius Maximus (9,2,ext.3) and Memnon (31,4) put the number at 80,000. See Magie (1950) 217, 1103.

16 See Hatzfeld (1919) *passim*.

situation.[17] I argued in Chapter 1 that Roman law was the default system for economic interaction and conflict resolution in Puteoli, the result of a path dependent process. Puteoli—a Roman colony relatively close to Rome, directly in its economic orbit as a harbor town—had been exposed to the Roman legal system from early on in its history. This had paved the way for making this system the accepted and expected standard. As we have seen, outsiders living or doing business in Puteoli in their interaction with the local population adopted the rules they encountered locally, and I think this finding can safely be extrapolated to Ostia and Rome. But for cities outside Italy things were obviously different.

Roman traders living in the province of Asia will inevitably have followed local customs, but the presence of the governor and his staff also meant that Roman law was introduced. The model as I presented it for the Italian cities is therefore not applicable in the same way. It does not matter here that the reception of Roman law in the East was gradual, patchy, and in the end never complete.[18] As a 'trade diaspora', Roman settlers do not conform to the model of the expatriate U.S. traders in Mexican California mentioned in Chapter 2, at least from the moment officials were present alongside them to administer the legal system of the imperial state.[19]

The reception of Roman law outside Italy has received a fair bit of scholarly attention. A focal point of research has been the extent to which Roman law made inroads into Greek (and other) modes of legal thinking: to what degree did local customs and rules remain in force, and to what degree were they supplanted by the legal system introduced by the Romans? To what extent did local customs in their turn influence the imperial legal system?[20] This approach is valuable, and has yielded important insights. However, in my discussion I will not attempt to establish the ratio between state law and local law, although the balance between the two will be a theme.

The previous three chapters were concerned almost exclusively with the social position of private groups of immigrants, but to analyze the situation in the Roman provinces we explicitly need to include the actions

---

17 Mitteis (1891) 61–79; Marshall (1980).

18 There are traces of Greco-Hellenistic law, Egyptian law, and Syrian law in the eastern provinces well after the *Constitutio Antoniniana*. Mitteis (1891) 159–205; Lintott (1993) 156.

19 Because of state involvement with naval backing, a better parallel is perhaps the Portuguese trade diaspora in the Indian Ocean during the sixteenth century. See Curtin (1984) 137–148.

20 Mitteis (1891) is still the fundamental work. See also Lintott (1993) 154–160; Marshall (1980).

of the state. This chapter therefore consists of two essential parts. The first discusses the impact of Roman rule on the legal system in Asia; the second focuses on the Roman merchants who left Italy and who went to live in the province. I will try to argue that, despite the presence of the Roman state in Asia, organizations of Roman businessmen were comparable in their purpose to those of immigrant traders in Italian cities. The main reason for making this argument is that government enforcement of private contracts was lacking in the provinces, just as it was in Italy; the need for personalized networks to facilitate long-distance trade will therefore have existed in the provinces, just as it did in Italy.

Law and Life of Asia

It is virtually impossible to determine the depth and speed of legal change after the Romans had taken control of the old Pergamene Kingdom. The evidence points to a large degree of change, but at the same time to a large degree of continuity. This is reflected in the following, mostly chronological discussion which presents a picture of continuing co-existence of Roman and Greek legal institutions, mostly unproblematic, but sometimes resulting in an uneasy cohabitation.

Of central importance for the judicial administration of the province was the system of hearings ('conventus' or 'διοίκησις' in Greek) at assize centers, cities which the governor would visit on a tour around the province to dispense justice and grant audiences. The present state of our evidence does not allow us to know for certain when or by whom the assize system was set up; our earliest evidence for it dates to the mid-first century BC, although it probably predated that time by a considerable margin. The date of the system has spurred much debate. It has been suggested that it built on a Pergamene precursor, although no real evidence for this hypothesis exists. Circumstantial evidence is provided by the list of Pergamene mints which shows a remarkable resemblance to the later list of assize centers.[21] The most that can be said on the basis on that resemblance, though, is that the cities involved apparently already enjoyed some prominence as administrative centers in Hellenistic times.

Other sources make a Roman date more plausible. Strabo notes that initially the assize system caused confusion among the native population

[21] The main minting centers of the Asian cistophoric coinage were: Pergamum, Ephesus, Tralles, Laodicea on the Lycus, and Apamea. Mitchell (1999) 24/25.

because the district boundaries cut through the old tribal divisions.[22] He also says that the first governor of Asia, Manius Aquillius, came over as consul (in 129 BC) and organized the province 'into the form of government that still now endures'.[23] This seems an unlikely reference to the Asian road system or to the province's overall territorial extent (which, moreover, had been altered by Strabo's own time), so it most probably refers to the assizes. On balance, then, it seems more likely it was a Roman innovation, all the more so since it was not confined to Asia but seems to have been common to all proconsular provinces.

Size, convenience, and ease of access largely determined which cities on the governor's circuit were appointed the status of assize center; they consisted mainly of the major cities connected by the province's artery roads. Our evidence for the governor's travel schedule is late, but suggests the itinerary and annual dates were predictable and widely known. Plutarch, for instance, speaks of multitudes coming together 'with yearly visitations stirring up Asia, which must come for law-suits and litigation at certain stated times'.[24] Changes were made to the assizes over time—larger areas were divided up, some cities were elevated to the status of assize center, others demoted—but the main pattern remained constant from the mid-first century BC onward. The list of centers seems slowly to have grown over time. As we will see below, there were eight around 50 BC; during the reign of Caligula there were probably thirteen all told, namely: Synnada, Miletus, Pergamum, Alabanda, Cyzicus, Apamea, Cibyra, Ephesus, Adramyttium, Philomelium, Halicarnassus, Smyrna, and Sardis.[25]

---

[22] Strabo 13,4,12. Mitchell (1999) 24; Burton (1975) 97–99; Marshall (1966) 233; Magie (1950) 171/172, 1059–1063.

[23] Strabo 14,1,38 'διέταξε τὴν ἐπαρχίαν εἰς τὸ νῦν ἔτι συμμένον τῆς πολιτείας σχῆμα'. Tr.: H.L. Jones, Loeb (1960). The decree of the Senate from 129 BC concerning the boundaries of Pergamene land (*RDGE* nr. 12) was published in Adramyttium, Smyrna, and Ephesus, which could indicate that already by that time they were all assize centers. Mitchell (1999) 22, 26/27.

[24] '... ἀλλ' ὥσπερ ἐτησίοις περιόδοις ἀκμὴ νοσήματος ἐκτραχύνουσα τὴν Ἀσίαν ἐπὶ δίκας καὶ ἀγῶνας ἐμπροθέσμους ἥκουσαν ἐνταῦθα συμβάλλει'. Plutarch *Mor.* 501F. Tr.: W.C. Helmbold, Loeb (1939). See also the Martyr act of Pionius (martyred ca. 250 AD); Lane Fox (1987) 462–492, esp. 484–490; Mitchell (1999) 26. Similar evidence exists for Africa Proconsularis (martyrdom of Cyprian), Burton (1975) 96.

[25] Evidence from the time of Caligula: *I.Dyd.* 148. The 'Customs law of Asia', in a section dating to 17 BC, lists the same cities, minus Alabanda, perhaps by mistake; Mitchell (2008) 193–197. For the continued status as assize centers of six of these, evidence from Flavian times exists: *I.Eph.* I, 13, see Habicht (1975). See also Burton (1975) 92–94; Mitchell (1999) 23.

It seems likely that the majority if not all retained that status at least until the mid-third century AD.

One of our earliest epigraphic sources related to the legal system in the province of Asia is an inscription datable to a period shortly after 120/119 BC, that is to say at a time we do not yet posses evidence on the assize system, although it may already have been implemented. It contains a decree from the city of Colophon, honoring a certain Menippos for defending the city's free status.[26] The inscription makes it apparent that this 'freedom' meant the city could maintain its own courts. This right gave Colophonian tribunals the power to try cases involving Roman citizens, whether as defendants or as plaintiffs, a prerogative explicitly confirmed by the Senate.[27]

Menippos was honored, among other reasons, because he had 'saved a fellow city-member' who was held responsible for the death of a Roman and who was 'summoned for a capital charge'.[28] It is not entirely clear what incident this refers to, but what exactly had transpired is probably deliberately kept vague in the inscription. One possible explanation is that a Colophonian had killed a Roman and, cleared of charges by a local court, was ordered to appear in Rome to stand trial there. An alternative explanation would be that a Colophonian tribunal had condemned and executed a Roman citizen, a verdict of which the Roman consuls had subsequently gotten wind. The consuls, not amused, in turn sought to execute the culprit (the accuser or else perhaps the leading judge) 'pour encourager les autres'.[29] But whatever the story may have been, Menippos, on an embassy to the Senate, evidently succeeded in getting the Roman authorities' demands revoked, reconfirming the city's free status in judicial matters.

Another early source testifying to Roman involvement in legal affairs is an inscription from Ephesus, containing both a treaty between Ephesus and Sardis and two letters to those cities by Q. Mucius Scaevola, the

---

[26] H.W. Pleket, *SEG* 39 (1989) nr. 1244. See also H.W. Pleket and R.S. Stroud, *SEG* 39 (1989) nr. 1243. Text and extensive commentary on both inscriptions in Robert and Robert (1989).

[27] 'τῆς συγκλήτου δεδογματικείας καὶ τὸν ἀδικοῦντα καὶ τὸν ἐνκαλοῦντα τινὶ τῶν ἡμετέρων πολιτῶν Ῥωμαῖον κρίνεσθαι παρ' ἡμῖν', column I line 42–44.

[28] 'τόν τε κατηιτιάμενον πολίτην ἐπὶ Ῥωμαικῶι θανάτωι καὶ μετάπεμπτον γενόμενον πρὸς ἔγκλημα κεφαλικὸν καὶ κριτηρίωι παραδιδόμενον ἅμα τῆι πόλει μετὰ τῶν νόμων ἀνασέσωκεν', column I line 44–48.

[29] Ferrary (1991) 567–572 makes a case for the latter reading. Robert and Robert (1989) 86/87 prefer the first explanation. See also Magie (1950) 1052 nr. 9.

governor of Asia in 98/97 BC (or 94/93 BC; no consensus exists on the exact date).[30] Scaevola had, through diplomatic efforts, managed to resolve some sort of spat between the two towns, apparently revolving around the question of where citizens of one city should be required to litigate with a citizen of the other in civil suits for damages. Scaevola had suggested a meeting between envoys of the two communities, and had sent his own representative—an Athenian Greek (now anonymous)—to facilitate negotiations. The two parties jointly nominated Pergamum as an arbitrator and in the end managed to conclude a treaty, the essence of which was that civil suits involving citizens of either city were to be held in the city of the defendant. Scaevola's efforts had apparently been instrumental in getting the issue resolved, and in a show of gratitude, games were instituted in his honor. The impression we get from this inscription is that the Roman authorities at this early date still treaded fairly lightly in matters to do with civil litigation. They shaped events, but limited themselves to diplomacy, leaving decisions largely to the local communities. This rather hands-off approach may have been general policy but may also have been generated by Ephesus' (and perhaps Sardis') status as a free city.[31]

In an inscription dating from 78 BC we have definite evidence for Roman courts operating in Asia. A bronze tablet, found in fragments in Rome, contains a *Senatus Consultum* conferring extraordinary honors and privileges on three Greek naval captains: Asclepiades of Clazomenae, Polystratus of Carystus, and Meniscus of Miletus.[32] They had distinguished themselves in the service of Rome during 'the Italic War' ('τοῦ πολέμου τοῦ Ἰταλικοῦ'), which most likely refers to the war of 90/89 BC but could also mean the Sullan war of 83/82 BC. As a reward they were made 'friends of the Roman people' ('amici populi Romani'), were given financial benefits (freedom from liturgies, restitution of property sold during their years of service), and were granted such high honors as the right to offer sacrifice on the Capitol and the right to speak in the Senate.

30 *RDGE* nr. 47 (= *I.Eph.* I, 7). On the date of Scaevola's governorship, see Sherk's commentary in *RDGE*; Magie (1950) 1064 nr. 47. Tr. of the letter to Ephesus: Sherk (1984) 68/69.

31 Ephesus: Magie (1950) 117, 474, 955. In light of recent evidence from Aphrodisias, the status of Ephesus is problematic though; the city was almost certainly not free under the Principate. See Millar (1999) 108–110. On Sardis, see Magie (1950) 156, 1046 (who takes the treaty inscription as evidence that the city was indeed free).

32 Most recent edition (with photos and a translation): Raggi (2001) 77–84. Also *RDGE* nr. 22; tr. in Sherk (1984) 81–83.

Apart from fiscal and honorary privileges, they were also offered a legal privilege: whether litigating as plaintiffs or as defendants, they could choose between appearing before the local court of their own cities, before Italian judges and the Roman magistrate, or before the courts in free cities that had been long-standing 'amici' of the Roman people. It is expressly stated that with the first option their own city-laws should apply. However, what laws were to be followed in the other two instances is not made explicit. The issue has been hotly debated in modern scholarship, the majority view still being that in effect this meant a choice of court, not of law, so that in both cases Greek law would apply.[33] If so, that would lead to the conclusion that Roman officials in Greek cities could on occasion be expected to pronounce judgment entirely on the basis of local, non-Roman laws.

In a comparable document from elsewhere in the Greek East dating to the triumviral period, Octavian conferred similar privileges to a certain Seleucus of Rhosus (Syria). He, too, was given a choice of jurisdiction, but there is one capital difference: Seleucus, unlike the three valiant naval captains, was made a Roman citizen.[34] This complicates matters a bit. Did a choice of court imply a choice of law in his case? If not, which rule-set would be applicable, Greek or Roman? If Roman law applied in all cases, would Seleucus then be judged under Roman law when appearing before a Greek court?[35] Inconceivable as that may seem, the alternative view that Greek law always prevailed and that therefore a citizen would be judged by Roman magistrates on the basis of non-Roman law is equally problematic. Opinions are divided, and barring the discovery of new evidence there is no definite solving this matter.

At all events, grants of this nature were doubtless not run-of-the-mill but they seem hardly to have been a rarity either. In Cyrene at least, there were clearly large numbers of people possessing all sorts of tax exemptions and special benefits; the Aphrodisians in 39 BC were given special

---

33 For a summary of the discussion, see Raggi (2001) 98–109. See also Sherk's commentary to *RDGE* nr. 22, 58.

34 Raggi (2004) with a translation; *RDGE* nr. 58; Sherk (1984) 106–109. See also Raggi (2001) 89–109.

35 Cf. the episode where C. Valerius Flaccus, governor of Nearer Spain in 87 BC, had the local senators of the non-Roman town of Contrebia be judges in a dispute between two other Spanish communities, and had them follow a Roman formula: 'Roman concepts were to be applied to non-Roman realities by non-Roman judges'; Galsterer (1986) 21/22.

privileges collectively.[36] The bronze tablet with the decree for the naval captains was set up on the Capitol where we know there were many more; Vespasian attempted to find copies of 3,000 such tablets destroyed by fire and containing 'alliances, treaties, and special privileges granted to individuals'.[37]

It is also important to note that for both the captains and Seleucus the newly conferred rights were in addition given to their children, wives, and descendants; the grant to Seleucus may even have been part of a collective one extended to a unit of veterans. A grant of this nature to an individual, in other words, created a larger number of people with a choice of jurisdiction down several generations. Provincial courts, whether Roman or Greek, may perhaps have been asked to deal with people possessing such rights more often than we might imagine. This does not seem to have put an enormous strain on either Greek or Roman legal institutions; apparently courts in the East were quite flexible in handling the interaction between Greek and Roman law. The fact that we are left guessing about the exact nature of Seleucus' and the three captains' legal privileges is itself significant in that respect. No further explanation was deemed necessary in the documents, suggesting that to contemporaries it was perfectly self-evident how these rights should be interpreted.

Troubled though the early history of Asia may have been—war with the usurper Aristonicus in the 130s BC, the Mithridatic War in 89–85 BC—when Cicero's brother Quintus was proconsul the province was tranquil, so much so that Cicero, writing in 59 BC, warned Quintus not to become somnambulant: 'Your portion is perfect peace and calm; and yet if the helmsman falls asleep he could go to the bottom in such weather, while if he keeps wide awake he may actually enjoy it'.[38] The governor's tasks seem almost entirely to have consisted of judicial activities.

---

[36] Cyrene edicts: Oliver (1989) nr. 8–12 (= J.J.E. Hondius, *SEG* 9 [1944] 11–16, nr. 8). See also *RDGE* nr. 31. Tr. in Oliver (1989) 46–50 and Sherk (1984) 127–132. See also Sherk's commentary to *RDGE* nr. 22. Decree to the Aphrodisians: Reynolds (1982) nr. 8.

[37] 'instrumentum imperii pulcherrimum ac vetustissimum, quo continebantur paene ab exordio urbis senatus consulta, plebi scita de societate et foedere ac privilegio cuicumque concessis', Suetonius *Vesp.* 8,5. Tr.: J.C. Rolfe, Loeb (1914). The decree granting benefits to the Aphrodisians was also set up on the Capitol, inscribed on a bronze plaque: Reynolds (1982) nr. 8 line 91/92. See also Eck (2009).

[38] 'tibi data est summa pax, summa tranquillitas, ita tamen ut ea dormientem gubernatorem vel obruere, vigilantem etiam delectare possit'. Cicero *QF* 1,1,5. Tr.: D.R. Shackleton Bailey, Loeb (2002). Cicero's explicit mention of peace in the province may be to emphasize that Quintus had nothing to fear from a provision in the *Lex Iulia de repetundis* about governors' military conduct; Fallu (1970) 197.

Cicero continues: 'As it seems to me, the administration of Asia presents no great variety of business; it all rests in the main on the dispensation of justice'.[39] He clearly imagined his brother traveling around on such official business, urging him not to allow his slaves to misbehave themselves while journeying the province: 'as though you were travelling down the Appian way, let them not suppose it makes any difference whether they have arrived in Tralles or in Formiae'.[40] This is an early allusion to a governor's visit to an assize center. Tralles appears again in Cicero's speech *Pro Flacco* delivered at the time of Quintus' governorship. Cicero asks his opponent C. Appuleius Decianus rhetorically: 'You like being in business. Why not at Pergamum, Smyrna, Tralles, where there are many Roman citizens and justice is administered by our magistrates?'[41] (Implied answer: 'because you like doing your shady business away from prying eyes and outside of the law'.) This remark shows Roman courts now forming an integral part of the Asian legal system.

In an inscription dating from shortly after, we see a more complete picture of the assize circuit. It was probably set up in 51/50 BC, the years Cicero was governor of Cilicia (a Cicero, in fact, is mentioned, although which one and in what context is uncertain). It contains a letter written by the governor of Asia, in all likelihood Q. Minucius Thermus. Its preoccupation with the dissemination of information and a remark about writing in Greek make it an extraordinary document:

> ... For these reasons I have written to the *koinon* of the Greeks, to you, to Ephesus, Tralles, Alabanda, Mylasa, Smyrna, Pergamum, Sardis, Adramyttium in order that (each of) you to the cities in your own judiciary district might dispatch (copies of this letter) and see to it that in the most conspicuous place on a pilaster of white stone there is engraved this letter, so that in common for all the province justice might be established for all time, and that all the other cities and peoples might do the same thing among themselves, and that they might deposit (a copy of this letter) in the archives of the *nomophylakia* and the *chrêmatistêria*. The reason for which I wrote in Greek, do not ask, since it was my intention that nothing contrary to the (correct) interpretation of my letter could possible be in your mind.

39 'ac mihi quidem videtur non sane magna varietas esse negotiorum in administranda Asia, sed ea tota iuris dictione maxime sustineri'; Cicero *QF* 1,1,20. Tr.: D.R. Shackleton Bailey, Loeb (2002).

40 '... ut ita se gerant in istis Asiaticis itineribus ut si iter Appia via faceres, neve interesse quicquam putent utrum Trallis an Formias venerint'; Cicero *QF* 1,1,17. Tr.: D.R. Shackleton Bailey, Loeb (2002).

41 'negotiari libet; cur non Pergami, Smyrnae, Trallibus, ubi et multi cives Romani sunt et ius a nostro magistratu dicitur?'; Cicero *Pro Flacco* 71. Tr.: C. MacDonald, Loeb (1977).

> This letter I have given to Timokles (son) of Anaxagoros, and Sosikrates (son) of Pythion, envoys from Magnesia on the Maeander.[42]

The seven cities mentioned, along with Miletus ('you') where the inscription was found, surely constituted the full complement of assize centers at the time of writing.[43] Evidently, the Roman authorities were attempting to achieve some uniformity in the judicial procedures in these places, although in what area we can now only speculate. The larger part of the inscription is lost, and it is most unfortunate that we no longer know what prompted the governor to compose this sternly-worded missive. He confessed amazement that the addressees endured the 'shamelessness of certain persons' ('τήν τινων περὶ [ταῦτα ἀ]ναίδειαν'), which does not really narrow down the range of possibilities much. Perhaps infringements of the *Lex Iulia de repetundis* were the cause, or else perhaps defaults on business deals of some kind.[44]

However, the gubernatorial concern for judicial uniformity expressed in the letter should not lead us to overestimate Roman legal influence. Cicero's letters as governor of the province of Cilicia provide information on the day-to-day application of the legal system in Asia as well. In a letter to Atticus he comments on his policy: 'Indeed I have followed many of Scaevola's provisions, including that one which the Greeks regard as their charter of liberty, that cases between Greeks should be tried under their own laws'.[45] Cicero thus extended to Cilicia the edict that Scaevola had

---

[42] '...δι' ἃς [αἰτίας] πρός τε τὸ κοινὸν τῶν Ἑλλήνων γέγραφα, [πρὸς ὑ]μᾶς, Ἐφεσίους, Τραλλιανούς, Ἀλαβανδεῖς, Μ[υλ]ασεῖς, Σμυρναίους, Περγαμηνούς, Σαρδιανο[ύς], Ἀδραμυτηνούς, ἵνα τε ὑμεῖς πρὸς τὰς ἐν τῆι δ[ιοικ]ήσει τῆι ἰδίαι πόλεις διαποστείλησθε ἔν τε τῶι ἐπ[ι]φανεστάτωι τόπωι ἐν στυλοπαραστάδι ἐπὶ λίθου λευκοῦ ἐνχαραχθῆναι φροντίσητε τ[αῦ]τα τὰ γράμματα, ἵνα κοινῶς πάσηι τῆι ἐπαρχεία[ι τὸ] δίκαιον ἐσταμένον ἦι εἰς τὸν αἰεὶ χρόνον, αἵ τε ἄλλαι πᾶσαι πόλεις καὶ δῆμοι τὸ αὐτὸν παρ' αὐτοῖς ποιήσωσιν, εἴς τε τὰ δημόσια ἀποθῶνται νομο[φυλά]κια καὶ χρηματιστήρια. τὴν δὲ αἰτίαν δι' ἣν ἑλλη[νι]κοῖς ἔγραψα, μὴ ἐπιζητήσητε· κατὰ νοῦν γὰρ [ἔσ]χον, μή τι παρὰ τὴν ἑρμηνείαν ἔλασσον τὰ [γεγραμμ]ένα νοῆσαι δύνησθε· τὴν δὲ ἐπιστολὴ[ν ἔδωκα Τι] μοκλῆι Ἀναξαγόρου καὶ Σωσικράτηι Πυ[θίωνος πρ]εσβευταῖς Μαγνήτων τῶν πρός τ[ῶι Μαιάνδρ]ωι'; *RDGE* 52 l. 42–60. Tr. Sherk (1984) 96–98. See Ando (2000) 83; Burton (1975) 93.

[43] Governors used the assize centers to publish important announcements. So for instance *RDGE* nr. 65: Paulus Fabius Maximus, governor of Asia in 9 BC, wanted his directive concerning a new calendar published 'ἐν ταῖς ἀφηγουμέναις τῶν διοικήσεων πόλεσιν' (D line 65). See Mitchell (1999) 27.

[44] Sherk prefers the latter interpretation, speculating it refers to the loans of Cluvius of Puteoli to Asian cities (Cicero *Ad Fam.* 13,56); *RDGE* nr. 52 note 6. Another possibility is that the date is not 51/50 BC but 29 BC, making Octavian the author, and the Cicero in line 39 the famous orator's son; Habicht (1975) 69; Sherk (1984) 97, nt. 2.

[45] 'multaque sum secutus Scaevolae, in iis illud in quo sibi libertatem censent Graeci datam, ut Graeci inter se disceptent suis legibus'; Cicero *Ad Att.* 6,1,15. Tr. (with modifications): D.R. Shackleton Baily, Loeb (1999). See Hatzfeld (1919) 319/320 with nt. 1.

already implemented in Asia in the 90s BC, and that had been held up as exemplary ever since.[46]

Clearly Cicero recognized a partition between Greek and Roman law, although precisely what judicial liberty he—and, by implication, Scaevola—had granted the Greeks is not immediately apparent. It seems inconceivable that all litigation in the province, including all litigation involving Greeks, had previously been taken over by the Roman governor and was now by edict returned to the competence of the Greek courts; the state apparatus that would have been necessary for such jurisdictional shifts would have been enormous. A more logical reading would be that this is a reference to 'international' cases between disputants from different cities; only these cases the Roman governor had claimed jurisdiction over, something we can imagine as actually being practicably feasible. The Greeks were now allowed again to continue their old practice of making legal treaties and of calling on the help of arbiters from other Greek cities, hence Cicero's otherwise somewhat puzzling remark: '[t]he natives are jubilant because they have alien judges'.[47] A recently discovered inscription from Aphrodisias (discussed further below), though dating from much later, now lends some support to this interpretation.[48]

In a somewhat problematic passage, Cicero adds that his edict consisted of two parts. The first is 'specifically provincial, including municipal finances, debt, interest, bonds, also all items connected with tax farmers'. The other 'comprises such matters as cannot conveniently be handled without an edict, as possession of inheritances, possession of property, appointment of receivers, sale of property, things which are usually both litigated and otherwise transacted in accordance with edict'.[49] He then goes on to say that a third category to do with the administration of justice he 'left unwritten' ('ἄγραφον reliqui'), limiting it to a statement that his rulings would conform to the edicts published in Rome. The most sensible explanation for the mention of this enigmatic 'unwritten' third part is that

---

[46] Galsterer (1986) 17; Magie (1950) 173–176.

[47] 'Graeci vero exsultant quod peregrinis iudicibus utuntur'; Cicero *Ad Att.* 6,1,15. Tr.: D.R. Shackleton Baily, Loeb (1999). Reading first suggested by Marshall (1980) 656–658.

[48] On the Greek tradition of calling on the help of judges from other cities, see Robert (1973). The Aphrodisias inscription is published in: Reynolds (2000) 5–15.

[49] 'breve autem edictum est propter hanc meam διαίρεσιν, quod duobus generibus edicendum putavi; quorum unum est provinciale, in quo inest de rationibus civitatum, de aere alieno, de usura, de syngraphis, in eodem omnia de publicanis; alterum quod sine edicto satis commode transigi non potest, de hereditatum possessionibus, de bonis possidendis, magistris faciendis, <bonis> vendendis, quae ex edicto et postulari et fieri solent'; Cicero *Ad Att.* 6,1,15. Tr.: D.R. Shackleton Baily, Loeb (1999).

Cicero was taking other provincial edicts—the one by Scaevola evidently among them—as models. These edicts included many provisions which were pertinent, but which Cicero thought unnecessary to copy in his own version because no explicit reference to them was required in litigation.[50] In any case, Cicero obviously implemented Roman law directly in Cilicia, incorporating and publishing it in his edict. At the same time, he displayed concern for native law, just as Scaevola had done over a generation earlier in Asia; Greeks litigating among themselves were to continue using their own rules.

In 39 BC, Aphrodisias saw its position as friend and ally of the Roman people renewed in response to an embassy to the Senate. The envoy's task sent over to Rome was doubtless made easier in no small measure by Marc Antony and Octavian who, as triumvirs, also cared to speak on Aphrodisias' behalf. The Senate in a lengthy decree duly heaped a wide variety of special honors and benefits on the city and its inhabitants, among other things: tax exemptions, freedom from levies, freedom from billeting by Roman magistrates, the temple of Aphrodite granted the rights of asylum like the temple of Artemis at Ephesus. Apart from these privileges, the city was guaranteed the use of its own laws and courts.[51] This grant of judicial autonomy was unusually comprehensive in its scope in that it explicitly included future local legislation: '(the Aphrodisians) are to be free in all respects and immune from taxation and are to enjoy their own traditional laws and those which they pass among themselves hereafter'.[52]

Aphrodisias was understandably proud of her privileged status, and inscribed several imperial letters referring to this special position—even some addressed to other cities—on a wall of her theater. These inscriptions show that Aphrodisias' rights were respected and reconfirmed over and over by the Emperors, at least into the mid-third century. A letter from Trajan to the Smyrnaeans, for instance, warns them that no one from a free city was to be forced into performing Smyrna's liturgies, least of

[50] Marshall (1964). See also Galsterer (1986) 17. Of course, Cicero's solution of referring to the edicts published in Rome begs the question: how exactly were provincials supposed to know about those edicts? Perhaps local archives (on which, Burton [1975] 103/104; Ando [2000] 80–96) contained copies, but in that case no reference to Rome would have been needed.

[51] Reynolds (1982) nr. 8, line 45/46 '[?...ἀλλ]ὰ ἐλευθέρους εἶναι τῷ (τε) δικαίῳ καὶ ταῖς [ἰδίαις κρίσεσιν ἕνεκεν τοῦ] δήμου τοῦ Ῥωμαίων τὴ[ν] πολειτήαν τὴν Πλαρασέων καὶ Ἀφροδεισιέων χρῆσθαι'. See also Pierobon-Benoit (1994) 307.

[52] '[ἀ]λλὰ ἐλεύθεροι καὶ ἀτελεῖς ὦσιν, νόμοις τε ἰδίοις π[ατρί]οις καὶ οὓς ἄν μετὰ ταῦτα ἐν ἑαυτοῖς κυρ<ώ>σ<ω>σιν χρῶν[ται...]', line 61/62. Tr.: Reynolds.

all anyone from Aphrodisias since that city had been removed from the *formula provinciae*. A letter from Hadrian to Aphrodisias also alludes to this fact, and confirms that the city was not to pay a tax on iron nails.[53]

A recently discovered Aphrodisian inscription (reused in a road-surface and probably not part of the theater's 'archive wall') contains four letters by Hadrian, the first one of particular interest in the context of local courts. In a reply to an embassy, Hadrian confirmed Aphrodisias' right to have civil cases ('τῶν χρηματικῶν δί[κων') fall under the jurisdiction of its courts as long as the disputants were Aphrodisians.[54] However, he seems to have added that in cases involving an Aphrodisian and a Greek from another city, the trial had to take place 'under Roman law and in the province' ('κατὰ Ῥωμ]αίων νόμους καὶ ἐν τῇ ἐπαρχίᾳ'). In Hadrian's day, 'international' cases involving Greeks from different cities were apparently to be tried by the Roman authorities, even in the free city of Aphrodisias. From the Cicero passage discussed above, in which Cicero talks about following Scaevola's edict, it would seem that once not just free but even unprivileged cities in Asia possessed such jurisdiction. If so, this loss of jurisdictional competence seems a marked diminution of Aphrodisias' legal autonomy. It is not clear whether this was the result of a decision by Hadrian or whether this had already happened at some earlier point in time.

But the Roman authorities' encroachment on the competence of Aphrodisian courts over 'international' cases notwithstanding, letters from later Emperors all underscore the city's rights. So, for example, two letters from Septimius Severus and Caracalla, and a third from Severus Alexander.[55] The dossier of imperial correspondence continues into the third century with two epistles, one from Gordian III and one from Decius, all guaranteeing the city preservation of its freedom and enjoyment of its rights.[56] One other letter written by Gordian III is particularly noteworthy: it is addressed not to the city of Aphrodisias but to a private individual, a certain Aurelius Epaphras. The Emperor wrote to him about 'the matter of Polydorus', advising him to explain 'the original tradition' to the Roman prefect in order to have him allocate the case to Aphrodisias' own

53 Reynolds (1982) nr. 14, 15 (= Oliver [1989] nr. 48, 69). *Formula provinciae* is rendered as 'τοῦ τύπου τῆς ἐπαρχείας' in Greek. On the *formula provinciae*, Lintott (1993) 28–32. See also Robert and Robert (1989) 86, who compare these two Aphrodisian inscriptions to the Colophonian decree for Menippos.

54 Reynolds (2000) 5–15.

55 Reynolds (1982) nr. 17, 18, 19 (= Oliver [1989] nr. 218, 219, 278).

56 Reynolds (1982) nr. 20, 21, 25 (= Oliver [1989] nr. 279, 281, 284).

court.[57] This remark shows that the city's autonomous judicial status was still being preserved by the Emperor almost three centuries after the triumviral period. This continuation of official policy is, of course, all the more surprising since the affair postdates the *Constitutio Antoniniana* by several decades.

Another remarkable source attesting the prevalence of local courts is formed by an inscription from Chios, dating to Augustan times. From this text we learn that in 80 BC under Sulla's settlement of the East the city had been declared free, and had been granted the privilege of making the Romans living there subject to her laws.[58] Around 4 AD the proconsul of Asia had been asked to arbitrate in a dispute where, it would seem, the Chian court had thought the case too awkward or too politically sensitive to pronounce judgment on its own authority. It decided to play it safe and to put the matter to the governor. The specifics of the case remain elusive, but the most likely explanation of what happened is that a Roman citizen had attempted to challenge the jurisdiction of a Chian court since the proconsul in a written reply expressed as his opinion that resident Romans ought to comply with the laws of Chios. From the rescript it appears that the governor had treated the request diligently and conscientiously, investigating what the policy of his predecessors in like cases had been.[59] He evidently felt that the privileges Chios had received as a reward from Sulla—the city had been mostly loyal to Rome in opposing Mithridates and had suffered the consequences—were to be respected.[60] Whatever the exact content of those privileges, the inscription demonstrates the continued jurisdiction of Greek civic courts under Roman rule, in this case even where Romans were concerned.

The Chian inscription may be unique in its reference to Romans under Greek law, but other sources as well show that in the Principate Greek legislation and customs continued to be respected. A grave marker from Magnesia on the Maeander, dating to imperial times, commemorates

[57] 'Εἰ τοίνυν προσιὼν τις τῷ φίλῳ μου καὶ ἐπάρχῳ τῆς πατρίδος τῆς ἐμῆς Φλαβίῳ Λατρωνιανῷ ὑπὲρ ὧν ἐνέγραψας διδάσκοις τὸ ἐξ ἀρχῆς ἔθος ἀναπέμψαι προνοήσεται τὴν περὶ τοῦ Πολυδώρου κρίσιν τῷ οἰκείῳ δικαστηρίῳ'. Reynolds (1982) nr. 22 (= Oliver [1989] nr. 282).

[58] *RDGE* nr. 70, tr. in Sherk (1984) 138/139. Chios as a free city, see also Appian *BM* 61.

[59] The way the dispute was resolved—through the proper legal channels—does not point towards abuse by the resident Romans. Hatzfeld, less plausibly in my view, sees the inscription as support for his argument that Romans in the East were exploiting their legal status; Hatzfeld (1919) 319 with nt. 3.

[60] Magie (1950) 224. For a different interpretation of the Chian inscription, see Marshall (1969) who argues that it has nothing to do with jurisdiction, but instead with a Chian administrative law concerning real estate.

Democharis, son of Procles.[61] It contains a warning not to violate the grave, and the threat leveled at the potential perpetrator is that he would be held 'liable under the (imperial) edicts and under the ancestral laws' ('ὑπεύθυνος ἔσται τοῖς διατάγμασι καὶ τοῖς πατρίοις νόμοις'). This somewhat surprising juxtaposition of imperial legislation and native law shows that even under the Principate local regulations continued to be in force, apparently without causing any offense to the Roman administration. In fact, there seems to have been a continuing Roman policy of respecting regional rules. Several instances can be found in the *Digest*. The Severan jurist Callistratus, for example, cites a rescript by Marcus Aurelius and Lucius Verus, prescribing that a magistrate in a province, when summoning witnesses, should take local customs into consideration.[62] Elsewhere in the *Digest* another rescript by the same Emperors is quoted as saying: 'The measures and prices with which tradesmen deal in wine are a matter for the contracting parties; no one is obliged to sell, if dissatisfied with the price or the measures, especially when nothing is done contrary to the custom of the region'.[63]

Many Greek civic courts continued to operate wholesale under the Empire, as can be seen in a story about the sophist Polemo. Sometime in the reign of Hadrian, Polemo founded his school at Smyrna, to the great delight of the natives, and proceeded to dole out sage advice to the city's leading factions. One area in which he counseled them concerned law suits: criminal trials for adultery, sacrilege, and murder, he urged, were to be driven out of the city, for their neglect 'bred malice' ('ἄγη φύεται') and they 'required a judge with a sword' ('δικαστοῦ γὰρ δεῖσθαι αὐτὰς [δίκας] ξίφος ἔχοντος').[64] Those last words almost certainly refer to the authority of the Roman proconsul who possessed the 'right of the sword' ('*ius gladii*'), meaning the power to inflict the ultimate punishment: death.[65]

---

61 *I.Trall* Anhang, 221/222 nr. 13 (= A. Hauvette-Besnault and M. Dubois, *BCH* 5 [1881] 344/345 nr. 5). Mitteis (1891) 101; Lintott (1993) 158/159. The provenance of this inscription is unclear; apparently found in Işıklı, and later brought to Aydın (Tralles), it is said to originate from Ine Bazar (Magnesia on the Maeander); E. Preuner, *AM* 46 (1921) 22/23 nr. 37.

62 Callistratus *Dig.* 22,5,3,6.

63 Papirius *Dig.* 18,1,71: 'quibus mensuris aut pretiis negotiatores vina compararent, in contrahentium potestate esse: neque enim quisquam cogitur vendere, si aut pretium aut mensura displiceat, praesertim si nihil contra consuetudinem regionis fiat'. Tr.: Watson (1985). See also Ulpianus *Dig.* 25,4,1,15.

64 Philostratus *VS* 530–532. See Garnsey (1968) 52/53 with nt. 14.

65 See Garnsey (1968) who argues that all governors (proconsuls as well as *legati Augusti pro praetore*) from late Republican times onward automatically possessed the '*ius gladii*', a power that encompassed the right to execute both civilians and soldiers.

Because Smyrna was an assize center, Polemo cannot have been saying that criminal trials were literally to be held outside the city;[66] instead, he was moralizing, saying that such trials should not arise in Smyrna in the first place. With his pronouncement he was presumably exhorting the Smyrnaeans not to let charges of criminal behavior devolve into blood feuds and personal vendettas. Civil suits on the other hand ('those over money', 'τὰς ὑπὲρ χρημάτων') were to be settled domestically ('οἴκοι'), that is to say, not by judges from another Greek city according to Hellenistic tradition.[67]

Another story about the same Polemo reveals that more than two centuries after Scaevola had brokered a deal between the Ephesians and the Sardians regarding litigation over damages, the Greek civic courts in Sardis were still functioning. Polemo, we are told, came to the city to plead a case before the '(court of) the Hundredmen by whom Lydia was judged' ('ἐν τοῖς ἑκατὸν ἀνδράσιν, ὑφ' ὧν ἐδικαιοῦτο ἡ Λυδία').[68] It is a pity that Philostratus, who tells the story, does not give us any further details about this body of judges, but almost certainly this was a Greek, not a Roman court. Apart from the fact that 'Hundredmen' sounds rather exotic,[69] if this was an assize-hearing the role of the governor would surely have been mentioned. Moreover, the court was said to have jurisdiction over 'Lydia' and, as mentioned above, Strabo remarks that the assize boundaries did not follow but cut through such old ethnically defined territories.[70] The case to be tried before the court was obviously of some import. It concerned a wealthy Lydian who was in danger of losing his property. That serious money was at stake is clear from the fact that Polemo, who acted for the defense, was paid the handsome sum of two talents for his trouble.

What makes these stories about Polemo all the more striking is, of course, that both Smyrna and Sardis had been assize centers from the earliest days the system was implemented, and that both cities had never

[66] Aelius Aristides *Or.* 50,85 provides evidence for Smyrna's continued status as an assize center; Burton (1975) 93, 95; Behr (1981) 440, nt. 146. A court of the Roman curator was apparently also present at Smyrna, at least in Flavian times; Philostratus *VS* 512 tells us of the falling-out between the Roman curator Rufus and the Sophist Nicetes (who refused to appear before Rufus' court). See Garnsey (1970) 81, nt. 3.

[67] Marshall (1980) 633–640; Robert (1973).

[68] Philostratus *VS* 524/525.

[69] The name itself is, of course, reminiscent of the ancient court of the '*Centumviri*' in Rome. There does not seem to be any logical connection between the Roman Centumviral and this Lydian court though.

[70] Strabo 13,4,12. The territory of the assize center of Smyrna, in fact, comprised part of Lydia. See Marshall (1966) 233, 237.

lost that status (as Tralles would in the early Principate).[71] If we accept these passages as an authentic reflection of the reality in the province of Asia, then we can conclude that local Greek courts continued in operation even where the influence of Rome was supposedly felt most.

All of this evidence for a continuation of Greek laws and courts notwithstanding, the arrival of a higher power on the scene seems to have altered the dynamic of Greek bickering. Plutarch in his essay *Precepts of Statecraft* complained that greedy and litigious prominent citizens of the Greek cities, quarreling among themselves, constantly invoked the authority of the Roman governor. In so doing, they diminished the influence and legitimacy of local governments and courts. Although the *Precepts* (probably written shortly after 96 AD) is written as a general essay, Plutarch in all likelihood had the situation at Sardis in mind.[72] He employs muscular language and evokes powerful images—all without a hint of irony—leaving no doubt about the question of where power ultimately rested:

> However, the statesman, while making his native State readily obedient to its sovereigns, must not further humble it; nor, when the leg has been fettered, go on and subject the neck to the yoke, as some do who, by referring everything, great or small, to the sovereigns, bring the reproach of slavery upon their country, or rather wholly destroy its constitutional government, ... those who invite the sovereign's decision on every decree, meeting of a council, granting of a privilege, or administrative measure, force their sovereign to be their master more than he desires. And the cause of this is chiefly the greed and contentiousness of the foremost citizens; ... they call in those who are mightier; and as a result (local) senate, popular assembly, courts, and the entire local government lose their authority.[73]

---

[71] Tralles lost its status as an assize center probably around 26/25 BC; Mitchell (1999) 23; Habicht (1975) 70/71. See also Burton (1975) 93; Magie (1950) 1061. The youngest secure evidence for Sardis as an assize center (*I.Eph.* I, 13) dates to the time of Vespasian; Habicht (1975). Burton (1975) 93/94 takes the story about the 'Hundredmen' as evidence for Sardis' continued status as an assize center, but it seems clear this was a local court.

[72] *Mor.* 815D mentions events that took place 'recently under Domitian'. The essay is addressed to Menemachus who must have hailed from Sardis; his fellow city-member Pardalas was a Sardian native: 813F, 825D.

[73] 'Ποιοῦντα μέντοι καὶ περέχοντα τοῖς κρατοῦσιν εὐπειθῆ τὴν πατρίδα, δεῖ μὴ προσεκταπεινοῦν μηδὲ τοῦ σκέλους δεδεμένου προσυποβάλλειν καὶ τὸν τράχηλον, ὥσπερ ἔνιοι, καὶ μικρὰ καὶ μείζω φέροντες ἐπὶ τοὺς ἡγεμόνας, ἐξονειδίζουσι τὴν δουλείαν, μᾶλλον δ'ὅλως τὴν πολιτείαν ἀναιροῦσι, ... οἱ παντὶ δόγματι καὶ συνεδρίῳ καὶ χάριτι καὶ διοικήσει προσάγοντες ἡγεμονικὴν κρίσιν ἀναγκάζουσιν ἑαυτῶν μᾶλλον ἢ βούλονται δεσπότας εἶναι τοὺς ἡγουμένους. Αἰτία δὲ τούτου μάλιστα πλεονεξία καὶ φιλονικία τῶν πρώτων· ... ἐπάγονται τοὺς κρείττονας· ἐκ τούτου δὲ καὶ βουλὴ καὶ δῆμος καὶ δικαστήρια καὶ ἀρχὴ πᾶσα τὴν ἐξουσίαν ἀπόλλυσι'; Plutarch *Mor.* 814E–815A. Tr.: F.C. Babbitt, Loeb (1936). See Ando (2000) 58.

Plutarch may have been complaining about Asian provincials constantly turning to the proconsul forcing him to be a 'master more than he desired' but, in the words of Andrew Lintott, 'it is worth stressing Plutarch's implied point, that, if cases and problems were not referred upwards, politics and jurisdiction could have proceeded in an autonomous fashion, without intervention by the Romans'.[74] Of course, Roman policy in the provinces itself had enabled and even encouraged the behavior bemoaned by Plutarch. The Roman authorities had superimposed a jurisdictional layer on Greek legal institutions by creating the possibility of a higher, previously non-existing appeal to their magistrates and ultimately to the Emperor.[75] The famous edicts from Cyrene, dating to 7/6 BC and 4 BC, already show the Emperor Augustus directly interfering in a provincial court system, laying down new revised rules for the composition of juries in capital trial-cases and for the arrangement of appeals for trials for extortion by public officials.[76] The evidence from Asia Minor as well shows traces of this centralizing policy.

An inscription from Cos, dating to the reign of Claudius, contains a letter to the Coans by the proconsul, Cn. Domitius Corbulo.[77] The text is badly mutilated, but clearly deals with an appeals case. A Coan, it seems, had issued an appeal directly to the Emperor, bypassing the proconsul and perhaps also omitting to put down the required deposit of 2,500 *denarii*. With his letter, Corbulo probably intended to point out to the Coan city-council—which seems to have been implicated in all of this somehow—that such behavior was unacceptable. He stressed that his proconsular instructions stipulated that appeals to the Emperor should be submitted to his preliminary scrutiny. Especially the mention of instructions ('ἐντολαῖς') is interesting, and indicative of a central policy regarding appeals as early as the Julio-Claudian period. Prior to the discovery of this inscription, it was generally believed that the issuing of instructions ('*mandata*', 'ἐντολαί') to proconsuls did not occur until the time of

[74] Lintott (1993) 159. See also Mitteis (1891) 87–89 nt 3, B.

[75] See Ando (2000) 162/163; Garnsey (1970) 67–72. Rome, of course, inherited the position of the Pergamene Kings with whom cities had maintained relations previously. The Kings seem to have made little attempt to interfere with the administration of justice though (see Jones [1940] 105–108), and it seems unlikely the assize system already existed at the time of their rule; Mitchell (1999) 22–25.

[76] Cyrene edicts, Oliver (1989) nr. 8–12 (= J.J.E. Hondius, *SEG* 9 [1944] 11–16, nr. 8). See also *RDGE* nr. 31. Tr. in Oliver (1989) 46–50 and Sherk (1984) 127–132. See also Ando (2000) 143/144, 148; Marshall (1980) 658–660.

[77] *I.Cos* ED 43 (= *IGRR*, IV, 1044 = A. Chastagnol, J. Gagé, M. Leglay, H.-G. Pflaum, *AE* [1976] 187/188, nr. 648). Tr. in Levick (2000) 12/13.

Hadrian, at the earliest. Cassius Dio, who claimed that the practice was established by Augustus, was thought to project the situation of his own time back into history.[78]

Aelius Aristides seems to be suggesting that trials of appeal were a fairly common occurrence in the provinces. Of course, he gives his own rhetorical twist to this statement: so fair and just were these trials that those who first handled the cases were as apprehensive of the final verdict as were the litigants, 'so that one would say that people now are governed by those sent out to them in so far as it pleases them'.[79] A rescript by Severus Alexander to the Bithynian *koinon* also deals with appeals, in this case to the Emperor himself: 'I do not see how anyone may be prevented from appealing by his judges, since it is permissible (for him) to make use of another route to the same end and to reach me more quickly'.[80] Copies of this rescript have been found on Egyptian papyri, showing its larger relevance outside Asia Minor.[81] Although it postdates the *Constitutio Antoniniana*, the evidence just discussed shows it was not the product of a Severan innovation but a continuation of long-standing policy.

To sum up, the Romans encountered a deeply-rooted Greco-Hellenistic system of laws and dispute settlement in the area they found themselves masters of after the bequest by Attalus III. Their most important innovation in many ways was to create an additional judicial layer with the proconsular court—with the ultimate possibility of appeal to the Emperor—and to organize the governor's court sessions in the assize system. The end result was a patchwork of direct Roman control and influence on the one hand, and a large number of local tribunals using local legislation on the other. The latter continued to try many cases that, simply for reasons of expediency, would never come to the attention of any Roman magistrate.

---

78 Cassius Dio 53,15,4. See Burton (1976).

79 'ὥστε φαίη τις ἂν τοσαῦτα ἄρχεσθαι τοὺς νῦν ὑπὸ τῶν πεμπομένων, ὁπόσα ἂν αὐτοῖς ἀρέσκῃ'. Aelius Aristides *Or.* 26,37–39. Tr. Behr (1981) 81.

80 'Ἐκκαλεῖσθαι μὲν πῶς ἂν τις κωλύοιτο ὑπὸ τῶν δικαζόντων, οὐχ ὁρῶ, ὁπότε ἔξεστιν τὴν ἑτέραν ὁδὸν τρεπόμενον ταὐτὸ ποιεῖν καὶ θᾶττον πρός με ἀφικνεῖσθαι'; Paulus *Dig.* 49,1,25. Tr.: Watson (1985).

81 *P.Oxy.* xvii, 2104; xliii, 3106 (= Oliver [1989] nr. 276A; 277B). See Kantor (2009) 256–258; Ando (2000) 109.

Romans Resident in Ephesus

Resident Roman traders in Ephesus seem to have operated conjointly from early on; an inscription dating to around 100 BC mentions the freedman P. Veturius Rodo, a 'director in charge of buying wine containers' ('mag(ister) in emendum dolariu[m').[82] The inscription is written on an architrave, and although the text is hopelessly mutilated it suggests that the construction (or refurbishment) of the building it once belonged to was decreed by the association: '[?]pidianum ded[it] ex decretu conlegei'. If so, Rodo may have been in charge of the construction project. The *collegium* organization with appointed *magistri*, the activities of which centered on a communal building, will have given the Roman community a high degree of visibility and recognizability.[83]

This community must have suffered heavily during the first Mithridatic War; Appian refers specifically to Ephesus while describing the horrific events that took place in 88 BC.[84] According to his narrative, the Ephesians voluntarily joined the rebellion, turning against the Romans in their midst, killing even the ones who had fled to the great temple of Artemis. However, he also tells us that the Ephesians, having been under Mithridates' rule for a few years, rose up against him, incarcerating and then killing his general Zenobius.[85] An inscription confirms this story; set up in the mid-80s BC, it commemorates the event and in verbose fashion proclaims the loyalty of the Ephesians to the name of Rome. Apparently, the Ephesians had somewhat belatedly realized which way the wind was blowing, and had opportunely changed sides. Needless to say, the inscription makes no mention whatsoever of any earlier support for the Pontic King, making it seem as if Ephesus had been taken against its will and by means of force.[86]

---

[82] *I.Eph.* VI, 2074, 'dolarium', perhaps a misspelling, is an unusual word but should, on the analogy of the single noun *doliarium*, probably be interpreted as 'wine containers' (Wankel and Merkelbach in *I.Eph.* comment: 'Doliarium = Weinkeller'). The inscription can not be precisely dated, but Hatzfeld (1919) 47 suggest Rodo was the freedman of P. Veturius, the father of a L. Veturius P. f. who was *magister* of a *collegium* on Delos at the end of the second century BC.

[83] *Scholae* of professional *collegia*, see Waltzing vol. 1 (1895) 217–231.

[84] Appian *BM* 23.

[85] Appian *BM* 48.

[86] *I.Eph.* Ia, 8. See Magie (1950) 214/215, 224/225. Note, incidentally, that Mithridates should perhaps better be called a 'Cappadocian king': 'The "kingdom of Pontus" is a modern construction'; Mitchell (2008) 176.

The Romans either never disappeared completely from the city or returned quickly after hostilities ceased. An inscription most likely dating to the 60s BC consists of a dedication to L. Agrius, L.f. Publeianus by the 'Italians who do business in Ephesus' ('Italicei quei Ephesi negotiantur').[87] Two other inscriptions are also dedications to people who had apparently earned the gratitude of the local Roman businessmen. The first is a dedication by the 'society of Roman citizens who do business in Ephesus' ('conventus c. [R.] quei Ephesi negotiantu[r]') to the consul M. Cocceius Nerva, possibly the great-grandfather of the later Emperor, in office in the year 36 BC.[88] Honorary inscriptions to Nerva are known also from Stratonicea and Teos, showing his activities spanned a larger part of Asia; he may have been a provincial governor at some point, but no definitive evidence exists.[89] The second inscription, written in Greek and unfortunately rather damaged, but probably dating to the same time as the dedication to Nerva, honors a certain (...?) Gallus, son of Publius who is called 'our savior and benefactor'.[90] Gallus may himself have been a member of the Roman mercantile community; alternatively he may have been their patron. One would like to have known why honors were bestowed upon Gallus and, especially, the consul Nerva, but whatever the reasons may have been, we can be reasonably confident that their actions somehow furthered the interests of the Roman traders.

A grand Ephesian grave monument—located on 'Curetes street', a main city-street and processional route—provides evidence for the ties of one famous Roman to Ephesus, although the implications go beyond the individual. It is the colossal mausoleum that C. Memmius, literary maecenas and one-time son-in-law of Sulla, built for his son around 50 BC.[91] Memmius, governor of Bithynia in 57 BC, stood for the consulship in 54 BC but was forced into exile when a bribery scandal broke during his campaign.

---

[87] *I.Eph.* VI, 2058. Cicero mentions a L. Agrius, a Roman knight and likely the same person, in *Pro Flacco* 31 (a speech dating from 59 BC); Hatzfeld (1919) 102. Italian traders, see also *I.Eph.* III, 884 (heavily emendated).

[88] *I.Eph.* III, 658 (= J. Gagé, M. Leglay, H.-G. Pflaum, P. Wuilleumier, *AE* [1968] 149/150, nr. 480). M. Cocceius Nerva, cos. 36 BC, was already proposed as the honoree in both editions; this was confirmed by a later epigraphic find; D. Knibbe, H. Engelmann, B. İplikçioğlu, *JöaI* 59 (1989) Beiblatt 235/236 nr. B2.

[89] Teos: J.J.E. Hondius, *SEG* 4 (1929), nr. 604 (= Y. Béquignon and A. Laumonier, *BCH* (1925) 310/311, nr. 8) (in both editions erroneously identified as the Emperor Nerva [see previous note]); Stratonicea: *I.Strat.* 509.

[90] 'ἐν Ε[φέσῳ πραγματε]υόμενοι ἔμπο[ροι Ἰταλικοὶ τὸ]ν ἑαυτῶν σω[τῆρα καὶ εὐεργέ]την'; *I.Eph.* III, 800.

[91] *I.Eph.* II, 403. See Torelli (1997) 152–174.

He withdrew to the East (Mytilene and Athens) and may, at the time his son died, have been sojourning in Ephesus, where he could probably count on a friendly reception from the immigrant Roman businessmen; he was likely the patron of some of them. An Ephesian grave inscription, roughly contemporary with the construction of the mausoleum, was set up for a L. Memmius T. f. Ouf., hailing from Tarracina, a town south of Rome where the Memmii owned real estate. Since the eminent branch of the Memmii belonged to the Menenia and Galeria tribes, not the Oufentina, this L. Memmius was likely a member of a client family.[92]

In Augustan times Ephesus prospered as a center of business. Strabo describes the city as the largest emporium in Asia west of the Taurus Mountains, growing daily because of its advantageous position.[93] With Ephesus' increasing size and mercantile importance likely came more Roman settlers. In 29 BC, according to Cassius Dio, Octavian used the presence of Romans in the city as a medium to institute what would grow into the imperial cult: 'Caesar, meanwhile, besides attending to the general business, gave permission for the dedication of sacred precincts in Ephesus and in Nicaea to Rome and to Caesar, his father, whom he named the hero Julius ... He commanded that the Romans resident in these cities should pay honour to these two divinities ...'[94]

In the 40s AD, two inscriptions were set up by the 'society of Roman citizens who do business in Asia' ('conventus civium Romanorum qui in Asia negotiantur'), an organization that, as we have seen above, had already been active in Ephesus from at least 36 BC. Exactly what the Romans' organization looked like and what the term 'conventus' denotes is a moot question that has greatly exercised scholars in the past. There is no need to go into the matter in detail here; suffice it to say it seems unwise to assume the term applied to a formalized, uniform organization adopted

---

[92] *I.Eph.* VI, 2285, see Torelli (1997) 163. Torelli posits that Memmius had much political clout in Ephesus through his *clientes*. However, his hypothesis relies heavily on his reading 'ex pequnia [publica]' in the inscription on the Memmius mausoleum. That reading is by no means certain though; Wankel and Merkelbach in *I.Eph.* emendate: 'ex pequni[a sua]'.

[93] 'ἡ δὲ πόλις τῇ πρὸς τὰ ἄλλα εὐκαιρίᾳ τῶν τόπων αὔξεται καθ' ἑκάστην ἡμέραν, ἐμπόριον οὖσα μέγιστον τῶν κατὰ τὴν Ἀσίαν τὴν ἐντὸς τοῦ Ταύρου'; Strabo 14,1,24.

[94] 'Καῖσαρ δὲ ἐν τούτῳ τά τε ἄλλα ἐχρημάτιζε, καὶ τεμένη τῇ τε Ῥώμῃ καὶ τῷ πατρὶ τῷ Καίσαρι, ἥρωα αὐτὸν Ἰούλιον ὀνομάσας, ἔν τε Ἐφέσῳ καὶ ἐν Νικαίᾳ γενέσθαι ἐφῆκεν· ... καὶ τούτους μὲν τοῖς Ῥωμαίοις τοῖς παρ' αὐτοῖς ἐποικοῦσι τιμᾶν προσέταξε· ...'; Cassius Dio 51,20,6/7. Tr.: E. Cary, Loeb (1980 [1917]).

all over the Empire.[95] In any case, both inscriptions set up by the 'conventus' honor the Emperor Claudius; one is inscribed on a base that seems to have supported a statue of the Emperor on horseback.[96] Whether all this was still a result of Augustus' attempt to establish Emperor worship through Roman settlers or whether we see here a reciprocation for benefactions of Claudius is hard to tell. But whichever was the case, patently a group of Romans, cooperating in a local organization and with business interests as their motive, had moved to Ephesus for the long term.

Romans Resident in Magnesia and Tralles

A first-century BC inscription from Magnesia informs us that the city-council and the people's assembly honored Numerius Cluvius, son of Manius. The honoree, showered with praise, had acted as a benefactor somehow, and in return was presented with a gold crown.[97] A certain N. Cluvius M'. f. is also known from two Puteolan inscriptions dating to the mid-first century BC; he was a regional notable who had been a *duumvir* at both Nola and Capua, and a *quattuorvir* at Caudium.[98] Cluvius is an uncommon *nomen*, almost certainly originating from the area between Capua and Puteoli. Because the name is region-specific and because of the close correspondence in date between the Puteolan and the Magnesian inscriptions, the suggestion has been made to equate the two men.[99] If we accept that the inscriptions refer to the same person, it need not mean that Numerius Cluvius ever lived in Magnesia; he might only have traveled there. But all the same, he seems to have had a lot of leverage in the area, which is not really surprising given what else we know about the Cluvii. An inscription from Delos refers to a M'. Cluvius who operated on the island in the late second and early first centuries BC, and in Cicero's letters we hear of a Puteolan Cluvius who was involved in money-lending

95 The idea of the *conventus* as a uniform, Empire-wide organization was put forward in the late nineteenth century (see Waltzing, vol. 1 (1895) 54, nt. 1; vol. 2 (1896) 177, nt. 4). The idea was challenged by Hatzfeld (1919) 257–265. See also La Piana (1927) 252/253 with nt. 10.

96 *I.Eph.* II, 409; *I.Eph.* VII, 1 3019.

97 'Ἡ βουλὴ κ]αὶ ὁ δῆμος ἐτίμησαν Νεμέ[ρ]ιον Κλούιον Μανίου υἱὸν ταῖς τε ἄλλαις τιμαῖς καὶ χρυσέῳ ἀριστείῳ στεφάνῳ...'; *I.Magn.* 139.

98 *CIL* X 1572, 1573. Cluvius was *duumvir* at Capua, not *quattuorvir*, Bispham (2000) 39.

99 Bispham (2000) 51, 68; Hatzfeld (1919) 123/124.

to cities in Caria.[100] The Cluvii, in other words, seem to have been an eminent Campanian *gens* with commercial ties to the Greek East.

Whether or not Numerius Cluvius ever moved to Magnesia at some point in his life, a larger community of resident Roman citizens seems to have been present there. An unfortunately badly damaged inscription gives a list of men with exclusively Latin names. The precise meaning of the text is no longer intelligible, but it seems certain enough it contained a list of donations for the embellishment of an edifice of some sort; the word 'κόσμον' appears a number of times as does the word 'κίονα', 'column'. Were these men Roman citizens paying for a communal building, a sort of clubhouse for Romans who had moved to the city?[101] Tempting though the assumption may be, unfortunately the information is insufficient to be certain.

Tralles provides much better information on a community of resident Romans. Cicero mentions that there were many Roman citizens living in the city by which, speaking in 59 BC, he can really only have meant immigrants from Italy, not local men who had acquired citizenship.[102] Five inscriptions as well contain evidence for a community of Roman residents. Not all have firm dates, although all but one seem to belong to the second century AD. The one inscription that falls outside that time-frame has been dated to the first century AD. It contains an honorary decree to T(i?) Iulius Claudianus who had acted as a benefactor to the city-council; he had established an endowment from which each councillor would, on an annual basis, be paid 250 *denarii*.[103] The inscription does not say how many Trallian councillors were to benefit, but even if their numbers were relatively modest the capital sum of the foundation must have been quite substantial indeed. We cannot know the exact figure which, apart from the number of councillors, depends on whether the foundation was real estate-based or cash-based. But either way it likely ran in the millions of *sestertii*.[104]

---

[100] P. Jouguet, *BCH* 23 (1899) 64/65, nr. 12, datable to 99/98 BC; the inscription mentions a freedman of M'. Cluvius in a list of *competaliastes*. Cicero *Ad Fam.* 13,56. See Bispham (2000) 50/51, 68.

[101] *I.Magn.* 118. Suggestion made by Hatzfeld (1919) 124.

[102] Cicero *Pro Flacco* 71.

[103] *I.Trall.* 145. See Magie (1950) 586.

[104] With 100 councillors (a conservative estimate, Broughton [1938] 814), the annual sum to be distributed would be 25,000 *denarii*. Assuming the foundation was real estate-based with 5% annual revenue (Duncan-Jones [1982] 33), the capital sum amounted to 500,000 *denarii*. If cash-based, annual revenue was perhaps as high as 10% (Broughton [1938] 900), giving a capital sum of 250,000 *denarii*. See Zuiderhoek (2009) 28–35.

Obviously, Claudianus was a man of considerable wealth. His role in the city was multifaceted, to say the least. He had been *stephanêphoros* (a high-ranking official with unknown responsibilities, perhaps also charged with the performance of sacred rites),[105] secretary of the people's assembly, president of the city-council, a magistrate charged with police tasks, overseer of markets, a member of the guards, and city treasurer.[106] He had apparently also been a priest, had been involved in organizing sacred festivals,[107] and had performed the duties of *dekaprôtos*, meaning he had been responsible for the orderly payment of taxes and had perhaps served as an intermediary between the city and the governor.[108] He had beautified the *agora* by erecting twenty columns there as well as an exedra decorated with marble incrustation and a mosaic pavement, all of which he had done 'for nothing' ('ἀντ' οὐδενός') meaning: without receiving any honorary magistracy in return.

An interesting line of the inscription mentions that Claudianus had twice brought in grain from Alexandria ('σιτωνήσαντα ἀπὸ [Ἀλεξα]νδρείας δίς'). The meaning of this phrase, also in light of other evidence, is unambiguous: Claudianus had bought Egyptian grain for distribution in the city, presumably selling it to the populace at a reduced price. Although 'it seems astonishing that the fabulously fertile valley of the Maeander could not supply the people with [food]'[109] such benefactions seem to have been a fairly regular occurrence.[110] As we will see below, on at least one occasion an imperial visit to Tralles seems to have furnished the reason. The instances alluded to in this inscription, on the other hand, may have been necessitated by food shortages. But whatever the explanation, redirecting shipments of Egyptian grain—the crop that fed the imperial capital—was not within every provincial benefactor's reach.[111] It probably shows Claudianus to have been a man of some political heft.

---

105 Magie (1950) 836–839.

106 'τὸν στεφανηφόρον καὶ γραμματέα τοῦ δήμου, βουλαρχήσαντα, εἰρηναρχήσαντα, ἀγορανομήσαντα... [πα]ραφυλάξαντα, ἀργυροταμιεύσαντα'.

107 'χρυσοφορήσαντα' ('adorned with gold', probably a priestly title) 'παν[ηγ]υριαρχήσαντα'.

108 See Poljakov's commentary to *I.Trall.* 145 line 9; Magie (1950) 1516/1517.

109 J.R.S. Sterrett, *PASA* I (1882) 108/109 nr. 10. See also Pierobon-Benoit (1994) 308. On cereal production, crop failures, and food imports into Asia Minor, see Broughton (1938) 607–609.

110 See the commentary on *I.Trall.* 80 (= *CIG* 2927) by Migeotte (1984) 314–316 nr. 100a.

111 Such purchases would need imperial approval, shown by Oliver (1989) nr. 187, an inscription containing a letter by an unidentifiable Emperor (Marcus Aurelius? Hadrian? Antoninus Pius?) to Ephesus, promising the city the right to buy Egyptian grain on the

Claudianus had, to conclude the long list of his activities, performed secretarial duties ('γραμματεύσαντα') for the council of elders (the *gerousia*), for the association of youths (the *neoi*), and for 'the Romans' ("Ρωμαίων'), which finally brings me to the Roman citizens resident in Tralles. The latter apparently possessed an organization well-defined enough to require having a secretary, although unfortunately no information is given on their activities. It is questionable if Claudianus, though a Roman citizen, belonged to their organization himself. He was clearly independently wealthy, and given his many other public functions and probable political connections he seems more likely to have been a local bigwig, a patron and honorary member of just about every civic body, organization, and club in the city. It seems unlikely that the organization of Romans consisted of men with the financial wherewithal and political clout of Claudianus. More probably, then, he was their patron or was otherwise affiliated with them in some honorary capacity.

In another, later inscription a certain A. Fabricius Priscianus Charmosynus is honored for providing the city with 60,000 *modii* of Egyptian grain, having paid for the load itself as well as its transport to Tralles.[112] It is explicitly stated that the Emperor Hadrian had decided on the shipment and on its quantity, and it has been credibly argued that in this particular case the Emperor's visit to Tralles occasioned the event. If indeed we should place the inscription in the context of Hadrian's journey through Asia Minor then it can be dated roughly to the year 129 AD.[113] The reason for the Emperor's decision to redirect Egyptian grain was probably his wish to ease the burden of the cities on his itinerary of accommodating the large imperial entourage; Ephesus had already received this treatment in the course of the same trip.[114] Charmosynus, by providing ready cash in support of the Emperor's gesture, probably recognized an opportunity to ingratiate himself with the people of Tralles and perhaps even with the people surrounding the Emperor. He will *de facto* have acted mostly as a short-term creditor, putting up the sum to buy grain in bulk but probably expecting some repayment as it was sold to the populace (though at a nominal or a reduced price).

---

proviso that the harvest be sufficient, and that the needs of the city of Rome be met first. See also Pierobon-Benoit (1994) 308; Pleket (1984) 21/22; Wörrle (1971).

112 *I.Trall.* 80 (= *CIG* 2927).

113 Halfmann (1986) 138/139, 204; Migeotte (1984) 314–316 nr. 100A; Wörrle (1971) 335/336.

114 *I.Eph* II, 274. See Wörrle (1971) 335; Halfmann (1986) 126/127, 138/139.

Unfortunately, the first line of the inscription is missing, but it almost certainly mentioned the city-council and the people's assembly as co-dedicators. The second line, however, without doubt shows that 'the Romans resident (in Tralles)' were also honoring Charmosynus. The phrase 'resident Romans' ('κατοικοῦντες Ῥωμαῖοι'), as we have seen in the previous chapters, shows that we are dealing with a group of settlers from a different community, not with a club consisting of locals who had acquired citizenship.[115] I would suggest that they were outsiders who had moved to the city from Italy.[116] At the same time, it is interesting to note that in the case of the honoree Charmosynus, Tralles is said to be his fatherland ('τῇ πατρίδι αὐτοῦ'). He is in addition called patriotic ('φιλόπατριν'); at the bottom of the text it is 'the fatherland' ('ἡ πατρὶς' i.e. Tralles) which praises him for his civic service. Most likely, then, he was a native Trallian who had acquired Roman citizenship. However, it is not inconceivable that he was of Italian origin, and that the designation of the city as his *patris* should be seen as a sign of the strong way in which he had come to identify with his adopted city. A possible parallel for this phenomenon is provided by the epigraphic material from Apamea, discussed below; Apamea is called the *patris* of Roman citizens who likely were Italian immigrants, or direct descendants of Italian immigrants.[117]

A third honorary inscription gives us another bit of information on the organization of Romans in Tralles. The first line is lost, but probably named the city-council and the people's assembly; if correct, these two civic bodies together with the council of elders, the association of youths, and 'the Romans in Tralles' ('οἱ ἐν Τράλλεσι Ῥωμαῖοι') honored Tib. Claudius Panychus Eutychus Coibilos.[118] The inscription, dated to the second century AD, praises Coibilos for his benefactions (he too, we learn, had imported Egyptian grain into the city) and for his civic service. His relationship to the resident Romans is made explicit: he acted as their curator ('κουρατορεύσαντα τῶν Ῥωμαίων'). In the previous two chapters we have seen the phenomenon of curators of foreign trade organizations a number

[115] Tyrians in Puteoli ('οἱ ἐν Ποτιόλοις κατοικοῦντες', *OGIS*, 595); Berytians in the same city ('qui Puteolis consistunt', *CIL* X 1634). See Waltzing vol. 2 (1896) 176–182. See also Mitteis (1891) 144/145.

[116] On the probably southern Italian provenance of many Romans in the East, see Hatzfeld (1919) 238–245; Broughton (1938) 543–554. The hypothesis that the Romans were descendants of colonists, sent by Augustus in 15 BC to revive the city after an earthquake, is discussed, and dismissed, by Hatzfeld (1919) 170–172.

[117] See Ramsay (1895) 426/427, 460; Hatzfeld (1919) 167 nt. 6.

[118] *I.Trall.* 77 (= *CIG* 2930).

of times, and this case seems to fit that pattern. Coibilos' functions were not all related to trade though: he had been commander of the night-watch, a magistrate in charge of tax collection, city treasurer, and temple warden.[119] However, he had also been overseer of markets and had, from his own money, set up twelve marble tables and their bases in the fish market.[120] In addition, he was involved in money-lending somehow, although the details of that activity remain obscure.[121]

Of a fourth honorary inscription only the first three lines survive: the city-council, the people's assembly, the council of elders, the association of youths, and an unidentifiable group in Tralles ('οἱ ἐν Τράλλεσι ...') honored someone whose name is now lost.[122] It is not certain the Romans are the missing group, but it seems a safe assumption since the list of dedicators is similar to the one in the inscription honoring Coibilos and since this inscription too has been dated to the second century AD. Unfortunately, we know nothing about the honoree or about his possible relations with the resident Romans.

The final inscription equally is too damaged to be certain the Romans figured in it, although it seems highly likely. From the few remaining words it would seem that the Emperor Hadrian addressed a group of people 'resident in Tralles' ('Trallibus consisten[tibus]').[123] Probably the inscription was the text of a letter, immortalized in stone, by Hadrian to this group. The second-century date, the fact that, as far as we know, the Romans were the only group in the city referred to as 'resident' ('consistentes', 'κατοικοῦντες'), and the circumstance that the letter (if indeed it was one) was written in Latin all support the idea that the addressees were indeed 'the Romans resident in Tralles'. Perhaps the inscription should be placed in the same context of Hadrian's visit to the city mentioned earlier, which would imply a date of approximately 129 AD.

---

119 'στρατηγήσαντα τὴν νυκ{υ}τερινὴν στρατηγίαν, δεκαπρωτεύσαντα, ἀργυροταμιεύσαντα ... νεωποιήσαντα'.

120 'ἀναθέντα δὲ ἐκ τῶν ἰδίων καὶ τὰς ἐν τῇ ὀψαριοπώλει<δι> μαρμαρίνας τραπέζας ιβ' σὺν ταῖς βάσεσιν <ι>β'' 'fish market', rather than 'meat market'; Broughton (1938) 766.

121 Coibilos was 'ἐκδανείσαντα'. The verb 'ἐκδανείζειν' ('to lend out money at interest') often refers to loans made by cities to individuals, but for the inscription to call Coibilos a debtor to the city makes little sense in this context. One solution would be to suppose that Coibilos had lent money to, rather than borrowed money from the city (see Migeotte (1984) 120/121 for an Aristotle passage where 'ἐκδανείζειν' seems to have that meaning). Another solution would be to suppose that Coibilos acted as a magistrate who managed the loans made by the city to private individuals; Migeotte (1984) 315/316.

122 *I.Trall.* 93.

123 *I.Trall.* 19 (= *CIL* III 444).

Romans Resident in Apamea

The city of Apamea provides excellent epigraphic source material for Romans domiciled there. As in Magnesia and Tralles, and in contrast to Ephesus where the oldest evidence dates to around 100 BC, the Apamean inscriptions seem all to belong to imperial times, with an unusually late, third-century cut-off date. The only possible exception (late first century BC?) consists of a marble column bearing the words '[...] qui Apameae negotiantur h(onoris) c(ausa)'. This type of Latin inscription in the Greek East often refers to Roman businessmen; since a community of Romans is well-documented in Apamea, the lacuna could have read 'cives Romani', or else perhaps 'conventus civium Romanorum'.[124]

To my knowledge, the oldest inscription in which Roman settlers appear for certain can not be firmly dated but must belong roughly to the early Empire since it is a dedication to a priest of Rome; such priesthoods of simply 'Rome' are rarely found in later times when Emperors were worshipped personally.[125] In the inscription a certain Mytas, son of Diocles, besides a priest of Rome also a secretary of the Apamean people's assembly, is honored by, in that order, the assembly and the resident Romans ('οἱ κατοικοῦντες Ῥωμαῖοι'). The inscription shows the imperial cult already to have penetrated deeply into Asia at an early date and to have acquired an institutionalized form. Presumably the reason the Roman settlers honored Mytas had to do with his priesthood, but that is about as much as we can say about their motives.

An inscription that can not be far removed in date from the one just discussed (it definitely belongs to the Julio-Claudian era) contains a dedication to the Apamean people's assembly by five men with full Roman names, all holding high civic office.[126] It would seem that it was set up to commemorate that for the first time in history a particular municipal board of magistrates consisted entirely of Romans ('ἄρξαντες ἐν τῷ λ' καὶ ρ' ἔτι Ῥωμαῖοι πρώτος'). Unfortunately, the inscription does not make clear what kind of office the Romans were holding. It could have been the supreme magistracy; in an inscription dating to Flavian times

---

[124] *CIL* III 365, with *CIL* III p. 977 ad. 365 (= *MAMA* VI, p. 146, nr. 109*). Hatzfeld (1919) 122 tentatively dates this inscription to the end of the first century BC. On the designation 'negotiantur', see Hatzfeld (1919) 193–196.

[125] *CB* nr. 302. See also Hatzfeld (1919) 168.

[126] *CB* nr. 290, attributed to 54/55 AD (= *IGRR* IV 792, dated there to 45/46 AD). See also Hatzfeld (1919) 167.

L. Atilius L. f. Pal. Proclus, son of one of the five men, is honored (he had acted as an envoy to Rome for the city), and the civic service of both Proclus himself and of his ancestors is emphatically alluded to, strengthening the interpretation that his father had indeed held the highest office.[127] Against that view, however, speaks that in no later inscription do we witness any Roman holding the supreme magistracy again, let alone several at the same time. But in any case, the mere fact that five Romans held some lofty office simultaneously is telling about the prominent role Roman settlers played in Apamean civic life.

In no fewer than nine honorary inscriptions the Romans appear alongside the Apamean city-council and people's assembly. The formula is invariably 'the *boulê*, the *dêmos*, and the resident Romans (are honoring)', and this practice remained constant from the mid-first century AD all the way to at least the third century AD. The, to date, oldest known Apamean inscription bearing this formula must have been set up at around the same time as the dedication by the five Roman office holders.[128] The honoree is a certain L. Rutilius L. f. Vel. Proclus, a man who, because of his unmistakably Roman name and because of the context of praise by a group of resident Romans, is thought to have been an immigrant from Italy. Nonetheless, Apamea is called his *patris* and the inscription stresses his civic service to the city.[129] Unless we discount this praise as pure rhetoric, it can be taken as indicative of the good relationship between the Roman community and at least the Apamean governing class.

A similar case is presented by an honorary decree, Flavian in date, to Proclus Manneius P. f. Rom. Ruso.[130] Ruso was in all likelihood of Italian stock, although his family must have settled at Apamea; the inscription praises the benefactions of both himself and his ancestors, and mentions how he had often provided the city (referred to as his *patris*) with food in

---

127 *CB* nr. 305. '…δικαίως ἐκ προγόνων πολιτευόμενον…' Hatzfeld (1919) 167 nt. 6 prefers an Antonine date for the inscription.

128 *CB* nr. 298. In both this inscription and the one by the five Roman office holders, the Greek spelling 'Λεύκιος' for 'Lucius' (rather than 'Λούκιος', cf. nr. 305) indicates an early date.

129 Rutilii are well-known from the epigraphic record from Delos; Wilson (1966) 109/110. Hatzfeld (1919) 167 nt. 6 remarks on the unusual use of the word *patris* in the inscriptions for L. Atilius Proclus, L. Rutilius Proclus, and Proclus Manneius Ruso (likely all Italian immigrants), taking it as a sign that they were deeply integrated into the Apamean society.

130 *CB* nr. 299 (= Doublet and Bérard [1893] nr. 8, 313–315). 'Πρόκλον' is probably an engraver's error for 'Πόπλιον' since Ruso was the son of a Publius. Hatzfeld (1919) 168 nt. 4 prefers an Antonine date for the inscription.

times of need. The immediate reason Ruso was honored, though, was that he had served as an envoy to Rome on behalf of Apamea. Perhaps the city planned to build a temple for the imperial cult; in that interpretation Ruso managed to get the Emperors' (Vespasian and Titus?) consent and also managed to receive a grant for the proposed temple from the college of high-priests of Asia.[131] Somewhat surprisingly, no mention is made of Ruso undertaking the embassy at his own expense, a usual addition in inscriptions like these, which might signal that the journey itself was not much out of the ordinary for him and that he traveled back and forth to Rome on a regular basis. The inscription does provide an interesting detail about the decision-making process behind the honorary decree, saying it had taken place in a general assembly of Romans and Apameans ('πανδήμου ἐκκλησίας'). It is perhaps tempting to suppose this phrase refers to some sort of formal civic body composed of representatives of the two communities. However, this is the only instance where these words appear and it seems safer to see them as a reference to some *ad hoc* gathering.

'The *boulê*, the *dêmos*, and the resident Romans' did not just honor private benefactors; they set up honorary decrees and statues for Emperors and (wives of) high Roman officials as well. In one inscription, for instance, this triad is seen honoring the Emperor Vespasian.[132] Some 60 years later, they set up a dedication and statue to Sossia Polla, the wife of Q. Roscius Pompeius Falco, proconsul of Asia.[133]

In four inscriptions, dating to the mid-second century AD and set up in two pairs, a father and son with the somewhat unwieldy names of Tiberius Claudius Tib. Cl. f. Quir. Piso Mithridatianus and Tiberius Claudius Tib. Cl. f. Quir. Granianus are honored by, once again, *boulê, dêmos*, and resident Romans.[134] Both men had been *gymnasiarch*—the father when the assizes were held in Apamea, which must have brought added responsibility—and both are praised for their civic service. Both were clearly Roman citizens, but it is doubtful they were of Italian origin. The son's

131 The word '*archiereis*' (the meaning of which is not entirely clear) in this interpretation refers to a council of high-priests of Asia, controlling funds belonging to the Asian *koinon*, and empowered to make grants to Asian cities. Ramsay (1895) 465.

132 *MAMA* VI, 177.

133 *CB* nr. 291 (= Doublet and Bérard [1893] nr. 4, 305/306). See also *CB* nr. 292 (= *MAMA* VI, 182).

134 *CB* nr. 294/295 (= *IGRR* IV, 790); *CB* nr. 296/297 (= *MAMA* 6, 180 = Doublet and Bérard [1893] nr. 6, 308–313).

cognomen, Granianus, could point to some distant Campanian roots.[135] However, his father's and grandfather's cognomina, Mithridatianus and Mithridates respectively, make it more likely the family descended from an Anatolian clan that had received citizenship sometime during the reign of Claudius. If so, the resident Romans were not honoring their own in this case.

The family to which father and son belonged must have been very well-off indeed, probably counting among the wealthiest families in Apamea. Mithridatianus, the inscriptions record, had promised not to use the 15,000 *denarii* allotted him by the city for his expenses as *gymnasiarch* if his son were to be elected to the same office. His liberality (in oil for the gymnasium and also in cash for the purchase of oil) in the end allowed the city to amass 34,000 *denarii*, money that was used as the capital sum for a foundation. From the annual rent, payments were made towards some sort of deficit Apamea had apparently incurred; Mithridatianus' generosity allowed the city to do away with the annual 'curators' ('κουράτορας' i.e.: of the gymnasium) who, as some sort of liturgy, were burdened with financing the debt.[136]

The youngest known Apamean inscriptions set up by *boulê, dêmos*, and resident Romans are all dedications to benefactors as well. In one, dating to either the 160s or the 170s AD, the imperial freedman M. Aurelius Zosimus is honored; no specifics are given about his munificence.[137] Two inscriptions seem to be late in date. One honors M. Aurelius Ariston Euclianus, in all likelihood a Greek whose family had acquired citizenship in Antonine times. The inscription seems to belong to the early third century AD, and the references to times of need and to Euclianus' efforts to feed the city ('θρέψαντα τὴν πόλιν ἐν δυσχρήστοις καιροῖς') may point to the disorganization of the time.[138] However, the phrase appears also in the honorary decree to Ruso (a Flavian inscription); the references in the Trallian source material to imports of Alexandrian grain too seem to

[135] Granius is a *nomen* associated with Campania, more specifically with Puteoli. See e.g. the Puteolan businessman Granius involved in Sicilian trade, summoned as a witness in Cicero II *Verres* 5,154.

[136] This is the explanation given by (Doublet and) Bérard (1893) 312/312 (followed by W.H. Buckler and W.M. Calder in *MAMA*). Ramsay (in *CB*) gives a different one: the curators were Roman officials, imposed on the city to oversee its finances, and to control its revenue. However, it seems hard to understand how the city could unilaterally have decided to do away with these imperial curators, even with the windfall of the foundation.

[137] *MAMA* VI, 183. The (almost certainly) same man appears in *IGRR* IV, 749.

[138] *CB* nr. 300 (= Doublet and Bérard [1893] nr. 2, 302–304).

suggest that even under peaceful circumstances, handouts of food were on occasion necessary in the Maeander Valley.[139] The youngest inscription is a dedication to Julius Ligys, an equestrian *primipilarius*. By the third century, the *primipilatus* formed a step towards the procuratorship, and the inscription can thus reasonably securely be dated to that time period.[140] As with the imperial freedman Zosimus, we are left in the dark about the nature of his benefactions.

The Roman Settlers' Social Position

From the discussions above it has become clear that in Ephesus, Tralles, and Apamea there were groups of Roman settlers. In Ephesus the evidence shows that at least some of these groups were mercantile and professional in nature ('negotiantur', 'conlegei'). Although in Tralles it is nowhere explicitly stated that the resident Romans were businessmen, their group characteristics fit the pattern that emerged from the evidence discussed in the previous chapters: outsiders settling locally and cooperating in an organization with a curator and other officials (a secretary, perhaps patrons). In Apamea as well the resident Romans are nowhere described as businessmen, but given the city's position as a central node on an East-West trade route, a route that saw the movement of goods from Italy, a connection between their presence and trade is likely. In the inscriptions from all three cities, little is said about communal buildings, but we know that at least in Ephesus Roman wine merchants possessed a structure of some sort as early as the first century BC. In the evidence from nearby Magnesia we may have further evidence for a building sheltering a Roman club. The question is: were the Roman groups in these cities performing the same task as the immigrant groups in Italian towns? Was their purpose, in other words, essentially to establish trust and to maintain stable relations for reasons of trade?

Of course, Roman businessmen living in Asia were not just one group of immigrants among many such as the Tyrians living in Puteoli; they were representatives of the militarily and politically dominant people. This situation must have had much significance especially in the period

[139] See in general on Asia Minor, Pierobon-Benoit (1994) who attributes the phenomenon of food shortages mostly to increased urbanization.

[140] *CB* nr. 301 (= *IGRR* IV, 786). Abbreviation 'ΠΠ' read as *primipilarius* both by W.M. Ramsay in *CB* and G. Lafaye in *IGRR*.

just following the creation of the province, when the Romans arrived as the heirs to royal power; with them had come armies, officials, and tax collectors. A century later, as we have seen, Augustus used the presence of Romans in Ephesus to implement a new imperial branch of religion: Emperor worship. Immigrants such as Nabataeans and Syrians brought their native religions with them to Italy, where they constructed temples and continued to venerate their gods. The introduction of the imperial cult by Romans in the East, though, was decidedly of a different social and political significance.[141] The sense that the relationship between Italy and the eastern provinces was one of conquerors and conquered may have been felt less acutely over time ('Graecia capta ferum victorem cepit') but in the second century AD there was still no question of what was center and what periphery.[142] Aelius Aristides neatly summarized the relation between the two. Though a son of Asia himself, he cheerfully proclaimed that the city of Rome did not need a defensive wall because its wall was the *limes imperii*.[143]

In Asia, governors and their staff toured the province and held assizes; they appointed judges and juries, and in general attempted to uphold the rule of law. Roman businessmen living in Ephesus and Apamea had the governor's court on their doorstep, so to speak, and although Tralles was stripped of its status as an assize center sometime in Augustus' reign, Ephesus was not far away. Unlike provincials coming to Italy, Roman businessmen in Asia therefore had access to the officials of their homeland, officials who, to boot, were representatives of the ruling imperial state. On the face of it, the position of Roman traders, certainly the ones living in the assize centers, seems therefore to have been far easier than the position of immigrant traders living in Italy.

Still, there are important caveats. How often exactly do we suppose the governor held court? During his one-year appointment he most likely visited all the assize centers in his province only once, if that often.[144] Dio Chrysostom informs us that in Apamea these visits happened only every other year, and that there was talk of making them even more infrequent.[145] If the amount of litigating the Sulpicii were doing is anything to go by, this

[141] See Price (1984) esp. 101–132.
[142] Horace *Ep.* 2,1,156.
[143] Aelius Aristides *Or.* 26,79/80. See also Appian *Praef.* 7; Herodian 2,11,5.
[144] Burton (1975) 97–99; Marshall (1966).
[145] Dio Chrysostom *Or.* 35,15–17. See Ramsay (1895) 364/365, 428/429.

would imply a much greater demand for court-sessions than were available through the governor's assize hearings.

The governor did naturally have recourse to physical force, an option he no doubt occasionally needed to revert to in the course of his duties. However, this power was his exclusive prerogative; he could not cede it to a deputy.[146] Since the governor was but one man who could only be in one place at any given time, the exercise of this power was limited and probably somewhat haphazard. Besides, the governor and his legates were interested most of all in cases with a direct impact on Roman rule: cases of a diplomatic nature between communities, criminal cases, and cases to do with administrative matters and taxation.[147] Ordinary trade disputes, if given any attention at all, probably got short shrift. More important still, there is one crucial similarity between the Italian and the provincial situation that deserves to be made explicit: as in Italy there is no indication that ordinary inhabitants of Asia—whether natives or resident Romans—could count on the government to enforce their contracts. The Roman provincial authorities did simply not see it as part of their duty to put their coercive powers in the service of private individuals.

Contract enforcement aside, could Roman merchants living in Asia still draw much everyday business advantage—perhaps unfair advantage—from the presence of Roman power? It is extremely tempting to assume *a priori* that they somehow benefited a great deal from the circumstance that a magistrate and his staff were present on the ground to administer the province. That they did not at all seems unlikely. For one thing, Roman officials were charged with fighting piracy and with making the waters safe for sailing and seaborne trade, which was in the Roman merchants' direct interest (though not just in theirs).[148] The edict, mentioned in the *Digest*, that Antoninus Pius issued when serving as governor of Asia also shows concern for suppressing brigandage; it contained instructions to the *eirênarchai* (local police officials) to arrest and interrogate robbers,

---

146 The powers of a governor of Asia and Macedonia in the Republican period are conveniently itemized in the *Lex de provinciis praetoriis*, section Cnidos IV 31–39; Crawford I (1996) 242, 255, 265/266. See also Lintott (1993) 56; Ferrary (2002) 136.

147 Roman provincial officials thin on the ground: Galsterer (1986) 25/26. Traveling governors: Marshall (1966); Burton (1975). Governors' concern for peace and security, see the edict issued by Antoninus Pius as governor of Asia: Marcianus *Dig*. 48,3,6,1 (see also Garnsey [1968]). Lines 147, 150 of the 'Customs law of Asia' are badly mutilated, but it is clear they contain provisions for jurisdiction in fiscal matters; Cottier and Crawford (2008) 82/83, 161–163.

148 *Lex de provinciis praetoriis* (dating from 100 BC), section Cnidos II 6–11 and Cnidos III 31–35; Crawford I (1996) 238/239, 253/254, 258/259, 261. See Ferrary (2002) 134/135.

draw up reports, and send sealed copies to the Roman magistrate.[149] But other, more specific and more personal benefits Roman traders may have been enjoying are harder to pinpoint.

The literature on the subject often presupposes a hand-in-glove cooperation between Roman traders and officials.[150] However, it is important to recognize that the one-year tenure of proconsuls formed a serious impediment to any such tight cooperation. Roman settlers were permanent residents of the province, having migrated for life or at least for the long term. Governors, on the other hand, were career officials who normally came and went every year. As we have seen, instructions were given to governors, and there will have been a certain consistency of official policy. But still, the province annually had to get acquainted with a proconsul, new to the area, and new to his task. Differences in personality between subsequent officials aside, this short-term tenure will have rendered it exceedingly difficult for Roman merchants to forge a close personal relationship with the proconsul.

Perhaps unsurprisingly, it is hard to find concrete examples of official favoritism. The best instance is probably provided by the decree from the free city of Colophon, dating to the early days of the province, already discussed at the beginning of this chapter. It honors the Colophonian Menippos among other things because he had 'freed the inhabitants of the city from the legal guarantees and from the power of the governor'.[151] The latter statement for certain refers to Colophon's free status; the governor had apparently been pronouncing judgment in the city, although strictly it fell outside his jurisdiction. After two pleas before the Senate in Rome, Menippos had managed to obtain a *Senatus Consultum* which put a halt to this infringement of local autonomy. The interpretation of the first statement about guarantees, however, is less clear-cut. It has been taken to mean that Greeks, when summoned by a Roman citizen, were required by the governor to pay a certain sum as security. This, so the reasoning goes, was a systematic and deliberate policy leaving Greeks involved in

---

149 Marcianus *Dig.* 48,3,6,1. See Ando (2000) 363/364; Magie (1950) 630, 647. See also Nippel (1995) 100–112.

150 Ferrary (2002) 134–139; Magie (1950) 162/163; Hatzfeld (1919) 321.

151 H.W. Pleket, *SEG* 39 (1989) nr. 1244: 'τοὺς δὲ κατοικοῦντας τὴν πόλιν ἐλευθέρωσε κατεγγυήσεων καὶ στρατηγικῆς ἐξουσίας', column I line 37–39 (see also column I line 23–27); Robert and Robert (1989) 63–66, 70, 86. See also H.W. Pleket and R.S. Stroud, *SEG* 39 (1989) nr. 1243 (roughly contemporary) in which another Colophonian seems to be honored for similar feats (column II line 51–61; Robert and Robert [1989] 13, 38–40). See also Lintott (1993) 62/63.

legal actions with Romans at a disadvantage.[152] Both circumstances have been adduced as proof that governors interfered in legal matters when it was in the interests of Roman citizens: they were willing to exceed their jurisdictional limits, and were creating favorable conditions for litigating Romans.

However, there are compelling arguments against that view. Apart from the fact that reconstructing exactly what had been going on in the Colophonian courts is hardly a straightforward matter, drawing conclusions on the basis of the events in one city during the early years of the province is risky. More importantly, it is crucial to note that the violation of Colophon's freedom was in the end checked by the Roman Senate itself. Besides, the same inscription tells us that Menippos—apparently a staunch defender of Greek interests—was subsequently enlisted as a sort of 'ambassador' by Roman officialdom, negotiating in that capacity with other Greek cities in the area. His past dealings with the Senate, crowned by the trophy of the *Senatus Consultum*, must have given considerable weight to his interferences.[153] If Roman magistrates really were systematically favoring their compatriots in a court setting, it seems incongruous they would have created such a nuisance for themselves.

Other evidence too hardly suggests a situation in which imperial officials were at beck and call of the Roman merchants. Cicero, as governor of Cilicia, dispatched his friend Q. Volusius to Cyprus for a few days 'so that', as he wrote to Atticus, 'the few Roman citizens who carry on business there should not say they had no one to try their cases—Cypriots cannot legally be summoned out of the island'.[154] To conclude that Roman citizens had the right to summon all eastern provincials except Cypriots to appear before the magistrate seems to me to be stretching the meaning of this passage. And in any case, it certainly does not imply that magistrates sprang into action whenever a Roman citizen was involved in litigation.[155] Cicero's tone rather betrays he grudgingly lent somewhat token support.

In analyzing the relations between governor and traders, we also have to reckon with a process of profound change. The members of the

---

[152] Ferrary (1991) 566/567; Ferrary (2002) 139. For his interpretation that this indicates abuse of legal guarantees, Ferrary points to Gaius *Inst.* 4,88/89; 101/102; 184/185 (*satisdatio*).

[153] Column III line 5–15; commentary, Robert and Robert (1989) 101/102. See also Ferrary (1991) 576.

[154] 'Q. Vulusium ... misi in Cyprum ut ibi pauculos dies esset, ne cives Romani pauci qui illic negotiantur ius sibi dictum negarent: nam evocari ex insula Cyprios non licet'. Cicero *Ad Att.* 5,21,6. Tr.: D.R. Shackleton Bailey, Loeb (1999). See Marshall (1966) 244.

[155] Ferrary (2002) 138/139.

collegium in Ephesus in approximately 100 BC lived in a different political and cultural world—a much more alien world—than the Romans in Tralles during the reign of Hadrian. When the province of Asia was created, the contrast between Roman merchants and the local population was still stark.[156] Over time, though, a process of increasing 'Romanization' took place in the East.[157] The term is somewhat nebulous, but whatever else it is taken to encompass, one thing is certain: from roughly the mid-40s BC onward more and more Asian Greeks acquired Roman citizenship.[158] Roman citizens, in other words, were no longer exclusively outsiders. Whatever advantage immigrants from the Italian peninsula living in Asia may have drawn from their legal status in the first century BC likely eroded away when citizenship was no longer their exclusive group characteristic.

But to return to my main theme, in Asia, as in Italy, the state did not enforce private contracts. I think it bears repeating that this circumstance, though easy to overlook, is of vital importance for understanding the mechanisms that supported long-distance trade. The implication is that the situation of groups living abroad, maintaining links with the homeland, facilitating the circulation of information, and providing for a social network to support enforcement is likely to have existed overseas as well as in Italy. My argument is therefore that the Romans we encounter in Ephesus, Tralles, and Apamea were indeed in essence a phenomenon comparable to the foreign groups in Puteoli, Ostia, and Rome.

Roman businessmen trading with the local community will almost have been obligated, at least in part, to play by the local rules and to use local institutions of arbitration. Of regional courts, there was no shortage in Asia, as I have shown above. The scarcity of proconsular court sessions will have forced traders—Roman citizens or no—to use them. Confirmation of the resulting necessity to adopt local rules comes from an unexpected source: a document in the Sulpicii archive. It is the maritime insurance-contract, already discussed in Chapter 2, dating to 38 AD and drawn up by the shipper Menelaos from Ceramus. The first half of the

[156] Romans had been coming to the East in small numbers from much earlier on, but the process really accelerated from the mid-second century BC onward. Wilson (1966) 85–93; Hatzfeld (1919) 17–51.

[157] For a particularly insightful discussion, with references to older literature, see Woolf (1994).

[158] Sherwin-White (1973) 306–311; Mitteis (1891) 148/149. See also *RDGE* nr. 58 (discussed above). Aelius Aristides *Or.* 26,64 alludes to the large number of provincials holding dual citizenship.

contract is written in Greek following a Greek contractual model, so that the result is a sort of Hellenistic-Roman hybrid. Even traders in Puteoli while dealing with itinerant Asians at times had to adjust to Asian rules and customs. This will have held true *a fortiori* for the Roman merchants actually resident in the province.[159]

It seems likely that in the coherence of groups of Romans living in Asia, as in the case of immigrant groups in Italy, provenance was the main ingredient. However, though the Romans presented themselves as a distinct group, unlike immigrants in Italian cities the labels they used do not reveal much about their exact geographical origin ('Roman' not, or at least not necessarily, meaning 'coming from the city of Rome'). No specific places are mentioned, and the only possible geographical pointer is provided by the term 'Italici' used in Republican times in Ephesus. Strabo tells us that originally 'Italia' only designated the extreme southern part of the peninsula, from the Strait of Sicily to the Gulf of Salerno. Already in Hellenistic times, however, the term included territory up to the Alps, as Polybius' description of Italy makes clear. The identifier 'Italici' slowly fell out of use in the Greek East in the decades following the conclusion of the Social War, but by adopting it the Italians in Ephesus may have kept a memory of their southern origin alive.[160] But either way, although a larger geographical area as a marker of provenance is not without parallel (see for example the Baeticans doing business in Rome) the consistency with which settlers called themselves 'Italians' or 'Romans', never e.g. 'Puteolans' or 'Ostians', is striking.[161] Does this lack of geographical specificity mean that the Roman groups consisted of people drawn indiscriminately from all over the Italian peninsula? That seems unlikely. The settlers united in local clubs and organizations, and it stands to reason that they co-opted from a network of people they knew, coming mostly or exclusively from a particular area or city, probably even from particular families.[162]

A wholly satisfactory explanation for the observed phenomenon is hard to devise. Complicating matters is that the meaning of both the term

---

159 *TPsulp*.78.

160 Strabo 5,1,1; Polybius 2,14,4–12.

161 This consistency is not confined to Ephesus, Tralles, and Apamea but encompasses all of Asia Minor and Greece. None of the labels the settlers used—whether 'Italici', 'Rhomaioi', or 'cives Romani'—reveal much about their exact geographical origin. Hatzfeld (1919) 238–245.

162 Just over fifty *gens* names appear in the epigraphic record, some only once or twice, some frequently. Much of the evidence points to a southern Italian origin. Wilson (1966) 152–155.

'Romans' ('cives Romani', 'Rhomaioi' and variants) and 'Italici' by migrating Italians cannot be assumed to have been the same before the Social War as after. Before the war 'Romans' might well have been employed because citizenship was deemed more important in self-representation than precise geographical origin, at least for purposes of public display such as inscriptions.[163] This might also explain the use of the term 'Italici', an ambiguous term with at least partly a geographical connotation. Use of this label might initially have been a way for migrating *socii*, or mixed groups of citizens and *socii*, to gloss over the lack of citizenship of all or some of their members.[164]

However, after the war and into imperial times, in the Greek East the term 'Roman' continued to be favored over references to individual cities. In the later period the word is less likely to have been intended to highlight citizenship, which all Italians now possessed and provincials increasing also acquired, and perhaps did refer mainly to geographical origin. If so, then Italian provenance as such had perhaps become the overriding identity in self-representation, trumping the identities from particular cities. All of this will have to remain speculative, but if that reading is correct then what we see in the post-Social War evidence might be a reflection of the same Italy-centric view of Empire promoted by Aelius Aristides.

A striking feature of the evidence mainly from Apamea, but also from Tralles, is that the Roman settlers seem to have played an active role in municipal affairs, much more so than foreign settlers in Italian cities. In Apamea, individual Romans held high office, and the Romans communally, together with the city-council and the people's assembly, dedicated honorary inscriptions to benefactors, Emperors, and high-ranking imperial officials. In Tralles, the Romans as a group appear in honorific inscriptions alongside Trallian social and political institutions such as the council of elders, the association of youths, the city-council, and the people's assembly. This Roman prominence in public life, though not as much in evidence in Ephesus as in Apamea and Tralles, conforms to a larger pattern

---

163 I think it is important to recognize that in all time periods it is *self*-representation we see. Hatzfeld (1919) 243 seems largely to miss this point: '... ils [i.e. Greeks] leur ont appliqué à tous le terme de "Ρωμαῖοι", inexact et imprécis comme tous ceux par lesquels les Orientaux ont désigné de tout temps les gents d'Occident'.

164 The word perhaps lent itself for such use because its meaning was not well-defined: 'La parola *Italicus* non ha un significato costante nelle nostre fonti'; Ilari (1974) 3/4 nt. 9. See also Hatzfeld (1919) 242/243: 'Ce mot ne comportait aucune unité ethnique,... ni juridique...; mais au moins exprimait-il une certaine unité géographique'.

of Roman expatriate behavior in the Greek East.[165] In contrast, nowhere in the evidence from Puteoli or Ostia do we see immigrants collectively participating in a similar way, the only possible exception being the Tyrians resident in Puteoli financing the local Ox-Sacrifice Games.

As is well known, the arrival of Rome on the Greek scene led to a deep and lasting transformation of the political process in Greek cities. The Roman government unabashedly favored the propertied classes—establishing property qualifications for office, enlarging the power of city-councils and local magistrates—and over time Greek cities became increasingly oligarchic, eventually being governed by a largely hereditary upper-class.[166] Given this dynamic, it is perhaps tempting to ascribe the cooperation of Roman residents and Greek civic bodies to a shift in power, seeing it as the product of a relationship between Roman rulers and Greek ruled. However, I think that interpretation would be to overestimate how much the power imbalance was felt in the day-to-day interaction of relatively few Romans living in a Greek environment. What it rather signifies is the wish of Roman permanent settlers to be a part of Greek civic life. The Romans, in other words, tried to assimilate and to forge a bond with at least the well-to-do section of the host population. Because of the greater cultural prominence of civic institutions in Greek city-life, their behavior differed from that of immigrants in Italian cities, but the mechanism was similar. I can probably do no better than quote Malcolm Errington here: '[Romans] had to live amicably together with the citizens in the cities where they resided and with whom they did business.... Where, for numerical reasons, cultural and local political domination was impossible, there remained simply the choice between ignoring what was going on in local civic life—which, given the traditionally intimate connection between wealth and civic life in Greek cities could only be extremely bad for business—or trying to adapt to it'.[167]

This brings me to somewhat of a historical problem, namely the relationship between the native Greek population and the Roman traders in the run-up to the first Mithridatic War. Since part of the Ephesian source material dates to the period just prior to and immediately following the conflict, it is worth addressing the question here. We have seen how Roman merchants before the war made themselves visible in Ephesus

---

165 Broughton (1938) 880/881; Hatzfeld (1919) 309–315.

166 See Ando (2000) 59; Jones (1940) 170–191.

167 Errington (1988) 145. On urban Greek elites and trade, see Pleket (1984).

with a *collegium* organization and a communal building flagged by a public inscription. Roman traders did also not hesitate to draw attention to their presence in the city in the 60s BC, with the massacre of their compatriots still within living memory. These public inscriptions might be taken as a sign that relations between the merchants and at least part of the local population were on the whole not unfriendly.

Stronger signs in Asia more generally include Romans marrying local women, Romans acting as benefactors and being awarded honors in return, Romans and their sons participating in Greek sporting festivals, Roman youths enrolling in the *ephêbate*, and Romans joining Greek religious associations.[168] Inscriptions provide the bulk of the evidence, and although caution is called for with the notoriously rhetorical epigraphic material, obviously not all of this can be dismissed as mere rhetoric. Yet, despite the many indications that relations between the Romans and the native population in Asia were civil or at times even cordial, the Romans were famously on the receiving end of brutal aggression almost as soon as Mithridates' campaign was underway.[169] The discrepancy between the seemingly collegial coexistence of Romans and Greeks on the one hand and the anti-Roman violence that erupted in the East on the other begs the question of how these two things can be reconciled.

Jean Hatzfeld, in what is still the fundamental work on Romans migrating to the East, was alert to the contradiction; he sought the explanation for the dislike of all things Roman in the use of a double legal standard.[170] The Romans, he posits, had recourse to both Greek and Roman law and could, according to circumstances and at the expense of their Greek business partners, choose the system that best suited their interests. To support his claim he points to the passage in Cicero's *Pro Flacco* where Cicero accused Decianus of having abused his legal position in the city of Apollonis (mid-way between Pergamum and Sardis)[171] in order to acquire an estate. If Cicero is to be believed, Decianus—exploiting what seems to have been a case of domestic strife within a prominent local family—initially went about his nefarious business using Greek law, but later, with the deal under threat, attempted to secure his acquisition by registering it in the Roman census.[172]

---

[168] Hatzfeld (1919) 291–315; Errington (1988).
[169] On the Mithridatic War, see Magie (1950) 199–231.
[170] Hatzfeld (1919) 315–332. Ferrary (2002) 142–145 struggles with the same problem.
[171] Strabo 13,4,4.
[172] Cicero *Pro Flacco* 70–80. See Marshall (1969) 267–270; Hatzfeld (1919) 319/320.

However, it is debatable whether this episode really provides firm evidence for Roman businessmen cherry-picking whatever laws they preferred. It is doubtful whether Decianus—an aristocrat, a senator's son, politically well connected in Rome—was representative of the group of Roman traders. Moreover, the transaction and certainly the circumstances—purchase of real estate, a family feud—were hardly typical of everyday trading activities. More importantly, Hatzfeld's thesis seems improbable because of its logical inconsistency. For Roman merchants domiciled in Greek cities, bullying, maneuvering, and conniving was a poor long-term strategy in establishing relations with the native trading community; no solid foundation for conducting long-distance intercommunity trade could ever be laid that way.[173]

Another hypothesis seems to do better justice to the sources, although the actions of Decianus still seem indicative of the larger problem. In my view it seems more probable that it was not so much the expatriate merchants and their families living permanently in Asian cities who were responsible for provoking the resistance to Rome; primarily, it was rapacious governors, greedy publicans, and unscrupulous and powerful men of the ilk of Decianus, out for a short-term gain.[174] Examples of maltreatment and fleecing in the East are not hard to find, even decades after the war and many years after the reforms of Lucullus in Asia, when one might perhaps expect things to have improved somewhat.[175] In 51 BC, for instance, Marcus Scaptius the prefect of Cyprus, demanding repayment of debts, allegedly besieged the local senate-house in Salamis with the aid of a cavalry troop until five senators died of starvation.[176] Conduct of that nature cannot have done much to endear Romans of whatever creed or color to the local population.

Things may not have gotten quite that bad anymore in Asia, but governors still faced serious difficulties reining in the tax farmers. Cicero, writing to Atticus at the time his brother Quintus was proconsul of Asia,

---

173 Not that bullying never occurred. From the Cyrene edicts I, 4–12 we learn that among the 215 Romans with the highest census valuation (2,500 *denarii*) there were groups who were blackmailing Greeks, serving as both accusers and witnesses in capital trials' cases; Oliver (1989) nr. 8–12 (= J.J.E. Hondius, *SEG* 9 [1944] 11–16, nr. 8 = *RDGE* nr. 31). Augustus, with his Cyrenaic legal reform, intended to check this abuse.

174 Hatzfeld too thinks this is at least part of the explanation: 'Les massacres de 88 eurent pour mobile beaucoup moins la haine des *negotiatores* italiens que celle de domination romaine'; Hatzfeld (1919) 331. Ferrary reaches a similar conclusion; Ferrary (2002) 144/145.

175 Wilson (1966) 178/179; Magie (1950) 252/253.

176 Cicero *Ad Att.* 6,1,6. See Hatzfeld (1919) 327.

weighed his thoughts on the demands of the publicans with regard to harbor dues; he considered that those demands ran counter not just to the interests of Roman businessmen but to those of 'the whole of Asia' ('universae Asiae').[177] Indeed, he regarded the question of how to control the behavior of the tax farmers Quintus' 'only really difficult administrative problem'. To his brother he wrote: '... to manage that you satisfy the tax farmers, ..., without letting the provincials go to ruin seems to call for capacity more than human—which is to say, it calls for yours'.[178] What is remarkable about this long letter is that it was not written in the first, but in the third—and last—year of Quintus' governorship. It was therefore not intended as a manual for a freshman proconsul (although superficially it reads that way), and Cicero may have had an ulterior motive in composing it: shielding his brother from extortion charges under the newly promulgated *Lex Iulia de repetundis*.[179] If that was the case it must be telling about the publicans and their actions that Cicero emphatically tried to disassociate Quintus from them.

Cicero's correspondence is hardly the only source for taxes and tax farming causing conflicts in Asia; such sources date back to the earliest days of the province. In 129 BC, a dispute arose between Pergamum and the tax-gatherers over the boundaries of the Pergamene territory. Both parties sent envoys to the Senate in Rome explaining their point of view; the Senate responded by sending out a magistrate to conduct an official inquiry.[180] Strabo tells us how Ephesus managed to wrest the taxes accruing from the traffic to a sacred lake back from the publicans.[181] The city, Strabo mentions, had dispatched Artemidorus on an embassy to this end, which helps date the story to approximately 100 BC. The 'Customs law of Asia', when discovered in 1976, provided important new information

---

[177] Cicero *Ad Att.* 2,16,4. The publicans probably demanded that custom dues be paid a second time on goods coming into an Asian harbor, even when harbor dues had already been paid once before in another Asian harbor; Magie (1950) 253/254. See also Hatzfeld (1919) 235, 322; Fallu (1970) 192.

[178] 'haec est una, si vere cogitare volumus, in toto imperio tuo difficultas', 'hic te ita versari ut et publicanis satis facias, ..., et socios perire non sinas divinae cuiusdam virtutis esse videtur, id est tuae'; Cicero *QF* 1,1,32/33. Tr.: D.R. Shackleton Bailey, Loeb (2002). See, Mitchell (1999) 26.

[179] This is the main argument of Fallu (1970).

[180] *RDGE* nr. 12, tr. in Sherk (1984) 47/48. The date of this document is disputed: either 129 BC or 101 BC. On the answer depends how we understand the content of the *Lex Sempronia* from 123/122 BC. Did that law mark the beginning of the collection of taxes by publicans in Asia or were taxes levied in the province before the law was passed? Mitchell (1999) 26/27.

[181] Strabo 14,1,26.

on how the Romans annexed their newly acquired province and how they arranged its tax regimen. It shows that—contrary to what had been believed previously[182]—right from the start the tax burden fell on all communities, including free cities; they too were liable for the payment of customs dues.[183] The 'freedom', so much cherished by Greek cities, did not imply exemption from all Roman taxes; in light of general Roman foreign policy '... indisputable evidence for a highly intrusive act of economic imperialism'.[184]

All of these sources combined form a strong reminder—if a reminder were ever needed—that the situation in the East was one of an imperial power lording it over a dependent territory. This backdrop makes the story of the position of Roman merchants domiciled in the province of Asia different and more complex than the one of provincial traders in Italian cities. The comportment of the imperial state and the impact its presence had on conditions in the province should explicitly be incorporated into that story. But the difference between the Italian and the provincial situation notwithstanding, I have tried to argue that in both cases we should see the phenomenon of immigrant traders settling permanently overseas in essentially the same light of the need to establish personalized networks to support long-distance trade.

Conclusion

In Asia, the Roman authorities encountered a highly developed legal system, different from their own. Instead of replacing it wholesale, they created Roman proconsular courts alongside it while leaving much of the existing legal institutions in place. The result was that many local Greek courts continued to try cases, continued to apply local laws, and continued to be—at least nominally—autonomous. However, although it is hard to trace with any great precision, Rome's impact on Greek judicial institutions was felt increasingly over time. Governors and later also Emperors—would intervene directly in legal affairs; the longevity of Roman rule combined with the creation of appeals and petitions to Roman magistrates and the Emperor led to a growing Roman influence.

182 Mitchell (2008) 184, 186. See e.g. Magie (1950) 114.
183 Cottier and Crawford (2008) 35/36, line 22–26, §9; commentary 110–112.
184 Mitchell (2008) 201.

On the face of it, the position of Roman traders resident in the province was therefore entirely different from the position of immigrant traders in Italian cities. Asia was a dependent territory in Rome's Empire, and migrating Romans were moving out to the imperial periphery, the reversed dynamic from provincials coming to the imperial center. State officials administered Asia as Rome's representatives, and a large part of their task consisted of attending to judicial matters. But although it is often assumed that Roman merchants drew much advantage from this circumstance, I have tried to show that the evidence does not point in that direction. There is, in truth, not much indication that strong-arming with the use of official power was practiced on a wide scale by ordinary Roman businessmen. The surviving evidence rather shows Roman settlers making a concerted effort to fit in with their new Greek environment, acting conjointly with social and civic bodies of Greek cities, and participating in social life.

This behavior can be explained by the key similarity between the Asian and the Italian situation: in both, there was no government enforcement of private contracts. Roman traders wanting to do long-term business in Asia therefore had to rely on the social dynamics of reputation and trust. Focusing specifically on Ephesus, Tralles, and Apamea I have shown that in Asian cities there were resident Romans who were not local men with citizenship but foreign immigrants. I have tried to argue that the role these Roman groups played was essentially the same as the one played by foreign organizations in Italian cities: facilitating trade by building trust, by providing access to information, and by providing a basis for contract enforcement.

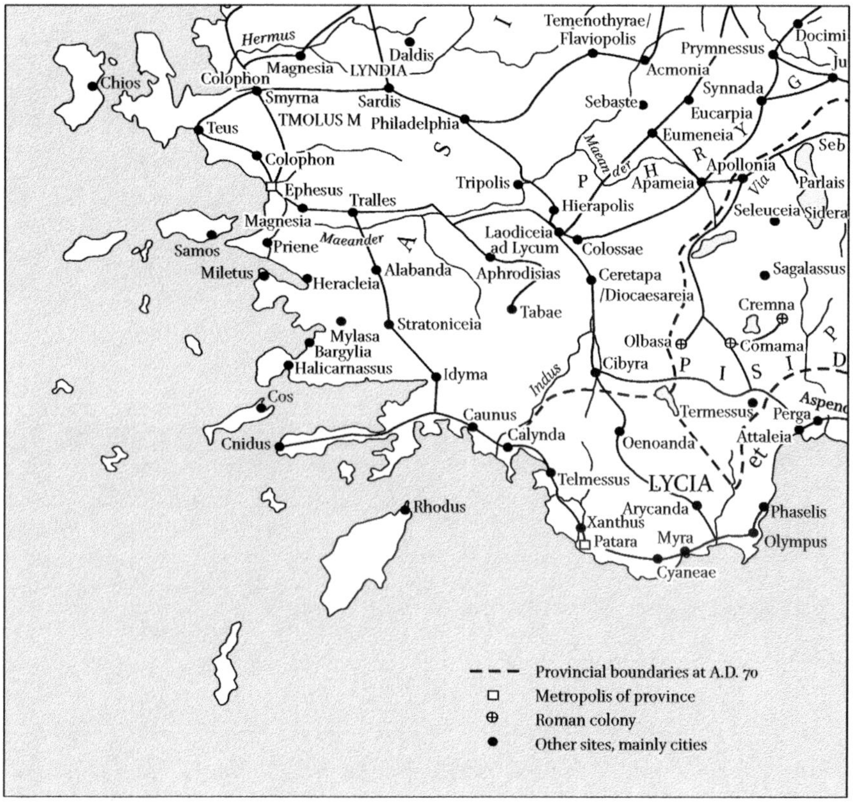

Figure 4. Roman Asia Minor.

CONCLUSION

In this book I have presented a model of Roman long-distance trade, addressing the question of how merchants in the Roman world enforced their contracts in the absence of state help, and how they managed the problem of slow information. I have argued that personalized networks based on geographical provenance formed the foundation for such trade. Information about members' conduct circulated within provenance-based networks; the fear of loss of reputation within, or expulsion from the networks formed the instrument of enforcement.

I developed this model in five specific and interlocking case-studies, each addressing either a part of the theory or adducing more evidence for the larger model. To summarize the line of argument in general terms: a specific set of rules for economic interaction will have been dominant in each individual city in the Roman Empire. This will have been Roman law for cities in Italy, and a mix of Roman law and local law in the provinces, the composition depending on circumstances and time period. Traders from different communities moving to another place—whether provincials coming to Italy or Italians going to the provinces—had to adapt to the rule-set they encountered overseas. Because such traders effectively became part of the community they moved to, and were thus compelled to conform to local mores, they were trustworthy business partners to their new social environment.

Outsiders from particular cities moving overseas would not settle as individuals but would group together along lines of geographical origin; foreign communities would therefore enjoy collective reputations that transcended those of their individual members. Since groups of settlers built up trust and a good name locally, they could serve as a trading 'bridge' between their home and their adopted community; they could also serve as a local foothold for traveling members of their native city, being able to vouch for their itinerant compatriots. The networks themselves must have had internal conventions, laws, and customs to regulate the behavior of their members. Because geographical origin formed the foundation of trade networks, expulsion from the group will have been a serious punishment. Traders could not easily join another network, and the networks as institutions therefore had a strong position vis-à-vis their individual members. The effect was that trade networks possessed the power to force their members to respect whatever set of customs governed the collective.

The legal framework of Roman law has been a theme throughout this book, and although it has not been the subject of this study *per se*, it has formed an important element of the argument. I will therefore direct my concluding remarks to the possible implications of my model for the way Roman law might have spread. The topic of state versus local law has received much scholarly attention, and the importance of the diffusion of Roman law for the process of 'Romanization' has been explicitly recognized, exemplified by the words of Andrew Lintott: '... if we seek to investigate the degree of political and social coherence in the Roman empire, the acceptability of Roman law to the dependent peoples is an obvious yardstick'.[1] However, the adopted approach has often been to try to establish the ratio of local to imperial law; to find evidence for either regional persistence or central dominance. I will here offer some thoughts on how the process of 'Romanization' in legal matters might have worked from the perspective of my model, the emphasis being on commercial incentives and trade networks.

It is likely that the internal rules that governed the organizations of foreign traders as we have seen them operating on, for instance, the Ostian 'piazzale delle corporazioni' were increasingly influenced by the rules of Roman law. We know nothing about those rules, much as we know virtually nothing about the 'merchants' law' that governed the coalition of the Maghribis. However, the evidence shows that outsiders doing business in Puteoli mostly used the laws of the Roman legal system in their economic and legal interaction with the Puteolan trading community. The same will, without much doubt, have held true for the situation in Ostia and Rome.

There is no way of knowing for certain, but it seems likely that the code of laws in force in the wider society influenced the internal control mechanisms of provenance-based networks. Because settlers from overseas trading in Italy adopted Roman law in dealing with the outside world, it is possible that they adopted it also within their own expatriate community. Traders could well have increasingly aligned the rules used within their own origin-based networks—their 'merchants' law'—with Roman rules in order to facilitate mercantile interaction. It is imaginable that, for instance, the Tyrians resident in Puteoli slowly internalized Roman legal

[1] Lintott (1993) 160.

concepts, jettisoning Tyrian customs in force only within their own group so as to synchronize their internal regulation with the dominant legal conventions of the Puteolan business world. If this process affected not just the resident but also the itinerant members of the coalitions, then trade networks increasingly using Roman law for their internal regulation could have had the effect of 'radiating' Roman law outward from the imperial center. If this inference is correct, we can see the networks and the contacts they maintained in Italian cities through local settlers as a vehicle for the spread of the Roman legal system.

Within Roman trade networks operating overseas—networks consisting of citizens—the internal rules governing economic interaction and conflict resolution will likely have been those of Roman law to begin with. As we have seen, the conclusion seems almost inevitable that Roman businessmen trading in the provinces had to litigate in non-Roman courts and had to adapt to regional customs and local practices. Undoubtedly, those regional customs and local practices always continued to exists, but with ongoing Roman imperial rule, with an increasing number of provincials acquiring citizenship, and with the tendency of governors and Emperors to impose uniformity through rescripts, the imperial legal system must increasingly have made itself felt. Groups of Romans resident overseas—like small islands in a foreign world, regulating the behavior within their own groups according to Roman law—can be seen as a contributing factor to this larger process of legal 'Romanization' in the provinces.

If these ideas are approximately right, then this dynamic would add a third social vector to the two identified in previous scholarship as facilitating the diffusion of Roman law: provincial elites and the military.[2] The process of the slowly spreading use of Roman law through trade networks may have been in an advanced stage by the time Caracalla granted citizenship to all inhabitants of the Empire in 212 AD, easing the transition from a personal to a territorial legal system. The process I have just outlined may, in that sense, have contributed to paving the way for the *Constitutio Antoniniana*. Apart from another way of looking at Roman long-distance trade, then, my model may also offer another way of looking at 'Romanization'. Exploring this aspect in-depth would require a separate book, though, different from this one.

---

[2] Galsterer (1986) 26.

BIBLIOGRAPHY

Adams, James N., 'The Latinity of C. Novius Eunus', in: *ZPE* 82 (1990) 227–247.

Alföldy, Géza, *Studi sull'epigrafia augustea e tiberiana di Roma* (Rome, 1992).

Ando, Clifford, *Imperial Ideology and Provincial Loyalty in the Roman Empire* (Berkeley, 2000).

Andreau, Jean, *Les affaires de monsieur Jucundus* (Rome, 1974).

——, 'Affaires financières à Pouzzoles au Ier siècle ap. J.-C.: Les tablettes de Murecine', in: *REL* 72 (1994) 39–55.

Andreau, Jean, *Banking and Business in the Roman World* (Cambridge Eng., 1999).

Ankum, Hans, 'Tabula Pompeiana 13: ein Seefrachtvertrag oder ein Seedarlehn?', in: *Iura* 29 (1978) 156–173.

Arias, Gino, *I trattati commerciali della repubblica fiorentina* (Florence, 1901).

Aubert, Jean-Jacques, *Business Managers in Ancient Rome: A Social and Economic Study of* Institores, *200 B.C.–A.D. 250* (Leiden, 1994).

Badian, Ernst, *Publicans and Sinners: Private Enterprise in the Service of the Roman Republic* (Ithaca NY, 1972).

Bang, Peter F., *The Roman Bazaar: A Comparative Study of Trade and Markets in a Tributary Empire* (Cambridge Eng., 2008).

Battistelli, Paolo and Gabriella Greco, 'Lo sviluppo architettonico del complesso del teatro di Ostia alla luce delle recenti indagini nell'edificio scenico', in: *MEFRA* 114,1 (2002) 391–420.

Beard, Mary, John North and Simon Price, *Religions of Rome*, 2 vols. (Cambridge Eng., 1998).

Becatti, Giovanni, *Scavi di Ostia*, vol. 4, *Mosaici e pavimenti marmorei* (Rome, 1961).

Behr, Charles A., *P. Aelius Aristides: The Complete Works*, vol. 2, *Orations XVII–LIII* (Leiden, 1981).

Benefiel, Rebecca R., 'Pompeii, Puteoli, and the Status of a *Colonia* in the Mid-First Century AD', in: Felice Senatore (ed.) *Pompei, Capri e la penisola sorrentina* (Capri, 2004) 349–367.

Benoit, Jean-Pierre and Vijay Krishna, 'Finitely Repeated Games', in: *Econometrica* 53,4 (1985) 905–922.

Berdan, Frances F., 'Trade and Markets in Precapitalist States', in: Stuart Plattner (ed.) *Economic Anthropology* (Stanford, 1989) 78–107.

Bernstein, Lisa, 'Private Commercial Law in the Cotton Industry: Creating Cooperation through Rules, Norms, and Institutions', in: *Michigan Law Review* 99,7 (2001) 1724–1790.

Bispham, Edward, 'Carved in Stone: The Municipal Magistracies of Numerius Cluvius', in: Alison E. Cooley (ed.) *The Epigraphic Landscape of Roman Italy* (London, 2000) 39–75.

Bloch, Herbert, 'Ostia—Iscrizioni rinvenute tra il 1930 e il 1939', in: *N.d.sc.* 7 (1953) 239–306.

Bollmann, Beate, *Römische Vereinshäuser: Untersuchungen zu den* Scholae *der römischen Berufs-, Kult- und Augustalen-Kollegien in Italien* (Mainz, 1998).

Borsari, Luigi, 'Del gruppo di edificii sacri al sole nell'area degli orti di Cesare', in: *Bull.Com.* s.3.15 (1887) 90–95.

Bove, Lucio, '*TPSulp.* 80 (= *Tab. Pomp.* 47): un *mandatum per epistulam* (con χειρέμβολον: Ulp. D. 4.9.1.3)?', in: Marina Silvestrini, Tullio Spagnuolo Vigorita, and Giuliano Volpe (eds.) *Studi in onore di Francesco Grelle* (Bari, 2006) 21–25.

Broughton, Thomas Robert S., 'Roman Asia Minor', in: Tenney Frank (ed.) *An Economic Survey of Ancient Rome*, vol. 4 (Baltimore, 1938) 499–918.

Brunt, Peter A., *The Fall of the Roman Republic and Related Essays* (Oxford, 1988).

Bruun, Christer, 'L'amministrazione imperiale di Ostia e Portus', in: Christer Bruun and Anna G. Zevi (eds.) *Ostia e Portus nelle loro relazioni con Roma* (= *Acta Instituti Romani Finlandiae*, vol. 27) (Rome, 2002) 161–192.

Buranelli Le Pera, Susanna and Luca D'Elia, '"Sacra via" : note topografiche', in: *Bull.Com.* 91,2 (1986) 241–262.

Burrell, Barbara, *Neokoroi: Greek Cities and Roman Emperors* (= *Cincinnati Classical Studies*, new series nr. 9) (Leiden, 2004).

Burton, Graham P., 'The Issuing of *Mandata* to Proconsuls and a New Inscription from Cos', in: *ZPE* 26 (1976) 63–68.

——, 'Proconsuls, Assizes and the Administration of Justice under the Empire', in: *JRS* 65 (1975) 92–106.

Caldelli, Maria L., '*Curia athletarum, iera xystike synodos* e organizzazione delle terme a Roma', in: *ZPE* 93 (1992) 75–87.

Calza, Guido, 'Il piazzale delle corporazioni e la funzione commerciale di Ostia', in: *Bull. Com.* 43 (1915) 178–206.

Calzini Gysens, Jacqueline, 'Dieux ancestraux et Baals syriens attestés à Rome', in: Gloria M. Bellelli and Ugo Bianchi (eds.) *Orientalia Sacra Urbis Romae: Dolichena et Heliopolitana* (Rome, 1996) 261–276.

Camodeca, Giuseppe, 'L'ordinamento in *regiones* e i *vici* di Puteoli', in: *Puteoli* 1 (1977) 62–98.

Camodeca, Giuseppe, 'La *gens Annia* puteolana in età giulio-claudia: potere politico e interessi commerciali', in: *Puteoli* 3 (1979) 17–34.

——, 'Per una riedizione dell' archivio puteolano dei Sulpicii', in: *Puteoli* 6 (1982a) 3–53.

—— (ed.) 'Schede epigrafiche', in: *Puteoli* 6 (1982b) 143–161.

——, *L'archivio puteolano dei Sulpicii* (Naples, 1992).

——, '*Puteoli* porto annonario e il commercio del grano in età imperiale', in: *Le ravitaillement en blé de Rome et des centres urbains de débuts de la République jusqu'au Haut Empire* (= *CJB*, vol. 11) (Naples, 1994) 103–128.

——, 'L'élite municipale di Puteoli fra la tarda repubblica e Nerone', in: Mireille Cébeillac-Gervasoni (ed.) *Les élites municipales de l'Italie péninsulaire des Gracques à Néron* (Naples, 1996) 91–110.

——, *Tabulae Pompeianae Sulpiciorum: Edizione critica dell'archivio puteolano dei Sulpicii* (Rome, 1999).

——, 'Il credito negli archivi campani: il caso di Puteoli e di Herculaneum', in: Elio Lo Cascio (ed.) *Credito e moneta nel mondo romano: Atti degli Incontri capresi di storia dell'economia antica (Capri 12–14 ottobre 2000)* (Bari, 2003) 69–98.

Cantarelli, Luigi, 'Le *stationes municipiorum*', in: *Bull.Com.* s.5, 28 (1900) 124–134.

Casson, Lionel, *Ships and Seamanship in the Ancient World* (Princeton, 1971).

Cébeillac-Gervasoni, Mireille and Fausto Zevi, 'Révisions et nouveautés pour trois inscriptions d'Ostie', in: *MEFRA* 88,2 (1976) 607–637.

Cébeillac-Gervasoni, Mireille, 'Ostie et le blé au IIe siècle ap. J.-C.', in: *Le ravitaillement en blé de Rome et des centres urbains de débuts de la République jusqu'au Haut Empire* (= *CJB*, vol. 11) (Naples, 1994) 47–59.

Chausson, François, '*Vel Iovi vel Soli*: Quatre études autour de la Vigna Barberini (191–354)', in: *MEFRA* 107,2 (1995) 661–765.

Clay, Karen, 'Trade, Institutions, and Credit: Contract Enforcement on the California Coast, 1830–1846', in: *Explorations in Economic History* 34,4 (1997) 495–521.

Coarelli, Filippo, 'Il *forum vinarium* di Ostia: un'ipotesi di localizzazione', in: Anna G. Zevi and Amanda Claridge (eds.) *'Roman Ostia' Revisited: Archaeological and Historical Papers in Memory of Russell Meiggs* (London, 1996) 105–113.

——, *Il Campo Marzio dalle origini alla fine della Repubblica* (Rome, 1997).

Constable, Olivia Remie, *Housing the Stranger in the Mediterranean World: Lodging, Trade, and Travel in Late Antiquity and the Middle Ages* (Cambridge Eng., 2003).

Cornell, Tim J., *The Beginnings of Rome: Italy and Rome from the Bronze Age to the Punic Wars (c. 1000–264 B.C.)* (London, 1995).

Cottier, Michel, Michael H. Crawford et al. (eds.) *The Customs Law of Asia* (Oxford, 2008).

Crawford, Michael H. et al. (eds.) *Roman Statutes*, 2 vols. (= *Bulletin of the Institute of Classical Studies*, Suppl. 64) (London, 1996).

Cremer, Jacques, 'Cooperation in Ongoing Organizations', in: *Quarterly Journal of Economics* 101,1 (1986) 33–50.

Crook, John A., *Law and Life of Rome* (Ithaca NY, 1967).

Curtin, Philip D., *Cross-Cultural Trade in World History* (Cambridge Eng., 1984).

D'Arms, John H., 'Puteoli in the Second Century of the Roman Empire: A Social and Economic Study', in: *JRS* 64 (1974) 104–124.

——, 'Tacitus, Annals 13.48 and a New Inscription from Puteoli', in: Barbara Levick (ed.) *The Ancient Historian and His Materials: Essays in Honour of C.E. Stevens on His Seventieth Birthday* (Farnborough, 1975) 155–165.

——, *Commerce and Social Standing in Ancient Rome* (Cambridge MA, 1981).

David, Paul A., 'Clio and the Economics of QWERTY', in: *American Economic Review* 75,2 (1985) 332–337.

——, 'Why Are Institutions the "Carriers of History"?: Path Dependence and the Evolution of Conventions, Organizations and Institutions', in: *Structural Change and Economic Dynamics* 5,2 (1994) 205–220.

——, 'Path Dependence, Its Critics and the Quest for "Historical Economics" ', in: Pierre Garrouste and Stavros Ioannides (eds.) *Evolution and Path Dependence in Economic Ideas: Past and Present* (Cheltenham, 2001) 15–40.

Deininger, Jürgen, *Die Provinziallandtage der römischen Kaiserzeit: Von Augustus bis zum Ende des dritten Jahrhunderts n. Chr.* (Munich, 1965).

Del Vecchio, Alberto and Eugenio Casanova, *Le rappresaglie nei comuni medievali e specialmente in Firenze* (Bologna, 1894).

Deman, Albert, 'Avec les utriculaires sur les sentiers muletiers de la Gaule romaine', in: *Cah.Glotz* 13 (2002) 233–246.

Dennison, Walter, 'Some New Inscriptions from Puteoli, Baiae, Misenum, and Cumae', in: *AJA* 2,5 (1898) 373–398.

De Petra, Giulio, 'Degli oggetti di metallo prezioso e dei libelli scoperti in Pompei', in: *N.d.sc.* (1887) 415–420.

De Romanis, Federico, *Cassia, cinnamomo, ossidiana: Uomini e merci tra Oceano indiano e Mediterraneo* (Rome, 1996).

——, '*Cultores huius loci*: Sulle coabitazioni divine del *lucus Furrinae*', in: Beatrice Palma Venetucci (ed.) *Culti orientali: Tra scavo e collezionismo* (Rome, 2008) 149–157.

De Simone, Antonio, 'L'indagine archeologica in località Murecine a Pompei', in: Antonio de Simone and Salvatore Ciro Nappo (eds.) *Mitis Sarni Opes* (Naples, 2000) 49–78.

Dixit, Avinash K., *Lawlessness and Economics: Alternative Modes of Governance* (Princeton, 2004).

Doublet, Georges and Victor Bérard, 'Inscriptions de Dinair (Apamée)', in: *BCH* 17 (1893) 301–321.

Dubois, Charles, *Pouzzoles antique (histoire et topographie)* (= *BÉFAR*, vol. 98) (Paris, 1907).

Duncan-Jones, Richard P., *The Economy of the Roman Empire: Quantitative Studies*, 2nd ed. (Cambridge Eng., 1982).

——, *Structure and Scale in the Roman Economy* (Cambridge Eng., 1990).

Duthoy, Françoise and Jiri Frel, 'Observations sur le sanctuaire syrien du Janicule', in: Gloria M. Bellelli and Ugo Bianchi (eds.) *Orientalia Sacra Urbis Romae: Dolichena et Heliopolitana* (Rome, 1996) 289–303.

Eck, Werner, 'Öffentlichkeit, Politik und Administration: Epigraphische Dokumente von Kaisern, Senat und Amtsträgern in Rom', in: Rudolf Haensch (ed.) *Selbstdarstellung und*

Kommunikation: Die Veröffentlichung staatlicher Urkunden auf Stein und Bronze in der römischen Welt (Munich, 2009) 75–96.

Edwards, Jeremy and Sheilagh Ogilvie, 'Contract Enforcement, Institutions and Social Capital: The Maghribi Traders Reappraised' (March 2008) *CESifo Working Paper Series No. 2254*. Available at SSRN:http://ssrn.com/abstract=1107801.

Ellickson, Robert, C. *Order Without Law: How Neighbors Settle Disputes* (Cambridge MA, 1991).

Errington, R. Malcolm, 'Aspects of Roman Acculturation in the East under the Republic', in: Peter Kneissl and Volker Losemann (eds.) *Alte Geschichte und Wissenschaftsgeschichte: Festschrift für Karl Christ zum 65. Geburtstag* (Darmstadt, 1988) 140–157.

Étienne, Robert, '*Diffusor olei ad annonam Vrbis*', in: Marguerite Garrido-Hory and Antonio Gonzalès (eds.) *Histoire, espaces et marges de l'antiquité: Hommages à Monique Clavel-Lévêque*, vol. 2 (Besançon, 2003) 245–253.

Fabiani, Enrico, 'Bilingue iscrizione di Habibi', in: *Bull.Com.* 6 (1878) 153–161; 272–274.

Fallu, Élie, 'La première lettre de Cicéron a Quintus et la *Lex Julia de repetundis*', in: *REL* 48 (1970) 180–204.

Ferrary, Jean-Louis, 'Le statut des cités libres dans l'Empire romain à la lumière des inscriptions de Claros', in: *CRAI* 135,3 (1991) 557–577.

——, 'La création de la province d'Asie et la présence italienne en Asie Mineure', in: *Les Italiens dans le monde grec, IIe siècle av. J.-C.–Ier siècle ap. J.-C.: Circulation, activités, intégration* (= *BCH*, suppl. 41) (Athens Greece, 2002) 133–147.

Finley, Moses I., *The Ancient Economy*, 2nd ed. (Berkeley, 1973).

Flobert, Pierre, 'Le latin des tablettes de Murécine (Pompéi)', in: *REL* 73 (1995) 138–150.

Frederiksen, Martin, *Campania* (edited with additions by Nicholas Purcell) (London, 1984).

Frier, Bruce W., *The Rise of the Roman Jurists: Studies in Cicero's* Pro Caecina (Princeton, 1985).

Galsterer, Hartmut, 'Roman Law in the Provinces: Some Problems of Transmission', in: Michael H. Crawford (ed.) *L'impero romano e le strutture economiche e sociali delle province* (Como, 1986) 13–27.

Garnsey, Peter, 'The Criminal Jurisdiction of Governors', in: *JRS* 58,1 (1968) 51–59.

——, *Social Status and Legal Privilege in the Roman Empire* (Oxford, 1970).

——, 'Independent Freedmen and the Economy of Roman Italy under the Principate', in: *Klio* 63 (1981) 359–371.

——, 'Commerce and Social Standing in Ancient Rome', review, in: *Classical Philology* 79,1 (1984) 85–88.

Gawlikowski, Michel, 'Palmyra and Its Caravan Trade', in: *Palmyra and the Silk Road* (= *Les annales archéologiques arabes syriennes*, vol. 42) (Damascus, 1996) 139–145.

Gialanella, Costanza and Valeria Sampaolo, 'Note sulla topografia di Puteoli', in: *Puteoli* 4/5 (1980/1981) 133–161.

Gil, Moshe, 'The Jews in Sicily under Muslim Rule, in the Light of the Geniza Documents', in: Vittore Colorni et al. (eds.) *Italia Judaica: Atti del I Convegno internazionale, Bari 18–22 maggio 1981* (Rome, 1983) 87–134.

Goitein, Shelemo D., *A Mediterranean Society: The Jewish Communities of the Arab World as Portrayed in the Documents of the Cairo Geniza*, 5 vols. (Berkeley, 1967–1988).

——, *Letters of Medieval Jewish Traders* (Princeton, 1973).

Goldberg, Jessica, 'Choosing and Enforcing Business Relationships in the Eleventh-Century Mediterranean: Reassessing the "Maghribī Traders" ', in: *Past & Present* 216,1 (2012) 3–40.

Goldsmith, Raymond W., 'An Estimate of the Size and Structure of the National Product of the Early Roman Empire', in: *Review of Income and Wealth* 30,3 (1984) 263–288.

Gonzalez, Julian and Michael H. Crawford, 'The Lex Irnitana: A New Copy of the Flavian Municipal Law', in: *JRS* 76 (1986) 147–243.

Greif, Avner, 'Reputation and Coalitions in Medieval Trade: Evidence on the Maghribi Traders', in: *Journal of Economic History* 49,4 (1989) 857–882.

——, *Institutions and the Path to the Modern Economy: Lessons from Medieval Trade* (Cambridge Eng., 2006).

——, 'Contract Enforcement and Institutions among the Maghribi Traders: Refuting Edwards and Ogilvie' (July 2008) *CESifo Working Paper Series No. 2350*. Available at SSRN: http://ssrn.com/abstract=1159681.

——, 'The Maghribi Traders: A Reappraisal?', in: *Economic History Review* 65,2 (2012) 445–469.

Gröschler, Peter, *Die* tabellae-*Urkunden aus den pompejanischen und herkulanensischen Urkundenfunden* (Berlin, 1997).

Habicht, Christian, 'New Evidence on the Province of Asia', in: *JRS* 65 (1975) 64–91.

Halfmann, Helmut, *Itinera Principum: Geschichte und Typologie der Kaiserreisen im römischen Reich* (Stuttgart, 1986).

Harris, William V., 'Towards a Study of the Roman Slave Trade', in: John H. D'Arms and Elizabeth C. Kopf (eds.) *The Seaborne Commerce of Ancient Rome: Studies in Archaeology and History* (= *MAAR*, vol. 36) (Rome, 1980) 117–140.

——, *Ancient Literacy* (Cambridge MA, 1989).

——, 'Trade', in: Alan K. Bowman, Peter Garnsey, and Dominic Rathbone (eds.) *The Cambridge Ancient History*, vol. 11, *The High Empire, A.D. 70–192* (Cambridge Eng., 2000) 710–740.

——, 'A Revisionist View of Roman Money', in: *JRS* 96 (2006) 1–24.

Hatzfeld, Jean, *Les trafiquants italiens dans l'Orient hellénique* (Paris, 1919).

Heichelheim, Fritz M., *An Ancient Economic History from the Palaeolithic Age to the Migrations of the Germanic, Slavic, and Arabic Nations*, vol. 1 (Leiden, 1958).

Heilporn, Paul, 'Registre de navires marchands', in: Henri Melaerts (ed.) *Papyri in Honorem Johannis Bingen Octogenarii* (Leuven, 2000) 339–359.

Hermansen, Gustav, 'The *Stuppatores* and Their Guild in Ostia', in: *AJA* 86,1 (1982) 121–126.

Hopkins, Keith, 'Taxes and Trade in the Roman Empire (200 B.C.–A.D. 400)', in: *JRS* 70 (1980) 101–125.

——, 'Rome, Taxes, Rents and Trade', in: Walter Scheidel and Sitta von Reden (eds.) *The Ancient Economy* (New York, 2002) 190–230.

Horden, Peregrine and Nicholas Purcell, *The Corrupting Sea: A Study of Mediterranean History* (Oxford, 2000).

Houston, George W., 'The Administration of Italian Seaports during the First Three Centuries of the Roman Empire', in: John H. D'Arms and Elizabeth C. Kopf (eds.) *The Seaborne Commerce of Ancient Rome: Studies in Archaeology and History* (= *MAAR*, vol. 36) (Rome, 1980) 157–171.

Ilari, Virgilio, *Gli Italici nelle strutture militari romane* (Milan, 1974).

Jahn, Otto, 'Über die puteolanische Basis', in: *Berichte über die Verhandlungen der königlich sächsischen Gesellschaft der Wissenschaften zu Leipzig* 3 (1851) 119–151.

Johnston, David, 'Law and Commercial Life of Rome', in: *PCPS* 43 (1997) 53–65.

Jones, Arnold H.M., *The Greek City from Alexander to Justinian* (Oxford, 1940).

Jones, David F., *The Bankers of Puteoli: Finance, Trade and Industry in the Roman World* (Stroud, 2006).

Jongman, Willem M., *The Economy and Society of Pompeii* (Amsterdam, 1988).

——, 'Consumption in the Early Roman Empire', in: Richard Saller, Ian Morris, and Walter Scheidel (eds.) *The Cambridge Economic History of the Greco-Roman World* (Cambridge Eng., 2007) 592–618.

Kaimio, Jorma, *The Romans and the Greek Language* (= *Commentationes Humanarum Litterarum*, vol. 64) (Helsinki, 1979).

Kaizer, Ted, *The Religious Life of Palmyra: A Study of the Social Patterns of Worship in the Roman Period* (Stuttgart, 2002).

Kantor, Georgy, 'Knowledge of Law in Roman Asia Minor', in: Rudolf Haensch (ed.) *Selbstdarstellung und Kommunikation: Die Veröffentlichung staatlicher Urkunden auf Stein und Bronze in der römischen Welt* (Munich, 2009) 249–265.

Kaser, Max, *Das altrömische* ius: *Studien zur Rechtsvorstellung und Rechtsgeschichte der Römer* (Göttingen, 1949).

——, *Das römische Privatrecht*, vol. 1, *Das altrömische, das vorklassische und klassische Recht*, 2nd ed. (Munich, 1971).

——, *Das römische Zivilprozessrecht*, 2nd ed., revised by Karl Hackl (Munich, 1996).

Kelly, John M., *Roman Litigation* (Oxford, 1966).

Kessler, David and Peter Temin, 'The Organization of the Grain Trade in the Early Roman Empire', in: *Economic History Review* 60,2 (2007) 313–332.

Kunkel, Wolfgang, *Römische Rechtsgeschichte: Eine Einführung*, 5th ed. (Cologne, 1968).

Lacerenza, Giancarlo, 'Il dio Dusares a Puteoli', in: *Puteoli* 12/13 (1988/1989) 119–149.

——, 'Due nuove iscrizioni del tempio di Dusares dell'antica Puteoli', in: *AION* 54 (1994) 15–17.

Lancaster, Lynne, 'Building Trajan's Markets 2: The Construction Process', in: *AJA* 104,4 (2000) 755–785.

Lane Fox, Robin, *Pagans and Christians* (New York, 1987).

Langum, David J., *Law and Community on the Mexican California Frontier: Anglo-American Expatriates and the Clash of Legal Traditions, 1821–1846* (Norman, 1987).

La Piana, George, 'Foreign Groups in Rome during the First Centuries of the Empire', in: *Harvard Theological Review* 20,4 (1927) 183–403.

La Regina, Adriano (ed.) *Lexicon Topographicum Urbis Romae Suburbium*, 4 vols. (Rome, 2001–2006).

Lauffer, Siegfried, *Diokletians Preisedikt* (Berlin, 1971).

Lenormant, François, 'Jupiter Heliopolitanus', in: *Gazette archéologique* 2 (1876) 78–82.

Levick, Barbara, *The Government of the Roman Empire: A Sourcebook*, 2nd ed. (London, 2000).

——, 'The Roman Economy: Trade in Asia Minor and the Niche Market', in: *Greece and Rome* 51,2 (2004) 180–198.

Levinson, Daryl J., 'Collective Sanctions', in: *Stanford Law Review* 56 (2003) 345–428.

Lewis, David K., *Convention: A Philosophical Study* (Cambridge MA, 1969).

Lewis, Naphtali and Meyer Reinhold, *Roman Civilization, Selected Readings*, vol. 2, *The Empire*, 3rd ed. (New York, 1990).

Lintott, Andrew, *Imperium Romanum: Politics and Administration* (London, 1993).

Liu, Jinyu, *Collegia Centonariorum: The Guilds of Textile Dealers in the Roman West* (Leiden, 2009).

Lo Cascio, Elio, 'Ancora sugli "Ostia's services to Rome" collegi e corporazioni annonarie a Ostia', in: *MEFRA* 114,1 (2002) 87–110.

Lopez, Robert S. and Irving W. Raymond, *Medieval Trade in the Mediterranean World: Illustrative Documents*, 2nd ed. with a foreword and bibliography by Olivia Remie Constable (New York, 2001).

Magie, David, *Roman Rule in Asia Minor to the End of the Third Century after Christ* (Princeton, 1950).

Mahoney, Paul G. and Chris William Sanchirico, 'Norms, Repeated Games, and the Role of Law', in: *California Law Review* 91,5 (2003) 1281–1329.

Maiuro, Marco, 'What Was the Forum Iulium Used for? The *Fiscus* and its Jurisdiction in First-Century CE Rome', in: Francesco de Angelis (ed.) *Spaces of Justice in the Roman World* (Leiden, 2010) 189–221.

Malmendier, Ulrike, *Societas Publicanorum: Staatliche Wirtschaftsaktivitäten in den Händen privater Unternehmer* (Cologne, 2002).

Manacorda, Daniele, 'Anfore spagnole a Pompei', in: Maria Annecchino et al. (eds.) *L'*instrumentum domesticum *di Ercolano e Pompei nella prima età imperiale* (Rome, 1977) 121–133.

Manthe, Ulrich, 'Lucio Bove: *Documenti processuali dalle Tabulae Pompeianae di Murecine*', review, in: *Gnomon* 53,2 (1981) 150–161.

Marshall, Anthony J., 'The Structure of Cicero's Edict', in: *American Journal of Philology* 85,2 (1964) 185–191.
——, 'Governors on the Move', in: *Phoenix* 20,3 (1966) 231–246.
——, 'Romans under Chian Law', in: *Greek, Roman and Byzantine Studies* 10,3 (1969) 255–271.
——, 'The Survival and Development of International Jurisdiction in the Greek World under Roman Rule', in: *ANRW*, vol. 2,13 (Berlin, 1980) 626–661.
Mastroroberto, Marisa, 'Una visita di Nerone a Pompei: le *deversoriae tabernae* di Moregine', in: Antonio d'Ambrosio, Pier Giovanni Guzzo, and Marisa Mastroroberto (eds.) *Storie da un'eruzione: Pompei Ercolano Oplontis* (Milan, 2003) 479–523.
Matthews, John F., 'The Tax Law of Palmyra: Evidence for Economic History in a City of the Roman East', in: *JRS* 74 (1984) 157–180.
Meiggs, Russell, *Roman Ostia* (Oxford, 1973).
——, *Trees and Timber in the Ancient Mediterranean World* (Oxford, 1982).
Metzger, Ernest, *A New Outline of the Roman Civil Trial* (Oxford, 1997).
——, *Litigation in Roman Law* (Oxford, 2005).
Meyer, Elizabeth A., *Legitimacy and Law in the Roman World* (Cambridge Eng., 2004).
Migeotte, Léopold, *L'emprunt public dans les cités grecques: Recueil des documents et analyse critique* (Québec, 1984).
Millar, Fergus, '*Civitates Liberae, Coloniae* and Provincial Governors under the Empire', in: *Mediterraneo antico: Economie, società, culture* 2,1 (1999) 95–113.
Mitchell, Stephen, 'The Administration of Roman Asia from 133 BC to AD 250', in: Werner Eck and Elisabeth Müller-Luckner (eds.) *Lokale Autonomie und römische Ordnungsmacht in den kaiserzeitlichen Provinzen vom 1. bis 3. Jahrhundert* (Munich, 1999) 17–46.
——, 'Geography, Politics, and Imperialism in the Asian Customs Law', in: Michel Cottier, Michael H. Crawford et al. (eds.) *The Customs Law of Asia* (Oxford, 2008) 165–201.
Mitteis, Ludwig, *Reichsrecht und Volksrecht in den östlichen Provinzen des römischen Kaiserreichs* (Leipzig, 1891).
Moeller, Walter O., *The Wool Trade of Ancient Pompeii* (Leiden, 1976).
Mommsen, Theodor, *Gesammelte Schriften*, vol. 8, *Epigraphische und numismatische Schriften* (ed. Hermann Dessau) (Berlin, 1913).
Morley, Neville, *Trade in Classical Antiquity* (Cambridge Eng., 2007).
Moretti, Luigi, 'Sulle "stationes municipiorum" del foro romano', in: *Athenaeum* 36 (1958) 106–116.
Nippel, Wilfried, *Public Order in Ancient Rome* (Cambridge Eng., 1995).
Noonan, Benjamin J., 'Did Nehemiah own Tyrian Goods? Trade between Judea and Phoenicia during the Achaemenid Period', in: *Journal of Biblical Literature* 130,2 (2011) 281–298.
North, Douglass C., *Institutions, Institutional Change and Economic Performance* (Cambridge Eng., 1990).
Noy, David, *Foreigners at Rome: Citizens and Strangers* (London, 2000).
Oliver, James H., *Greek Constitutions of Early Roman Emperors from Inscriptions and Papyri* (Philadelphia, 1989).
Packer, James E., 'Housing and Population in Imperial Ostia and Rome', in: *JRS* 57 (1967) 80–95.
Pagano, Mario, 'L'edificio dell' agro Murecine a Pompei', in: *RendNap* 58 (1983) 325–361.
Panciera, Silvio, '*Olearii*', in: John H. D'Arms and Elizabeth C. Kopf (eds.) *The Seaborne Commerce of Ancient Rome: Studies in Archaeology and History* (= *MAAR*, vol. 36) (Rome, 1980) 235–250.
Pârvan, Vasile, *Die Nationalität der Kaufleute im römischen Kaiserreiche* (Breslau, 1909).
Paschetto, Ludovico, *Ostia colonia romana: Storia e monumenti* (Rome, 1912).
Paterson, Jeremy, 'Trade and Traders in the Roman World: Scale, Structure, and Organisation', in: Helen Parkins and Christopher Smith (eds.) *Trade, Traders and the Ancient City* (London, 1998) 149–167.

Pellegrino, Angelo, 'Il culto di Vulcano ad Ostia. Nuove testimonianze', in: *MGR* 10 (1986) 289–301.

Peterson, Roy M., *The Cults of Campania* (= *PAAR*, vol. 1) (Rome, 1919).

Pierobon-Benoit, Raffaella, 'L'Asia Minore e l'approvvigionamento in grano di Roma', in: *Le ravitaillement en blé de Rome et des centres urbains de débuts de la République jusqu'au Haut Empire* (= *CJB*, vol. 11) (Naples, 1994) 305–321.

Platner, Samuel B. and Thomas Ashby, *A Topographical Dictionary of Ancient Rome* (London, 1929).

Pleket, Harry W., 'Urban Elites and Business in the Greek Part of the Roman Empire', in: Peter Garnsey, Keith Hopkins and Charles R. Whittaker (eds.) *Trade in the Ancient Economy* (Berkeley, 1983) 131–144.

——, 'Urban Elites and the Economy in the Greek Cities of the Roman Empire', in: *Münstersche Beiträge zur antiken Handelsgeschichte* 3,1 (1984) 3–35.

——, 'Wirtschaft', in: Friedrich Vittinghoff (ed.) *Handbuch der europäischen Wirtschafts- und Sozialgeschichte*, vol. 1, *Europäische Wirtschafts- und Sozialgeschichte in der römischen Kaiserzeit* (Stuttgart, 1990) 25–160.

Pohl, Ingrid, 'Ostia. Piazzale delle corporazioni, portico ovest: Saggi sotto i mosaici', in: *N.d.sc.* Suppl. s. 8, nr. 32 (1978) 165–443.

Posner, Eric A., 'The Regulation of Groups: The Influence of Legal and Nonlegal Sanctions on Collective Action', in: *University of Chicago Law Review* 63,1 (1996) 133–197.

——, *Law and Social Norms* (Cambridge MA, 2000).

Posner, Richard A., 'Social Norms and the Law: An Economic Approach', in: *American Economic Review* 87,2 (1997) 365–369.

Price, Simon R.F., *Rituals and Power: The Roman Imperial Cult in Asia Minor* (Cambridge Eng., 1984).

Pulice, Domenico, 'Sviluppo costituzionale della colonia Puteoli in età repubblicana', in: *Puteoli* 1 (1977) 27–49.

Raggi, Andrea, 'Senatus consultum de Asclepiade Clazomenio sociisque', in: *ZPE* 135 (2001) 73–116.

——, 'The Epigraphic Dossier of Seleucus of Rhosus: A revised Edition', in: *ZPE* 147 (2004) 123–138.

Ramsay, William M., *Cities and Bishoprics of Phrygia: Being an Essay of the Local History of Phrygia from the Earliest Times to the Turkish Conquest*, vol. 1, part 2, *West and West-Central Phrygia* (Oxford, 1895).

Rathbone, Dominic, 'Monetisation, not Price-Inflation, in Third-Century A.D. Egypt?', in: Cathy E. King and David G. Wigg (eds.) *Coin Finds and Coin Use in the Roman World* (Berlin, 1996) 321–339.

Rauh, Nicholas K., *The Sacred Bonds of Commerce: Religion, Economy, and Trade Society at Hellenistic Roman Delos* (Amsterdam, 1993).

Rey-Coquais, Jean-Paul, 'Syrie romaine, de Pompée à Dioclétien', in: *JRS* 68 (1978) 44–73.

Reynolds, Joyce M., *Aphrodisias and Rome: Documents from the Excavation of the Theatre at Aphrodisias Conducted by Professor Kenan T. Erim, Together with Some Related Texts* (London, 1982).

——, 'New Letters from Hadrian to Aphrodisias: Trials, Taxes, Gladiators and an Aqueduct', in: *JRA* 13 (2000) 5–20.

Ricci, Cecilia, *Orbis in Urbe: Fenomeni migratori nella Roma imperiale* (Rome, 2005).

Richardson, Lawrence, *A new Topographical Dictionary of Ancient Rome* (Baltimore, 1992).

Robert, Louis, 'Les juges étrangers dans la cité grecque', in Ernst von Caemmerer et al. (eds.) *Xenion: Festschrift für Pan. J. Zepos*, vol. 1 (Athens Greece, 1973) 765–782.

Robert, Louis and Jeanne Robert, *Claros I: Décrets hellénistiques* (Paris, 1989).

Ronzevalle, Louis, 'Notice sur un bas-relief représentant le simulacre du Jupiter Heliopolitanus', in: *CRAI* 45,3 (1901) 437–482.

Rose, Kenneth F.C., 'Time and Place in the Satyricon', in: *PAPS* 93 (1962) 402–409.

Rougé, Jean, *Recherches sur l'organisation du commerce maritime en Méditerranée sous l'Empire romain* (Paris, 1966).
——, *La marine dans l'antiquité* (Paris, 1975).
Roussel, Pierre, *Délos, colonie athénienne* (= *BÉFAR* fasc. 111) (Paris, 1916).
Royden, Halsey L., *The Magistrates of the Roman Professional* Collegia *in Italy from the First to the Third Century A.D.* (Pisa, 1988).
Saller, Richard P., *Personal Patronage under the Early Empire* (Cambridge Eng., 1982).
——, *Patriarchy, Property and Death in the Roman Family* (Cambridge Eng., 1994).
Salomies, Olli, 'People in Ostia: Some Onomastic Observations and Comparisons with Rome', in: Christer Bruun and Anna G. Zevi (eds.) *Ostia e Portus nelle loro relazioni con Roma* (= *Acta Instituti Romani Finlandiae*, vol. 27) (Rome, 2002) 135–159.
Saloner, Garth, 'Old Boy Networks as Screening Mechanisms', in: *Journal of Labor Economics* 3,3 (1985) 255–267.
Santini, Pietro, 'Appunti sulla vendetta privata e sulle rappresaglie in occasione di un documento inedito', in: *Archivo storico italiano* 4 serie, t.18 (1886) 162–176.
Savage, Susan M., 'The Cults of Ancient Trastevere', in: *MAAR*, vol. 17 (1940) 26–56.
Schneider, Eugenia E., 'Il santuario di Bel e delle divinità di Palmira: Comunità e tradizioni religiose dei Palmireni a Roma', in: *Dialoghi di archeologia* 5,1 (1987) 69–85.
Scheidel, Walter, 'Roman Age Structure: Evidence and Models', in: *JRS* 91 (2001) 1–26.
——, 'From the "Great Convergence" to the "First Great Divergence": Roman and Qin-Han State Formation and Its Aftermath', in: Walter Scheidel (ed.) *Rome and China: Comparative Perspectives on Ancient World Empires* (Oxford, 2009) 11–23.
Sherk, Robert K., *Rome and the Greek East to the Death of Augustus* (= *Translated Documents of Greece and Rome*, vol. 4) (Cambridge Eng., 1984).
Sherwin-White, Adrian N., *The Roman Citizenship*, 2nd ed. (Oxford, 1973).
Smith, Martin S., *Petronii Arbitri Cena Trimalchionis, Edited by Martin S. Smith*, 2nd ed. (Oxford, 1982).
Sosin, Joshua D., 'Tyrian *Stationarii* at Puteoli', in: *Tyche: Beiträge zur alten Geschichte, Papyrologie und Epigraphik* 14 (1999) 275–284.
Squarciapino, Maria Floriani, *I culti orientali ad Ostia* (Leiden, 1962).
Starcky, Jean and Michel Gawlikowski, *Palmyre* (*Édition revue et augmentée des nouvelles découvertes*) (Paris, 1985).
Steinby, Eva M. (ed.) *Lexicon Topographicum Urbis Romae*, 6 vols. (Rome, 1993–2000).
Steuernagel, Dirk, *Kult und Alltag in römischen Hafenstädten: Soziale Prozesse in archäologischer Perspektive* (Stuttgart, 2004).
Taylor, Lily Ross, *The Cults of Ostia* (= *Bryn Mawr College Monographs*, vol. 11) (Bryn Mawr, 1912).
Temin, Peter, 'Estimating GDP in the Early Roman Empire', in: Elio Lo Cascio (ed.) *Innovazione technica e progresso economico nel mondo romano: Atti degli Incontri capresi di storia dell' economia antica (Capri 13–16 aprile 2003)* (Bari, 2006) 31–54.
Terpstra, Taco T., 'Roman Trade with the Far East: Evidence for Nabataean Middlemen in Puteoli', in Marco Maiuro and Federico de Romanis (eds.) *A Tale of Two Worlds: Comparative Perspectives on Indo-Mediterranean Commerce* (Leiden, 2013).
Thylander, Hilding, *Inscriptions du port d'Ostie* (= *Acta Instituti Romani Regni Sueciae*, vol. 6,1) (Lund, 1952).
Tirole, Jean, 'A Theory of Collective Reputations (with Applications to the Persistence of Corruption and to Firm Quality)', in: *Review of Economic Studies* 63 (1996) 1–22.
Torelli, Mario, *Il rango, il rito e l'immagine: Alle origini della rappresentazione storica romana* (Milan, 1997).
Torrey, Charles C., 'The Exiled God of Sarepta', in: *Berytus* 9 (1948/1949) 45–49.
Tran tam Tinh, Victor, *Le culte des divinités orientales en Campanie en dehors de Pompéi, de Stabies et d'Herculanum* (Leiden, 1972).

Udovitch, Avrom L., 'Formalism and Informalism in the Social and Economic Institutions of the Medieval Islamic World', in: Amin Banani and Speros Vryonos Jr. (eds.) *Individualism and Conformity in Classical Islam* (Wiesbaden, 1977) 61–81.

Ulrich, Roger B., 'Julius Caesar and the Creation of the Forum Iulium', in: *AJA* 97,1 (1993) 49–80.

Van der Meer, Lammert B., 'The Temple on the Piazzale delle Corporazioni in Ostia Antica', in: *Bulletin Antieke Beschaving* (= *Annual Papers on Mediterranean Archaeology*) 84 (2009) 169–176.

Verboven, Koenraad, *The Economy of Friends: Economic Aspects of* Amicitia *and Patronage in the Late Republic* (Brussels, 2002).

——, 'The Sulpicii from Puteoli, *Argentarii* or *Faeneratores*?', in: Pol Defosse (ed.) *Hommages à Carl Deroux*, vol. 3, *Histoire et épigraphie, droit* (= *Collection Latomus*, vol. 270) (Brussels, 2003a) 429–445.

——, 'The Sulpicii from Puteoli and Usury in the Early Roman Empire', in: *Tijdschrift voor Rechtsgeschiedenis* (= *Revue d'histoire du droit/Legal History Review*) 71,1–2 (2003b) 7–28.

Virlouvet, Catherine, 'Encore à propos des *Horrea Galbana* de Rome: Entrepôts ou *ergustules*?', in: *Cah.Glotz* 17 (2006) 23–60.

Veyne, Paul, 'Vie de Trimalcion', in: *Annales: économies, sociétés, civilisations* 16,2 (1961) 213–247.

Visconti, Carlo L., 'Escavazioni della Vigna Bonelli, fuori della Porta Portese negli anni 1859 e 60', in: *AdI* 32 (1860) 415–450.

Visonà, Paolo, 'The Bilingual Inscription for the Holy God of Sarepta', in: *Puteoli* 9/10 (1985/1986) 50–57.

Von Lübtow, Ulrich, *Das römische Volk: Sein Staat und sein Recht* (Frankfurt am Main, 1955).

Wallace-Hadrill, Andrew (ed.) *Patronage in Ancient Society* (London, 1989).

Waltzing, Jean-Pierre, *Étude historique sur les corporations professionnelles chez les Romains depuis les origines jusque'à la chute de l'Empire d'Occident*, 4 vols. (Leuven, 1895–1900).

Watson, Alan, *Rome of the XII Tables: Persons and Property* (Princeton, 1975).

——, *The Digest of Justinian: Latin Text Edited by Theodor Mommsen with the Aid of Paul Krueger, English Translation Edited by Alan Watson*, 4 vols. (Philadelphia, 1985).

——, *The State, Law and Religion: Pagan Rome* (Athens GA, 1992).

Wenning, Robert, 'The Nabataeans in History', in: Konstantinos D. Politis (ed.) *The World of the Nabateans* (Stuttgart, 2007) 25–44.

Wieacker, Franz, *Römische Rechtsgeschichte: Quellenkunde, Rechtsbildung, Jurisprudenz und Rechtsliteratur*, vol. 1 (Munich, 1988).

Wilson, Alan J.N., *Emigration from Italy in the Republican Age of Rome* (Manchester, 1966).

Wolf, Joseph G., 'Das sogenannte Ladungsvadimonium', in: Johan A. Ankum, Johannes E. Spruit, and Felix B.J. Wubbe (eds.) *Satura Roberto Feenstra: Sexagesimum Quintum Annum Aetatis Complenti ab Alumnis Collegis Amicis Oblata* (Freiburg, 1985) 59–69.

——, 'Haftungsübernahme durch Auftrag? Eine Urkunde aus dem Jahre 48 n. Chr', in: Dieter Nörr and Shigeo Nishimura (eds.) *Mandatum und Verwandtes: Beiträge zum römischen und modernen Recht* (Berlin, 1993) 69–91.

——, 'Der neue pompejanische Urkundenfund, zu Camodecas "Edizione critica dell'archivio puteolano dei Sulpicii" ', in: *Zeitschrift der Savigny-Stiftung für Rechtsgeschichte, romanistische Abteilung* 118 (2001) 73–132.

Woolf, Greg, 'Becoming Roman, Staying Greek: Culture, Identity and the Civilizing Process in the Roman East', in: *PCPS* 40 (1994) 116–143.

——, *Becoming Roman: The Origins of Provincial Civilization in Gaul* (Cambridge Eng., 1998).

Wörrle, Michael, 'Ägyptisches Getreide für Ephesos', in: *Chiron* 1 (1971) 325–340.

Yakobson, Alexander, *Elections and Electioneering in Rome: A Study in the Political System of the Late Republic* (Stuttgart, 1999).
Zabehlicky, Heinrich, 'Preliminary Views of the Ephesian Harbor', in: *Ephesos, Metropolis of Asia: An Interdisciplinary Approach to Its Archaeology, Religion, and Culture* (Valley Forge, 1995) 201–215.
Zayadine, Fawzi, 'The Spice Trade from South Arabia and India to Nabataea and Palestine', in: Konstantinos D. Politis (ed.) *The World of the Nabataeans* (Stuttgart, 2007) 201–215.
Zuiderhoek, Arjan, *The Politics of Munificence in the Roman Empire: Citizens, Elites and Benefactors in Asia Minor* (Cambridge Eng., 2009).

INDEX

Columbia Studies in the Classical Tradition publishes monographs by members of the Columbia University faculty and by former Columbia students. Its subjects are the following: Greek and Latin literature, ancient philosophy, Greek and Roman history, classical archaeology, and the classical tradition in its medieval, Renaissance and modern manifestations.

1. MONFASANI, J. *Georg of Trebizond.* A Biography and a Study of his Rhetoric and Logic. 1976. ISBN 90 04 04370 5
2. COULTER, J. *The Literary Microcosm.* Theories of Interpretation of the Later Neoplatonists. 1976. ISBN 90 04 04489 2
3. RIGINOS, A.S. *Platonica.* The Anecdotes concerning the Life and Writings of Plato. ISBN 90 04 04565 1
4. BAGNALL, R.S. *The Administration of the Ptolemaic Possessions outside Egypt.* 1976. ISBN 90 04 04490 6
5. KEULS, E. *Plato and Greek Painting.* 1978. ISBN 90 04 05395 6
6. SCHEIN, S.L. *The Iambic Trimeter in Aeschylus and Sophocles.* A Study in Metrical Form. 1979. ISBN 90 04 05949 0
7. O'SULLIVAN, T.D. *The* De Excidio *of Gildas: Its Authenticity and Date.* 1978. ISBN 90 04 05793 5
8. COHEN, S.J.D. *Josephus in Galilee and Rome.* His Vita and Development as a Historian. 1979. ISBN 90 04 05922 9
9. TARÁN, S.L. *The Art of Variation in the Hellenistic Epigram.* 1979. ISBN 90 04 05957 1
10. CAMERON, A.V. & J. HERRIN (eds.). *Constantinople in the Early Eighth Century: the Parastaseis Syntomoi Chronikai.* Introduction, Translation and Commentary. In conjunction with Al. Cameron, R. Cormack and Ch. Roueché. 1984. ISBN 90 04 07010 9
11. BRUNO, V.J. *Hellenistic Painting Techniques.* The Evidence of the Delos Fragments. 1985. ISBN 90 04 07159 8
12. WOOD, S. *Roman Portrait Sculpture 217-260 A.D.* The Transformation of an Artistic Tradition. 1986. ISBN 90 04 07282 9
13. BAGNALL, R.S. & W.V. HARRIS (eds.). *Studies in Roman Law in Memory of A. Arthur Schiller.* 1986. ISBN 90 04 07568 2
14. SACKS, R. *The Traditional Phrase in Homer.* Two Studies in Form, Meaning and Interpretation. 1987. ISBN 90 04 07862 2
15. BROWN, R.D. (ed.). *Lucretius on Love and Sex.* A Commentary on *De Rerum Natura* IV, 10301287 with Prolegomena, Text and Translation. 1987. ISBN 90 04 08512 2

16. KNOX, D. *Ironia*. Medieval and Renaissance Ideas about Irony. 1990. ISBN 90 04 08965 9
17. HANKINS, J. *Plato in the Italian Renaissance*. Reprint 1994. ISBN 90 04 10095 4
18. SCHWARTZ, S. *Josephus and Judaean Politics*. 1990. ISBN 90 04 09230 7
19. BARTMAN, E. *Ancient Sculptural Copies in Miniature*. 1992. ISBN 90 04 09532 2
20. DORCEY, P.F. *The Cult of Silvanus*. A Study in Roman Folk Religion. 1992. ISBN 90 04 09601 9
21. AUBERT, J.-J. *Business Managers in Ancient Rome*. A Social and Economic Study of Institores, 200 B.C.–A.D. 250. 1994. ISBN 90 04 10038 5
22. BILLOWS, R.A. *Kings and Colonists*. Aspects of Macedonian Imperialism. 1994. ISBN 90 04 10177 2
23. ROTH, J.P. *The Logistics of the Roman Army at War (264 B.C.–A.D. 235)*. 1999. ISBN 90 04 11275 1
24. PHANG, S.E. *The Marriage of Roman Soldiers (13 B.C.–A.D. 235)*. Law and Family in the Imperial Army. 2001 ISBN 90 04 12155 2
25. MARCONI, C. (ed.). *Greek Vases: Images, Contexts and Controversies*. Proceedings of the Conference sponsored by The Center for the Ancient Mediterranean at Columbia University, 23–24 March 2002. 2004. ISBN 90 04 13802 1
26. HARRIS, W.V. & G. RUFFINI (eds.). *Ancient Alexandria between Egypt and Greece*. 2005. ISBN 90 04 14105 7
27. HARRIS, W.V. (ed.). *The Spread of Christianity in the First Four Centuries*. Essays in Explanation. 2005. ISBN 90 04 14717 9
28. VOLK, K. & G.D. WILLIAMS (eds.). *Seeing Seneca Whole*. Perspectives on Philosophy, Poetry and Politics. 2006. ISBN-10: 90 04 15078 1, ISBN-13: 978 90 04 15078 2
29. HOLLANDER, D.B. *Money in the Late Roman Republic*. 2007. ISBN 978 90 04 15649 4
30. MARZANO, A. *Roman Villas in Central Italy*. A Social and Economic History. 2007. ISBN 978 90 04 16037 8
31. BAROLINI, T. & H. WAYNE STOREY (eds.). *Petrarch and the Textual Origins of Inter-pretation*. 2007. ISBN 978 90 04 16322 5
32. CICCOLELLA, F. *Donati Graeci*. Learning Greek in the Renaissance. 2008. ISBN 978 90 04 16352 2
33. HARRIS, W.V. & B. HOLMES (eds.). *Aelius Aristides between Greece, Rome, and the Gods*. 2008. ISBN 978 90 04 17204 3

34. LIU, J. Collegia Centonariorum: *The Guilds of Textile Dealers in the Roman West.* 2009. ISBN 978 90 04 17774 1
35. DE ANGELIS, F. (ed.). *Spaces of Justice in the Roman World.* 2010. ISBN 978 90 04 18925 6
36. BARRETT, C.E. *Egyptianizing Figurines from Delos.* A Study in Hellenistic Religion. 2011. ISBN 978 90 04 20797 4
37. TERPSTRA, T.T. *Trading Communities in the Roman World.* A Micro-Economic and Institutional Perspective. 2013. ISBN 978 90 04 23860 2

www.brill.com/csct